The Queer Bookishness
of Romanticism

The Queer Bookishness of Romanticism

Ornamental Community

Michael E. Robinson

LEXINGTON BOOKS
Lanham • Boulder • New York • London

Published by Lexington Books
An imprint of The Rowman & Littlefield Publishing Group, Inc.
4501 Forbes Boulevard, Suite 200, Lanham, Maryland 20706
www.rowman.com

6 Tinworth Street, London SE11 5AL, United Kingdom

Copyright © 2021 The Rowman & Littlefield Publishing Group, Inc.

All rights reserved. No part of this book may be reproduced in any form or by any electronic or mechanical means, including information storage and retrieval systems, without written permission from the publisher, except by a reviewer who may quote passages in a review.

British Library Cataloguing in Publication Information Available

Library of Congress Cataloging-in-Publication Data Available

ISBN: 9781793607935 (cloth) | ISBN: 9781793607959 (pbk)

Library of Congress Control Number: 2020948218

For Shayna and Ayla

Contents

Acknowledgments	ix
Introduction: Romantic Bookishness	1
1 Collecting the Ladies of Llangollen	31
2 Thomas F. Dibdin's Club for Ornamental Gentlemen	81
3 The Punk Antiquarianism of Charles Lamb	117
4 Henry Buxton Forman and Thomas J. Wise, a Curious Pair of Bookmen	159
Bibliography	207
Index	221
About the Author	233

Acknowledgments

In writing this book, I was fortunate to have the support of a bookish community of supportive colleagues and advisors based primarily in that unlikeliest of book-collecting hubs, Los Angeles, California. I want to express my deep gratitude to those who inspired me and those who have generously contributed advice and assistance. Large is the debt I owe to Margaret Russett at USC, with whom I had many conversations about this book's argument as I began to develop it. Her suggestions, insights, and rigorous questions productively complicated my first attempts to engage with Romantic bookishness. I owe a similarly large debt to James R. Kincaid. In addition to the example of his teaching and writing, the knowledge and advice he offered during conversations about methodologies and evidence were invaluable. He also read and provided feedback on an early draft. Elinor Accampo also has my gratitude for reading and commenting on a draft.

Others who generously helped me develop or express the core ideas include Joseph Dane, who read a rough draft and provided feedback and encouragement at a key stage. Conversations with Rebecca Lemon and Joseph Boone were very helpful as I initially framed the book's central questions and developed claims. I am grateful to them and to my undergraduate advisor Julian Wolfreys, generally speaking for his devotion to his lucky advisees and particularly for remembering me years later and starting a conversation that led to my writing this book. But, by a wide margin, my largest debt belongs to Shayna for her unwavering faith and support. Always ready with a joke and smile at just the right time, she never once asked me why I was still spending time on that puerile book about book collecting. Whatever virtues this book has are due to their influence. The faults are my own.

Material support for the writing of this book has come from a number of sources, including the Andrew M. Mellon Foundation, which provided a Short-Term Award to conduct archival research at the H. E. Huntington Library, Art Museum, and Botanical Gardens in San Marino, California. This award enabled the discovery of evidence at the heart of chapter 2. I am particularly grateful to the foundation and the Huntington for the ability to publish some of the library's large collection of manuscript letters to and from Thomas Frognall Dibdin dating to 1807–1844. Following the term of this fellowship, continued manuscript reading privileges at the Huntington helped essentially in the revision of chapters 2 and 3. Funding from the USC English Department was crucial to the writing of an early version of the argument. A travel bursary from the North American Society for the Study of Romanticism (NASSR) enabled me to present part of an early version of chapter 2 at the association's annual conference. I am also grateful to the John Hay Library in Providence, Rhode Island, for giving me access to key sources for chapter 1.

I also want to acknowledge the dedicated and collegial editors at Lexington Books. Jessica Thwaite has my gratitude for her interest in the project and Holly Buchanan for her unflagging commitment to it and her overall professionalism. Also, an anonymous reviewer's generous and detailed feedback materially improved the argument and its expression.

Portions of chapter 2 rework material from "Ornamental Gentlemen: Thomas F. Dibdin, Romantic Bibliomania, and Romantic Sexualities," *European Romantic Review* 22 no. 5 (2011). A section of chapter 3 expands on an article that will appear in the *Charles Lamb Bulletin* at around the same time this book is published, "An 'Ungentle' Punk: Revisiting Charles Lamb's Bookishness" (No. 172, Winter 2020). I am grateful to the publishers for permission to reuse material.

Introduction
Romantic Bookishness

In William Thackeray's *Vanity Fair* (1847–1848), young Squire Pitt, heir to the Queen's Crawley estate and unenthusiastic suitor of Lady Jane Sheepshanks, has a curious reading habit:

> Pitt meanwhile in the dining-room, with a pamphlet of the Corn Laws or a Missionary Register by his side, took that kind of recreation which suits romantic and unromantic men after dinner. He sipped madeira: built castles in the air: thought himself a fine fellow: felt himself much more in love with Jane than he had been any time these seven years, during which their *liaison* had lasted without the slightest impatience on Pitt's part—and slept a good deal. When the time for coffee came, Mr. Bowls used to enter in a noisy manner, and summon Squire Pitt, who would be found in the dark very busy with his pamphlet.[1]

That Pitt likes to get "busy" with a pamphlet in the dark hints at the scandalous potential of certain relations with print, to the point where Pitt's reading habit resembles a morally problematic sexual one akin to onanism: his handling and nonreading of a pamphlet are bound up with an extravagant self-embrace ("thought himself a fine fellow," "felt himself much more in love") followed by a nap. Superficially, the passage freights a style of cultural consumption with sexually dissident implications, implying that Pitt is an abuser of culture as well as himself. The satire's exact target remains tantalizingly vague, however. Does Pitt's provoking busyness merely serve to hint satirically at other, more shameful or embarrassing acts? Is there something sexually suspect about the act of not reading itself? Is the genre of the pamphlet, rather than Pitt's uses of it, the point? In other words, do ephemeral and hobby-horsical pamphlets intrinsically merit the kind of reader who would "busy" himself with print?

The ambiguous but clearly judgmental meanings operating in this representation of a solitary man enjoying a piece of print illustrate a nexus of ideas about cultural production and consumption that circulated around bookish people in the nineteenth century. The vagueness of Thackeray's satire is noteworthy in itself for suggesting the existence of sexualizing yet scatter-shot hostility to a target that resists precise identification. Such indeterminacy reflects the mechanism of phobias.[2] While the exact target of the satire remains obscure, the means of Pitt's transgression is clear enough. However mysterious, the exact pathology associated with it, the symptom, the pamphlet, is undeniable. This symptom draws focus to an object's particularity and physicality: Pitt's abuse is not of literature or ephemeral print culture in the abstract but of a physical object in particular. Hence, the mystery of Pitt's problematic sexual activity—his busyness—is tied to printed material. Rather than reading, failing to read has drawn the aim of ambiguous satire binding sexual dissidence with literary materiality.

An association with paper and books is an easily overlooked aspect of the deficient manliness of Pitt, a figure for the Prince Regent. In fact, the retiring bookishness of this "man of books" figures in the text's overall rendering of this Romantic-period figure as sexually suspect.[3] Pitt's unmanly bookishness extends beyond the conventional boundaries of gendered identity, suggesting an antisocial mode of affective life independent of, but also encompassing, effeminacy. In other words, Pitt's modes of consuming and producing culture are intimately bound up with his "frigid[ity]."[4] Consequently, the novel organizes a portrait of a sexual dissident around the use, as well as the misuse, of literature. Simultaneously, it also acts as a geography of literary pleasures and deviations: Pitt's fetishism of the literary is doubly obscene—literally, "off-stage," or out of place—because his bad reading occurs outside the library, a traditionally masculine domestic space within the home, a traditionally feminine one. Pitt has a bookish and queer, or queerly bookish, sensibility that simultaneously conforms to and deviates from the rubrics of gender difference and sexual difference, along with conventional notions of reading and reading spaces. Pitt's dissidence is unclear in part because its ostensible object, a piece of print, is not normally recognizable as a subject-defining object of desire.

A DISSIDENT EMBRACE OF A PROVOKING THING

Not unique, as it is a goal of this study to demonstrate, *Vanity Fair*'s linking of bookishness to "bad sex," to sexual behaviors that lie on the wrong side of what Gayle Rubin has famously called the "imaginary line" distinguishing socially sanctioned sexual practices from nonnormative ones, belongs to a tradition of literary representation of sexual dissidents that stretches across the long Romantic period in Great Britain.[5] In Romantic culture, bookish folks often appear to be queer in various ways. The phobic representation of bookish people, such as collectors, joined more familiar expressions of anxiety about readers, reading, and books that are commonly seen as Romantic anxieties. This rich and multifaceted, as well as anxious and even angry, discourse about book use and ownership is at its bedrock a discourse about affect, or, more precisely, about pleasure and its power to bind as well as rend community.[6] For this reason, it belongs to the discourse of sensibility, that unruly theme that, as Christopher Nagle argues in *Sexuality and the Culture of Sensibility in the British Romantic Era*, makes a case for the long nineteenth century as a redefined Romantic era that could be termed the "Long Age of Sensibility."[7]

Thackeray's evident anxiety about literary materiality hints at the long span of Romantic interest in dissident and bookish pleasures. Consequently, this book identifies a similarly apt example of the intersection of dissidence and bookishness in the illegitimate works of a pair of Victorian forgers, Thomas J. Wise (1859–1937) and Henry "Harry" Buxton Forman (1842–1917). Partners in crime who met through a literary society that celebrated and reprinted Percy Shelley, Wise, and Forman collected Romantic authors, and Forman edited standard editions of Shelley and John Keats. They later gained infamy as forgers of literary rarities, and their forgeries exemplified an abstract form of dissidence on the level of production. In producing fake first editions of Romantic writers, they exploited and exposed the discursive foundations of the singular author. At the other end of the Age of Sensibility, the famed "Ladies of Llangollen," Eleanor Butler (1739–1829) and Sarah Ponsonby (1755–1831), fostered a network of dissidents connected by bookish habits. This group's bookish sensibility blurred the boundaries between literature and architecture while illustrating the power of consumerism to bind dissident community in contexts where more conventional literary expressions of self were impossible or personally dangerous.

These examples suggest that bookishness is a neglected thread of Romanticism that informed styles of not only consumption but also production. These styles suggest the prominence of materiality in both marginal communities' shared identities and the expression of individual desire, while presenting a challenge to conceptions of sexuality that confine affect exclusively to the sphere of the human, even in the context of the discourse of sensibility. In a nod to one Romantic collector's description of himself as an "ornamental Gentleman," I have termed the groups that I examine here ornamental communities.[8] Romantic ornamental communities were defined by a provoking attachment to the materiality of the literary. In varying ways, matter bound and gave expressive power to marginalized groups whose subcultural tastes and activities fostered shared identity and prompted phobic representation in the broader culture. Romantic ornamental communities illuminate a wide framework around the sexual: the social mechanisms that have historically informed dissident sexual expression were triggered by affective relations with objects.

In this study, the above two cases of bookend examples of dissident book love that connect works and practices of a range of differently marginal Romantics, literary figures whose identities were defined by literary materiality in ways more prominent Romantics' identities were not. In contrast to writers defined, by themselves or others, in terms of transcendence, ornamental figures occupied positions adjacent or supplementary to the mainstream and canonical productive forces of the period—editors, a magazine writer, a bibliographer, and collectors. Ironically, these liminal figures and their subcultures shed a different light on themes central to Romanticism, including the author cult, the Gothic, and antiquarianism, unveiling the bookish underside of Romanticism. Sharing material attachments to the objects of literary culture, the groups nonetheless expressed a love of the literary. For one ornamental community, the objects of this love were incunabula and auction culture; for another, the detritus of the retail market for books; for another, the queer Gothic; and, for a Victorian ornamental community, Romantic culture itself. Distinct modes of loving literature shared exclusion from Romanticism's charmed circle—the realm of reified signifiers—while this exclusion undergirded the discursive production of singular authorship and normative sexuality. The queer status of ornamental communities reflected in part the operation of these discourses, meaning that the wider culture's phobic responses to "bookmen," antiquaries, collectors, and forgers were symptomatic.

As Ina Ferris argues in *Book-Men, Book Clubs, and the Romantic Literary Sphere*, community had a presently neglected but important role in the fostering of Romantic bookishness. The book collector figure and his less noxious kin the bibliophile illustrate a general tendency during the period to imagine bookishness in terms of the habits and interests of an individual and male type, but, as Ferris points out, the Romantic culture of bookishness had not only a fundamentally "associational" character but also a more diverse membership than its phobic image suggests. Walter Scott's founding in the 1820s of the Bannatyne Club, despite being modeled after the exclusive Roxburghe Club, spawned imitators serving the middle classes, and women and laborers also belonged to book clubs. The fact that the story of this kind of bookish community, which found common cause and interest in appreciating and reprinting rare books, has gone largely untold reflects, on the one hand, a long-running tension between the literary sphere and the bookish one and, on the other, the eventual hegemony of the literary. The foundation of the literary is the very premise of its distinction from bookish community—or, to use Ferris' apt terms for this, "a disjunction between literary culture and book culture"—and bookish conceptions of print and the modern book. Despite this abjection of book culture, book clubs did not merely serve as channels for transmission and exchange; rather, they produced an alternative form of print culture—making their members who authored books that much more problematic to gatekeepers in the properly "literary" realm. The different systems and chains of production, reflected in the new genres and formats, such as the club book, that the clubs marshaled, troubled the literary not by virtue of their radical difference but, as Ferris acutely observes, by their similarity and nearness. The liminal and, as Ferris says, "outlier" status of book club culture

> helps to account for the strangely vehement response to the apparently inoffensive print phenomenon of bookmen and book clubs within the literary sphere. The critique represents not just a pushing out of what does not belong (a territorial imperative); rather, it answers to the more unsettling recognition of alien trajectories within book and literary culture in uncomfortable proximity to its own.[9]

One such alien trajectory was the oddly excessive style of bookish prose, which Ferris terms the "language of book fancy." Reflecting book culture's alternative perspective on the materiality of the medium of print, book fancy takes print as what Ferris calls its "literal ground," indulging in incessant figures and ornaments of many kinds. These uncannily camp effects of bookish discourse, arguably best represented by the works of Dibdin, prompted sharp critique, mockery, and imitation beyond the confines of the subculture. Far from a merely comic tic of an enthusiastic coterie, this playful excess on the level of style has serious implications regarding technology and subjectivity. Ferris' compelling point about the style is that it reflects a broader cultural construct along the lines of the nature/culture divide according to which technique, as in Alan Liu's formulation, constitutes a cultural, as opposed to natural, exercise of technology independent of use-value. From this view, bookish style's camp effects reflect an alternative valuation and focus on the materiality of print such that the discourse amounts to a playful exercise of the medium's possibilities rather than an extension of the uniformity and notional transparency that makes the ideology of disembodied singularity possible. The indulgence in "linguistic pleasure" on offer in a Dibdin text can be seen as a performative, material manipulation of the medium of print with provocative implications for the ideology of both authorship and subjectivity.[10]

As I claim in this book, the style's pleasures and echoes of sensibility also redound to the history of sexuality, fusing the histories of sexuality and authorship while uncannily expressing forms of dissidence, including a form of male love, through their detailed inventory of embodied and shared pleasure in things. Simultaneously, the style exemplifies a historically central form of affect and identity-formation—consumerism—while embodying what Lee Edelman has described as the "literariness" inherent in queer subjectivity and what Thomas A. King has described as the hyper-material, "residually pederastic" character of queer embodiment.[11] In the light of the fraught status of bookish community and discourse in the Romantic literary sphere as well as the history of sexuality, what Dibdin facetiously calls the "book madness" transcended the status of any one historical event, such as the Romantic book boom, and any one subcultural form of luxury consumerism, such as aristocratic book collecting.[12] Instead, "bookish" names a queer practice and discourse with importance to men and women of letters whose marginal styles of consumption and production played an antithetical role in the elaboration of the twinned, spiritualizing ideologies of sexuality and authorship in Romanticism and its Victorian afterlife.

The topic of reading, including the appearance of new readers and the spread of the practice, has overshadowed the importance of bookishness to Romanticism. This emphasis on reading reflects Romanticism's historical significance in the broader context of the democratization of literary culture. In *The Reading Nation in the Romantic Period*, the historian William St. Clair identifies the period with "great change" in the history of reading. It saw the spread of the reading "habit," as distinct from the reading of Bibles, chapbooks, and ballads, to less-educated and lower-income groups along with a broad expansion of reading options.[13] As David Allan says in *A Nation of Readers*, "[r]eading may safely be described as one of the great collective obsessions of the eighteenth- and nineteenth-century English society."[14] Indeed, the "more highly educated members of society," as St. Clair says, also consumed more print and read more widely than before.[15] New genres, such as the Gothic and the sensation novel, reflected the changing audience. Related to these developments was the success of women writers such as Felicia Hemans and Maria Edgeworth. Edgeworth was among the most successful English novelists, in both commercial and critical terms, of the Romantic period and the very best paid until Scott.[16] The spread of the reading habit sponsored another new cultural tradition: classed and gendered commentary on Britain's new consumers of print. Comprising anxious reaction to the specter of "masses" and the genres and formats they consumed, high-pitched responses came from surprising quarters.

Some in the avant-garde, including those espousing radical political views, responded anxiously to the "explosion of reading."[17] Edmund Burke's infamous (but, as J. C. D. Clark has noted, arguably misinterpreted) image of the "swinish multitude" found telling echoes in Samuel Taylor Coleridge's "reading fly" and "learned pig."[18] In the "Essay, Supplementary to the Preface" (1815), Wordsworth dismisses the reading public as "small, though loud" and describes it as an unthinking collective governed by "factitious influence."[19] In Biographia *Literaria* (1817), Coleridge writes condescendingly of circulating libraries, which gave many lower-income people their only opportunity to read: "[A]s to the devotees of the circulating libraries, I dare not compliment their pass-time, or rather kill-time, with the name of reading."[20] The explosion of reading produced new writers and women writers invoked special ire. Hemans's popularity elicited heated responses from both Byron and the Lake poets—writers having little else in common. Byron was fond of referring to Hemans as "Mrs. Hewomans"—so alarming was her violation of what he perceived to be a woman's proper social role—and to Maria Edgeworth as having a "pencil under her petticoat."[21] In attacking the allegedly excessive embodiment of new readers, these responses suggest that concern about the broadening of access to print was displacing an awareness of entrenched material advantages in the cultural sphere onto the bodies of the marginalized.

While reading spread and associated figures of new consumers and producers prompted and reflected anxiety, the material means of cultural production underwent its own transformation. The mechanization of print was a Romantic innovation, the seeds of this traceable to the Didot company in Essonnes, France, and the work of Louis-Nicholas Robert, creator in 1799 of the first machine for making paper.[22] As Lucien Febvre and Henri-Jean Martin note in *The Coming of the Book*, although mechanization met the new reading public's demand for information, new technologies also served a niche market for consumers less interested in information than in collecting. A library habit, much smaller than the reading habit, spread among the wealthy. The relative few who could afford to indulge in it stocked personal libraries with illustrated books, leading to a renewal of the genre. Deluxe reissues of unlikely texts by Montesquieu (*Temple of Gnidus*) and Jean-Benjamin de Laborde (*Choix de Chansons*) appeared in France, and methods of engraving developed for this market eventually saw wider use.[23] In England, lithography made possible the antiquarian genre of the illustrated "tour," which was popular among middle-class and aristocratic collectors alike. Examples of Thomas Pennant's (1726–1798) contributions to this genre, including *A Tour in Scotland* (1769) and *A Tour in Scotland, and Voyage to the Hebrides; 1772* (1774), were owned by the businessman father of Thomas De Quincey (1785–1859), who cited them as a powerful influence. In a discussion of his father's library in *Sketches of Life and Manners* (1834), De Quincey recalls the unforgettable impression made by tour books' many illustrations. De Quincey's father also wrote his own tour book.[24] In the digressive *A Short Tour in the Midland Counties of England* (1775), Thomas Quincey (the family posthumously added the "De") calls himself "a gleaner, a collector" of views.[25]

Judith Pascoe remarks in *The Hummingbird Cabinet: A Rare and Curious History of Romantic Collectors* that the period witnessed the democratizing of collecting, a phenomenon evinced partly by the many periodicals devoted to the habit.[26] In this light, it is curious that the figure of the collector became provoking in much the same way as the new readers. The book collector Oldbuck in Sir Walter Scott's *The Antiquary* (1816) is an antisocial miser faulted even for the weakness of his addiction: at least Don Quixote sacrificed land, rather than mere money, for books.[27] In Dr. John Ferriar's satirical poem *The Bibliomania, an Epistle to Richard Heber, Esq.* (1809), book collectors are similarly scorned for lacking heroism, and, ironically, the heroism they lack is the kind described by Homer, Horace, and Tully in books left unbought only because their margins were too small to attract a collector's "haggard eye."[28] In his 1834 autobiography, Sir Samuel Egerton Brydges confesses to a youthful period of "book-fever" that lamentably distracted him from "original composition." Collecting, Brydges says, is one of the "minor labors" on which "intellectual powers" are "grievously" wasted.[29] The figure of the collector, and in particular the collector of old books, prompted anxiety focused on such perceived ills as waste, exclusion, distraction, and monopoly. Simultaneously, literary materiality acquired a dark cast, suggesting that the period's "obsessions" with books, to use Allan's term, extended beyond abstract notions of and ostensibly immaterial relations with culture.[30] Readers, not the only consumers of print, were not the only targets for criticism.

An event that drew attention to collectors was the "book boom," a period of rapid price inflation and feverish buying and selling of rare books that peaked in the 1820s.[31] The prices of rare books and manuscripts rose by as much as 400 percent during the boom, which was comparable to the Dutch Tulip Madness and the South Sea Bubble.[32] In *A Gentle Madness: Bibliophiles, Bibliomanes, and the Eternal Passion for Books*, Nicholas Basbanes says that in one twelve-month stretch, from November 1806 to November 1807, a total of 149,200 books were auctioned off by only three auction houses. A single auction netted £23,397 for more than 9,000 books. A single collector active during the boom, Richard Heber (1773–1833), spent over £100,000 on books. Another boom-period collector, Sir Thomas Phillips (1792–1872), styled himself a "vello-maniac" and said he intended to collect "every book in the world." He ended up accumulating a collection of manuscripts that eventually sold for the same sum Heber spent.[33] As prices rose and auctions made news, the boom brought new attention to the largely male, homosocial subculture of collectors who attended high-profile book auctions, collected books, and produced bibliographies. Their activities prompted a facetious vocabulary describing their circle and its shared passion: terms such as "bibliophilia," "bibliomania," "bookman," "book-fool," "bibliomane," and "goldbeater" (one who strips a book's illuminations of precious metals, as Basbanes notes) entered the lexicon or regained currency.[34] Stereotypically, these men were fetishists who lacked interest in the "contents" of their books.

Collectors became objects of psychological scrutiny, and in some cases the collectors were their own analysts. In texts about collecting by collectors, the practices and pleasures associated with the book-object get detailed description. Sometimes conceiving of their activities as manifestations of a desire both to accumulate for self and preserve for others, which is how Phillips, for example, described his love of collecting books, this eroticized and typically male figure was one whose individual affective life defined him individually and connected him to the wider culture. About his passion for books, Phillips wrote,

> As I advanced, the ardor of the pursuit increased until at last I became a perfect vello-maniac (if I may coin a word), and I gave any price that was asked. Nor do I regret it, for my object was not only to secure good manuscripts for myself, but also to raise the public estimation of them, so that their value might be more generally known, and consequently more manuscripts preserved. For nothing tends to the preservation of anything so much as making it bear a high price.[35]

This collector writes as if the whole community of readers (the "public") has a stake in his erotic life (his "ardor"). Hence, the self-portrait sketched here is of a being both sensual and sensible, and the portrait mirrored in telling ways an active discourse conducted by non-collectors who imagined they, too, had an interest in his pleasures. Pathological in varying degrees of seriousness (as Phillips' facetious labeling of himself a "maniac" suggests), these pleasures were subject to discussion and debate because they were thought to have social implications. Registering individual and communal stakes, the discourse of bibliomaniacal passions overlapped with the discourse of sensibility. In the latter context, pleasures had social functions enabled by culture. As Nagle says, Romantic sensibility resembled a network that "works to connect others through its stimulating effects—to plug into them through the technology, not merely to plug into the technology itself."[36] Bibliomaniacs like Phillips conceived of their desires as both self-defining and as having the potential to bind or rend the public sphere.

Thus, it is hardly surprising that this collector figure became a popular-psychological patient, or "case study," to borrow a phrase from Deidre Shauna Lynch's *Loving Literature: A Cultural History*.[37] Writers performed diagnoses of the collector in books with dramatic titles like *Bibliomania, or, Book-Madness: A Bibliographical Romance* (1811) and *The Bibliographical*

Decameron (1817). These are works by Thomas F. Dibdin (1776–1847), a kind of clerk at bibliomaniacal court who recorded aristocratic collectors' activities and whose celebration of the book boom helped establish a community of collectors while, in other quarters, acting as an irritant. In addition to writing books about collectors, he was a cleric and marginal figure on the auction circuit who cataloged the library of Lord George John Spencer (1758–1834). Whereas others, such as Phillips and Brydges, implied concern about the social consequences of collecting, Dibdin's works present almost the opposite "case." Rather than diagnose antisocial pathologies, they enthusiastically describe shared pleasures. They produce the discourse of sensibility in an insular context and on a small scale because desire tied together the members of a subculture. As I will discuss in more detail in this book's second chapter, commentary elicited by Dibdin's works indicate that the subculture's discourse about relations with books could be irritating to outsiders.

Lynch has attributed this reaction partly to the fear that collectors' possessiveness threatened an ongoing effort to widen access to literature through inexpensive reprinting, which, in the form of anthologies, sponsored a new way of relating to literature. One could now love literature as such—relate immaterially to texts in a way shaped by the form of the anthology and, therefore, uncannily like the collector's material relations with books. Ironically, loving literature begot novel forms of fetishistic attachment, as collectors such as the liberal writer and activist Leigh Hunt nourished selves forged in the reading of anthologies by collecting books in ways distinct from those of the aristocratic collectors.[38] As this conclusion suggests, Lynch's incisive and nuanced approach to disciplinary history enables her to trace the source of now-commonplace conceptions of English as a subject to be loved to the political structure of the literary field and the materiality of the literary. Beyond the discipline of English, bookishness has intrinsic importance and particular relevance to the history of sexuality. The present study addresses this intrinsic importance of bookishness and, specifically, its capacity to shed light on queerness as expressed through and mediated by relations with things. One aspect of this queerness relates to expressions of bookish desire, which reflected the socialization of books and took pornographic form.

Although the book boom was a Romantic phenomenon, the expression of dissident passion has arguably always figured prominently in bookish discourse. Book lovers talk about their habit in strikingly odd ways—using words like "fetish," "addiction," "mania," and, of course, "love." This tendency may not distinguish books from other collectibles, but collectors' tendency to anthropomorphize the book-object in this context arguably does. *Books Are People: A Bookman's Credo* is the title of a recent book by the collector Ethel R. Sawyer. A Romantic example can be found in the 1769 King James Bible, where John the Apostle renders Jesus of Nazareth as a book ("the word made flesh"), one that in Neoplatonic fashion John subordinates to divine speech.[39] Texts have "bodies," books "spines," and letters "limbs" and "lobes." Type has a "face." A copy can be "castrated" (or not, if an editor is faithful). From a sociological perspective, this anthropomorphism reflects the socialization of books. As Arjun Appadurai has observed, the uncanniness of objects can effectively endow them with a kind of life, resulting in a situation in which "persons and things are not radically distinct categories."[40]

One outgrowth of this blurring of thing and human is erotic discourse about books, or, colloquially, "book porn." In the nineteenth century, this mode's institutional home was the collecting society, which fostered texts chronicling men's erotic attachments to books. Illustrating Romantic book porn is a rare text attributed to William Beckford (1760–1844), a collector of collections and the notorious author of *Vathek* (1782, 1786). The mock-heroic text, "Rare Doings at Roxburghe Hall. A Ballad" (1821), narrates a shocking scene of auction-house jousting, or "tilting," for rarities among different classes of male collectors. In the text, competition among some book "puppies" (a common term for less affluent collectors), who gulp book "jelly" and "foam," serves as a prelude to more serious action between two "noble champions." The competition between these noblemen, Earl Spira and Baron Blandish, starts out as hand-to-hand combat but gradually builds in intensity: "At last these noble champions met, / Both maniacs in good plight, / With lion-strength their blows laid on, / And made a cruel fight." As the battle continues, the sight of a new lot compels the warriors to unsheathe their sizeable weapons: "The golden prize exposed to view, / Their fierce desires provoke; / And massive blades of temper'd steel, / Brought blood at every stroke." In the course of combat, Blandish's assaults have special power: "With that [Blandish] rais'd his falchion high, / And made so fierce a thrust, / That would have thrown a weaker knight / E'en prostrate in the dust." A well-armed jouster, Iulus, joins the fray, and the narrator says, "A stouter weapon ne'er was borne by knight or trusty squire." The ultimate outcome is climactic as well as ambiguous. First, a wounded Blandish recovers himself and aims a long arrow at Spira's buttocks. Then, the "arrow of a cloth-yard long" connects, hitting Spira's "flank." Humiliated, the earl's pocket tears and "in streams of pactolian flowing down, / His ammunition went."[41]

Among the unlikely jokes in this brazenly queer text is the one rendering, in Freudian fashion, money as filthy lucre.[42] Another, more ambiguous, joke seems to concern the wages of sodomitical "sin." In the end, the earl clearly wins by losing—or does he? The answer seems to depend on whether one locates the object of the satirical discourse in the auction room, the bedroom, or somewhere in between. As far as bookish *double entendres* go, Beckford's here are representative of some bibliomaniacal discourse in being scandalously suggestive yet resistant to interpretation. Rather than identify a singular, human object of the facetious discourse, and "tilt" in one direction only, the reader is invited to share the writer's pleasure in the transgressive potential of erotic discourse about men whose desire is shared but also directed elsewhere, at things. Authors of such texts seem to be enjoying a rare freedom—one that reflects the multiplicity of bookish desire—to traffic in signifiers of homoerotic pleasure while maintaining deniability and expressing desires that span and extend past the human.

Alongside privately printed pamphlets, a medium for discourse like this was the collector's periodical. In 1871, *The Book Collector's Miscellany* reprinted a notable piece of early modern book pornography in which simultaneous fetishism of a man's body and a book illustrates the uncannily queer effects of some bookish discourse. Called "Trimming Thomas Nashe, Gentleman" (1597), it was the last sally in a vicious "paper war" between Nashe and Dr. Gabriel Harvey. The battle of words was violent enough for the Archbishop of Canterbury to intervene. The piece, written in the voice of a fictional barber to whom Nashe had dedicated an earlier work aimed at Harvey, imagines the murder-by-castration of Nashe by a barber-surgeon metaphorically as a book-binder's loving yet brutal attention to an uncut copy.[43] Fantasizing acts of violence, the piece is not conventionally erotic, which is why it aptly exemplifies the strange effects and echoes of bookish discourse, in which eroticism can move through strange yet uncannily familiar channels of longing, and human and nonhuman objects attract a shifting but consistently attentive gaze. The piece lingers over a body and book, conflating them in a series of explicit details that conjures the notoriously ineffable qualities of pornography. It merits a lengthy quotation:

> You see how lovingly I deal with you in my epistle, and tell of your virtues, which (God forgive me for it) is as arrant a lie as ever was told; but to leave these paregastrical speeches, and to come to your trimming. Because I will deal roundly with you I will cut you with the round cut, in which I include two cuts: first, the margin cut; secondly the perfect cut. The margin cut is nothing else but a preparation to the perfect cut, whereby I might more perfectly discharge that cut upon you; for as in a deep standing pool, the brinks thereof, which are not unfitly called the margins, being pared away, we may the better see thereinto; so the margins, which fitly we may term the brinks of your stinking standing pool (for it infects the ear as doth the stinking pool the smell) being cut away, I may the better finish this perfect cut, and rid myself of you.[44]

Reflecting the fact that pornography is reductive detail in pursuit of an impossible goal—an attempt to represent an "unattainable" object, as Slavoj Žižek says in *Looking Awry*—the ultimate object is everything and nothing to this discourse.[45] Its object could be described as an enemy's mutilated corpse, a virginal book, or both at once. Affirming Appadurai's characterization of the human relationship with objects, this collector's sensual pleasure ("I may the better finish this perfect cut") is not typically loving nor consistently human-centered, but it remains decidedly erotic. Also, despite having a violent aim, the attention to Nashe's body strikes queer and pornographic notes due to the abundant pleasure taken in attending to a male form ("but to leave these paregastrical speeches, and to come to your trimming"), and this attentiveness to male bodies and pleasures is something bookish discourse shares with its focus on the book-object. Attention to the physical characteristics of individual copies was among Dibdin's more important contributions to the field of bibliography, which suggests that continuities existed between bibliographical discourse and collectors' erotic relations with books as discussed in "extracurricular" contexts like this one.

Bookish discourse is psychological as well as sensual, a vibrant subgenre being the mock diagnosis. When collectors psychologize their habit, an erotic attachment becomes uncannily sexual as a discourse of pleasure gains self-describing power. Some collectors define themselves overtly in terms of bookish desires. "I choose books," wrote the forger and Romanticist Henry Buxton Forman in a letter to a close male friend in which Forman describes his difficulties relating to women.[46] Some collectors diagnose others. The contemporary works of Basbanes interweave descriptions of visits to collectors and libraries with this type of analytical discourse. In *Patience and Fortitude*, Basbanes describes the author, artist, and collector Maurice Sendak's fondness for books explicitly in terms of object-cathexis and selfhood (or, in other words, sexuality): "Books are more than containers of information for him; they are 'love objects,' and there is no question that the love he feels for them is total in every respect."[47] Basbanes is echoing tropes of nineteenth-century bibliophile psychology here. Dibdin's *Bibliomania; or Book-Madness; A Bibliographical Romance* (second edition, 1842) takes the form of a mock-medical treatise on the book-collecting "malady," for example.[48] The character Lysander cries out, "I will frankly confess . . . that I am an arrant BIBLIOMANIAC—that I love books dearly."[49] Dibdin, in turn, is echoing early modern psychological discourse about bibliophiles. However satirical, the figure of the Book-Fool in Sebastian Brant's *Das Narrenschiff* (*Ship of Fools* [1494]), who dusts his books but "take[s] no wysdome by them," suggests that book love has long elicited not only pornographic but also psychological discourse.[50]

A watershed moment in the history of the Romantic psychosexual pathology of bookishness was the sale of a collectible book with sexual associations of its own, a very rare copy of Giovanni Boccaccio's *Decameron*, the "Valdarfer Boccaccio," which was printed in 1471 by the Venetian printer Christopher Valdarfer and thought lost until 1812. (Considered at the time to be a unique copy and the first edition, the Valdarfer has been superseded by the undated "Deo Gratias" edition, printed in Naples by Francesco del Tuppo around 1470.[51]) The first society that served book collectors exclusively was founded in celebration of this sale. Dibdin established the group, the still-active Roxburghe Club, in 1812 following the auctioning off of the Duke of Roxburghe's book collection. At the auction, the Boccaccio sold for the record-setting price of £2,260, the rough equivalent of £1.5 million today. The sale was well publicized and widely noticed at the time. De Quincey, a collector whose book habit rivaled his better-known opium habit, attended it and then satirized a club member's account. Critical accounts appeared in the press, portraying the members as imbeciles, hedonists, gluttons, and snobs.[52] One attack in particular is noteworthy. In 1834, an anonymous article appeared in *The Athenæum* ostensibly reviewing *Roxburghe Revels*, the unintended memoir of a club member, Joseph Haslewood. The article's author, who was later identified as James Silk Buckingham, uses the piece as a platform to make sexually phobic insinuations, invoking the classical *effeminatus* figure to portray the club's membership as immoral enemies of the "cause of letters."[53] The article also refers to a sex scandal involving Heber, a club member, and another man. In the article's rendering, collectors are uncreative in a starkly immoral way that redounds to their essential being. Implicit is a concept of literature as a field of manly competition in service to the nation. Receiving more detailed analysis in this study's second chapter, the collectors of the Roxburghe Club appear in the article as social parasites and monstrous bodies whose out-of-control passions have disqualified them for battle.

Although, as this attack makes evident, critics faulted book clubs for their perceived interest only in the materiality of existing, usually old, books, evidence of their activities takes the form of cultural products, reflecting the fact that many bibliophiles were producers as well as consumers. In its early years, the Roxburghe Club was a publishing house, producing small, bibliophile-friendly runs of scholarly reprints on antiquarian subjects. As John V. Richardson, Jr., has observed, this publishing activity effectively makes the club the first publishing society, anticipating the work that Frederick J. Furnivall, the founder of the (Percy) Shelley and Browning Societies later in the century, would make into a cottage industry.[54] Furnivall's societies were also elemental to the Victorian cult of Romantic poets (which, especially in Shelley's case, was shot through with male love) and instrumental in their canonization. In fact, the costs associated with bibliophile reprinting bankrupted Furnivall's Shelley Society.[55]

The bibliophile-quality reprinting that was the primary output of book clubs reflects the fact that Romantic bookishness was a subculture and not simply an object of fascination or a "habit" existing in subordinate relation to cultural production. In this way, bookish culture displayed the hallmarks of subcultures in which, as Dick Hebdige says in *Subculture: The Meaning of Style*, consumption serves the aims of expression and affiliation.[56] Unlike twentieth-century subcultures as described by Hebdige, bookish Romantics did more than repurpose consumer goods, and the products of ornamental communities included literature and architecture. Nonetheless, like punks and other modern youth subcultures, bookishness attracted and connected dissidents for whom books served signifying purposes (along with other possessions, many of which were antiquarian), even if many of these dissidents were motivated to express their love of books in the form of new products. The collecting of Horace Walpole (1717–1797) suggests the extent to which bookishness was a productive style as well as a habit. Walpole's home, Strawberry Hill, was itself a Gothic collection, as Sean Silver has observed.[57] It housed a private press, as Barrett Kalter has noted, along with a manuscript collection, and the home's design was a bookish product with cues making it continuous with the collection.[58] Walpole decorated the walls of his "paper fabric" castle with manuscript ornaments (*fleurs-de-lis*).[59] Walpole's novel *The Castle of Otranto* (1764), the first Gothic novel, is another bookish product containing similar themes. In it, the magical helmet of Alonso represents the materiality of the literary. (An overdetermined figure for the press, the helmet makes a mechanical racket ["the clank of more than mortal armor"], sends a powerful political message while remaining mute, and gets aligned thematically with vision and contrasted to speech throughout the text.)[60] Together with these themes, Walpole's fictional framing narrative of the novel representing it as a found manuscript makes *Otranto* a bookish text. In this way, it anticipated another touchstone of the literary queer Gothic, Beckford's *Vathek*. Beckford, like Walpole, made antiquarianism and dissident desire conjoined literary themes.

Bookish architecture in the lineage of Walpole's Strawberry Hill includes Fonthill Abbey, the massive but fragile and short-lived home of Beckford, and the extant Plas newydd, the famed home of the Ladies of Llangollen and a version of the rural ornamental cottage used by the "romantic friends" to undertake a queer and trans mode of domesticity in Wales. As I claim in the first chapter of this book, the bookish queer Gothic, as pioneered by Walpole in architecture and fiction, recurred in the hyper-ornamental design of Plas newydd, the remodeling of which, like Strawberry Hill's by Walpole, emphasized the library.[61] Butler and Ponsonby, who are not usually invoked in discussions of the queer Gothic, like Walpole nonetheless gravitated aesthetically to a highly ornamental style of Gothic architecture continuous with the literary. What a biographer of the couple has referred to as the home's kitschy "riot" of ornamentation recalled the Walpolian Gothic and paralleled the Ladies' materialistic style of literary consumption.[62] In this light, they adopted a general style that, like that of bibliomaniacs, was consumerist without being confined to consumption and that drew attention to the materiality of signifiers.

The productions and prose styles of some Romantic writers for the magazines offer another example of the intersecting themes of bookishness and dissidence. As Deidre Lynch and Margaret Russett have argued, writers such as Leigh Hunt (1784–1859), Thomas De Quincey, and Charles Lamb (1775–1834) acknowledged their "minor" status in the literary field by representing literature and their relations with it in materialistic, embodied ways.[63] The personal essays of Lamb in particular, the focus of this study's third chapter, deployed a camp prose style that melded antiquarianism and book love in the frame of a prototypically bohemian worldview. Lamb's works are particularly notable for the ways they integrate dissident themes and a distinctive, antiqued authorial voice, rendering authorship as practically continuous with consumerism.

Psychoanalytic theory offers insights relevant to the consumerist culture of Romantic bookishness. The culture of Romantic bookishness embodied queerness by virtue of its focus on materiality. Socially, bookishness organized dissidents otherwise linked by the expressed, as opposed to repressed, materiality of their subjectivity—by a queerness that, to paraphrase Lee Edelman's Lacanian theory of queerness in *No Future: Queer Theory and Death Drive*, exposed the materiality of the signifier.[64] Collecting served as a refuge perhaps because it would have been an extension and echo of self—an embodied metaphor for the queer experience. Books belonged to a broader world of ornamental culture—encompassing the Gothic, kitsch, and camp —in which the overtness of gesture and posture, which Susan Sontag's definition of camp registers in terms of "artifice," illuminated and extended the more general materiality of the self.[65] In its embrace of materiality, bookishness also put glaring light on an opposing relation to the literary—authorship—along with the latter's different sexual politics. Authorship, as theorized in the nineteenth century in terms of disembodied voice, stands in the same relation to literary materiality as does normativity to queerness, redeeming what Edelman calls the "lifeless machinery" of the letter and infusing this with the "'spirit' of futurity."[66]

The ways bookishness materialized subjectivity reflected the broader discourse about sexuality during the period. As Richard C. Sha's discussion of Romantic aesthetics and science in *Perverse Romanticism: Aesthetics and Sexuality in Britain, 1750–1832* has revealed, pleasure preoccupied thinkers due to its relevance to debates about utility, necessity, and hierarchy in the industrial age. Science could find no function for bodily pleasure, but a dominant strain of aesthetic theory elevated purposeless pleasure, or perversion, to the standard of disinterestedness. In light of Kantian purposiveness, eroticism, which represented mutual and nonreproductive pleasure, seemed to hold radical potential for more equal social relations and an existence free of the tyranny of tradition, matter, and instinct.[67]

Perverse pleasure acquired radical potential, but matter threatened a new image of the social founded on disinterestedness and equality. Meanwhile, as Russett and Martha Woodmansee have observed, the author-function became enshrined in theoretical and legal discourse as an irreducibly singular voice transcending materiality.[68] Ringed in opposition to the singular author were vexing materialists including the pirate and forger. In *Fictions and Fakes: Forging Romantic Authenticity, 1760–1845*, Russett shows how the forger's perceived over-closeness to literary matter made him a useful foil for the singular author.[69] A claim that I offer more detailed support for in the last chapter of this book is that the bibliophile should be classed with the forger as a foil for the author-function. Bookish ornamental cultures were particularly vexing because they embodied a mode of eroticism that invoked queerness, the aristocratic world of surfaces and bodies, and the embrace, rather than the transcendence, of materiality.

THE MATERIAL TURN

Although book love is a traditional aspect of the literary consumer's experience, this perspective has not always featured prominently in the history of the book. Book history and research in literary studies drawing on book history are in the midst of a bookish moment, however, as scholars attend to the behaviors and habits of the consumers, as opposed to producers, of print. In the context of book history, the work of Robert Darnton, David C. Hall, and William St. Clair can be cited as foundational to a shift in focus on the consumer, which St. Clair describes in *The Reading Nation in the Romantic Period* as the "history of reading."[70] This focus represents a departure from the production- and producer-oriented work of scholars such as Elizabeth Eisenstein (*The Printing Press as an Agent of Change* and *The Printing Revolution in Early-modern Europe*). The agency granted to technology in Eisenstein's work is a corollary of a certain distance from the consumer's experience. Influential for arguing that the introduction of print sparked a cultural revolution, Eisenstein has charted the broad social impact of the "move from the copyist's desk to the printer's workshop." Eisenstein's more recent book *Divine Art, Infernal Machine*, while not, like her previous book, a flashpoint for debate about technology's agency within the history of the book, addresses "attitudes towards printing and printers," not toward readers and owners.[71] Likewise, as Joseph Dane notes in *The Myth of Print Culture*, Eisenstein's distinction between scribe and printer has also had influence on the field.[72]

In an essay, Darnton expresses frustration with much book history and praises the work of scholars influenced by the *Annales* school of historians because they explored "the literary experience of ordinary readers."[73] Hall similarly strives to capture the "consumption of books" in *Cultures of Print*, where Hall endorses a "double vision" encompassing traditional power centers and authorities as well as those at society's margins whose consumption has often been neglected by book historians. The accounts of "readers and their books" that Hall's volume tells emphasize, on the one hand, cross-class transmission and, on the other, cultural uniformity. One chapter deals with cultural representations of book use, but it does so at the level of social class and print-culture distribution trends.[74] St. Clair has shared with Hall an interest in the broad social impacts of print culture. In *The Reading Nation in the Romantic Period*, he sets out to determine the actual "consequences" of print matter's distribution across time and space.[75]

These scholars' varying methods share with Roger Chartier's work (*The Order of Books: Readers, Authors, and Libraries in Europe Between the 14th and 18th Centuries*) a debt to Darnton. Darnton's adoption of the "philosophy of praxis," to use Antonio Gramsci's term from the *Prison Notebooks*, deserves much credit for orienting the field toward the user.[76] In *The Business of Enlightenment*, Darnton attends to the "lived experience of literature among ordinary readers." In doing so, the book engages questions not only about the distribution and readership of the *Encyclopédie* but also philosophical ones about the influence of materiality on form. Darnton's study of the *Encyclopédie*'s readership finds that the book's audience was mainly composed of educated readers outside the middle class.[77]

All such work reflects the influence of Richard D. Altick's *The English Common Reader: A Social History of the Mass Reading Public 1800–1900*, the first social history of nineteenth-century readership and the first sociology of the reading public. Altick's argument ties the advent of the "common reader" to industrialization: rising wages increased demand for cheap publications, for example, and newly alienating work in factories required a new, compensatory form of leisure. Additionally, Altick identifies the three requisites of a reading public as "literacy, leisure, and a little pocket money." Atypically, Altick relies heavily on literary evidence, drawing on an array of authors' views of readers. Wilkie Collins is cited for his ideas about the new "Unknown Public," for example.[78]

Some histories of the library have contributed to this social history of the book. Allan's *A Nation of Readers* is a history of eighteenth- and nineteenth-century libraries, including the circulating library, reading society, and subscription library.[79] In *The Making of English Reading Audiences, 1790–1832*, Jon P. Klancher conducts "a social as well as interpretive conception of 'reading.'" One of Klancher's goals is to reclaim the social collective and, hence, the reading audience from the school of "semiotic cultural history," comprising work by Clifford Geertz, Lynn Hunt, and François Furet, while negotiating, like his Romantic lights Samuel Taylor Coleridge and Percy Shelley, the gap between the "unmistakable realm of social class" and the "classless" realm of the signifier. Klancher faces a limitation in the anonymity of readers, so he relies on writers' efforts to create audiences and address them. A key conclusion is that radical and middle-class writers construct the social position of their imagined readerships differently. The former kind addresses a class and the latter a reader distinct from class.[80]

Although, in presenting a theory of Romantic bookishness, the present study contributes to the field of book history, it belongs primarily to the field of literary studies. Nonetheless, I have drawn inspiration from book historians, and this study's overall subject and methodology share ground with their discipline. In the spirit of the work of Hall, Darnton, St. Clair, and Klancher, for example, the present study's approach to the book-object privileges consumption over production, the consumer's perspective being of paramount importance. I am primarily interested, in other words, in what Darnton calls this figure's "lived experience," and my evidence, to this extent like Altick's, is literary representation. A difference is that my goal, to explore the sexual dissidence of Romantic bookishness, means that I must often veer away from the representative or "mass" experience toward the exceptional one. Ultimately, this means that the analysis arrives at not the center but an overlooked margin.

This book's use of book-historical methods puts it in good company. In recent years, both Romanticists and Victorianists have used book history to uncover a rich discourse about books in Romantic literature. Drawing on Klancher, Altick, and other social historians of the book, a number of scholars, including Nagle, Heather J. Jackson, Leah Price, Ferris, Lynch, Barbara M. Benedict, and Paul Keen, have addressed the complex role of print in consumers' affective lives. Considered in light of these scholars' shared focus on the materiality of the literary and book users' embodied experiences, this work belongs to the larger material turn in literary studies—a "turn of attention to material objects and practices conducted by scholars who have traditionally focused almost solely on texts," to use Maureen Daly Goggin's apt description.[81] Far from confirming stereotypical representations of bookish folks as antisocial misfits—book closet cases—these scholars' work has uncovered an intimacy between bookishness and the production of new communities along with new, communal art forms. Lynch, for example, has studied the particular ways that discourse on the affective charge associated with reading have helped give shape to the British canon. In one essay, Lynch sketches an emergent affective community around the canon in the eighteenth century—"an ideal of readerly health," "sense of comfort," and community that writers like Samuel Johnson associated with canonical works.[82] Lynch's *Loving Literature* claims that Romantic essayists such as Hazlitt, De Quincey, and Lamb invented a newly affective relationship to literature in their representation of the book-object as a monument to poetic genius.[83] Similarly focusing on the book-related memories of Romantic essayists, Ferris has also identified a connection between the book and new imaginary communities. Ferris has argued that essayists were responsible for contributing a new "book-sentiment" to culture that, rather than being possessive, imagined "a new public" founded on the "quasi-bodily pleasure of books." Consequently, given the broader reification of the reader's body over the course of history, the early nineteenth century witnesses "something of a swerve," as a return to "bookishness . . . restor[es] to view the body of the reader through a foregrounding of the body of the book."[84] Also, as mentioned earlier, Ferris' *Book-Men, Book Clubs and the Romantic Literary Sphere* uncovers the forgotten role played by the provoking materialism of the bookmen and their "associational" networks in the broader, gradual cultural absorption of print and consolidation of the modern literary sphere through opposition to bookishness.

Tracing, like Ferris, Lynch, and St. Clair, the ties between reading and shared mentalities in the context of Romanticism, Heather J. Jackson has used a quasi-bibliographical method to locate a form of the public sphere in readers' material engagement with books. In *Marginalia: Readers Writing in Books* and *Romantic Readers: The Evidence of Marginalia*, Jackson looks to annotations for evidence of a shared language ("the common codes of reading") and individuals' senses of the act of annotation, which Jackson terms a "social art." Jackson's *Marginalia* integrates the methods of bibliography and literary analysis to conduct a "genre study" of the "annotator's art" spanning 300 years.[85]

Leah Price has turned from the politics of culture to the construction of literature through lenses colored by race, class, and gender. In *How to Do Things with Books in Victorian Britain*, Price studies nineteenth-century conceptions of the uses of print. In the process, Price finds that "mythic" idealization of textuality at the expense of literary materiality was a gendered, racialized, and classed phenomenon. Canonical novels are shown to uphold the myth, but Price also uncovers texts that challenge the notion that the reification of materiality, which is perceivable in the ideology of literary property, was uniform. In products of the Evangelical press like anonymous pieces in religious periodicals ("The History of an Old Packet Bible," *History of a Religious Tract Supposed to Be Related by Itself*), for example, the book-object, as opposed to any disembodied text, has heroic status.[86]

In studying collectors and their institutions, Barbara M. Benedict has also approached the problem of social division rather than the project of social cohesion. Benedict's *Curiosity: A Cultural History of Early Modern Inquiry* approaches the topic from the perspective of gender and sexuality, looking at the cultural tradition aligning curiosity with deviance. This tradition lies behind a traditional dissident type of the collector, whose knowledge has traditionally been associated with affect. This knowledge is an object of desire, and curiosity is a psychosexual symptom. Ancient Mesopotamia and ancient Greece produced the dangerous figures Eve and Pandora, for example—women both curious and object-focused in their seeking and finding. These figures expose the historical gendering of curiosity as feminine.[87] The latter resembles a collector, keeping evil in a jar until "the woman unstopped the jar and let it all out," as Hesiod says in *Works and Days*.[88]

Curiosity, as Benedict also argues, has long attracted associations with transgressions of various kinds. In the early modern period in particular, curiosity represented a problematic desire for mastery, self-aggrandizement, fetishism, and appropriation. This is true even if Sir Hans Sloane and Samuel Johnson exemplify well-regarded curious men whose interests were thought to provide a clear benefit to the public. In *Rasselas* and elsewhere, Johnson himself expressed views highly critical of the insubordinate and tormenting desire for knowledge.[89] The virtuoso, an effeminate seventeenth-century version of the type, was a collector who kept his "knacks," a slang term for "testicles," in cabinets.[90]

This dissident type is also perceivable in responses to nineteenth-century archaeology and, specifically, the discovery of the Elgin marbles and similar artifacts. Antiquaries not only infamously plundered Greece's national treasures but also, in the form of the Elgin marbles' representation of male beauty, brought "Greek love" uncomfortably close to home. Object-focused and queer, this dissident type linked accumulative desire, cultural expertise, and consumerism to classical antiquity and the people, usually men, who studied it. In the nineteenth century, the figure of the collector simultaneously extended and enriched an old tradition of sexually phobic associations of male queerness with connoisseurship and collecting.

The political conservatism of some among the critics of collectors was not happenstance, as scholars focused on Romantic aesthetics have discovered. The phobic representations of connoisseurs suggest the perceived dissidence of pleasure taken in objects as well as knowledge from them, and Sha has identified the former as a thread through Romantic aesthetics and science. Specifically, Sha identifies a connection between Kant's notion of the nonutilitarian nature of the beautiful and Romantic science's skepticism about biological determinism, finding that the Romantics imagined political liberation in terms of sexual perversion.[91] The discourses produced by and about collectors during the period affirms Sha's general thesis concerning the period's imagining of a kind of freedom in useless pleasure.

The provocation presented by collectors speaks to the broader, heterosexist repression of affect in the discipline of history, which Elizabeth Freeman has examined. In other words, intellectual history offers helpful context for understanding the negative thrust of these phobic associations accrued by the figure of the collector. In *Time Binds: Queer Temporalities, Queer Histories*, Freeman proposes an alternative method of historiography, "erotohistoriography," as a counterweight to traditional historiography's repressive tendencies. In practice, erotohistoriography locates affective communities whose binding forces are "nonsequential" and, therefore, hidden from history, where sequential chronology dominates. Freeman's method also serves to trace the lineaments of historiography's repressive force, showing in the process how pleasure has been a "loser" in intradisciplinary conflict over proper historical practice.[92] Freeman's work illuminates the sexual politics informing the fate of another discourse, "wild bibliography." As Klancher has argued in an article about Dibdin, an unruly and eventually superseded version of bibliography practiced in the early nineteenth century relied on a practice in which collecting and history overlapped. The work of Freeman and Klancher suggests that the status of the collector can be explained in part by an evolving contest between sensibility and repression in the context of intellectual history.

The origins of modern history may have had a still closer connection to the phobic construction of antiquarians, as Mike Goode has argued in *Sentimental Masculinity and the Rise of History, 1790–1890*. Male sensibility was conceived of as integral to historical practice, but the body's prominence in historiography also invoked grosser passions, prompting a crisis in masculinity. The antiquarian's queerness emerged as a foil for the proper conduct of history, which Goode illustrates with Thomas Rowlandson's salacious cartoon depicting a perverse antiquarian groping a Greek statue, *Modern Antiques*.[93]

Some recent scholarship has identified a tradition associating specifically bookishness and reading with deviance. Nagle notes that, beginning in the eighteenth century, reading was viewed as potentially harmful due to readers' perceived private enjoyment of "excessive pleasures." Citing the work of Patricia Meyer Spacks, Nagle observes that the fears linked to reading reflected a more general anxiety about privacy, with its inevitable associations with sexuality.[94] Whereas Lynch and Ferris and, to a lesser degree, Price find that the book has a binding function in communities, the present study, in a way in keeping with the observations of Benedict and Nagle, finds that the book is more often a marker of difference rather than a means of bridging it. In the cases this book examines, the promise of sensibility, conventionally understood, fails as often as it succeeds: desire, while revealed to be dynamic and, at times, disturbingly unpredictable, often does not bring human subjects to common ground. Instead, desire is most often either a classed and sexualized marker of difference (or both), as in the case of the representation of Dibdin's collecting society; a compensation for social alienation, as in the case of the imposturous culture of Wise and Forman; or an eccentric form of consumerism, as in the case of Lamb's proto-bohemian *flâneurship* and book collecting. These examples suggest that when literature appears to be a fetish, the sensibility oriented toward it is seen as a liability rather than a promise of community and parity.

CHAPTER SUMMARY

This examination of Romantic ornamental communities organized by book love begins in the Gothic eighteenth century with the queer radicalism and domestic dissidence of the Ladies of Llangollen. Glamorgan Pottery's popular, pirated "Ladies of Llangollen" china pattern (1825) speaks to the widespread interest in this couple's defiantly public "romantic friendship." Rather than corrupting it, the prominence of books and other things in the lives and legacy of the couple, Butler and Ponsonby, points to the extensive network of object relations binding the women to each other and to a number of men and women across time. This network encompassed a broader circle of intimates, including women such as Princess Charlotte and Anna Seward. Men with whom the couple was close to sustained the famed material legacy embodied in their self-consciously antiquarian home, a pastiche of Walpole's Strawberry Hill complete with Gothic follies and a highly ornamented library. Integral to this queer community was a nationalist, imperialist, and, as commemorative relics suggest, commodified image of Wales in the English imaginary—a version of the Grand Tour's transnational queer eroticism that was closer to home. In drawing attention to this transnational and intergenerational ornamental community, united by shared antiquarian possessions, including Wales itself, the first chapter identifies such materialism as a powerful form of imaginative, medial extension enabling the expression of queer communities and ways of being irreducible to the conventional framework on human sexuality.

For the Ladies, bookish consumerism was at once radical and compensatory in the way it afforded the dissident women community and self-empowering pleasure. In the period, bookishness also took a more public form: the male, homosocial collecting society. To commemorate the sale of a very rare fifteenth-century copy of Giovanni Boccaccio's The *Decameron* at auction in 1812, for a price not surpassed until 1884, Dibdin founded the first such group, the still-active Roxburghe Club. His works and the image of his circle of collectors in the periodical press serve as the focus of the second chapter.

Other members of the group included the book's winner, Lord Spencer, and one of its meetings may have been attended by Walter Scott, who corresponded with Dibdin. The club celebrated aristocratic consumption but also produced antiquarian culture. Independently, Dibdin was an ambitious, but frustrated and financially insecure, self-published bibliographer and poet. His works, including a mock-heroic dialogue modeled after Boccaccio's *Decameron* and the incomplete long poem *Bibliography* (1812), like the Ladies' architectural text Plas newydd, afforded the imagining of another, more welcoming world—in Dibdin's case a "faery-land of bibliography" peopled by male "converts" to the "bibliographical cause" who express love for vellum pages and "black-letter" text. His works also mark the entrance of the book collector into a public discourse of something like sexuality. Dibdin, as noted by Lennard J. Davis in *Obsession: A History*, also had an interest in medical science, which is reflected in the quasi-medical approach he takes to diagnosing what he facetiously calls the "book-disease." Dibdin's discourse is uncannily queer, being to an indeterminable extent the production of an effect of the history of sexuality, if not a queer subject. The origins of its queerness relate sexual identity not only to textuality and rhetoric, as in the work of Edelman, but also to the very materiality of language. The bibliomaniac's bookish desires, in other words, ran counter to notions of national and individual intellectual property and returned the repressed literariness of sexuality to legibility, revealing in the process close ties between ideas about literary materiality, authorship, and queerness.

In 1834, Dibdin's group of "ornamental gentlemen" attracted the notice of an anonymous writer for *The Athenæum* magazine, whose ostensible purpose was to review the unintended publication of a memoir by a deceased member of the club. The writer of the magazine piece, who may have been James Silk Buckingham, argues that rare book collecting poses a risk to the health of the "republic" of British letters, and the article's image of this threat is a hypersensual male connoisseur. This figure recalls traditional models of male queerness such as the seventeenth-century virtuoso with his collectible "knacks" as well as the effeminatus, the origins of which Linda Dowling has located in classical republican discourse.[95] The attack also associates the club with the famous collector Richard Heber. Heber, like Beckford before him, had been embroiled in a scandal involving a younger man. The article's insinuations and veiled attacks suggest a public, overtly phobic and unambiguously queer version of Dibdin's earlier and more ambiguously queer collector—one that resembles later homophobic representations of gay men.

Histories of book collecting focus almost exclusively on the activities of wealthy collectors, but Dibdin, a hanger-on at bibliomaniacal court whose financial desperation is evident from his correspondence, shows that interest in rare books extended beyond the confines of aristocrats' libraries, while simultaneously focusing on the worlds of the auction room and private library. Bibliophile taste was far from monolithic during the period and reached places far removed from aristocratic spaces. The third chapter of this study addresses ways that the dissident culture of bookishness also manifested itself outside the auction room and aristocratic culture more broadly. Addressing an ornamental culture in a middle-class context, this chapter examines the prototypically bohemian styles of a "minor" Romantic who wrote for the magazines, Charles Lamb.

Lamb was a paid writer for magazines at a time when professionalization and publication itself were stigmatized by the *avant-garde*. In the Elia essays, Lamb self-consciously registers his liminal position in British letters through representation of his own consumerism—a love of literature that simultaneously conformed to and departed from aristocrats' collecting practices. Scholars such as Lynch and Russett have drawn connections between such a unique, affective relationship to literature and the condition of canonical minority. As this chapter sets out to show, however, the significance of Lamb's bookishness goes beyond the political structure of the literary field. The collecting practices of this "gentle" and bookish "hero" of the *London Magazine*, along with Lamb's Elia essays, including "Oxford in the Vacation" and " The South-sea House," are the foci of this chapter. Lamb, whose works have in the past enjoyed canonical status, is due for the kind of revival of critical interest that De Quincey, another master of the personal essay, has received. Drawing on the work of Colin Campbell and Hebdige, this chapter argues that Lamb's self-conception as a London writer and his self-conscious preference for dog-eared volumes culled from London's used bookshops—his "ragged regiment of book-tatterdemalions"—play a role in a populist and prototypically bohemian style as well as merge a version of camp aesthetics with a bookish and queer mode of authorial subjectivity, which Lamb's "gentle" moniker references.[96]

Lamb's articulations of opposition in the theory and praxis of bibliomania recurred in one of its legacies, the Victorian literary society. Instrumental in the construction of a canon of Romantic writers during the Victorian period, clubs like Frederick J. Furnivall's Shelley Society continued the tradition of private printing begun by Dibdin's Roxburghe Club. In the Victorian clubs, bookish consumerism offered a haven for dissidents in the spirit of the Ladies' Plas newydd. Some members of Furnivall's societies were united by sexual dissidence and a love of Romanticism indistinguishable from a fetishism of literary materiality. Two active members of several such clubs were the bibliographers and collectors Wise and Forman. Wise was an eminent bibliographer whose own collection, which included the manuscript of Shelley's *Queen Mab*, became famous as a result of his catalog *Ashley*

Library. Forman was an esteemed editor of Keats and Shelley whose editorial practices, which created the modern preference for the "correct" text of a work, were not only revolutionary but also reflected a bibliophile's values. The pair is more widely known, however, for a fraudulent form of Romantic cultural reproduction that grew out of innocent hobbyist reprinting by the societies to which they belonged. This work involved the highly profitable creation of "creative forgeries"—fake first editions—the authenticity of which was subsequently validated by the pair's own bibliography. Advances in bibliographic science ultimately exposed their forgeries, but only after Forman had died and when Wise was very old. A famous edition of Elizabeth Barrett Browning's *Songs from the Portuguese* is among their illicit works. In the context of a queer reading of their illicit project and works, drawing on both sociological and psychoanalytic approaches to forgery and imposture, the fourth chapter argues that the illicit, bookish culture of Wise and Forman identifies Romanticism as a "curious" artifact of bibliomania and forgery as a queer foil for authorship.

NOTES

1. William Makepeace Thackeray, *Vanity Fair* (Oxford: Oxford University Press, 1998), 421 (emphasis original).
2. Sigmund Freud, "From the History of an Infantile Neurosis ('Wolf Man')," in *The Freud Reader*, ed. Peter Gay (New York: Norton, 1989).
3. Thackeray, *Vanity Fair*, 569.
4. Thackeray, *Vanity Fair*, 569.
5. Gayle Rubin, "Thinking Sex: Notes for a Radical Theory of the Politics of Sexuality," in *The Lesbian and Gay Studies Reader*, ed. H. Abelove, M. A. Barale, and D. M. Halperin (New York: Routledge, 1993), 4.
6. Christopher Nagle, *Sexuality and the Culture of Sensibility in the British Romantic Era* (New York: Palgrave Macmillan, 2007), 5–6.
7. Nagle, *Culture of Sensibility*, 4.
8. Thomas F. Dibdin to William Nichol (16 October 1828) (emphasis in original), H. E. Huntington Library, San Marino, CA.
9. Ina Ferris, *Book-Men, Book Clubs, and the Romantic Literary Sphere* (Houndmills, UK: Palgrave Macmillan, 2015), 6.
10. Ferris, *Book-Men, Book Clubs, and the Romantic Literary Sphere*, 2–7.
11. Lee Edelman, *Homographesis: Essays in Gay Literary and Cultural Theory* (New York: Routledge, 1994), xiv; Thomas A. King, *The Gendering of Men, 1600–1750* (Madison: University of Wisconsin Press, 2004), 1.111.
12. Thomas F. Dibdin, *Bibliomania, or, Book-madness: A Bibliographical Romance, in Six Parts, Illustrated with Cuts* (London: Longman, Hurst, Rees, Orme, and Brown, 1811).

13. William St. Clair, *The Reading Nation in the Romantic Period* (Cambridge: Cambridge University Press, 2004), 10–11.

14. David Allan, *A Nation of Readers: The Lending Library in Georgian England* (London: The British Library, 2008), 1.

15. St. Clair, *Reading Nation*, 10–11.

16. Marilyn Butler, *Maria Edgeworth: A Literary Biography* (Oxford: Clarendon Press, 1972).

17. Butler, *Maria Edgeworth*, 103.

18. Edmund Burke, *Reflections on the Revolution in France*, ed. J. C. D. Clark (Stanford: Stanford University Press, 2001), 242; Samuel Taylor Coleridge, *The Statesman's Manual; or The Bible the Best Guide to Political Skill and Foresight: A Lay Sermon, Addressed to the Higher Classes of Society*, ed. R. J. White, in *The Collected Works of Samuel Taylor Coleridge*, ed. Kathleen Coburn and Bart Winer (London: Routledge & Kegan Paul, 1983), 6.37–38.

19. William Wordsworth, "Essay, Supplementary to the Preface," in *The Prose Works of William Wordsworth*, ed. W. J. B. Owen and Jane W. Smyser (Oxford: Clarendon Press, 1974), 3.84.

20. Samuel Taylor Coleridge, "Biographia Literaria, or Biographical Sketches of My Literary Life and Opinions," in *Collected Works of Samuel Taylor Coleridge* ed. James Engall and W. Jackson Bate, 7.48.

21. George Gordon Lord Byron, *Byron's Letters and Journals*, ed. Leslie A. Marchand (Cambridge, MA: Harvard University Press, 1977), 7.217.

22. Lucien Febvre and Henri-Jean Martin, *The Coming of the Book*, trans. David Gerard (London: Verso, 1976).

23. Febvre and Martin, *Coming of the Book*.

24. Thomas De Quincey, *The Works of Thomas De Quincey, Vol. 11: Articles from Tait's Magazine and Blackwood's Magazine, 1838–41*, ed. Julian North (London: Pickering & Chatto, 2000).

25. Thomas Quincey, *A Short Tour in the Midland Counties of England; Performed in the Summer of 1772. Together with an Account of a Similar Excursion, Undertaken September 1774* (London: M. Lewis, 1775), 78–79.

26. Judith Pascoe, *The Hummingbird Cabinet: A Rare and Curious History of Romantic Collectors* (Ithaca, NY: Cornell University Press, 2006).

27. Walter Scott, *The Antiquary* (London: Ward, Lock & Co., 1883).

28. Ferriar, John. M. D., *The Bibliomania, an Epistle, to Richard Heber, Esq.* (London: T. Cadell and W. Davies, 1809), 43, Google Books.

29. Sir Samuel Egerton Brydges, *The Autobiography, Times, Opinions, and Contemporaries of Sir Egerton Brydges* (London: Cochrane and McCrone, 1834), 2.196, Google Books.

30. Allan, *Nation of Readers*, 1.

31. Philip Connell, "Bibliomania: Book Collecting, Cultural Politics, and the Rise of Literary Heritage in Romantic Britain," *Representations* 71 (2000): 43n4.

32. Connell, "Bibliomania."

33. Nicholas A. Basbanes, *A Gentle Madness: Bibliophiles, Bibliomanes, and the Eternal Passion for Books* (New York: Henry Holt, 1995), 114, 123, 120.

34. Basbanes, *Gentle Madness*, 120.

35. L. M. M., "Phillips, Sir Thomas (1792–1872)," in *The Dictionary of National Biography*, ed. Leslie Stephen and Sidney Lee (London: Smith, Elder, & Co., 1896), 45.193, Google Books.

36. Nagle, *Culture of Sensibility*, 6.

37. Deidre Shauna Lynch, *Loving Literature: A Cultural History* (Chicago: University of Chicago Press, 2015), 114.

38. Lynch, *Loving Literature*.

39. *The 1769 King James Bible*, John 1: 14, https://en.wikisource.org/wiki/Bible_(King_James)/John#Chapter_1.

40. Arjun Appadurai, "The Thing Itself," *Public Culture* 18, no. 1 (2006): 15.

41. William Beckford, *Rare Doings at Roxburghe Hall. A Ballad* (London: J. F. Dove, [1821]), inserted in William Clarke, *Repertorium Bibliographicum* (San Marino, CA: H. E. Huntington Library).

42. Sigmund Freud, "Character and Anal Erotism," in *The Freud Reader*, ed. Peter Gay, trans. James Strachey (New York: Norton, 1989), 296.

43. J. P. C., "Introduction," in "The Trimming of Thomas Nash, Gentleman," in *Miscellaneous Tracts* (n.p., n.d.), v, Google Books.

44. Richard Lichfield [Gabriel Harvey], "The Trimming of Thomas Nashe," in *The Old Book Collector's Miscellany: Or a Collection of Readerly Reprints of Literary Rarities, Illustrative of the History, Literature, Manners, and Biography of the English Nation*, ed. Charles Hindley (London: Reeves & Turner, [1597] 1871–3), 1.9, Google Books.

45. Slavoj Žižek, *Looking Awry: An Introduction to Jacques Lacan through Popular Culture* (Cambridge, MA: MIT Press, 1991), 110.

46. John Collins, *The Two Forgers: A Biography of Harry Buxton Forman and Thomas J. Wise* (New Castle, DE: Oak Knoll, 1992), 40.

47. Nicholas A. Basbanes, *Patience and Fortitude: A Roving Chronicle of Book People, Book Places, and Book Culture* (New York: HarperCollins, 2001), 234.

48. Thomas F. Dibdin, *Bibliomania, or, Book-madness: A Bibliographical Romance, in Six Parts, Illustrated with Cuts*, 2nd ed. (London: 1842), v.

49. Dibdin, *Bibliomania* (1811), 4.

50. Sebastian Brant, *Ship of Fools*, ed. T. H. Jamieson, trans. Alexander Barclay (Edinburgh: William Paterson, 1874), http://www.gutenberg.org/files/20179/20179-h/20179-h.htm.

51. Gaetana Marrone, Paolo Puppa, and Luce Sonigli, *Encyclopedia of Italian Literary Studies* (New York: Routledge, 2007).

52. Barbara M. Benedict, *Curiosity: A Cultural History of Early Modern Inquiry* (Chicago: University of Chicago Press, 2001), 183.

53. [Buckingham, James Silk?], Rev. of *Roxburghe Revels*, *The Athenæum* 323–325 (January 1834): 2.

54. John V. Richardson, Jr., "Dibdin, Thomas Frognall (1776–1847)," in *Oxford Dictionary of National Biography*, ed. H. C. G. Matthew and Brian Harrison (Oxford: Oxford University Press, 2004), http://www.oxforddnb.com/view/article/7588.

55. Nicolas Barker and John Collins, *A Sequel to an Enquiry into the Nature of Certain Nineteenth Century Pamphlets by John Carter and Graham Pollard* (London: Scolar Press, 1983).

56. Dick Hebdige, *Subculture: The Meaning of Style* (New York: Methuen & Co, Ltd, 1979).

57. Sean Silver, "Visiting Strawberry Hill: Horace Walpole's Gothic Historiography," *Eighteenth Century Fiction* 21, no. 4 (2009), Academic Search Complete.

58. Barrett Kalter, *Modern Antiques: The Material Past in England, 1660–1780* (Lewisburg, PA: Bucknell University Press, 2011).

59. Austin Dobson, *Horace Walpole: A Memoir* (New York: Dodd, Mead and Co., 1893), 225, Google Books.

60. Horace Walpole, *The Castle of Otranto*, ed. W. S. Lewis and E. J. Clery (Oxford: Oxford University Press, 1998), 162.

61. Elizabeth Mavor, *The Ladies of Llangollen: A Study in Romantic Friendship* (London: Michael Joseph, 1971).

62. Mavor, *Ladies of Llangollen*, 176.

63. Lynch, *Loving Literature*; Margaret Russett, *De Quincey's Romanticism: Canonical Minority and the Forms of Transmission* (Cambridge: Cambridge University Press, 1997).

64. Lee Edelman, *No Future: Queer Theory and the Death Drive* (Durham, NC: Duke University Press, 2004).

65. Susan Sontag. "Notes on Camp," in *Against Interpretation and Other Essays* (New York: Dell Publishing Co., 1969).

66. Edelman, *No Future*, 27.

67. Richard C. Sha, *Perverse Romanticism: Aesthetics and Sexuality in Britain, 1750–1832* (Baltimore: Johns Hopkins University Press, 2009).

68. Margaret Russett, *Fictions and Fakes: Forging Romantic Authenticity, 1760–1845* (Cambridge: Cambridge University Press, 2006); Martha Woodmansee, *The Author, Art, and the Market: Rereading the History of Aesthetics* (New York: Columbia University Press, 1994).

69. Russett, *Fictions and Fakes*.

70. St. Clair, *Reading Nation*, 9.

71. Elizabeth L. Eisenstein, *The Printing Press as an Agent of Change: Communications and Cultural Transformations in Early-modern Europe* (Cambridge: Cambridge University Press, 1979), 1.5; Elizabeth L. Eisenstein, *Divine Art, Infernal Machine: The Reception of Printing in the West from First Impressions to the Sense of an Ending* (Philadelphia: University of Pennsylvania Press, 2011), ix.

72. Joseph Dane, *The Myth of Print Culture* (Toronto: University of Toronto Press, 2003).

73. Robert Darnton, *The Case for Books: Past, Present, and Future* (New York: PublicAffairs, 2010), 178.

74. David D. Hall, *Cultures of Print: Essays in the History of the Book* (Amherst: University of Massachusetts Press, 1996), 1, 2, 119, 169–87.

75. St. Clair, *Reading Nation*, 2.

76. Antonio Gramsci, *Selections from the Prison Notebooks*, ed. and trans. Quintin Hoare and Geoffrey Nowell Smith (New York: International Publishers), 384.

77. Robert Darnton, *The Business of Enlightenment* (Cambridge, MA: Belknap Press of Harvard University Press, 1979), 3.

78. Richard D. Altick, *The English Common Reader: A Social History of the Mass Reading Public, 1800–1900* (Chicago: University of Chicago Press, 1957), 306, 5.

79. Allan, *Nation of Readers*.

80. Jon P. Klancher, *The Making of English Reading Audiences, 1790–1832* (Madison: University of Wisconsin Press, 1987), 9, 6–8.

81. Maureen Daly Goggin, "Introduction: Threading Women," in *Women and the Material Culture of Needlework and Textiles, 1750–1950*, ed. Maureen Daly Goggin and Beth Fowkes Tobin (Abingdon, UK: Routledge, 2016), 5.

82. Deidre Shauna Lynch, "Canons' Clockwork: Novels for Everyday Use," in *Bookish Histories: Books, Literature, and Commercial Modernity, 1700–1900*, ed. Ina Ferris and Paul Keen (Basingstoke: Palgrave Macmillan, 2009), 89–91.

83. Lynch, *Loving Literature*.

84. Ina Ferris, "Book-love and the Remaking of Literary Culture in the Romantic Periodical," in *Bookish Histories: Books, Literature, and Commercial Modernity, 1700–1900*, ed. Ina Ferris and Paul Keen (Basingstoke: Palgrave Macmillan, 2009), 114–15.

85. Heather J. Jackson, *Romantic Readers: The Evidence of Marginalia* (New Haven: Yale University Press, 2005), xi; Heather J. Jackson, *Marginalia: Readers Writing in Books* (New Haven: Yale University Press, 2001), 6–7.

86. Leah Price, *How to Do Things with Books in Victorian Britain* (Princeton: Princeton University Press, 2012), 16, 115, 16.

87. Benedict, *Curiosity*, 25.

88. Hesiod, *Theogony* and *Works and Days*, trans. M. L. West (Oxford: Oxford University Press, 1988), 39.

89. Benedict, *Curiosity*.

90. King, *Gendering of Men, 1600–1750*, 2.98–100.

91. Sha, *Perverse Romanticism*.

92. Elizabeth Freeman, *Time Binds: Queer Temporalities, Queer Histories* (Durham, NC: Duke University Press, 2010), xi, 95.

93. Mike Goode, *Sentimental Masculinity and the Rise of History, 1790–1890* (Cambridge: Cambridge University Press, 2009).

94. Nagle, *Culture of Sensibility*, 6.

95. Linda Dowling, *Hellenism and Homosexuality in Victorian Oxford* (Ithaca: Cornell University Press, 1994).

96. E. V. Lucas, ed., *The Works of Charles and Mary Lamb* (London: Methuen, 1903), 2.191.

Chapter 1

Collecting the Ladies of Llangollen

Glamorgan Pottery's "Ladies of Llangollen" china pattern (1825) depicts two figures draped in riding attire and sitting astride horses on a serpentine path around a shallow pond (fig. 1.1). In the foreground, a farmer stands in midstride with his back to the viewer, a reaper in one hand and a lunch pail in the other. He looks up at the stately riders. In the middle distance sits a quaint cottage, its chimney quiet and water wheel still. An imposing castle dominates the far background, its four domed towers joined by crenulated walls. This pastoral and Gothic scene is Llangollen Vale, home to the famous "Llangollen Ladies," or "Ladies of Llangollen," Eleanor Butler (1739–1829) and Sarah Ponsonby (1755–1831), the most famous queer women of the eighteenth and nineteenth centuries. The life that Butler and Ponsonby built in Wales in Llangollen Vale, to which they fled, initially with reservation, in 1778, and where they had both died by the winter of 1830, has made them by turns eccentric dowagers, "romantic friends," lesbian icons, and "sapphists."[1]

With its subjects and feudal and Gothic overtones, the Glamorgan pattern presents an image of Plas newydd as paradisiacal in an antiquarian and dissident mode—as an object, in other words, of retrospective but also transgressive longing. Hence, it embodies the roles played by material culture and consumerist desire in the lives and legacy of these iconic dissidents. By their example and powerful influence, Butler and Ponsonby sponsored a small boom in consumer goods including, in addition to the Glamorgan pattern, other pieces of pottery featuring their image, an engraving of them wearing men's clothes seated in their library, a pirated version of the same engraving in which the women appear to be wearing top hats and tails in their garden, and even cookies stamped with the same image.[2] In *The Ladies of Llangollen: Desire, Indeterminacy, and the Legacies of Criticism*, Fiona Brideoake aptly

Figure 1.1 Glamorgan China Pattern. Image courtesy of Andrew J. Pyle, Lovers of Blue and White China Specialists, Royston, Hertfordshire, England.

terms this collection of goods a "commodity cluster" and includes in this inventory tapestries, ashtrays, guidebooks, and porcelain fairings available from the Denbighshire County Council.[3] While sponsoring others' desire for things, the Ladies' own relationship with materiality was intimate and laden with affect. Through friends and acquaintances, objects bound an intergenerational queer community inspired by their example. Their home, Plas newydd, and its location, Wales, an object of commodified longing among antiquaries and tourists seeking sublime experiences or an alternative to the traditional Grand Tour, should themselves be numbered among these objects of consumerist desire.[4]

This chapter focuses on the role of such objects in the still-vibrant community that the Ladies created. Objects are not usually the central players in their story, however. Instead, the perceived radicalness of their "choice to live together without men," as one scholar has put it, has fired imaginations and debates since their own lifetimes.[5] While scholarly discussion of the Ladies has reflected the dominance of the asexual "romantic friendship" thesis championed by Elizabeth Mavor, outside academic discourse, the Ladies' adventurous elopement to Wales figures prominently in lesbian-themed cultural production.⁶ Mary Gordon's *Chase of the Wild Goose* (1936, 1975), which Leonard and Virginia Woolf's Hogarth Press issued, draws on sources such as the women's journals and contemporaries' correspondence to offer an imaginative retelling of their story as a trailblazing love affair. As Ellen Crowell has also noticed, the narrative includes some remarkably sultry dialogue.⁷ In Gordon's description of the couple's reunion at a dance, Ponsonby says to Butler, "Heart of my heart! I could kiss you for a year."⁸ The central characters are heroic in their commitment to self-determination and to each other, despite resistance in the form of relatives' self-serving plans for their lives. The book's history includes the tidbit, as relayed by Brideoake, that Gordon told Leonard Woolf that she received a visitation from the Ladies' ghosts.⁹

Colette took inspiration from the publication of Butler's journal in 1932 to rewrite the couple's biography in *Ces plaisirs* (*The Pure and the Impure*), depicting them as asexual dowagers.¹⁰ More recently, Doris Grumbach based a novel, *The Ladies* (1984), on their lives, and the lesbian rock group Frank Chickens recorded a song about them, "Two Little Ladies" (1990).¹¹ They also make a surprising appearance in the former Second Lady Lynne Cheney's disclaimed 1981 novel *Sisters*, where the main character dismisses a traditional narrative that posits them as exemplars of chaste friendship and identifies with the hidden sensuality of their bond.¹²

The neutralizing friendship narrative invoked in Cheney's text reflects the more complex and shifting picture of the Ladies that scholars have produced. In *The Literature of Lesbianism*, which includes excerpts from Butler's diaries, Terry Castle says the couple's "life together continues to inspire lesbian fantasy" despite the fact that "the exact nature of their relationship is unclear."¹³ Castle's evident frustration at the resistant opacity of the Ladies' relationship illustrates the position of the couple at a crossroads where conflicting views on the proper roles of historiography, identity, and theory in the study of gender and sexuality collide. Castle herself has elsewhere expressed critical views of the Ladies' famed chastity, lamenting its far-reaching influence on lesbian stereotypes.¹⁴ As Brideoake has astutely noted, the long-running debate among scholars over how to define the Ladies' relationship reflects, on the one hand, the influence of an ahistorical deployment of categorical identity common in the study of sexuality and, on the other, a specific moment in the field informed by Second-Wave feminist discourse, which happens to be the moment when Mavor's standard text on the Ladies, *Ladies of Llangollen: A Study in Romantic Friendship*, appeared.¹⁵ Mavor argues that the Ladies enjoyed a mode of chaste "romantic friendship" common among women of the time but rendered impossible in modernity by biological conceptions of sexuality that influence not only the broader cultural construction of sexuality but also women's own behavior and self-conceptions.¹⁶ Testifying to the staying power of Mavor's influence, Crowell has discussed the spectral power that

Butler and Ponsonby's "friendship" and, as already mentioned, their remarkable "choice to live together without men" has had over Irish women writers, including Maria Edgeworth, Elizabeth Bowen, and Molly Keane.[17] A competing tradition has employed the identitarian and sexualizing logic of the "female husband" typology, a tradition active during the women's own time.[18] As Lisa L. Moore says in *Dangerous Intimacies: Toward a Sapphic History of the British Novel*, their elopement aroused fears that they would replace men.[19] (Moore's own perspective on the Ladies can be seen ultimately to agree with Mavor's, however).[20] Taking a view more nuanced than either of these traditions, Susan S. Lanser, in *The Sexuality of History: Modernity and the Sapphic, 1565–1830* as well as an article in Richard C. Sha's collection *Historicizing Romantic Sexuality*, has cited the Ladies as exemplary of a paradoxically virtuous yet sexually suspect form of attachment she terms "sapphism," finding their ambiguous and evolving status—being sometimes celebrated as virgins and other times mocked as deviants—in the cultural imaginary to reflect shifting, class-bound representational traditions that alternatively victimized and empowered dissidents.[21] In her book on the Ladies, Brideoake similarly avoids ontological questions altogether, taking, similarly to Lanser, the "dialectical recurrence" of the competing frameworks as a subject in its own right. This very tension, Brideoake says, "evidences [the Ladies'] queerness, constituted by their strikingly public resistance to sexual specification, rather than either their nonnormativity or fulfillment of specific identitarian criteria."[22]

Like Lanser and Brideoake's analyses, the present discussion takes a broad view on the queerness of the women's ornamental community rather than engage ontological questions about their identities or ambiguously sexual relationship. Focusing on their community's desire for, production of, and exchange of objects and literary products in particular, I explore ways that the desire that bound the community—hallmarks of which ironically invoke reductive clichés about queer identity, in fact—transcended the human to comprise consumerist desire and accumulation. Examples of this consumerism include the women's bookish and Gothic take on homemaking and their attraction to Wales, a form of consumption speaking to the popularity of antiquarian and picturesque travel in the Romantic period. Bookish in itself, such tourism was mediated by the literary genre of the "tour." As Brideoake has observed, the literary qualities of Northern tourism recall the bookishness of the Grand Tour, "a primarily literary phenomenon, undertaken by individuals whose itineraries, attitudes, and observations were conditioned by travel journals, guidebooks, collected letters, and popular archaeology."[23] Tours, akin to today's coffee table books, were made possible by new printing technology that allowed for the wide distribution of images.[24] The bookishness of tourism and travel was part and parcel with the Ladies' domestic habits. Their grand and ornate library became an attraction in its own right, fostering a wide network of literary lights and sponsoring the Ladies' fame. It was, as Brideoake says, one of the "textual, material, and sociable means" by which they created an "anodyne public image" to distract from their "unconventional relationship."[25] Their private consumption habits interleaved the intimate with the literary. An entry in Butler's diary, begun in 1788, illustrates their shared bookishness: "My beloved and I went to the new garden. Reading. Drawing. Read 'Davila.' Then my beloved read 'La Morte d'Abel.' Nine till twelve in the bedchamber reading. . . . A day of sweet and delicious retirement."[26] Not only literature but also the repeated expression of a bookish and antiquarian sensibility centrally occupied the couple's domestic intimacy and "delicious" homemaking. Registering the dissident power of this trope, Gordon devotes an entire page of *Chase of the Wild Goose* to a list of the many times the phrase "delicious retirement" appears in the journals.[27] What an exclusively human-centered and conventionally identitarian lens on the Ladies fails to capture is the key role of objects in their intimacy.

Objects also mattered in the Ladies' intergenerational community of dissidents, as they particularly have in other dissident communities across time and space. Hence, like Brideoake's approach to the Ladies, the focus of this argument finds support in Ann Cvetkovich's insights into the prominent role played by material culture in queer lives. This importance is difficult to disentangle from the methods and products of queer history. In *An Archive of Feelings: Trauma, Sexuality, and Lesbian Public Cultures*, Cvetkovich suggests that discrimination against nonnormative persons has contributed to this prominence of the material in queer communities. More specifically, Cvetkovich observes that, because histories of sexuality and affect often fail to find written form ("sex and feelings [being] too personal or ephemeral to leave records"), scholars of queer history frequently rely instead on nonliterary materials, including the camp effluvia of pop culture, due to the lacunae created by mainstream disregard for queer history.[28] What is known of the Ladies' community implies parallels between homosocial collecting societies and other Romantic subcultures for whom pleasure in objects acted as an affectively charged social binder and, as in the cases of *virtuosi* and bibliomaniacs, a signifier of difference. While contextualizing them in the broader scope of queer history and linking them to dissident men such as Horace Walpole, the materialism integral to the Ladies' nonnormative erotic lives should not be taken as implying their equivalence to male dissidents. As David Halperin has argued, the structure of patriarchy, through its imposition of compulsive heterosexuality, produces radically different stakes for women's and men's nonnormative sexualities. Men's queerness merely alters patriarchy; women's threatens it.[29]

Objects have extended the Ladies' community generationally, as the Ladies' contemporaries and succeeding generations have passed down and renovated a home, exchanged a multitude of cultural products with or about the Ladies, toured Llangollen, and produced or consumed representations of Butler and Ponsonby. Hence, this chapter situates their story within the broader history of things in the history of sexuality. This chapter's contextualization of the Ladies in the history of sexuality and materiality begins with a discussion of parallels between the Ladies and other queer folks across time and space, focusing on the Ladies' status as refugees (or "Two Fugitive Ladies," as the title page of Ponsonby's travel journal, *Account of a Journey in Wales* [1778], says).[30] The argument then turns to a material example of the Ladies' belonging to this broader terrain: Plas newydd. Analysis of Plas newydd as a queer Gothic text finds it to exemplify queer and transgendered Gothic architecture and consumerism, as well as to embody an economistic process undertaken by a sexually diverse, and therefore queer, consumerist subculture. Despite the problematic status of objects in the history of women, which the following section acknowledges, the self-extension afforded by Plas newydd reflects the resemblance of the Ladies' ornamental community to an "object culture" in theorist Bill Brown's sense. Of fundamental importance to this culture were books, as I ultimately claim, before discussing the role of an appropriately bookish style of tourism in the Ladies' elopement and settlement in Wales.

The elopement made them icons in their own lifetimes. A strand running through their iconography implies the importance of objects for the counterintuitive reason that the pattern features the compulsive abjection of the physical. Among the many famous admirers and visitors to the Ladies in Llangollen at their *cottage ornée* was William Wordsworth. His sonnet "To the Lady E. B. and the Hon. Miss P" (1824) celebrates the "love" shared by the "sisters" by stressing the ideality of their union:

A Stream to mingle with your favorite Dee
Along the VALE OF MEDITATION flows;
So styled by those fierce Britons, pleased to see
In Nature's face the expression of repose;
Or, haply there some pious Hermit chose
To live and die—the peace of Heaven his aim;
To whom the wild sequestered region owes,
At this late day, its sanctifying name.
GLYN CAFAILLGAROCH, in the Cambrian tongue,
In ours the VALE OF FRIENDSHIP, let *this* spot
Be nam'd; where, faithful to a low roof'd Cot,
On Deva's banks, ye have abode so long;
Sisters in love, a love allowed to climb
Ev'n on this earth, above the reach of Time![31]

Notably spiritualizing their sisterly love, the poet takes pains (with the diction "Heaven" and "sanctifying") to forestall any interpretation of the couple's bond in terms of a physical or conventionally romantic tie. Far from an embodied, human relation, their "love" is ethereal and transcendent, "climb[ing]" beyond the reach of "time" itself. Anna Seward likewise made the pilgrimage and commemorated her visit with a poem. Her *Llangollen Vale* (1796) places the Ladies in a mythical and Gothic context, complete with death personified and a ruined "pile," while, like Wordsworth's poem, implying that the exceptional purity of their affective lives makes them superhuman:

Thro' Eleanora, and her Zara's mind,
Early tho' genius, taste, and fancy flow'd,
Tho' all the graceful Arts their powers combin'd,
And her last polish brilliant life bestow'd,
The lavish promiser in youth's soft morn,
Pride, pomp, and love, her friends, the sweet enthusiasts scorn.
Then rose the fairy palace of the vale,
Then bloom'd around it the Arcadian bowers;
Screen'd from the storms of Winter, cold and pale,
Screen'd from the fervours of the sultry hours,
Circling the lawny crescent, soon they rose,
To letter'd ease devote, and friendship's blest repose.[32]

Their super "powers" have caused a "fairy palace" to blossom like a magical flower in a wilderness. Other notable devotees wrote about them in similarly transcendent terms. Hester Lynch Piozzi (formerly Thrale, 1741–1821) and her friend Leonard Chappelow both visited. Piozzi is known for her reminiscences of Johnson, *Anecdotes of the Late Samuel Johnson, LL.D.* and *Letters to and from the Late Samuel Johnson, LL.D.*, and her own correspondence. Relating to Piozzi that a visit to Llangollen inspired a dream about the Ladies, Leonard Chappelow describes "a most heavenly retreat—a Convent in miniature" where "Aeolian Harps heightened this Scene of Enchantment." There, he, a "trembling Stranger," was greeted by immortal "Genij of the Place" who described to him their otherworldly retreat in verse. The Genij says "no turbulent Desires intrude" on the couple's "Repose" in "the deep Recess of dusky Groves."[33] In Chappelow's rendering, the Ladies are heroes of chastity for whom nature's secluded spaces are pleasure enough.

Piozzi, tongue-in-cheek, similarly describes the Ladies as "fair and noble Recluses" living an otherworldly and magical life in a "famous Cottage."[34] In 1800, when the couple faced the prospect of losing their home, Piozzi called it a "dear and celebrated Cottage—which never never must slip from the Possession of Ladies which have made its very Name Immortal."[35]

Elsewhere, Piozzi, like Chappelow, gravitates to the mock-heroic in order to render the strangeness of the place and its owners: "[T]wo Days were delightfully disposed of with the Recluses at Llangollen Cottage, where you would I think leave your Heart a willing Prisoner. They conquer an' keep in their *Enchanted Castle* all Travellers passing that particular Road—at least all those for whome they spread their Nets—Harriett Lee escaped by some Poetical Chance, but they like her Book."[36]

Other notable pilgrims included Robert Southey, Walter Scott, who visited Plas newydd with his godson John Lockhart, and Thomas De Quincey.[37] De Quincey found them courteous but disappointingly unimpressed by himself or his conversation. To his frustration, they also proved difficult to convince of Wordsworth's genius. As he said afterward, "I grieve to say that my own feelings were not more ardent towards *them*."[38] Byron also knew of them, mailing a copy of *The Corsair* to Plas newydd in 1814.[39] Butler's diary contains many entries about unexpected visitors. Some the Ladies admitted to the grounds but not the cottage. Some they hid from: "Saw a Lady walking before the door. Mrs. Otway's compliments. Beg'd leave to see the garden. Permitted. Staid in the potager till she, her little girl, and Dog were gone."[40]

Only by the 1970s, as Mavor observed then, had their international celebrity dimmed.[41] The chronology is notable: their fame waned as the modern gay rights movement began, suggesting that their example of dissidence, blunted by unusual social privilege and the shroud of romantic friendship, was less galvanizing for the nascent movement than it was emblematic of inherited, oppressive power structures and self-hindering ways of being. Curiously, a stream of backhanded compliments and quasi-phobic characterization has followed them into modernity. Mavor recalls the couple's being labeled "suffragettes, spies, nymphomaniacs, men dressed as women, women dressed as men."[42] In a feature story appearing around the same time as Mavor's book, the *Chicago Tribune* refers to them as "enchantresses" and "the two most celebrated virgins in Europe," attributing the label to Prince Puckler Puskau.[43] *The Hamwood Papers*, a collection containing excerpts from Butler's diary, opens with the same quote.[44]

Their galvanic role in a discourse shaped by fraught and shifting politics has obscured aspects of their story that uncannily invoke common aspects of the queer relationship to the material world. Despite their story's seeming incompatibility with the stories of less-privileged gender and sexual dissidents, aspects of it are familiar. One such was the key process of physical movement that brought them to their "vale of friendship." In light of this movement, their story mirrors the "migration-to-liberation" narrative common among sexual orientation and gender identity, or SOGI, asylum claimants today.[45] David Murray has discussed such claimants' ambivalence toward their countries and communities of origin, speaking to the complexity in SOGI refugees' notions of home. Interviews with asylum-seekers suggest that some SOGI refugees today feel ambivalent about or hostile toward their home communities, preferring "to look forward rather backward."[46]

One can see continuity between contemporary refugees' ambivalence toward home and the Ladies' futurist orientation in their own process of physical resettlement and homemaking. Although primarily associated with Wales, they were not natives. Mavor remains a useful resource for detailed information about their backgrounds. Children of the Irish aristocracy, both Butler and Ponsonby grew up in estates near Kilkenny. Butler was descended from Margaret Ormonde, and Ponsonby from a family of Cromwell loyalists, including a viscount and an earl. Butler spent part of her youth in a Norman castle called Woodstock. Ponsonby, whom a cousin of her deceased mother may have adopted, grew up in a Georgian mansion in Inistiogue. Their families' connection through marriage brought them together. After trying and failing to elope, the women won the grudging approval of their families to embark on a life together. An aggravating factor was the difference in their ages, Ponsonby being forty and Eleanor twenty-three at the time of the move. Even so, the two could initially count on a modest income (£280).[47] This degree of tolerance, while striking, is consistent with experiences described by other British women of the aristocracy at the time.[48] The ability of such women to live together is the historical exception proving the rule such that familial obligations and financial dependency limited the ability of women outside the aristocracy to live together with any noteworthy frequency until around 1870.[49] Even so, despite their unusual privilege, even Butler and Ponsonby narrowly escaped forced marriage or imprisonment in a convent.[50] Hence, while their home in Llangollen Vale was a quasireligious site and "shrine" to their transcendent "friendship," it was also a literal refuge.[51] When they arrived there, they called their home Plas newydd, or New Place. It became a virtual colony united by things—the site of an intergenerational queer community bound by a shared love of literature in general and the Gothic in particular.

A piece of journalism about them from the 1790s underlines the fact that Wales was a more than metaphorical refuge:

> Miss Butler and Miss Ponsonby, now retired from the society of men into the wilds of a certain Welch [sic] vale, are extremely attached to each other. . . . The Ladies concerted, and executed a fresh elopement:—each having a small sum, and having been allowed a trifling income, the place of their retreat was confided to a female servant of the Butler family, who was sworn to secrecy: She was only to say, that they were well and safe; and hoped that their friends, without farther inquiry, would continue their annuities.[52]

This period document makes plain that some saw the remoteness and wildness of their rural destination as protective in themselves, especially given that retirement to the place is supposed to preclude all contact with men. It also clearly suggests that the women were fearful for their financial security following the elopement ("hoped their friends . . . would continue their annuities") and feared for their personal safety ("sworn to secrecy"). A scholar has nonetheless cited the document, which appeared in a Welsh publication, as an example of phobic representation of the Ladies.[53] As Moore says, the story's writer faults Butler for being "tall and masculine" and indistinguishable from "a young man if we except the petticoats which she still retains."[54] The Ladies consulted Edmund Burke about pursuing a libel case against the periodical, but he cautioned that a case would attract still more unwelcome attention.[55] Although derogatory and phobic, the article describes the material dangers the Ladies faced by offering details about their physical whereabouts and appearance and, therefore, endangering them. A sense of physical risk, not simply risk to their reputations, likely prompted the libel case in the hope that it would, as Burke says, deflect attention. Emphasizing their social status and relative freedom obscures, in the spirit of the period's iconography, the various ways that the material world defines their story and ties it to common representations of other dissidents across time and space. Among these commonalities were bookishness in general and the antiquarian example set by a queer luminary of the eighteenth century, Horace Walpole, in particular.

A WELSH STRAWBERRY HILL

Plas newydd has served as an object of singular importance to the Ladies and their community. Although eccentric, the structure, which still stands, is highly traditional if one's reference point is the Romantic queer Gothic as established by Walpole through his home and novels. Considering Plas newydd exclusively in light of aesthetic tropes of the Gothic nonetheless obscures the role of consumerism in the Ladies' personal style as the home embodies this. In addition to invoking, as an artifact, the queer Gothic, Plas newydd stands as the result of a process, having been produced by, while embodying, a mode of queer and antiquarian consumerism. Along with the Gothic, camp taste appears in the architectural form of the *cottage ornée*, historically associated with the working classes, as Brideoake has said, and the heightened degree of ornamentation the Ladies applied in their remodeling of their home.[56] However prominent in the outcome of this process, the Gothic and camp were also integral to the consumption that led to it, a process subversive and dissident in its own right, apart from its cultural and architectural products. One form of dissidence integral to this consumerism and its outcome was the subversion of traditional, gendered notions of rural retirement and the *cottage ornée*.[57] I will be arguing that, with this home, the couple subverted both sexual and gender imperatives, founding an intergenerational queer community bound not simply by aesthetic tropes but also by consumerism.

In focusing on the role of consumption in the production of an object, in this case, a home, and the cultural forms it could also be said to contain and, like a text, cite, the present analysis approaches the object from the perspective of Marxian discourse about commodity fetishism, on the one hand, and Marshall McLuhan's discussion of cultural products, on the other. In a well-known section of *Capital*, Marx explores the history of the commodity and its special qualities contrasted to objects of utility. Marx breaks with political economists such as Adam Smith and David Ricardo in critiquing the abstraction that defines commodities' value in terms of generalized labor. Ultimately, Marx's logic serves a larger aim to uncover the alienation of workers partly through the discourse of political economy. In making this larger argument, Marx invests objects with irreconcilable and mysterious histories. These are, in effect, secret, quasi-human lives that reflect something actual—namely, the diversity within the human labor process—as well as something perspectival—namely, a distance produced by the conceptual framing of bourgeois economists. The discourse of political economy has made the commodity mysterious by attempting, through abstract determinations of value, to reconcile the irreconcilable. Such is the "fetishism" of commodities in discourse.[58] Marx's famous example of this fetishism is the commodified table, which, as if mocking civilization itself, "stands on its head, and evolves out of its wooden brain grotesque ideas, far more wonderful than 'table-turning' ever was."[59] For Marx, this playful and Gothic anthropomorphism reflects not simply the perverse facts of a market economy, by virtue of which objects have social lives while the working classes experience fragmentation, but also a deeper mystery—namely, the production of a lost history that observers struggle to reconcile with the physicality of things. The paradoxically artificial yet real mystery has an antiquarian valence, considering that Marx describes it as a "social hieroglyphic": "[W]e try to decipher the hieroglyphic, to get behind the secret of our social products; for to stamp an object of utility as a value, is just as much a social product as language."[60] These features of the commodity combine to make it interpretable like a text or any other cultural product. Marx goes so far as to specify linguistic communication as a point of comparison. Although traditional literary exegesis often rests on the assumption of singular authorship and unitary meaning, as in the case of the New Criticism, the Marxian notion of the commodity emphasizes the processual and social bases of cultural products—the shared labor and cultural inheritance producing their mysterious meanings. In this way, *Capital* anticipates the poststructuralist critique of the author initially undertaken by Michel Foucault and Roland Barthes. Marx's analysis of the commodity is relevant to the present discussion because it offers a model for examining objects like Plas newydd. Specifically, Marx's analysis offers a bookish template and justification for reading nonlinguistic, nonmedial objects analytically like cultural products. Objects can be read like texts because, like texts, they are social creations situated in the broader economy that has been shaped by economic actors whose collective behaviors issue in products the social dimensions of which make them uncannily meaningful.

Like Marx, McLuhan sees objects that are not traditionally viewed as cultural products as signifiers and, also like Marx, sees the meaning of an object as a social production. In *Understanding Media: The Extensions of Man*, McLuhan's focus is on exploring the power, rather than the symptomatic character, of objects. For McLuhan, an object's meaning is a function of its particular extension of human capacity and its relationship to other objects. Rather than belonging to a market, objects belong to an evolving network. One of McLuhan's best-known theories of media is summed up by the slogan "the medium is the message."[61] By this, McLuhan means in part that a medium's significance (its message) is not its conveyance of information but its social impact—the way it further extends human capacities: "[T]he 'message' of any medium or technology is the change of scale or pace or pattern that it introduces into human affairs."[62] McLuhan's slogan also refers to another theory, one about the nature of medial interdependency: "[T]he 'content' of any medium is always another medium."[63] To support this claim, McLuhan observes that the "content" of the telegraph is print, the content of print is writing, and the content of writing is speech.[64] If media are recognizable as such by the acceleration or increase in scale they offer—by their "messages" in McLuhan's flexible sense—then nonlinguistic and non-representational objects can be media. Hence, McLuhan includes among his examples transportation technology—the wheel, the railroad, and air travel. What McLuhan's theory offers to an examination of the human relationship to the world of objects is a capacious definition of media focused on media's general functionality that also subordinates the particular function of representation to the more general extension of human power that objects can offer.

Objects embodying the Romantic queer Gothic have long offered a promise of extension. They are McLuhanesque in a double sense because they have empowered their owners while bearing wishes for liberation, possibility, and community. Illustrating ways queer Gothic objects can be social creatures, akin to Marx's commodity, and portents of change and possibility are Walpole's Gothic productions, including his own *cottage ornée*, which, as Brideoake has noted, inspired the design of Plas newydd.[65] Brideoake has also discussed parallels between Plas newydd and Strawberry Hill, along with Beckford's short-lived Fonthill Abbey, focusing on the role of the Gothic in compensatory architectural performances of gender normativity and nobility. In the view of Dale Townshend and Brideoake, Walpole used Strawberry Hill's exaggerated Gothic tropes to imply his possession of a rich English cultural and material patrimony despite his family's lack of a high-toned lineage.[66] The heaviness and seriousness of the Gothic can also be seen as having acted as a shield against references to his effeminate gender style in the press (mocking his "nature maleish" and "disposition female").[67]

If viewable as defensive in this way, the particular style of Strawberry Hill's version of the Gothic also illustrates extension and playful, outward-facing intertextuality. In fact, the home tropes and exaggerates the species of gap between signifier and signified upon which any false narrative of nobility would have been premised, making artifice a theme rather than a ruse. More specifically, the home, initially a cottage, has the design features but not the size of a Gothic castle. Also, the home's design choices wink at this disconnect with its materials, as Barrett Kalter has shown. These choices included wallpaper and an artificial type of masonry called Coade, which enabled relatively easy modification later.[68] In addition, the extensive role played by papier-mâché, as noted by Townshend among other critics, hints that the design's purpose was self-referentially to represent or cite, rather than faithfully reproduce, medieval architectural conventions.[69] A statement by Walpole in a letter about the home implies a knowing and ironic fondness for the structure's overt and literary artificiality: "[T]his *old, old, very old castle* that, as his prints called Old Parr, is so near being perfect that it will certainly be ready by the time I die, to be improved by India paper; or to have the windows cut down to the ground by some travelled lady."[70] This description of the structure, famed as a "paper house," as Townshend has noted, makes it an embodiment of critical definitions of camp by Sontag and, more recently, Andrew Elfenbein, which stress the sensibility's preference for the artificial and marginal.[71] As Townshend says, many critics have observed the prominence of paper as an architectural and interior design medium in the home.[72] In addition to thematizing impermanence and artifice, the material makes the home literary in the McLuhanesque sense that its surfaces represent its literary contents, these being the home's "message."[73] The home's many *fleurs-de-lis*, for example, a common textual ornament, make its bookish walls continuous with the manuscripts it housed.

These playful and eccentric ironies in the design drew attention to Walpole as its creator, but the home was not so much Walpole personified as a medium through which Walpole could embody his expressiveness. While enlarging him and his aesthetic sensibilities, it drew attention to the artifice of this grand self-expression. The Strawberry Committee, a subcommittee, as it were, of the still-on-going social aspect of this expression, reminds one that Strawberry Hill is not a text fixed in time but, as Kalter has stressed, an ongoing process the temporality and impermanence of which fascinated Walpole.[74] Its design initially reflected Walpole's sensibility and stood as an extension of his personality, but its embodiment of him resulted from a dynamic process of consumption of materials and services. Generations of people have continued this corporate process in order to maintain the home.

Thomas Macaulay toured it in the nineteenth century and recorded his impressions of its appealingly incoherent collection of curiosities:

> In his villa, every apartment is a museum, every piece of furniture is a curiosity; there is something strange in the form of the shovel; there is a long story belonging to the bell-rope. We wander among a profusion of rarities, of trifling intrinsic value, but so quaint in fashion, or connected with such remarkable names and events, that they may well detain our attention for a moment. A moment is enough. Some new relic, some new unique, some new carved work, some new enamel, is forthcoming in an instant. One cabinet of trinkets is no sooner closed than another is opened.[75]

Macaulay's account registers the power of Walpole's personality as reflected in the collection, which is a way of describing a style of collecting rather than a system or logic. For Macaulay, there was little to the collection because there was little of value intrinsic to the objects and little connecting them apart from Walpole himself—hence the collection's pleasant strangeness and jumbled insubstantiality ("quaint in fashion"). "Strange" is a term that could be used to describe the Ladies' tastes, as well, as we will see. Strawberry Hill appeared to Macaulay to be a mere "cabinet" of curiosities because it lacked the integrity conferred by an established organizing principle for a collection. Instead, its organization reflected a personal relationship to objects—Walpole's idiosyncratic process of consuming things and describing them ("connected with such remarkable names and events"). In this light, Macaulay's account suggests that the house and its collections functioned as media in McLuhan's sense—extensions and containers. Their visibility as such and, hence, artifice amplified the fact that they contained and extended Walpole's sensibility. While enlarging Walpole's tastes and collecting practices, the home bore the hallmarks of camp in its "trifling" oddness, artifice, and self-conscious ephemerality.[76] As Andrew Ross has theorized, a taste for exorbitance, which is evident in Walpole and the Ladies' love of decoration, also defines camp style.[77] Once again, Sontag's view of camp has particular relevance. To her, these very traits speak to the difficulty of defining the sensibility due to the fact that it is an "esoteric" style rather than a conceptual system.[78] Sontag also observes that camp prioritizes the decorative and domestic arts: "Clothes, furniture, all the elements of visual décor . . . make up a large part of Camp. For Camp art is often decorative art, emphasizing texture, sensuous surface, and style at the expense of content."[79]

Walpole's bookish home embodied not simply an individual's tastes but his capacious ability to have taste—to present the capacity for sensibility in the form of personal and real property. To borrow a metaphor from Marx's discussion of the commodity, the home self-referentially embodied a crystalline and "congealed" process of collection.[80] In being organized around an antiquarian's personality, it embodied a consumerist sensibility, even if historians of consumerism tend not to focus on real property. Such a home should be regarded not simply as a monument to self or antiquity but as a medium and instance of consumerism—self-extension through consumption.

"A RICH AND APPALLING RIOT OF CARVING"

Like Strawberry Hill in its Gothicism and hyper-materialism, Plas newydd acted as a medium of self-extension and a space of imaginative refuge for Butler and Ponsonby and the larger community that has taken inspiration from its otherworldly design. In light of the similar Strawberry Hill, the home has the hallmarks of camp and uses materiality self-consciously and overtly to create a norm-defying space. Brideoake has contrasted the two structures in terms of weight, noting the "lightness of touch" characterizing Walpole's playful design choices at Strawberry Hill and opposing these to Plas newydd's solidity and gravitas. Brideoake suggests the latter reflects an effort at conformity: the heavy use of oak by the Ladies, who used the material to ornament much of the structure, inside and out, could have been intended to put a strongly British and virtuous face on their unusual domesticity.[81] Like Walpole's "paper fabric" castle, however, Plas newydd features ornamentation so extravagant it appears to make artifice and materiality design themes, drawing attention to the surplus materiality, scalar disproportion, and general artificiality of the home.[82] In renovating it, the Ladies, like Walpole, redesigned a relatively small, rustic cottage—an example of the ornamental cottage, a staple of middle-class male identity and rural domesticity—to resemble a Gothic estate. Hyper-ornamentation characterizes features such as heavily carved oak window bays projecting strangely from the flat, white exterior walls. Reflecting this theme of material excess, ornamentation in the abstract became a fixture in the broader ornamental community centered on Plas newydd and stretched across time and space, to the point where pieces of carving served as official admission tokens at the home in the 1960s.[83] Again echoing Walpole, the Ladies also put conspicuous consumption in the service of eccentric expression, and this consumption had the "anal character" of any collection.[84] In fact, the Romantic-period auctioneer George Robins called Plas newydd a "museum of great interest and amusement."[85] In *Building Romanticism: Literature and Architecture in Nineteenth-Century Britain*, Reynolds describes the couple's renovations of the home as a process that extended their active interest in collecting.[86] The present section explores ways Plas newydd was the site of a camp and communal performance of queer masculinity enabled by this sort of consumerism.

At first, although sturdy and waterproof, the small, four-room cottage that would become Plas newydd probably had less to recommend it than its highly picturesque and sublime lot.[87] The parcel's irregular, rolling landscape included views of Dinas Bran, the ruined Gothic castle pictured on the Glamorgan platter; the Trevor rocks, some craggy rock formations; and the Berwyn mountain range. Locals believed the home to be haunted.[88] In fact, rumors of ghost sightings had scared off potential buyers for two years, during which the place sat uninhabited following the former owner's death.[89] These Gothic amenities were attractive to Butler, who made an offer on the house while stopping in Llangollen during a London trip.[90] The Ladies fled to the home in 1778.[91] As Brideoake has remarked, "their intention of never returning to their Irish homes" distinguished them from the upper-class tourists increasingly drawn to Wales for picturesque tourism.[92]

From the beginning of their ownership, the couple used things and services to project a dissident identity and create such a space. Mavor's revealing term for their taste in renovating the cottage is "grotesque," such was the degree of ornamentation.[93] Their hyper-material version of the Gothic, full of delightful strangeness, in fact applied the queer Gothic to the cottage format, drawing specifically on Walpole's example. Plas newydd's grounds eventually featured a folly, a garden featuring Gothic seating, a font borrowed from a nearby ruin, quaint ornamental bridges across a brook, and a new small cottage with a carefully selected set of books from the main library.[94] The Ladies' home embodied "the love of the exaggerated," and they, like Walpole, made winking exaggeration the heart of their style.[95] In camp fashion, they expressed strong opinions about the smallest details as they gradually medievalized their miniature country seat. Inside the main house, marble slabs would replace tile flooring that Butler abhorred. In her diary, Butler writes, "The stone cutter come to lay the stones in the Hall in the place of the odious Tiles which we have hated for so long."[96]

Like Walpole, they focused their energy on constructing a house worthy of their collections. First, they tackled the library, expanding it and adding three Gothic bay windows, marble flooring, ornamental canopies (gifts of the Duchess of St. Albans dated to 1798 and 1814), a porch featuring many *fleurs-de-lis*, worked columns, vaulted ceilings, chandeliers, trefoil windows, and a doorway sporting intricate carving in relief.[97] One noteworthy piece of decoration was a lamp that none other than Beckford would closely reproduce with a well-known octagonal device of his own in Fonthill Abbey.[98] In such choices, Mavor laments "a rich and appalling riot" of ornamentation, but not every witness has recoiled at the design.[99] Responses to the renovations by friends of the Ladies suggest enchantment with the otherworldliness of the place. In a letter, Seward described the lamp and another piece of décor in a manner conveying a sense of wonder at the home's Gothic femininity:

> The ingenious friends have invented a kind of prismatic lantern, which occupies the whole elliptic arch of the Gothic door. This lantern is of cut glass, variously coloured, enclosing two lamps with their reflectors. The light it imparts resembles that of a volcano, sanguine and solemn. It is assisted by two glow worm lamps, that, in little marble reservoirs, stand on the opposite chimney-piece, and these supply the place of the here always chastized day-light, when the dusk of evening sables, or when night wholly involves the thrice-lovely solitude. A large Eolian harp is fixed in one of the windows, and, when the weather permits them to be opened, it breathes its deep tones to the gale, swelling and softening as that rises and falls.[100]

Seward's enthusiastic figures (the metaphor of the "volcano," the anthropomorphic "breathes its deep tones") convey rapture at the way the couple has used objects to transform a wild environment into a protective, oceanic space of private, feminine nurturance ("swelling and softening as that rises and falls"). As described by Seward, the Ladies' inventive use of objects has thrown light on the service of manipulating time to create an enchanting and sensual space. Seward was so inspired by the couple's way of life that she made plans to create a similar home with Elizabeth Cornwallis. Unfortunately, she died before Cornwallis, whom she called Clarissa, and she could realize the dream.[101]

Piozzi's correspondence largely confirms Seward's observations. A letter to Piozzi from Chappelow recalls a visit to the cottage in a way that colors Plas newydd with angelic strangeness:

> Their House is literally a cottage—so you must rest at the Inn nocturnally. . . . They have Lived 18 years in their retreat—having never been absent but 2 nights in all that time. . . . They are indeed superior Beings, and a happy mixture between mortal and immortality.—I have a favour to beg of you.—tis this. They cannot any where get The Florence Miscellany.—May I give them mine?—The Book in their Custody would meet with an Apotheosis.[102]

Whereas Seward's vision presents a materialistic version of the pastoral organized around a protected and liberated feminine sensuality, Chappelow's makes materiality the focus (in the form of a book) but imagines the Ladies as superhuman agents of sublimation ("superior Beings," "happy mixture between mortal and immortality," "would meet with an apotheosis") and, as in Seward's account, masters of time ("in all that time"). For Chappelow, their liberated sensuality more closely resembles liberation from sensuality, in the spirit of Wordsworth's sonnet. Nonetheless, the responses of Seward and Chappelow both acknowledge the imaginative and materialistic mode of domesticity the women engaged in and the way they used objects creatively to produce a strikingly unusual space. Rather than social climbers, the Ladies appear in these accounts as dissidents for whom objects acted as media for self-expression and the construction of an empowering space for imaginative and quasi-spiritual reinvention.

Plas newydd's situation in space offers another view on the couple's dissident use of materiality. The gendered history of the type of home Plas newydd exemplified, the *cottage ornée*, an architectural staple of bourgeois manhood and rural leisure, suggests that their dissidently Gothic design choices belonged to a more generally transgendered version of the pastoral. The "ornamented cottage," as William Pocock refers to the architectural form in an 1807 book of architectural drawings, reflected masculine priorities such as convenience, recreational activities such as hunting, and comfort. It is "more calculated than any other description of building for the enjoyment of the true pleasures of domestic life."[103] In 1798, James Malton used phallic imagery to describe the ornamental cottage as the entitlement of the "matured eye" who enjoys both picturesque views and domesticity's "tender" pleasures:

> The matured eye, palled with gaudy magnificence, turns disgusted from the gorgeous structure, fair sloping lawn, well turned canal, regular fence, and formal rows of trees; and regards, with unspeakable delight, the simple cottage, the rugged common, rude pond, wild hedge-rows, and irregular plantations. Happy he! who early sees that true happiness is distinct from noise, from bustle, and from ceremony; who looks for it, chiefly, in his properly discharging his domestic duties, and by early planting with parental tenderness, the seeds of content in his rising offspring, reaps the glad harvest in autumnal age.[104]

In this view, the pastoral and ornamental cottage are media for a wide range of middle-aged male recreation, including the pleasures and responsibilities of procreation ("properly discharging his domestic duties . . . reaps the glad harvest"). Indeed, such "domestic duties," encompassing the "planting" of fatherly "seeds," are said to offer "unspeakable" pleasures to man's dissipated "eye." This discourse constructs the ornamental cottage as a sexualized extension of masculinity into the pastoral and extraction of pleasure from this feminized space.

When, in a letter from 1796, Seward playfully laments the length of time since her last "intercourse with the ornaments of Llangollen Vale," meaning Butler and Ponsonby, she provocatively invokes not merely their general fame and wit but also the implications of the women's material, obtruding presence in the vale. With the mischievous word "intercourse," Seward emphasizes the sensuousness of their incongruous presence and of the trio's relations.[105] However jesting, such a remark hints at the likely fact that Seward and others appreciated the incongruity of the couple's refashioning of an architectural genre associated with male pleasure and familial domestic life. The word "ornaments" points to their dissidence and material difference while raising the possibility that what *mattered* to Seward was the women's known material existence. Privileging transcendence, in the vein of Wordsworth and Chappelow, figuratively evaporated what must have mattered most to Seward and others like her taking inspiration from the Ladies—the fact that they had made their wishes actual. To name the fact that they physically ornamented a rural vale, a synonym of "hollow" and "valley," likely felt deliciously subversive in a number of ways, helping explain the draw of materiality per se as a theme of dissident self-expression beyond Seward's correspondence. In the context of the eighteenth-century discourse of the picturesque, self-conscious ornaments stuck out: they mocked and defied the reproductive logic of traditionally gendered ideas about space, its uses, and users. Malton's distaste for the formal (the organization and regularity of neoclassical beauty) and preference for "rugged" and "rude" simplicity in design exemplifies this masculinist and normative ideology, while illustrating the context and provocative implications of the Ladies' hyper-ornamental parody of the ornamental cottage. In light of the design discourse of the period, the Ladies' design choices resemble drag—a performance of identity that, like subcultural *bricolage*, exposes the discursiveness of identity itself (or in Jack Halberstam's terms on the subject of drag kings, a performance of masculinity that constitutes an "exposure of the theatricality of masculinity" itself).[106]

In this light, the widespread interest in couple's library during the period takes on added significance. Parallel to their use of a masculine vessel to occupy feminine space, the Ladies' library constitutes an appropriation of traditionally masculine domestic space within the feminine one of the home. Brideoake has said that the couple's focus on their library had the specific aim of embodying a performance—of class position. Specifically, they used the space to project an image of themselves as upper-class intellectuals rather than "sexually suspect spinsters." The space and its collection, which they accumulated at great expense, became "central to their assertion of the class prerogatives more typically held by landed gentlemen."[107] These physical aspects of their homemaking also have a gendered meaning, adding helpful context to what is known about their gender presentation from other sources. Their attention to the space of the library and proud display of folios there, congruent with their hyper-ornamentation of an ornamental cottage, has the uncanny appearance of a bookish and courageously public performance of female masculinity, to use Halberstam's term for masculine women of all kinds, including butch lesbians and drag kings.[108] This dissident self-presentation is on display in Lady Leighton's sketches of the couple from the 1820s in which they appear to be dressed in men's formal wear while seated at the table in the library. Butler is wearing her *Croix St. Louis* pendant, an award traditionally bestowed on soldiers for feats of valor.[109] Such are sources of the iconography that issued in the Glamorgan pattern and the pirated drawing of them in beavers, which resemble top hats, on the grounds of Plas newydd.[110]

Butler's diary offers a fuller sense of the radical charge of the Ladies' dissident use of space. Bridoake has emphasized the classed implications of their assumption of the identity of local gentry, but the Ladies' own descriptions of their day-to-day life in their "little demesne," as Butler refers to Plas newydd, present an image of women sharing the duties of traditionally male household leadership and enjoying the pleasures of aristocratic leisure in rural seclusion.[111] The diary is a record, moreover, of intellectual pleasures and leisure traditionally supported by women's labor in domestic and rural spaces; strikingly, it is not a record of the management of such a space for others, nor does it record effort spent to maintain a home. Rather it documents pleasure in the products of others' domestic labor. A "fracas" with a male servant offers a window onto the novelty of the Ladies' domesticity and how they sustained it.[112] Diary entries describe an incident involving insolent behavior on the part of the servant, Richard. The Ladies' habitual tour of the grounds—their "Home Circuit"—alerted them to the need for additional gravel in a new garden near the kitchen. When they asked Richard to do the work, he replied with a "warning." The Ladies promptly fired him:

> He gave us warning, which (to his infinite surprise and evident regret) we immediately accepted, being determined never while we retain our senses to be imposed upon by a servant. . . . Richard sent in his keys. We sent out his wages. He went away with great reluctance. But not chusing to let our servants change places with us, We resolved when He gave Warning in the morning that he should take the consequence of it in the afternoon. . . . A day of sweetly enjoyed retirement, the little Fracas of Richard's sauciness not having disturbed us, as we think we acted with becoming calmness and presence of Mind.[113]

Here one sees women equitably sharing in not only pleasure but also responsibility for a traditionally masculine domain—the rational exercise of authority over a rural household. Butler relates happily that Richard's impertinence only temporarily polluted the grounds. The diary's description of the return of equilibrium shows Plas newydd to be a feminine medium for intellectual leisure in the mode of the picturesque:

> Celestial lovely day. Reading, drawing. Saw a white lamb in the Clerk's hanging Field. The Parlour getting a general scouring, sweeping and cleaning. My Beloved and I went the Home Circuit. Walked round our empty garden many times, liked it infinitely better empty than occupied by that Drunken idle Richard. Sweetest lovely day, close, nay even sultry. Lambs bleating, Birds singing, everything that constitutes the Beauty of solitude and retirement. . . . Began Les Mémoires de Madame de Maintenon. I doubt whether the Vulgarity of stile, absurd anecdotes, and impertinent reflections will permit me to read it.[114]

The passage typifies Butler's descriptions of their ornamental cottage as an intellectual retreat sustained by pastoral pleasures ("garden," "lambs bleating," "birds singing," "beauty of solitude and retirement"). Significantly, as Gordon notes, the word "retirement" is a recurring touchstone in Butler's account of their household habits and management.[115] Leisure and, specifically, consumption here form a process through which the Ladies subverted gendered expectations and a medium they used to produce a strikingly different, and, indeed, transgendered version of domesticity.

Butler's diary paints them as playful ironists on the subject of this dissident homemaking, referring to a bedroom at Plas newydd as "the State Bedchamber" and the garden as "our Shrubbery and Gardens" (in capitals).[116] If they displayed an ironic wit about their performance of rural patronage, they did behave like lords. Butler proudly inventories in the diary the guests they hosted, the gifts they received, and the compliments they received ("Mary Davis, our Butcher and Bakers wife, sent us a present of Sago puddings. Fullerton came with compliments from Sir William and Lady Barker . . . ; they will be here immediately—how fortunate that the Hall is finished").[117] In 1788, they received a written appeal from a young mother convicted of infanticide ("Letter from the unfortunate Creature in Ruthin Gaol. What can we do for her?").[118] In describing a visit to the home of a local weaver, they adopted a patronizing air: "Went into the Weaver's garden. Never saw anything more near and comfortable. . . . The honest man just returned from Oswestry Fair where he had been to sell a piece of Cloth, three little children cleanly drest playing before the door. The Wife scouring her chairs and Tables."[119]

As Brideoake has said, the couple's collecting practices suggest those of male, landed patrons of the arts. They followed the practice of book collectors in producing a catalog of their library, the manuscript "A Catalog of Our Books" (1792), for example. The text's organization reflects an attempt at an institutional style of bibliography intended for use by a community, not an informal style of record-keeping merely for personal use. The text includes a description of the books' arrangement on the library's shelves, giving the project a bibliomaniacal air. This section of the MS also speaks to the attention they paid to the arranging of books. As Brideoake has noted, the Ladies seem to have used book arrangement as a way to project an image of themselves as belonging to the landed gentry: their duodecimos and octavos—formats associated with women readers that drew attention to their own "gender and unmarried status"—they stored in the bedroom, but their folios they displayed in the library.[120]

THE QUESTION OF IDENTITY

The Ladies' ironic appropriation of signifiers of masculine power and status has long raised thorny questions about identity and historiography. Mavor argues that images of them in what seemed to be men's clothing contributed to a queer mythology about the women that had little connection to reality. For example, their clothing was perhaps less masculine than it was a reflection of their trendy and Continental fashion sense. French women wore beaver hats, and the cropped "Titus" hairstyle had become popular among British women in the 1790s.[121] These circumstances offer helpful context but do not negate the masculine appearance of Butler (Ponsonby's gender style having a uniformly different perception).[122] Gordon represents Butler as wearing men's clothing as a young person.[123] The choice would not have been totally unheard of: a contemporary known for her many affairs with other women, the "lesbian seductress" Anne Lister, also dressed in clothing that resembled, while remaining slightly different from, men's clothing.[124] Also, the qualifications Mavor makes do not detract from the significance of the Ladies' reputation and legacy—in other words, from the fact that the Ladies' modes of self-expression contributed to a history of self-expression by dissident people and that others have perceived as dissident—with inspirational impact.[125] Among these was Lister herself, who believed the Ladies relationship "was not platonic."[126] Writing to a lover, Lister said, "Heaven forgive me, but I look within myself & doubt. I feel the infirmity of our nature & hesitate to pronounce such attachments uncemented by something more tender still than friendship."[127] Furthermore, as Brideoake has claimed, the indeterminacy of their sexuality in itself should compel one to read it as queer.[128]

Mavor's well-informed critique offers a salutary reminder about the dangers of ahistoricism in the study of gender and sexuality. To be fully valid, however, such a critique requires that intrinsic and fixed sexual or gendered identities be actual and recoverable sources of modes of gender and sexual expression. This raises methodological issues related to history and theory. In terms of history, the concept of homosexuality postdates the Ladies of Llangollen's deaths by decades. Also, a lack of empirical evidence makes determinations of their sexuality problematic from the perspective of historical practice. In theoretical terms, since the queer turn in the study of sexuality (marked by Foucault's *The History of Sexuality*) and gender (Judith Butler's *Gender Trouble*), scholars have recognized the logical flaws that ensue from attempts to draw a metaphorical line to essences from expressions or, to use Butler's famous term, performances.[129] In the wake of the queer turn, scholars such as David Halperin have used the concept of queerness to explore expressions of sexuality and modes of existing as independent of presumed characterological or biological essences. Halperin's definition of the term "queer" is illustrative: "[Q]ueer does not name some natural kind or refer to some determinate object. It acquires its meaning from its oppositional relation to the norm. Queer is by definition whatever is at odds with the normal, the legitimate, the dominant. There is nothing in particular to which it necessarily refers. It is an identity without an essence."[130]

While not necessarily implying any intrinsic state of being, behaviors not traditionally sexual in nature, such as dress or consumerism, can nonetheless have meaning in the broader history of human affective life and worth for analysis in their own right, independently of an allegedly natural and prior identity or intention. Hence, as Brideoake astutely observes, queerness is a "singularly useful concept" for analyzing the couple.[131] This approach does represent a departure from the model of chaste romantic friendship that has long dominated discussion of the Ladies. As Brideoake has noted, the reading of their relationship in terms of friendship actually does not fundamentally differ from the speculative conclusion that they were lesbians or, for that matter, chaste heterosexual women.[132]

The debate about the Ladies illustrates that the study of sexual minorities has suffered under an "inequitable burden of proof," to quote Susan S. Lanser, such that the dissidence of nonnormative figures must be demonstrated with much more certainty than must normativity.[133] Relatedly, acts and behavior must be documented to affirm or establish the dissident interior desires of subjects, when in other contexts a link between the two would not be required. Furthermore, in regimes of compulsory heterosexuality, evidence of sex cannot logically or morally be cited as valid evidence of desire. Outside the confines of this double standard, a wider range of erotic attachments can serve more broadly to illuminate a subject's affective life.[134]

For Lanser, the Ladies' case and others like it require a new lens on female intimacy, one that avoids the impossible double standard of certainty and the fetishism of sexual acts while remaining adaptable to different historical contexts' conceptions of erotic life. This lens is one that prioritizes the social elaboration of intimacy and de-emphasizes the methodologically unsound focus on specifically sexual behavior. Lanser terms the approach "sapphism": "I want to ask that we broaden our sense of the erotic, and hence also of what I am calling the *sapphic*, beyond explicit sexual acts or even overtly enunciated sexual wishes to encompass desires and penchants that give primacy—even momentary primacy—to same-sex bonds through words and practices amendable to an erotic rendering."[135] As Lanser writes elsewhere, sapphism, as opposed to lesbianism, serves as a broader "canopy" than traditional identity, encompassing "discourses, representations, and social phenomena that inscribe preferential desires, behaviors, and affiliations—whether explicitly sexual or just implicitly erotic, whether frankly female or . . . gender-queer."[136] The Ladies serve as an apt example of the sapphic: the two women in a committed, loving relationship publicly declared their love for one another, shared a home for most of their lives, and slept in the same bed.[137] Applying the traditional standard of sexual behavior, which the known evidence in the case cannot meet, would mean that their love had no name. But, as Lanser says, "[B]y no stretch would it make sense to consider Butler and Ponsonby either heterosexual or undesiring given the fact that they brooked rejection and penury to live together and stay together as passionately united partners until death."[138] Viewed through the lens of sapphism, the dissidence of the Ladies comes into focus as a mode of eroticism that nonetheless lacks traditional hallmarks of sexuality, or least the existence of this cannot be established.

Lanser's notion of sapphism can serve to illuminate occluded ways of being, but in entertaining asexual modes of eroticism while defining this exclusively in terms of human object-choices, this approach seems to impose an arbitrarily restrictive framework on affective life. If sexual acts alone can no longer define eroticism, then why are attractions to other people the only ones with subject-defining force? The prominence of objects in the story of the Ladies and in particular the role of objects in mediating affective relations between women and men in their community suggests that restricting critical focus to the human relations in the community would obscure a fundamental aspect of these people's erotic lives. By contrast, enlarging the critical focus to encompass the full range of objects, both animate and inanimate, freighted with erotic charge means considering the Ladies' ornamental community as akin to an "object culture" in Brown's sense—a culture in which things "mediate our sense of ourselves (as individuals and as collectivities) and our sense of others."[139] Brown goes on:

A given object culture entails the practical and symbolic use of objects. It thus entails both the ways that inanimate objects mediate human relations and the ways that humans mediate object relations (generating differences of value, significance, and permanence among them), thus the systems (material, economic, symbolic) through which objects become meaningful or fail to.[140]

For Brown, an object culture is a culture of meaning and, in particular, the meaning of the shared or different nature of being for individuals and groups—which is to say, a culture of epistemology. A community bound by fetishism of materiality—the kind of community I am here terming an ornamental community—resembles an object culture structurally, but distinguishing the former from the latter (along with queer space-time from a notion of lesbian identity rooted in knowledge of acts) is the aesthetic.

Such a focus on women's aesthetic relation to objects, even books, is not to be entered into lightly. The history of women's collective efforts at self-determination and liberation is marked by debates about the proper role of objects, and consumerism more generally, in women's lives.[141] Some of these debates have hinged on questions about the compatibility of feminism with participation in market economies.[142] The role of objects in women's erotic lives, however, has attracted comparatively less notice on the part of scholars.[143] Similarly, the role of objects in the erotic lives of dissidents remains underexplored. While the Ladies' intergenerational community suggests a positive role for objects as social binders, they have often appeared as a burden that a liberated femininity would ultimately discard. For example, feminists have expressed an aversion to the objects of domesticity, which, in the words of Rita Felski, "have often been viewed as an especially insidious form of endangerment and entrapment." For women, often the unasked-for sediment of domestic life, things "were the bricks that walled women into the desperation of small, unambitious lives."[144]

An avenue that presents itself as an alternative to this problematic focus on domestic materiality and women is a focus on the role of objects in the broader community of dissidents. In this context, the queer Gothic presents an opportunity to explore the role of objects in expressions of dissident eroticism. In the case of the Romantic queer Gothic, Walpole and Beckford loom large. The queer Gothic, as exemplified by these dissidents and Gothic progenitors, typified an antiquarian and consumerist mode of queerness that interwove dissident eroticism and heightened, eccentric consumerism, including active collecting of Gothic objects. This queer Gothic consumerism produced large collections of books, collections of Gothic objects such as suits of armor, and grand Gothic homes. Other notable figures and subcultures, including the bibliomaniacs and *virtuosi*, suggest that the aesthetic dimension of consumerism—meaning the lived experience of capitalism, including the desire for and accumulation of things—is bound up tightly with the history of sexual dissidence. In the spirit of the Ladies' bookish domesticity, this broader queer-historical context could be called an intergenerational ornamental community—one bound by dissidence and a shared embrace of surplus value, in the form of antiques, ornamental cottages and farms, and book-objects, all of which represent the subordination of utility to unproductive pleasure.[145] The desire that has established this community should be termed queer (rather than gay) precisely because it cannot be reduced to readily identifiable modes of dissidence or categories of identity. As Brideoake says about the ambiguity surrounding the Ladies, "While the hypostatized entity 'the Ladies of Llangollen' masquerades as immediately legible, it has come to signify an oppositional relationship to heteronormativity irreducible to a single meaning or identity position."[146] Taking Brideoake's skepticism about identity one step further, one could also say that, in the Ladies' case, desire bound a dissident community and exceeded the human altogether. While not recognizably sexual, consumerist desire integrated affective lives and human bonds while affording the expression of queer subjectivity. In such an ornamental community, objects primarily mediate affective relations, not the production of knowledge (e.g., about the essential identities of members as in sexological discourse).[147]

In one scholarly tradition within gay and lesbian history, the general intersection of material culture with dissidently affective community represents familiar territory. In a classic essay, John D'Emilio established this field by making a materialist and determinist argument about the relationship between capitalism and gay identity. Whereas Lanser has sought to expand the understanding of sexuality by disentangling identity and sex, D'Emilio's approach to identity is to use a certain notion of it to historicize sexuality. Polemicizing against "the myth of the eternal homosexual," D'Emilio contends that the historical emergence of wage labor produced homosexuality.[148] Wage labor created the conditions necessary for gays and lesbians to self-identify sexually and build communities. In D'Emilio's words, "the historical development of capitalism—more specifically its wage labor system— . . . has allowed large numbers of men and women in the late twentieth century to call themselves gay, to see themselves as part of a community of similar men and women, and to organize politically on the basis of that identity."[149] Hence, D'Emilio's argument challenges traditional and essentialist notions of sexual identity, contributing to the queering of LBGT scholarship that began in the late 1980s and early 1990s. This intervention produced approaches to understanding nonnormative identity that complicated biological notions of identity while integrating nonbiological and nonpsychological factors such as culture, history, and economics into the study of sexuality. Building on the foundation laid by pioneering gay and lesbian historians who had established the historical existence of dissident populations over time and throughout the world, while exposing the genocidal campaigns waged against them up to the present day, queer scholarship deconstructed the framework of identity itself, exploring topics such as the fluidity of desire, the populations marginalized or erased by monolithic identity categories, and the ultimately non-rational basis of the rigid binary concepts underlying traditional categories. D'Emilio's work is of a piece with queer scholarship that is, on the one hand, skeptical of the innateness and fixity of sexual identity and, on the other, open to the notion that identity is subject to cultural influence if not determination. In privileging abstract conceptions of labor and property, D'Emilio's work illustrates the fact that such discussions have necessarily skirted the concrete, lived experiences of consumers, however.

While this tradition of queer scholarship has established connections between capitalism and identity in the abstract, scholars in sociology and economics have explored connections between identity and consumerism in the concrete. Apart from the study of sexuality, these researchers have also explored ways that economic structures and phenomena have shaped human desire, even if they have not focused on the subject of sexuality overtly or on dissident populations. As Mike Savage has observed, in the field of sociology, this tradition is better exemplified by the Weberian interpretive tradition than by Pierre Bourdieu's revolutionary focus on the reproduction of classes through cultural, rather than solely material, means. According to Savage, Max Weber was the first sociologist to attend to the ways that modern people form status groups in addition to classes. Modern status for Weber is a function of possessions and what these signify for members of the middle classes—for example, clothing and property—which upon its historical emergence represented a significant shift in the cultural construction of social standing and distinguished status per se from "stande," sundering with it the traditional link between behavior (and virtue along with all aspects of inner life) and reputation (outer life).[150] Weber's work suggests that status is a function of the human relationship to the world of objects.

In the field of economics, scholars have focused more narrowly on consumerism and linked this type of behavior to identity. Frank Trentmann, for example, has found that consumerism has shaped modernity such that the identity of the consumer is a "master category" of identity and the political and cultural lodestar of the twentieth and twenty-first centuries, on par with the medieval chivalric knight.[151] Trentmann's work has shown how the modern concept of the consumer grew out of Free Trade ideology in the nineteenth century, when commercial interests successfully yoked consumption to citizenship in the mind of the British public, winning a debate with nationalists opposed to globalization and overturning traditional notions of consumption that associated it with acquisitiveness and selfishness.[152] In the cultural realm, the figure of the consumer evolved as thinkers considered anew the human relationship with the physical world. In *Empire of Things*, Trentmann argues that, in contrast to the view of the nineteenth-century worker offered by Marx, the modern self is not radically distinct from the world of things and, therefore, mystified as to her relationship to objects and other people, as Marx claims in *Capital*. Rather, the modern self is a dynamic product of the consumption process. As aptly exemplified by Mrs. Gereth in Henry James's *The Spoils of Poynton*, a character consumed by an obsession with collecting that dictates her (ultimately destructive) attitudes toward family members, the modern self uses "things . . . to build social identities and relations."[153] Trentmann places Marx alongside Weber and Jean-Jacques Rousseau, two others who have cast the relation in binary terms, in a conversation about the relationship of the human to the world of things.[154] Specifically, the human and thing exist in dialectical relationship to each other, suggesting that consumerism has produced a new frame for understanding the self and the relationship between the self and the world, a lens that integrates things with the self rather than separating them fundamentally from it. In this view, things have become integral to self-making in modernity, and consumerism in particular, not capitalism in the abstract, has come to define identity. Viewed from the perspective of the history of sexuality, a new identity category presents itself: the consumer, a figure defined by her relations with things. As Mrs. Gareth shows, these relations are not exclusively epistemological in nature. The consumer is a figure whose being is a product of affectively charged relations with material culture.

The Ladies and their community seem to offer an example of such a dialectical production of self and community. For them, books and other domestic objects served as tools for building a novel style of domesticity that, while retaining an association with the feminine, did not conform to limiting prescriptions of roles and identities. Things resembled tools for constructing an experimental mode of life; their cottage was a highly plastic medium. In fact, Seward's correspondence suggests that domesticity and its world of objects held almost magical possibility. The material world that Butler and Ponsonby literally and figuratively carved out of the pastoral was, for Seward, evidently not a hindrance to self-realization but a quasi-magical means for reinvention. Plas newydd was a "retreat," Seward writes, "which breathes all the witchery of genius, taste, and sentiment."[155] Writing about the garden in a letter, Seward says, "Beneath the wand of the enchantresses, Beauty starts up in her form divine, as Satanic grandeur did beneath the spear of Ithuriel."[156] Such passages offer a gendered theory of cultural production that offers an alternative to the phobic and gendered transcendentalism being advocated by the *avant-garde* and eventually canonical theorists of the period, such as Wordsworth and Coleridge, who identified pleasure taken from relations with objects (as represented, for instance, by the production of rhymes) as a degraded mode of production and a sign of pathology.[157] The contrast suggested by Seward's letters to the canonical Romantic scene of inspiration from the period's literary theory and poetry could hardly be clearer. The materiality rejected by Wordsworth and Coleridge in the founding texts of Romantic critical theory is here a crucible for rebellious self-making. Significantly, objects problematic, at least in women's hands, to the poets were domestic ones—gardens, books, and magazines. For Seward and others who took inspiration from Plas newydd, books and the domestic world of objects in general did not stand in contrast to the process of building a new world, literary or otherwise, but served as its shared medium. Furthermore, Seward's striking allusion to Milton's *Paradise Lost* (1) emphasizes the communal and self-consciously radical dimension of Plas newydd's potential. Dissidence has aggressive and communal valences here. Milton's Satan is not an isolated poet-seer but a "gen'ral," the leader of a radical movement.[158] Furthermore, Satanic charisma rests on the promise of self-making and exploration—the vision of new possibilities and a new world (as Satan says to his battalion of rebels in Book I, "Space may produce new worlds").[159]

A MATERIAL LEGACY

Fittingly, subsequent generations of women and men would follow Seward in taking inspiration from Plas newydd and the example of Butler and Ponsonby. As the history of the home will reveal, a thread binding this transgenerational and transgendered community was not a shared identity but a reimagined world of domestic objects. These included the most personal of things. An entry in Butler's diary hints at the degree to which domestic materiality at Plas newydd offered unspoken (if not also unspeakable) promises of self-extension, intimately binding a community through consumption and exchange: one day in 1790 Butler writes, "My beloved and I woke at seven. Found by our bed side Petticoats and Pockets, a new year's gift from our *truest* friends."[160] Mary Caryll, their servant of many years, had given these undergarments to them.

Better known in the history of Plas newydd is a remarkable triple memorial to the couple and Caryll, whose friendship was "the closest of all friendships outside their own."[161] An obelisk, this monument, which was built on the grounds of St. Collen's Church in Llangollen, enshrines the women's dissident and antiquarian revision of the pastoral in courageously permanent form. Designed with the help of Thomas Parker, as Mavor notes, it materially records a mode of queer community that transcended the dyad.[162] As such, as

Brideoake has argued, the monument represents a doubly queer relation by celebrating an affective bond that extended beyond the form of the bonded pair.[163] Noting the monument's "equilateral arrangement," Brideoake has claimed that the "tombstone materially marks Caryll's place within Butler and Ponsonby's family unit."[164] The monument also enshrines and extends the materialism that solidified the triple's bond. Mavor notes that their closeness was reflected in the exchange of tokens of affection. These included, in addition to the petticoats that Caryll presented to the couple in 1790, a seal Caryll made for Butler and presents that Butler and Ponsonby sent to Caryll's relatives.[165] Like these other objects, the monument represents bonds of love binding a triad—bonds from the contemporary vantage point irreducible to monogamy, homosexuality, or even sexuality as traditionally defined—while embodying a love of things through which they expressed their love. In the case of such objects, the medium is the message.

The dissidently communal aspect of the Ladies' domesticity transcended the intimate relationship with Caryll. Bound by antiquarianism and materiality, this community, taking inspiration of the women's iconic example of sexual and gendered dissidence, has spanned generations and genders. Seward and Piozzi belonged to the first generation of women and men inspired by the couple and bound to them by a shared love of objects and antiquarianism. Their letters, among which Seward's were published during the Ladies' lifetimes, offer many details about the Ladies and their home. Like Seward's poem about them, this record suggests a mischievous sense of possibility and excitement inspired by the objects the women surrounded themselves with and used at Plas newydd.

Mavor has detailed the history of this ornamental community as this relates directly to Plas newydd. Ownership and care of Plas newydd have reflected a proud and amiably disrespectful memorialization of the couple through care of the home. A series of illustrations of Plas newydd produced between 1788 and 1815 show that the ongoing and gradually more elaborate Gothicizing of the space that the "ornaments of Llangollen Vale" began was enthusiastically continued by others who shared their antiquarian interests and tastes.[166] After the sale of the home upon Ponsonby's death in 1831, it was bought by Amelia Lolly and Charlotte Andrew, local "spinster Ladies."[167] They enthusiastically continued decorating the cottage, likely in ways Butler and Ponsonby could not have foreseen. According to Mavor, the cottage's new owners

> caused a large stuffed bear to be set up at the corner of the cottage, and the white front palings . . . had sprouted a number of grotesque devices. Miss Sinclair herself glimpsed a "gim-cracked model of a wooden house stuck on a wooden pillar." It is not to be wondered that Miss Costello, visiting the cottage eleven years later, found the "whole place had a vulgar and commonplace appearance."[168]

In 1861, Andrew was interred under a Gothic tombstone next to Lolly, emulating the gravesite of Butler, Ponsonby, and Caryll.[169] After being owned by a relative of Lolly, Richard Lloyd Williams bought the house in 1876. Soon after, Williams sold it to General John Yorke, who had known the women as a young person. He continued the tradition of ornamenting the home and made it into a kind of shrine. Yorke's renovations included adding an entirely new wing, attaching Elizabethan-style battens to the front of the house, and erecting a neo-Gothic structure, the so-called "Hermitage," on the property.[170] The interior became a virtual cabinet of curiosities displaying the collar of Ponsonby's dog, Chance, and a brooch and bell once owned by Butler. These appeared alongside other curios: an artificial human leg, the head of a four-horned ram, and locks of hair.[171]

G. H. Robertson continued the tradition of reverently disrespectful curatorship of the place. Robertson, like Yorke, Lolly, and Andrew before him, took evident delight in continuing the "romantic friends'" extravagant reinvention of the site, rather than in carefully preserving the home as they had left it. All the subsequent owners arguably engaged in a curious process of memorialization. Their attentive materialism and consumption memorialized the spirit, or style, of the Ladies' dissident consumerism, rather than the objects this produced. Robertson, a cotton merchant, likely had the means to restore the home to its original state. He, like Yorke, revered Butler and Ponsonby. At one point during his curatorship, he held a grand ceremony to celebrate the couple. Mrs. Robertson played the part of Butler "in full hunting rig," "looking so dashing as to give everyone the most idealistic conception of the original."[172] Instead of restoring Plas newydd, however, Robertson expanded it on a grander scale than even Yorke, adding four bathrooms, multiple halls, eleven bedrooms, and seven parlors. Upon retiring, Robertson sold the property in 1910 to the last person to use it as a permanent residence, a woman from Lincolnshire. In 1932, the Llangollen Town Council came into possession.[173]

Generations later, the home still exerts a strong force of attraction. Testifying to this pull of Plas newydd is Gordon's experimental prose in an autobiographical section of *Chase of the Wild Goose*, where she describes breaking into the house at night in hopes of encountering the Ladies' ghosts and taking a surreptitious photograph of the ornamental woodwork, photographs of which appear in the book. She also describes the feeling of their uncanny presence in Plas newydd over one hundred years after their deaths. This feeling haunts her as she gazes at a few possessions they left behind: "They [the Ladies] followed me all over the house, either by my side or close behind me, and once seemed to stand, so that I could not pass, while I looked at an old watch in a little case of relics."[174] The feeling is also woven through description of their picturesque parcel of land, where Gordon "listened for any sound of movement or for rustling in the short bracken which covered the turf. I kept looking round about me and above and below, almost fearfully, although in the expanse before me not so much as a stray sheep was to be seen."[175] When the narrative turns to a conversation between Gordon and their ghosts, whom she encounters "on God's own hillside," Gordon repeats the introduction ritual familiar to readers of the Ladies' diaries, informing the Ladies that one book-object in particular is responsible for their time-bending meeting: "Some months ago I bought from a bookseller a large book which contained the 'Journal of E. B. and S. P., written by E. B. . . . With it were published many other papers which you could never have seen."[176] Gordon shares what is so meaningful about the journal, and the metaphor she uses to describe the time-spanning significance of the book is remarkable for the way it recalls that most social of objects, the commodity: "But in your journal the truth comes crystalline. It is as though you had been born and had lived together in . . . in a . . . in an amethyst. But really as things have turned out, are you not thankful that you wrote your own journal?"[177] The echo of Marx conveys the significance of this object so central to the Ladies' ornamental community with an image of material culture as social flux hardened in a crucible of oppression. Gordon suggests the power of objects with this image of a book-object as indelible proof of often invisible lives. The seemingly perverse mode of "preservation" in which the Ladies' community has engaged reflects Gordon's reverence for a testamentary archive that does not simply record but brings new life into being. To preserve Plas newydd in amber (or amethyst) would fail the Ladies' inspiring example of dissident materiality by refusing its promise of reinvention.

Gordon's retelling of their history in the vale, which draws on reliable sources while taking occasional flights of fancy, makes objects and the picturesque central to the Ladies' inspirational example of dissident femininity, but in light of the diverse legacy of curators of Plas newydd and the transgendered dissidence of the queer Gothic informing their style of consumerism, one must recognize the diversity within this population and its activities, even if doing so risks appearing to minimize the undeniably homoerotic currents also swirling around Llangollen Vale. Such diversity of persons and behaviors speaks to the flexibility of queer space. C. J. Nash, Amy L. Stone, and Halberstam have addressed ways in which certain spaces can nurture experimental, improvisational, dissident, and unstable affective and sexual bonds between their inhabitants, fostering what Stone has called "queer flexibility in gender and sexuality."[178] The dissident community fostered and inspired by the Ladies comprises the ambiguously erotic bond shared by the couple themselves, the diverse community of men and women who materially sustained the women's legacy in various ways, and the multitude of people subsequently inspired by their example. To this list must be added the non-human objects of desire mediating these relations, enabling this network, and circulating within this world.

The objects of desire circulating within and around Plas newydd pose a challenge to traditional ways of seeing queerness. Brideoake's notion of queer community and Reynolds's historically attuned reconstruction of rural retirement are powerful but, like the lenses of romantic friendship and lesbianism, these scholars' versions of queer community restrict the relevance of the Ladies to an anthropocentric sphere of community and culture. If relations with Seward and Caryll suggest a wider affective community than the dyad allows, the material devotion of the General and Robertson suggest an even broader community than this human one—a heterosocial network in which things mediated human bonds and humans mediated relations between things. Attention to the domestic spaces and objects this network shared offers a means of seeing a broader scope of queer desire than that viewable through the lens of conventional models of sexuality and affect.

Chief among the objects that attracted desire within this community were books. As Gordon's narrative illustrates, a shared love of books bound this intergenerational community. The Ladies were great readers who acquired extensive knowledge of literature and the literary world. Given the remoteness of Plas newydd, their knowledge of books and writers could seem magical. Piozzi's correspondence registers wonder at their knowledge; her detailed account of visits and interactions with the Ladies also shows the extent to which bookish topics and habits fostered bonds within their circle of acquaintances and friends. Writing of a visit in March 1800 to the "Vale," Piozzi remarks, "The unaccountable knowledge those Recluses have of all living Books and People and Things, is like Magic; one can mention no one of whom the private History is unknown to Them."[179]

The Ladies' rural seclusion also made them dependent on friends and acquaintances for the books they sought. Much correspondence with and about the Ladies reads like a record of literary transactions—bibliography. Highly involved in such transactions were Chappelow and Piozzi. In addition to the abovementioned *Florence Miscellany*, the quartet exchanged a series of book-objects and manuscripts. These included a transcription of Chappelow's "vision," which the Ladies requested from him, requiring Piozzi to copy part of a letter from Chappelow to her and then forward to Llangollen.[180] Another manuscript was promised by Piozzi on behalf of Chappelow: a work in progress by the latter, a poem about a swallow. Piozzi promises it because there must be no end to the giving of things: "what is there they do not deserve?"[181]

Piozzi's letters, for example, reveal she played the role of informal and unpaid book agent, fielding and relaying requests from the Ladies for particular titles. On the Ladies' behalf, Piozzi requested a copy of H. Bunbury's gruesome "Little Grey Man," which appeared in Matthew

"Monk" Lewis's *Tales of Wonder* (1801), from a friend, saying, "they are dying for it. They like those old Scandinavian tales and the imitations of them exceedingly."[182] Piozzi also fetched and borrowed books from the Ladies, for herself and others. One was Charlotte Brooke's *Reliques of Ancient Irish Poetry* (1789): "We shall spend a Day or two next Week with the Ladies of Llangollen, and I shall enquire for Miss Brooks' Reliques of ancient Poetry."[183] In fact, the Ladies' collection was an archive Piozzi relied on for hard-to-find works.[184]

Butler's diary offers a different perspective on this network of exchange, suggesting that the transactions were integral to the Ladies' bookish intimacy. One passage ends with a common refrain in the diary to the effect that the most bookish days were red-letter days: "Young Downes brought from our Barretts Sheridan's Life of Swift. . . . Post-bag from Wrexham. Letter from the bishop of St Asaph dated London 22nd, written in the handsomest and most flattering terms and promising to do something for poor Mrs. Jones in whose favour we wrote. Reading Sheridan's Life of Swift. A day of most delicious and exquisite retirement."[185]

In the context of their bookish community, one transaction in particular deserves special attention—the gift of a book from the Ladies to Anna Seward. Piozzi notes the growing intimacy shared by the Ladies and Seward: "I think Miss Seward never writes now. The Recluse Ladies at Llangollen who pick up every Rarety in Literature, are much her Admirers; Are *you* in Correspondence with her now?"[186] In a letter, Seward writes that their gift to her of Robert Southey's epic poem *Joan of Arc* (1796) not only touched her but also reflected their keen understanding of her taste. The book was a token of their intellectual intimacy: "Truly did they divine that its genius would attract my imagination," Seward writes to another correspondent.[187] Seward says that Southey's genius, if not his "unpatriotic" politics, impressed her.[188] So did the heroic and dissident character of Joan, the "warrior maid."[189] Seward's discussion of Joan conveys the significance of this book-object as a gift from the couple to Seward, who appreciated Southey's representation of Joan as a hero in the tradition of Milton's Adam and of Joan's courage in the face of certain death. Writing to Ponsonby, Seward favorably compares the scene of Joan's seeing her own ghost to Adam's vision of the murder of Abel in *Paradise Lost*: "Joan's apparition seems shown to her for more important purpose, viz. that the false hope of reward might have no share in stimulating her exertions. The consciousness of final martyrdom, given by this vision, extremely exalts her character."[190]

The bookish activities of the three women extended from consumption to production. They collaborated on an edition of Seward's *Llangollen Vale*. In a letter to Butler, Seward thanks them for arranging for the drawing and engraving of an illustration for the work but implores them to allow her to pay the engraver: "I have already expressed to Miss Ponsonby my delight in the scenic fidelity, and excellent execution of the vignette for Llangollen Vale; but I cannot cease to feel pain, in the idea that my receiving it as your and Miss Ponsonby's present, must render the publication expensive to you. If you will have the goodness to allow me to discharge the engraver's bill, you will extremely oblige me."[191]

CODA: WALES, THE PICTURESQUE, AND QUEER ANTIQUARIAN DESIRE

Literary representation of the vale is a thread running through the story of the Ladies' relationship with Llangollen and Plas newydd. The book produced with Seward may have given cultural form to an actual affinity for the place, but it also reissued desire that had long taken bookish form in the broader culture. The desire for spaces like the vale was a kind of cultural product in itself—the product of a literary genre, the "tour." The popularization of tourism was a Romantic-period phenomenon stemming not simply from an unmediated love of landscapes or antiquities but, as Tim Fulford has discussed, from a revolution in printing technology that enabled the dissemination of images on an unprecedented scale.[192] The mass reproduction of images of landscapes created demand for experiences in picturesque parts of England, Scotland, and Wales. Fulford's insight relates specifically to picture books, or "views," such as William Westall's 1818 *Views of the Caves Near Ingleton and Yorkshire* and Paul Sandby's *XII Views in South Wales*, but the technology used to produce the images in picture books, which Fulford says sponsored a "virtual" mode of topography in poetry that elevated the picturesque and combined word and image to prompt "metaphysical apprehension of the world," was the same as that used to create the images printed in "tours," which also feature many images, of landscapes as well as antiquities.[193] A case in point is the work of Dibdin, the subject of this book's next chapter, whose bibliophile tours married bibliography, antiquarianism, and inland tourism. His unpublished correspondence reveals the personal hazard he courted in overextending himself to furnish his books with illustrations, so important were they to the goals of his bibliophile, subscription-based productions. Butler and Ponsonby's attraction to Wales and bookish retirement there belonged to a cultural ecosystem akin to a feedback loop in which cultural products created desires, and desires produced cultural products in turn.

At first glance, Butler's choice of Wales (it being hers, not Ponsonby's) may seem out of character, given that Butler, known for her forward-looking and cosmopolitan taste, was educated in France and enjoyed London.[194] Her cutting-edge fashion sense as a young person, for example, attracted notice from the periodical press.[195] Many discussions of the Ladies emphasize the couple's rural isolation in Wales, and, as Mavor points out, Llangollen's location between London ports popular among Irish tourists and its low cost of living would have made it seem convenient, but the pleasures of inland tourism were fashionable.[196] In this light, the women's fondness for a place such as Llangollen was not so surprising, even if one could also argue that their migration had a politically radical aspect. Crowell has termed the Ladies "sexual and *national* rebels" due to their migration and rejection of their expected role as Irish "ascendancy Ladies" responsible for contributing to the nation's colonial project through marrying and bearing children.[197]

Wales was by the early nineteenth century a familiar destination among those engaging in picturesque tourism. In fact, thanks to William Gilpin's tour of the Wye (*Observations on the River Wye, and several parts of South Wales*, 1782), Welsh tourism arguably launched the phenomenon of the Home Tour among the British.[198] Travel writing and guides about Wales produced in Gilpin's wake illustrate the powerful influence of the picturesque. An eighteenth-century Welsh phrasebook for English speakers, Gambold's *Grammar of the Welsh Language* (first edition 1727), includes the phrase "Is there not a waterfall in this neighbourhood?"[199] Catherine Sinclair wrote a travelogue while touring Wales in the summer of 1833 that critiques some evidently destitute children who are "not ragged enough to be picturesque."[200] Ostensibly a complaint, this analysis is actually an application of Gilpin's analytical method, which, as Singer has noted, privileges lineal irregularity, to human subjects.[201] Applied to local people, Gilpin's method as used by Sinclair stretches the discourse of the picturesque to an extreme degree of aestheticism. The analysis speaks to the power of Gilpin's influence. At the same time, in collapsing foreground into background, as it were, and human into landscape, the critique reveals the pervasion of Welsh travel writing by a Rousseauian idealization of an allegedly more primitive, or "natural," human condition.[202]

Such primitivist longing extended to traditional Welsh folkways. Gwyneth Tyson Roberts has detailed a rising popular interest in Welsh culture, along with a corresponding exploitation of this, during the period. Such was the appeal of Wales to antiquarians and tourists that, when genuinely old cultural products were lacking, some were happy to manufacture them. Welsh harp songs experienced a resurgence, but, as the form was dying, adapted English songs often played the part. The popular tales of Llywelyn and his dog Gelert were invented to draw tourists to Beddgelert and elsewhere. Lady Llanofer contrived a Welsh "national costume" from examples of peasant clothing. The poet, antiquary, and forger Iolo Morgannwg reconceived the *eisteddfodau*, or festival, which had expired in the 1500s.[203] In this light, the politics of the *Ladies of Llangollen* china pattern's representation of local Welsh society are notable. In the image, a worker, a scythe resting on one shoulder and a lunch pail or toolbox in hand, seems to greet the Ladies on the viewer's behalf while striking a posture of receptive subservience. This figure, whose old-fashioned scythe had been displaced by a more modern farming tool, the cradle reaper, by the time the Ladies moved to Wales, synecdochically represents both the local society and Wales's romanticized past.[204] The historically inaccurate image of the region is one not so much rural or "pristine" but impossibly young—outside the flow of time and frozen in a non-existent past. The scythe instances a pattern incorporating many other representations of the Ladies that textured their history with Gothic and romantic trappings, as we have seen. The pattern reached even to the Ladies' self-conception as path-breaking individualists yet also feudal lords invested in the doctrine of noblesse oblige.[205] Rather than Roman Catholicism, as would have been the case with Butler, "the religion of noblesse oblige was the real practical religion of both the Ladies, as it is among many people throughout the world."[206] In the context of other similarly old-fashioned—not old—products designed to satisfy consumers' nostalgic longing, the image suggests that something of market value about Wales was the sense that experiencing it felt like travel outside time, as opposed to the sense that it was rural, "natural," or "primitive." Ironically, then, this mass-produced image of the Ladies affirms theoretical insights into queer culture, such as the notion that the utopian promise of movement through time often links sexual liberation, which incidentally involves economic liberation, to the notion of movement through space.[207] It bears recalling that the Ladies' own consumerism relied on a re-imagining of the past essentially similar to this mass-produced image of them. One conclusion to be drawn from such images of the Ladies is that the radical promise held out by dissident antiquarianism was subject to mainstream appropriation and, therefore, commodifiable. Another is that the status of Wales in the cultural imaginary suggested the popularity of antiquarian practices motivated by fetishistic and primitivist desire. Momentarily, I will discuss why the fetishism of poverty and working-class lifeways was a form of such longing.

A third conclusion touches on the medial quality of this picturesque and antiquarian longing. Writing about and by the Ladies illustrates the degree to which antiquarianism provided an attractive vocabulary for understanding and representing difference. An old-fashioned valence framed their timelessness. The tropes of romance, for example, served Seward in imagining the Ladies' heterodox and utopian domesticity, and, to Wordsworth, a mythical hermit's sojourn presaged the manner in which the Ladies' sisterly love stretched "above the reach of Time." The Ladies' own literary productions also illustrate the Gothic and antiquarian facets of their utopianism. Brideoake has noted the Gothic echoes that render the *Account of a Journey in Wales* Walpolian, including emphasis through a "florid" Gothic font of the key terms "'Ruins,' 'Priory,' 'Dungeon' and 'Monks.'"[208] This manipulation of textual ornamentation alerts one to the bookish aspect of the project: they enjoyed representing their migration materially. "They had no sooner set foot in Wales," Mavor says, "than Sarah, in her elegant hand, began recording their impressions. It was the first journal they had kept together, and was bound in marbled boards with a blue leather back and corners."[209] This little resembled a casual series of notes:

> "An Account of a Journey in Wales," announced the illuminated title-page, "Perform'd in May 1778," and then, with a self-consciousness all the more startling considering the trouble everyone had been put to on their account, she had added, "By Two Fugitive Ladies." The whole was dedicated to "Her most tenderly Beloved Companion," and on the opposite page she drew a rather lifeless sketch of Benton Castle, Milford Haven.[210]

Cynically, one could see this fanciful text with its bookish features as a vanity project—a product of youthful self-regard. But as McLuhan observes, media do not simply reflect but also extend our reach.[211] Media also allow us to "recognize . . . experience in a new material form" and "translate the outer world into the fabric of our own beings."[212] The timing of the journal speaks volumes. For the Ladies to bind their elopement not just to the classic medium of adventure, the literary romance, but also to the materiality of this medium implies an effort at re-creation through re-cognition, to use McLuhan's term. In order to get the benefits of media's extension of sensory experience and cognition, perhaps the Ladies felt a need to recast their difficult experience and then consume it, thereby re-living it differently, as a romantic adventure and travel narrative. Practitioners in the field of clinical psychology use a similar process to treat trauma. The treatment involves a combination of narrative and sensory repetition of traumatic events in order to access the "felt sense" and resolve traumatic symptoms by experiencing them differently.[213] Similarly, the antiqued frameworks of the romance and picturesque travel narrative genres could have offered the Ladies a means not simply of recasting their difficult migration in heroic terms but of re-experiencing it in self-affirming and constructive ones, perhaps as a way to turn a disruptive event into a foundation for a different kind of future. The possible need to use their limited resources in this way affirms the likelihood that significant stress or even trauma was associated with the elopement. Also, day-to-day life could not have been easy in the "wild sequestered region."[214]

Perhaps risk attends expanding the analytical context so far as to invoke the experience and treatment of trauma. Helpfully, imaginary temporal flux figured prominently in the Ladies' own process of reinvention in a new place. While real and imagined movement in space and time had critical relevance to the way that the Ladies lived, movement across space and time, virtually and actually, are additional features of the nonnormative experience. Hence, the proper context for a complete understanding of the Ladies' dissident antiquarianism extends far beyond Llangollen or even Wales to include international antiquarianism. Welsh tourism and the Home Tour in general were corollaries of Continental tourism, as Roberts and James Buzard have shown. During the Romantic period, inland travel afforded an alternative tour to British leisure travelers denied access to the Continent by the Napoleonic Wars and the revolution in France.[215] However different the attractions of the inland and Continental regions British people visited, the markets and, by extension, the desires animating the tourism overlapped.

The desires motivating Continental tourism among British people had many facets, including interests in antiquarianism, primitivism, and sexual expression. These have intersected in Continental tourism for as long as the Grand Tour has been seen as a rite of passage for young people, particularly men, from the upper classes. Encapsulating these intersecting interests during the period is the work of Richard Payne Knight, notoriously the author of the illustrated, privately printed *The Worship of Priapus* (1786). Knight also wrote a treatise on the picturesque, *An Analytical Inquiry into the Principles of Taste* (1805). In his work, dissidence intersects with Continental tourism and antiquarianism. More readily associated with sexuality than dissidence per se, *Priapus*, as its title suggests, devotes much attention to representation of the male reproductive anatomy. The simple representation of the male body has scandalously dissident implications in patriarchal culture, in which a "peculiar silence" and "taboo" surround the penis and the male body in general.[216] Knight's study of fertility symbolism in antiquity features detailed illustrations of sculpture representing male genitalia and relies on research that Knight, a collector whose antiquities were ultimately acquired by the British Museum in a gift authorized by a special parliamentary action, conducted while touring the Continent.[217] Knight wrote that his intended audience was the Society of Dilettanti, the male antiquarian society to which Knight belonged, that had had a significant role in the excavation of Herculaneum and Pompeii.[218]

Knight's research into the "generative principle" in *Priapus* illustrates how Continental tourism and its cultural products interwove sexually dissident themes, antiquarianism, and primitivism. Specifically, the book's primitivist thesis is that the Old World's fertility rites have persisted as the basis of modern religious imagery and practices. A striking example Knight cites is the "lucky coincidence" that the Christian cross is nearly identical to ancient images of the male reproductive system: "one of the most remarkable of these [symbols of the male organs] is a cross, in the form of the letter T, which thus served as the emblem of creation and generation, before the Church adopted it as the sign of salvation."[219]

The role of primitivism in the ideological structure of inland tourism has a different aspect. The political purpose of Continental tourism, as Buzard has noted, was to use the study of the generally "ennobling" culture of Europe to complete the education of young aristocrats, implying a sense of equivalence or inferiority to the Continent. The role of the picturesque in inland tourism, by contrast, reveals marked condescension on the part of the English.[220] Even in discourse sympathetic to the plight of native populations, the vocabulary of the picturesque served dehumanizing portrayals of native populations. According to Kevin Hutchings, this discourse employed stadial theory indebted to Adam Smith and others.[221] In contrast to Buzard and Hutchings, I want to emphasize that stadial theory was a framework that organized both Continental and inland tourism. Stadial theory was indebted to antiquarian discourse about the Continent, and appearing in this stadial framework were sexualized notions of the Old World. Notions of the Old World's relative immorality—its "moral decadence"—struck both an ethnocentric and a primitivist note: the disease-like influence of the colonists reflected a state of fuller development and greater sophistication.[222]

Hutchings's reading of "Primeval Nature's Child" in *The Excursion* (1814) is helpful here. Hutchings shows how Wordsworth's representation of indigenous people parallels the idealized relation between the poet/traveler and nature elsewhere in Wordsworth's poetry. Wordsworth's indigenous person displays a kind of fortitude based on an unmediated link to nature.[223] Hence, as Hutchings says, drawing on Fulford's discussion of Wordsworth, the indigenous person is virtually indistinguishable from Wordsworth's "introspective rustic" figure, the one whom Wordsworth himself strove to emulate in moving to the Lake District.[224] Using Hutchings, one could claim that Wordsworth's move to the region seems to resemble an unintentional parody of the colonial project. In life a kind of colonist of the Lake District, Wordsworth nonetheless clearly identified with indigenous populations bearing the brunt of colonial domination and expropriation.

There are other parallels. The attractions of undeveloped, rural areas for adventurous antiquarians and eco-tourists show the operation of imperial ideology. John Whale has noted the irony in the fact that, despite being motivated by new interest in the specifically "British" past, tourists thought of themselves as "discovering" North Wales.[225] The "tours" produced by Home Tourists suggests that a powerful draw of Wales was the perceived simplicity and wildness of the North in general.

All these facets of the Home Tour are on view, so to speak, in Butler and Ponsonby's story, which shows Wales's offering liberatory possibilities not only for bookish adventure in the fullest sense—aesthetic and antiquarian-inflected world-making sponsored by the mass production of images and reproduced by the adventurers themselves in literary form—but also for dissident self-expression. Tourism had long offered Britons escape from repression. Continental tourism in particular offered at least a temporary escape for sexual minorities from sexual phobia and the threat of violence. Dissident sex acts were a capital offense. Byron is a famous case of someone who found sexual freedom in Continental tourism.[226] Through the promise of rural seclusion and the safety of distance, "wild" spaces like Llangollen Vale offered a practical alternative to the Continent's literally escapist pleasures. The Ladies were not unique in constructing the rural as a picturesque opportunity for camp world-making, self-reinvention, and refuge. Wiltshire in southwest England was the site of "Beckford's Folly," the ill-fated Fonthill Abbey. Once-rural Twickenham in London is home to Strawberry Hill. The Ladies' movement and homemaking in Wales had a more direct parallel, however. At least one other Romantic ventured to Wales to experiment with freer sexual possibilities and overtly identified the North with liberation from sexual conformity and repression. The aforementioned bibliographer Dibdin conducted such experimentation in the context of antiquarian discourse in Wales. Dibdin's works include *A Bibliographical, Antiquarian and Picturesque Tour in the Northern Counties of England and in Scotland* (1838) and *A Bibliographical Antiquarian and Picturesque Tour in France and Germany* (1821). These bibliophile works use foreign contexts as "magical" settings for shared male pleasure in aesthetic "sweets."[227] Although little-read today, Dibdin's productions merit close attention in part because they offer a cultural analogue for the Ladies' resettlement in Wales. In Dibdin's subscription-based tomes, antiquarianism, sexual dissidence, and the picturesque intersect, and inland tourism is sometimes the context. In an odd discourse, Dibdin uses the discussion of rare books and other antiquities as an occasion for meditating on excited male bodies and vividly describing shared and avowedly scandalous passions. An illustrative quote from Dibdin's *The Library Companion; or, the Young Man's Guide, and the Old Man's Comfort, in the Choice of a Library*: "I know more than *one* friend who covets these precious *morsels* of blackletter rarity, with an ardour and insatiableness that promise never to be satisfied. Happy state of excitation!"[228] The context here is book collecting, but this ostensible focus is all but overwhelmed by the description of shared male pleasure.

    Bound up with the discourse of the sublime and picturesque and deriving from the antiquarian longing, consumerist enthusiasms, and the illicit pleasures associated with the Grand Tour, the popularity of the Northern Tour offers another context for understanding Butler and Ponsonby's settlement in

Wales and the character of their antiquarian practice—an adventurous, quasi-colonial enterprise of discovery and world-making free from the strictures of conventional British society and bound up with antiquarian and picturesque longing.

NOTES

1. Mavor, *Ladies of Llangollen*, 28.
2. Mavor, *Ladies of Llangollen*, 200–01.
3. Fiona Brideoake, *The Ladies of Llangollen: Desire, Indeterminacy, and the Legacies of Criticism* (Lewisburg, PA: Bucknell University Press, 2017), xxiii.
4. David Punter, "The Picturesque and the Sublime: Two Worldviews," in *The Politics of the Picturesque: Literature, Landscape and Aesthetics since 1770*, ed. Stephen Copley and Peter Garside (Cambridge: Cambridge University Press, 1994), 221.
5. Ellen Crowell, "Ghosting the Llangollen Ladies: Female Intimacies, Ascendancy Exiles, and the Anglo-Irish Novel," *Éire-Ireland* 39, no. 3 (2004): 204.
6. On the history of the "romantic friendship" thesis, see Brideoake, *Ladies of Llangollen*.
7. Crowell, "Ghosting the Llangollen Ladies."
8. Mary Gordon, *Chase of the Wild Goose* (New York: Arno Press, [1936] 1985), 85.
9. Brideoake, *Ladies of Llangollen*.
10. Terry Castle, *The Literature of Lesbianism: A Historical Anthology from Ariosto to Stonewall* (New York: Columbia University Press, 2003).
11. Castle, *Literature of Lesbianism*.
12. Brideoake, *Ladies of Llangollen*.
13. Castle, *Literature of Lesbianism*, 334.
14. Brideoake, *Ladies of Llangollen*.
15. Brideoake, *Ladies of Llangollen*.
16. Mavor, *Ladies of Llangollen*, 11.
17. Crowell, "Ghosting the Llangollen Ladies," 204.
18. Brideoake, *Ladies of Llangollen*.
19. Lisa Moore, *Dangerous Intimacies: Toward a Sapphic History of the British Novel* (Durham, NC: Duke University Press, 1997).
20. Brideoake, *Ladies of Llangollen*.
21. Susan S. Lanser, *The Sexuality of History: Modernity and the Sapphic, 1565–1830* (Chicago: University of Chicago Press, 2014); "'Put to the Blush': Romantic Irregularities and Sapphic Tropes," in *Historicizing Romantic Sexuality: A Romantic Circles Praxis Volume*, ed. Richard C. Sha (*Romantic Circles*, 2006), 6, https://romantic-circles.org/praxis/sexuality/lanser/lanser.html.
22. Brideoake, *Ladies of Llangollen*, 20.
23. Brideoake, *Ladies of Llangollen*, 76.
24. Febvre and Martin, *Coming of the Book*.

25. Brideoake, *Ladies of Llangollen*, 49.

26. Eleanor Butler, Sarah Ponsonby, and Caroline Tighe Hamilton, *The Hamwood Papers of the Ladies of Llangollen and Caroline Hamilton* (London: Macmillan, 1930), 73.

27. Gordon, *Chase of the Wild Goose*, 149.

28. Brideoake, *Ladies of Llangollen*; Ann Cvetkovich, *An Archive of Feelings: Trauma, Sexuality, and Lesbian Public Cultures* (Durham, NC: Duke University Press), 244.

29. David Halperin, *How to do the History of Homosexuality* (Chicago: University of Chicago Press, 2002).

30. Brideoake, *Ladies of Llangollen*, 78.

31. William Wordsworth, *The Poetical Works of William Wordsworth*, ed. William Knight (London: Macmillan, 1896), 7.129, Google Books.

32. E. V. Lucas, *A Swan and Her Friends* (London: Methuen & Co., 1907), 282.

33. Hester Lynch Thrale, *Thraliana: The Diary of Mrs. Hester Lynch Thrale, 1776–1809* (Oxford: Clarendon Press, 1951), 2.957–58.

34. Hester Lynch Piozzi, *The Piozzi Letters: Correspondence of Hester Lynch Piozzi, 1784–1821 (formerly Mrs. Thrale)*, ed. Lillian D. Bloom (Newark: University of Delware Press, 1991), 2.534.

35. Piozzi, *Piozzi Letters*, 2.220.

36. Piozzi, *Piozzi Letters*, 2.478 (emphasis added).

37. Mavor, *Ladies of Llangollen*.

38. Thomas De Quincey, *De Quincey's Works* (London: James Hogg, 1856), 5.122.

39. Mavor, *Ladies of Llangollen*.

40. Butler, Ponsonby, and Hamilton, *Hamwood Papers*, 97.

41. Mavor, *Ladies of Llangollen*.

42. Mavor, *Ladies of Llangollen*, 214.

43. Gordon Rowley, "Enchantresses of Wales Still Lure Visitors," in *Chicago Tribune* (22 May 1977), C15. Proquest.

44. Butler, Ponsonby, and Hamilton, *Hamwood Papers*.

45. David Murray, "The Challenge of Home for Sexual Orientation and Gendered Identity Refugees in Toronto," *Journal of Canadian Studies* 48 (2014), Academic Search Complete.

46. Murray, "Challenge of Home," 133.

47. Mavor, *Ladies of Llangollen*.

48. Blanche Wiesen Cook, "'Women Alone Stir My Imagination': Lesbianism and the Cultural Tradition," *Signs* 4, no. 4 (1979), https://www.jstor.org/stable/3173368.

49. Martha Vicinus, "Distance and Desire: English Boarding-School Friendships," *Signs* 9, no. 4 (1984), https://www.jstor.org/stable/3173613.

50. Martha Vicinus, "'They Wonder to Which Sex I Belong': The Historical Roots of the Modern Lesbian Identity," *Feminist Studies* 18, no. 3 (1992), https://www.jstor.org/stable/3178078.

51. John Hicklin, *The Ladies of Llangollen, as Sketched by Many Hands: With Notices of Other Objects of Interest in that Sweetest of Vales* (Chester: Thomas Catherall, 1847), 39, Google Books.

52. "Extraordinary Instance of Female Friendship," *Parental Monitor* (1796), Adam Matthew Digital.

53. Moore, *Dangerous Intimacies*.

54. "Extraordinary Instance of Female Friendship," 101; Moore, *Dangerous Intimacies*.

55. Moore, *Dangerous Intimacies*.

56. Brideoake, *Ladies of Llangollen*.

57. Nicole Reynolds, *Building Romanticism: Literature and Architecture in Nineteenth-Century Britain* (Ann Arbor: University of Michigan Press, 2010).

58. Karl Marx, *Capital: A Critique of Political Economy*, ed. Edward Aveling (New York: International Publishers, 1967), 1.71.

59. Marx, *Capital*, 1.71.

60. Marx, *Capital*, 1.74.

61. Marshall McLuhan, *Understanding Media: The Extensions of Man* (New York: McGraw-Hill Book Company, 1964), 7.

62. McLuhan, *Understanding Media*, 8.

63. McLuhan, *Understanding Media*, 8.

64. McLuhan, *Understanding Media*, 8.

65. Brideoake, *Ladies of Llangollen*.

66. Dale Townshend, *Gothic Antiquity: History, Romance, and the Architectural Imagination, 1760–1840* (Oxford: Oxford University Press, 2019); Brideoake, *Ladies of Llangollen*.

67. Brideoake, *Ladies of Llangollen*, 109.

68. Kalter, *Modern Antiques*.

69. Townshend, *Gothic Antiquity*.

70. Horace Walpole, *The Letters of Horace Walpole, Fourth Earl of Orford* (Edinburgh: John Grant, 1906), 5.385, Google Books.

71. Townshend, *Gothic Antiquity*; Sontag, "Notes on Camp"; Andrew Elfenbein, *Romantic Genius: The Prehistory of a Homosexual Role* (New York: Columbia University Press, 1999).

72. Townshend, *Gothic Antiquity*.

73. McLuhan, *Understanding Media*, 7.

74. Townshend, *Gothic Antiquity*; Kalter, *Modern Antiques*.

75. Horace Walpole, *Horace Walpole and His World: Select Passages from his Letters*. (London: Seeley, Jackson, and Halliday, 1884), 14, Google Books.

76. Sontag, "Notes on Camp," 277.

77. Andrew Ross, *No Respect: Intellectuals and Popular Culture* (Abingdon, UK: Routledge, 2014).

78. Sontag, "Notes on Camp," 277.

79. Sontag, "Notes on Camp," 280.

80. Marx, *Capital*, 1.40.

81. Brideoake, *Ladies of Llangollen*, 112.

82. Walpole, *Horace Walpole and His World*, 14.

83. Brideoake, *Ladies of Llangollen*.

84. Freud, "Character and Anal Erotism," 297.

85. Reynolds, *Building Romanticism*, 93.
86. Reynolds, *Building Romanticism*.
87. Gordon, *Chase of the Wild Goose*, 68.
88. Gordon, *Chase of the Wild Goose*.
89. Gordon, *Chase of the Wild Goose*.
90. Gordon, *Chase of the Wild Goose*.
91. Mavor, *Ladies of Llangollen*.
92. Brideoake, *Ladies of Llangollen*, 76.
93. Mavor, *Ladies of Llangollen*, 112.
94. Mavor, *Ladies of Llangollen*.
95. Sontag, "Notes on Camp," 280.
96. Butler, Ponsonby, and Hamilton, *Hamwood Papers*, 80.
97. Mavor, *Ladies of Llangollen*.
98. Mavor, *Ladies of Llangollen*.
99. Mavor, *Ladies of Llangollen*, 176.
100. Anna Seward, *Letters of Anna Seward, Written Between the Years 1784 and 1807* (Edinburgh: Archibald Constable and Co., 1811), 4.99–100, Google Books.
101. Castle, *Literature of Lesbianism*.
102. Piozzi, *Piozzi Letters*, 2.323.
103. William F. Pocock, *Architectural Designs for Rustic Cottages, Picturesque Dwellings, Villas, &c.* (London: J. Turner, 1807), 8.
104. James Malton, *An Essay on British Cottage Architecture: Being an Attempt to Perpetuate on Principle, that Peculiar Mode of Building, which was Originally the Effect of Chance* (London: Hockham and Carpenter, Booksellers, 1798), 7.
105. Seward, *Letters*, 293.
106. On subcultural use of consumerism that resembles *bricolage*, see Hebdige, *Subculture*; Jack Halberstam, *Female Masculinity* (Durham, NC: Duke University Press, 1998), 232.
107. Brideoake, *Ladies of Llangollen*, 125.
108. Halberstam, *Female Masculinity*.
109. Mavor, *Ladies of Llangollen*.
110. Mavor, *Ladies of Llangollen*.
111. Brideoake, *Ladies of Llangollen*; Butler, Ponsonby, and Hamilton, *Hamwood Papers*, 91.
112. Butler, Ponsonby, and Hamilton, *Hamwood Papers*, 85.
113. Butler, Ponsonby, and Hamilton, *Hamwood Papers*, 85.
114. Butler, Ponsonby, and Hamilton, *Hamwood Papers*, 86.
115. Gordon, *Chase of the Wild Goose*.
116. Butler, Ponsonby, and Hamilton, *Hamwood Papers*, 94.
117. Butler, Ponsonby, and Hamilton, *Hamwood Papers*, 81.
118. Butler, Ponsonby, and Hamilton, *Hamwood Papers*, 85.
119. Butler, Ponsonby, and Hamilton, *Hamwood Papers*, 92.
120. Brideoake, *Ladies of Llangollen*, 129.
121. Mavor, *Ladies of Llangollen*.
122. Brideoake, *Ladies of Llangollen*.

123. Gordon, *Chase of the Wild Goose*.
124. Castle, *Literature of Lesbianism*, 390.
125. Anne Lister, *I Know My Own Heart: The Diaries of Anne Lister, 1791–1840* (New York: New York University Press, 1992), xv.
126. Castle, *Literature of Lesbianism*.
127. Moore, *Dangerous Intimacies*, 84.
128. Brideoake, *Ladies of Llangollen*.
129. Michel Foucault, *The History of Sexuality: Volume 1: An Introduction*, trans. Robert Hurley (New York: Vintage Books, 1990); Judith Butler, *Gender Trouble: Feminism and the Subversion of Identity* (New York: Routledge, 1990).
130. David Halperin, *Saint Foucault: Towards a Gay Hagiography* (New York: Oxford University Press, 1995), 62 (emphasis original).
131. Fiona Brideoake, "'Extraordinary Female Affection': The Ladies of Llangollen and the Endurance of Queer Community," *Romanticism on the Net* 36–37 (November 2004, February 2005), 5. http://www.erudit.org/revue/ron/2005/v/n36-37/011141ar.html?vue=resume.
132. Brideoake, "Extraordinary Female Affection," 5.
133. Susan S. Lanser, "Bluestocking Sapphism and the Economies of Desire," *Huntington Library Quarterly* 65, no. 1/2 (2002): 260, https://www.jstor.org/stable/3817740.
134. Lanser, "Bluestocking Sapphism."
135. Lanser, "Bluestocking Sapphism," 259–60.
136. Susan S. Lanser, *The Sexuality of History: Modernity and the Sapphic, 1565–1830* (Chicago: University of Chicago Press, 2014), 15.
137. Lanser, "Bluestocking Sapphism."
138. Lanser, "Bluestocking Sapphism," 261.
139. Bill Brown, "Objects, Others, and Us (The Refabrication of Things)," 187.
140. Brown, "Objects, Others, and Us," 188.
141. Hallie Lieberman, "Intimate Transactions: Sex Toys and the Sexual Discourse of Second-Wave Feminism," *Sexuality & Culture* 21, no. 1 (2017), Academic Search Complete.
142. Lieberman, "Intimate Transactions."
143. Lieberman, "Intimate Transactions."
144. Rita Felski, "Object Relations," *Contemporary Women's Writing*, 1, no. 1–2 (2007): 186, 185, https://academic-oup-com.uri.idm.oclc.org/cww.
145. Brideoake discusses the history of the *ferme ornée* (ornamental farm) in *Ladies of Llangollen*.
146. Brideoake, *Ladies of Llangollen*, xxiv.
147. Foucault, *History of Sexuality*.
148. John D'Emilio, "Capitalism and Gay Identity," in *Powers of Desire: The Politics of Sexuality*, ed. Christine Stansell Ann Snitow and Sharan Thompson (New York: Monthly Review Press, 1983), 101.
149. D'Emilio, "Capitalism and Gay Identity," 102.
150. Mike Savage, "Status, Lifestyle, and Taste," in *The Oxford Handbook of the History of Consumption*, ed. Frank Trentmann (Oxford: Oxford University Press, 2013), 555.

151. Frank Trentmann, *Empire of Things: How We Became a World of Consumers, from the Fifteenth Century to the Twenty-first* (New York: HarperCollins Publishers, 2016), 4; Frank Trentmann, "Knowing Consumers—Histories, Identities, Practices," in *The Making of the Consumer: Knowledge, Power, and Identity in the Modern World*, ed. Frank Trentmann (Oxford: Berg Publishers, 2005).

152. Frank Trentmann, *Free Trade Nation: Commerce, Consumption, and Civil Society in Modern Britain* (Oxford: Oxford University Press, 2009), 16–17.

153. Trentmann, *Free Trade Nation*, 232.

154. Trentmann, *Free Trade Nation*.

155. Seward, *Letters of Anna Seward*, 99.

156. Seward, *Letters of Anna Seward*, 149–50.

157. William Wordsworth, "Wordsworth's Prefaces of 1800 and 1802," in *Lyrical Ballads*, ed. R. L. Brett and A. R. Jones (London: Routledge, 1991).

158. John Milton, *Paradise Lost*, ed. Gordon Teskey (New York: Norton, 2005), 1.337.

159. Milton, *Paradise Lost*, 1.650.

160. Castle, *Literature of Lesbianism*, 338.

161. Mavor, *Ladies of Llangollen*, 150.

162. Mavor, *Ladies of Llangollen*.

163. Brideoake, "Extraordinary Female Affection."

164. Brideoake, *Ladies of Llangollen*, 47.

165. Mavor, *Ladies of Llangollen*.

166. Brideoake, "Extraordinary Female Affection."

167. Mavor, *Ladies of Llangollen*, 203.

168. Mavor, *Ladies of Llangollen*, 203–04.

169. Brideoake, "Extraordinary Female Affection."

170. Mavor, *Ladies of Llangollen*.

171. Mavor, *Ladies of Llangollen*.

172. Mavor, *Ladies of Llangollen*, 208.

173. Mavor, *Ladies of Llangollen*.

174. Gordon, *Chase of the Wild Goose*, 240.

175. Gordon, *Chase of the Wild Goose*, 243.

176. Gordon, *Chase of the Wild Goose*, 246–47.

177. Gordon, *Chase of the Wild Goose*, 249.

178. Catherine Jean Nash, "Trans Experiences in Lesbian and Queer Space," *Canadian Geographer* 55 no. 2 (2011): 205, Academic Search Complete; Amy L. Stone, "Flexible Queers, Serious Bodies: Transgender Inclusion in Queer Spaces," *Journal of Homosexuality* 60 no. 12 (2013): 1648, Academic Search Complete; Jack Halberstam, *In a Queer Time and Place: Transgender Bodies, Subcultural Lives* (New York: New York University Press, 2005).

179. Piozzi, *Piozzi Letters*, 2.173.

180. Piozzi, *Piozzi Letters*.

181. Piozzi, *Piozzi Letters*, 2.477.

182. Piozzi, *Piozzi Letters*, 2.508.

183. Piozzi, *Piozzi Letters*, 2.150.

184. Piozzi, *Piozzi Letters*.
185. Butler, Ponsonby, and Hamilton, *Hamwood Papers*, 80.
186. Piozzi, *Piozzi Letters*, 2.513.
187. Seward, *Letters of Anna Seward*, 290.
188. Seward, *Letters of Anna Seward*, 369.
189. Robert Southey, *Joan of Arc* (London: Henry Vizetelly, 1853), 1.105, Google Books.
190. Seward, *Letters of Anna Seward*, 297.
191. Seward, *Letters of Anna Seward*, 150.
192. Tim Fulford, "Virtual Topography: Poets, Painters, Publishers and the Reproduction of the Landscape in the Early Nineteenth Century," *RAVON* 57–58 (2010), https://id.erudit.org/iderudit/1006512ar.
193. Fulford, "Virtual Topography," 3, 23.
194. Gordon, *Chase of the Wild Goose*.
195. Gordon, *Chase of the Wild Goose*.
196. Mavor, *Ladies of Llangollen*.
197. Ellen Crowell, "Ghosting the Llangollen Ladies," 205.
198. C. S. Matheson, "'Ancient and Present': Charles Heath of Monmouth and the Historical and Descriptive Accounts . . . of Tintern Abbey 1793–1828," in *Travel Writing and Tourism in Britain and Ireland*, ed. Benjamin Colbert (Houndmills, UK: Palgrave Macmillan, 2012).
199. William Gambold, *A Compendious Welsh Grammar, or a Short and Easy Introduction to the Welsh Language* (Bala: R. Saunderson, 1833), 174.
200. Catherine Sinclair, *Hill and Valley: or, Wales and the Welsh* (Edinburgh: W. Whyte & Co., 1848), 170, Google Books.
201. Rita Singer, "Through Wales in the Footsteps of William Gilpin: Illustrated Travel Accounts by Early French Tourists, 1768–1810," *European Romantic Review* 30, no. 2 (2019), Academic Search Complete.
202. Singer, "Through Wales."
203. Gwyneth Tyson Roberts, "'Under the Hatches': English Parliamentary Commissioners' Views of the People and Language of Mid-nineteenth-century Wales," in *The Expansion of England: Race, Ethnicity and Cultural History*, ed. Bill Schwartz (London: Routledge, 1996), 174.
204. Rudi Volti, *Society and Technological Change*, 4th ed. (New York: Worth Publishers, 2001).
205. Gordon, *Chase of the Wild Goose*.
206. Gordon, *Chase of the Wild Goose*, 222.
207. Halberstam, *In a Queer Time and Place*.
208. Brideoake, *Ladies of Llangollen*, 78.
209. Mavor, *Ladies of Llangollen*, 52.
210. Mavor, *Ladies of Llangollen*, 52.
211. McLuhan, *Understanding Media*.
212. McLuhan, *Understanding Media*, 211.
213. Peter A. Levine and Ann Frederick, *Waking the Tiger: Healing Trauma* (Berkeley: North Atlantic Books, 1997), 121.

214. Wordsworth, *Poetical Works of William Wordsworth*, 7.129.

215. James Buzard, "The Grand Tour and After (1660–1840)," in *The Cambridge Companion to Travel Writing*, ed. Peter Hume and Tim Young (Cambridge: Cambridge University Press, 2002).

216. Peter Lehman, *Running Scared: Masculinity and the Representation of the Male Body* (Detroit: Wayne State University Press, 2007), 29–30.

217. Richard Payne Knight, *A Discourse on the Worship of Priapus, and Its Connection with the Mystic Theology of the Ancients to which is added an Essay on the Worship of the Generative Powers during the Middle Ages* (London: Privately Printed, 1865), Google Books.

218. Jana Funke, Kate Fisher, Jen Grove, and Rebecca Langlands, "Illustrating Phallic Worship: Uses of Material Objects and the Production of Sexual Knowledge in Eighteenth-century Antiquarianism and Early Twentieth-century Sexual Science," *Word & Image* 33, no. 3 (2017), https://www.tandfonline.com/doi/full/10.1080/02666286.2017.1294952.

219. Knight, *A Discourse on the Worship of Priapus*, 27.

220. Buzard, "The Grand Tour and After," 2.

221. Kevin Hutchings, *Romantic Ecologies and Colonial Cultures in the British Atlantic World, 1770–1850* (Montreal: McGill-Queen's University Press, 2009).

222. Hutchings, *Romantic Ecologies*, 35.

223. Hutchings, *Romantic Ecologies*, 157.

224. Hutchings, *Romantic Ecologies*, 157.

225. John Whale, "Romantics, Explorers and Picturesque Travellers," in *The Politics of the Picturesque: Literature, Landscape and Aesthetics since 1770*, ed. Stephen Copley and Peter Garside (Cambridge: Cambridge University Press, 1994), 177.

226. Louis Crompton, *Byron and Greek Love: Homosexuality in Nineteenth-century England* (Berkeley: University of California Press, 1985).

227. Thomas Frognall Dibdin, *A Bibliographical Antiquarian and Picturesque Tour in France and Germany* (London: Shakespeare Press, 1821), 1.205, 1.216.

228. Dibdin, *The Library Companion; or, the Young Man's Guide, and the Old Man's Comfort, in the Choice of a Library* (London: Harding, Triphook, and Lepard, 1824), 420.

Chapter 2

Thomas F. Dibdin's Club for Ornamental Gentlemen

In one of his lavish bibliographical tour books, *A Bibliographical Antiquarian and Picturesque Tour in France and Germany* (1821, 1829), Thomas F. Dibdin sketches, using an emphatic and erroneous style all his own, the scene of a valet taking a solitary break with some fifteenth-century pornography:

> The postboy having stabled and refreshed his horses, was regaling himself in the kitchen—but how do you think he was regaling himself?—Truly, in stretching himself upon a bench, and reading, as old Ascham expresses it, "a merry tale from Boccace." In other words, he was reading a French version of the Decameron of that celebrated author. Now, my friend, whether he had ever heard of the *Voldarfer* [sic] *Boccaccio*, is truly beyond my power of divination to affirm: but most certain it is that he *was* so occupied—thereby putting to shame perhaps the whole tribe of postillions in Great Britain! . . . We left the bibliomaniacal postboy to his Boccaccio, and prepared to visit the CASTLE.[1]

The "Valdarfer Boccaccio" had signal importance for Dibdin, who, in the *Bibliographical Decameron; or, Ten Days Pleasant Discourse upon Illuminated Manuscripts, and Subjects Connected with Early Engraving, Typography, and Bibliography* (1817), celebrates it as "[p]erhaps the most notorious volume in existence" and "certainly one of the scarcest, if not the very scarcest book that existed." Illustrating the bibliographer's innovative attention to the individual copy, he describes it as "a sound rather than a fine copy" in "a faded yellow morocco binding." Long sought after, as he says, "this very book had been a sort of bone of contention among the collectors in the reign of the first two Georges."[2] Notable for its nonjudgmental representation of same-sex love, Boccaccio's collection of ribald tales obsessed Dibdin's circle of "bibliomaniacs," a common term for rare book collectors in the early nineteenth century. Dibdin named his book-collecting and publishing society, the first such group (the still-active Roxburghe Club, or, in Dibdinese, the "Corpus Roxburghianum") after an auction featuring the sale of the book.[3] Dibdin also devotes space in the third volume of *Bibliographical Decameron*, modeled loosely on Boccaccio's text, to a mock-heroic account of this auction.

Dibdin's voyeuristic rendering of a solitary young man "regaling himself" with an illicit book points to the curious, ineffable dissidence of Romantic bibliomania: bookish discourse from the period strikes queer notes. "Curious," a keyword among bibliomaniacs, offers a window onto this surprising queerness. A passage from Dibdin's *A Bibliographical Antiquarian and Picturesque Tour in France and Germany* (1821) typifies the usage: "Having gratified our *curiosity*, as much as we were enabled, rather than as much as we wished, to do—we returned to the cabaret."[4] In this discourse, "curious" is a byword for shared male pleasure. The word's sexual implications were by then long-established. Edward Ward has recorded a reference to the patrons of an eighteenth-century Mollies' club as a "curious band of fellows," for example.[5] Nineteenth-century pornography offers an instance at the other end of the century. The narrator of *My Secret Life* (1888–1894) uses the word to describe his specifically sexual desire: "During one period of this erotic frenzy, being as it happened by myself in town alone, I was there nearly every night. My *curiosity* was insatiable."[6] According to the *Oxford English Dictionary*, one concurrent sense of the word was "of materials," especially "fine" or "delicate" ones, while another, older one was "strange, singular, odd; queer." Complicating this history is the cultural valence—and, specifically, negative associations—of intellectual curiosity. Benedict has found in the history of its queerness, alongside the approbation of free intellectual inquiry that stemmed from the Enlightenment, a much older tradition of inflammatory representation of curious people and the things and practices associated with them—with those who "[look] beyond."[7] While recalling McLuhan's theory of media as extensions of human capacity, this tradition identifies both collectors and the objects they collect with what Benedict terms an "ontological transgression." On the one hand, the intellectually ambitious, ambition being the "essence" of curiosity, are "monsters, 'queers,' and curiosities."[8] Such figures, including connoisseurs and scientists, traditionally appear as insatiable and narcissistic.[9] On the other, as Benedict further claims, their monstrous desire animates their objects. That bibliomaniacs of the Romantic period embraced such a loaded term carries with it an impossible and scandalous implication—namely, that the bibliomaniacal subculture was somehow queer in a way resembling the conventional, modern sense of the word. Simultaneously, the complex history of the word and the bookish context of its usage among bibliophiles points in completely divergent directions.

Nevertheless, one can safely begin by observing that the bibliomaniacs' community resembled the Ladies' in being an ornamental one—a consumerist subculture bound by a dissident embrace of objects. We have seen in the case of the Ladies' circle that consumption bound a community that used objects to practice a dissident mode of domesticity. This dissident homemaking drew on the queer Gothic, in itself a hyper-material form, to imagine and produce a new world. In the present chapter, the examination of Romantic bibliomaniacs, represented by Dibdin's works and circle, will reveal that queer desire could also be an uncanny effect of bookish discourse, blurring distinctions between human and object in scandalous yet ambiguous ways. I will argue that the figure of the compulsive bibliophile marked the entry of a dissident being into discourse, anticipating the later clinical production of the homosexual. While yoked, like the figure of the onanist, to a "medicalized personal identity," the figure of the bibliomaniac was not a prototypically gay subject but a collection of sexual identities.[10] A complicating factor was the close relationship between sexuality and textuality going back to the seventeenth century, when, according to Foucault, a "discursive explosion" on the subject of sex began.[11] More specifically, this production of sexuality was to an equally indeterminable extent also a reflexive one—a textual effect of the history of sexuality. Close analysis of a text by Dibdin will make the case that, like the Ladies' community, bibliomaniacal discourse suggests a way in which Romantic dissidence was bound up with its media, multiplying objects of desire and making any one, allegedly stable object difficult to identify. Discussion of Dibdin's life, circle, and works, including archival correspondence and papers, will also show how Romantic book love gave provocative and rare form to a taboo subject: sensual pleasure among men. A prominent feature of this discourse of book love is compulsion—desire so powerful it threatens.

The term "bibliomania," a French word Lord Chesterfield borrowed in 1750, referred to the compulsive book collecting of aristocratic rare book collectors and to the affliction—an addiction to the "black letter"—from which they suffered.[12] As Lynch has noted, attention to the figure corresponded to a "boom period" in the market for rare books stretching from the beginning of the century to the 1820s, so popular interest in bibliomaniacs waxed and waned with the prices of old books.[13] While it reflected the changing economics of book production and consumption during the period, the figure of the male bibliomaniac also reflected nineteenth-century scientific discourse concerning addiction, hence the "mania" in bibliomania.

The science of addiction in the period bore the influence of what George S. Rousseau, author of *Nervous Acts: Essays on Literature, Culture and Sensibility*, has termed "nervous social anthropology," many versions of which appeared between the late eighteenth century and the publication of

Origin of Species (1859). Nervous system development was thought to correlate with broader social development (rendered in scalar and evolutionary terms): increasing social complexity reflected the increasing complexity of the nervous system. For one influential nineteenth-century scientist, Robert Verity (Changes Produced in the Nervous System by *Civilization* [1839]), nutrition played a key role. Protein built more complex nervous systems, which meant stronger minds and bodies and, in turn, increasingly more effective institutions. What was true for the society was true for the individual, so "great men" had more nerves (being more "nervous"). Certain behaviors could "shatter" one's nervous system. Sedentary occupations in particular were thought to have this effect—hence the notion of "literary nerves," the supposed cause of melancholia and nervous disorders. Rousseau cites the case of the scholar John Addington Symonds (1840–1893) as an example of the way nineteenth-century science pathologized and sexualized "literary nerves." Specifically, Symonds diagnosed himself with "excessive erethism," or sexual overexcitement, after abandoning a fellowship at Oxford upon being accused of desiring students.[14] This diagnosis, common in late-Victorian neurology, illustrates, for Foucault, the phenomenon of "discursive erethism"—the transformation of sex into discourse.[15] In this way, scientific discourse defined certain modes of literary consumption as individual, social, and sexual dysfunctions. Against this backdrop in which sexologists understood bookishness in terms of sexual nonconformity—and "incitement"—the figure of the bibliomaniac appeared and attracted criticism.[16] In light of this medicalized discourse, Dibdin's scientific background is notable. He was a member of the Society for Scientific and Literary Disquisition (the "Lunatics") and the author, as Lennard J. Davis has noted, of a lost poem entitled "Vaccinia."[17] His psychological interest in the fetishism of literature, its perils and pleasures, reflected a mode of bibliography that was also a science of the nervous system. Rather than make him unique, Dibdin's quasiclinical purchase on bibliomania linked him to an ongoing tradition of theorizing about collecting, some of which overtly psychosexualizes collectors' practices. As Susan Stewart and Jean Baudrillard have observed, this tradition continues.[18]

In the popular imagination, the collector was an economic case study—and problem—in addition to being a psychological one. Interest in the figure focused on the imagined larger impact on literature of his compulsive possessiveness, for example. Consequently, the period saw the continuation of a traditional image of the book collector as a rich dilettante—the owner of more books than he had ever read or ever would. This image of the collector serves as a reference point for Dibdin's own gently ironic representations of bibliomaniacs. For instance, *Bibliomania* takes as its epigraph a quotation from Alexander Barclay's 1509 adaptation of Sebastian Brant's *Ship of Fools* (1494) dealing with the "Book-Fool" (although Dibdin fittingly credits instead of Barclay the book's printer, Richard Pynson).[19] The quotation, in black letter, satirizes the book collector as a compulsive and greedy fetishist: "Styll am I besy bokes assemblynge, / For to have plenty is a pleasant thynge / In my conceyt, and to have them ay in honde: / But what they mene I do not understonde."[20]

Another literary figure, the book collector Oldbuck in Walter Scott's *The Antiquary* (1816), illustrates the miserly and antisocial associations of the hobby at a time when, thanks to dropping printing costs, the wider diffusion of the reading habit and the popularity of the literary anthology, literature took on the aspect of public property.[21] The traits of Oldbuck evidently also reflected Scott's personal feelings about bookishness. Although Scott and Dibdin corresponded, and Scott praised his work, Scott saw his antiquarianism as distinct from the bibliomaniacs': "[M]y book-mania rather respects the matter than the size of my volumes."[22] In *The Antiquary*, contemporary bibliomania is at once luxuriant and impotent, the pale "imitation" of the bookish pursuits of an ancient warrior-class of collector. The "excess of expenditure" of the "lords, knights and squires of our own day" only dimly mirrors the power of Don Quixote's addiction, for instance, which compelled the man of La Mancha to trade his land for books.[23] Oldbuck, by contrast, takes more interest in money than books, his ledger being the book consulted in his meetings with Sir Arthur in the former's library, the "*sanctum sanctorum*" where the two "virtuosos" meet to discuss Arthur's debt.[24]

Philip Connell has argued that the notoriety of such conspicuous book hoarders reflected conflicting ideas about the practices of aristocratic collectors at a time of increasing literacy rates and decreasing book-making costs. The wider diffusion of the reading habit and greater popularity of the literary anthology, the production of which was supported by the activities of collectors like George John Spencer, whose library Dibdin cataloged, meant that the collector now simultaneously earned derision for his seeming encroachment upon a canon coming to be seen as a form of public property (a "national heritage") and laurels for his preservation of precisely this canon through his collecting.[25]

The practices of wealthy collectors came to define the collecting subculture. Spencer was a wealthy and socially prominent member of Dibdin's club, as was Richard Heber (1774–1833), but members of the group seem to have been united more by their bookish and antiquarian interests, not their wealth or social standing. Nonetheless, most prominent in writing about the bibliomaniac is the collector's unproductive, selfish, and acquisitive literary attachments. Generalizing about the status of the bibliomania later in the century, Connell argues that the Victorians moralized about the bibliomania in terms of acquisitiveness and licentiousness. If unalloyed by a healthy sense of obligation to the public, the collector's privatization of literature seemed,

Connell claims, to threaten the health of a culture coming to be regarded as an intellectual commons.[26]

Deidre Lynch has come to a similar conclusion about the economic basis of the Romantic bibliomaniac's negative stereotype. According to Lynch, the bibliomaniac was problematic because he "threatened the ideological sleight-of-hand that invited Britons to understand others' private properties as part of the common stock of the national heritage."[27] In Lynch's view, the bibliomaniac's symptomology, or problematic affective life, was a function of the perceived exclusivity of his cultural practices. More specifically, his desire for the "black letter" was the source of an antisocial kind of cultural consumption—a "book-disease" that was less a condition than an activity, one that was dangerous precisely because it could not be caught.[28]

A bug that could be caught was the love of literature. Thomas De Quincey famously adored Wordsworth's poetry, proselytizing to practically anyone who would listen, including, as we have seen, the Ladies. Charles Lamb wrote of his love of Elizabethan dramatists in his famous essays for the magazines. The same writers were dedicated materialists, however. The "opium-eater" De Quincey's other habit was book collecting: an anecdote in his *Confessions* tells of his comically unlikely escape from a boarding school with a large trunk full of books.[29] Unlike the bibliomaniacs, De Quincey preferred to collect new fiction and went into debt buying romances and works in other popular genres. At one point, his collection was so large it forced his growing family to move.[30] Lamb had a similarly eccentric collecting style, as the next chapter will discuss. The new, professionalized class of periodical writers represented by Lamb and De Quincey, who wrote for publications such as the *London Magazine* and *Blackwood's*, were bookish people who practiced a new style of consumption, as Lynch has said.[31] Conceiving of their relationship to literature in response to the popular image of the bibliomaniac, De Quincey, Lamb, William Hazlitt, and others adopted a romantic view of literary culture. They were "in effect the first professional lovers of literature." Their style of consumption reified materiality—constituting a "relocation of library culture ... within the psychic territory of people's intimate lives." This newly intimate relationship was ultimately strategic because it allowed self-conscious consumers to distinguish their stock from the "real capital" of aristocratic collectors.[32] The middle-class consumer's capital was cultural. Now, loving literature—being the first to appreciate Wordsworth's greatness, for instance, as De Quincey famously boasted—could mean loving the insides, not the outsides, of books.[33]

The magazine writers' love of literature suggests an alternative, internalized form of bibliomania. Discussion of bookishness by Leah Price suggests that the vexed role of materiality in these writers' affective relations with books reflects the hegemony of Cartesianism in intellectual discourse.

Cartesianism "teaches us to filter out the look, the feel, the smell of the printed page."³⁴ The Enlightenment had sponsored a Cartesian reification of literary culture. Similarly, Lorraine Piroux has argued that a "denial of the materiality of language" marked bourgeois ascendancy in eighteenth-century France, where the design of the *Encyclopédie* reflected a larger-scale idealism about media that played a role in the democratic project of the Enlightenment: "[T]he success of the Enlightenment [was believed to rest] on the printed book's ability to bring its readers into close and unhindered proximity with thought and ideas, or, to put it differently, on its ability to create a purely semantic text."³⁵ Generally speaking, the eighteenth century produced an "Enlightenment ideal of linguistic and bibliographic transparency," Price says.³⁶ The proper posture toward materiality nevertheless sparked debate, and scholars have recently begun to recover the evolving status of materiality in the Romantic period's history of ideas.

For example, Romantic bibliography invested grand ambitions in the materiality of signifiers. In 1802, for example, French bibliographer Gustave Peignot theorized bibliography as "the totality of human knowledge."³⁷ According to Jon Klancher, at this historical moment book history and literary studies were practically indistinguishable: proponents of the "new book history" of the period "believed it *was* literary history."³⁸ The period's interregnum fostered interdisciplinary scholarship that unified bibliography and literary history and anticipated the present practice of book history. Today, the work of media scholars and book historians, including Price, Klancher, and N. Katherine Hayles, has recuperated "wild bibliography," as Klancher calls it, and revealed the processes of reification and displacement supporting the construction of media as things without thingness—objects that exist apart from time and space. The present moment has witnessed a unification of disparate disciplines attuned, as Hayles says in *Writing Machines*, to the "materiality of the medium."³⁹ As Price notes, these fields include bibliography, literacy statistics, editing, and media studies.⁴⁰

In the contested, evolving status of the book-object lies an opportunity to uncover alternative social formations around the book during the period. The tension that Ferris has observed between the properly literary sphere and the bookish one, a tension informed by contestation over the uniformity and transparency of print and the singularity of authorship, speaks to the relatively open and fluid conceptions of print and society that Romantics held, along with the greater range of genres and networks of production the concepts enabled.⁴¹ An ornamental community seems to have been poised to transform reigning ideas about communication and materiality more broadly. The practices and ideas of bookish folks existed in tension with an ideological projection of community, the cultural sphere, and a concomitant negation of materiality, the singular author. For a time, the strange materialism of Dibdin seemed not so alien and may have offered the promise of more honest relations with objects of consumerist desire—relations that did not repress the materiality of its objects and displace materialism onto alleged dissidents. For a moment, according to Ferris, alternative conceptions of culture and community could be glimpsed. Specifically, a fruitful connection existed between the book-object and experimental "cultural identity-formations." Bookmen had the freedom to deviate in surprising ways: theirs was a "waywardness oddly sanctioned by a culture otherwise heavily invested in the powers of literacy to effect domestic order and definition."[42]

The bookish community was far from a monolith. The mythological power of bibliography, for instance, had a different status than auction-house antics. One lever acting on perceptions of collectors was homosociality. While the solitary bookishness of men like Jane Austen's Mr. Bennet in *Pride and Prejudice* (1813), which Heather J. Jackson has discussed, was normalized, the domestic and pastoral pleasures of homosocial bibliomaniacs had an altogether different image.[43] A puzzling and provocative record of this communal form of bookishness can be found in Dibdin's published works and correspondence. Together with journalism about his circle, Dibdin's works offer a window onto an ornamental community whose dissidence is inseparable from its form and, therefore, irreducible to conventional definitions of sexuality while pregnant with radical possibility.

BOOKS GLITTERING WITH ORNAMENTS

Although containing many factual and typographical errors, Dibdin's bibliographical efforts deserve credit for a major innovation in the field: the introduction of "the principle of first-hand examination of books." Dibdin may have created "the entire field of English bibliography and book collecting," in fact.[44] A literary form of bibliophilia, Dibdin's innovative attention to the materiality of the copy—the binding, paper, and illustrations—transforms into discourse the bibliomaniac's sensual mode of appreciating antique books. At the same time, some of Dibdin's bibliographical and poetic productions sketch the contours of a fictionalized bibliophile community, a homosocial subculture organized around the acquisition of luxury goods in which initiation, secrecy, and guilt are tropes in the representation of a pleasurable, acquisitive impulse. As I will argue in what follows, Dibdin's representations of homosocial bookishness convey an uncannily queer relation with literature.

Although little-read today, Dibdin once belonged to an intellectual vanguard entranced by the possibilities of object-centered bibliography. Unfortunately, his career lay astride the evolution of modern, author-centered bibliography out of this approach, as Klancher has observed. Before it was "notorious," the "wild bibliography" with which Dibdin is associated was briefly on the cutting edge of literary history and theory. In fact, some proponents of the form of book-historical bibliography practiced by Dibdin thought it an intellectual tool akin to Casaubon's "Key to all Mythologies"—a lens for understanding not only all of literature but also all of human thought.[45] As modern, author-centered bibliographical methods displaced the materialist approach of Dibdin's bibliography around 1825, however, the reputation of Dibdin, whose last lecture was attended by Coleridge, suffered the same fate as book history and its "garish twin" bibliomania.[46]

Dibdin's early life was even more dramatic. Orphaned at age four by a naval captain named Thomas, a hard-pressed sailor working as a rover in the Indian Ocean, and a woman named Elizabeth Compton whom his father married in Calcutta in 1775, Dibdin says of his life in the *Reminiscences of a Literary Life* (1836), "I have frequently compared myself to a floating piece of timber, in a wreck, which has accidentally and luckily reached the shore." Frail and sickly as a child, Dibdin had the good fortune to receive the attentions of a kindly schoolmaster named John Man and his wife. They "saved my life," he says. From Man, he "caught, or fancied I caught, the electric spark of the BIBLIOMANIA." As a commoner at St. John's College, Oxford, he lamented the "backwardness" of his provincial education ("The want, too, of an education at a *public school* was fancied to be felt") and did not receive his bachelor's degree until four years after leaving the university, in order to enter the priesthood. In between, Dibdin unsuccessfully pursued a legal career, briefly opening practices in London and Worcester. By the time of his resolution to take orders, his *Introduction to the . . . Greek and Latin Classics*, an initial effort at bibliography, had just been reissued (ultimately, it would have four editions by 1827). A seldom-noted aspect of Dibdin's biography is his relationship with the Royal Institution. There, between 1806 and 1808, he delivered a series of twenty-eight lectures on English literature, including a defense of *"black-letter* reading," which was at the time "held up to something like public ridicule or contempt." He enjoyed large audiences at the fashionable organization and knew some of the famous literary figures of the time. At a dinner hosted by Thomas Bernard, who was overseeing Dibdin's editorship of a short-lived journal called *The Director*, Dibdin met Coleridge sometime around 1807: "The viands were usually costly, and the banquet was at once rich and varied; but there seemed to be no dish like Coleridge's to feed upon!" He also dined more than once with Scott, who appears as Sir Tristrem in Dibdin's *Bibliomania* and who, along with Robert Southey, received a gift of one of Dibdin's works.[47]

Dibdin approached these lavish productions, "book[s] glittering with ornaments," like a speculative entrepreneur.[48] A striver, he cobbled together a literary reproduction of aristocratic culture on the margins of the middle class. That the "father of bibliomania" was not a wealthy collector himself reveals the danger of generalizing about Romantic bibliomania in terms of aristocratic culture and practices.[49] His unpublished correspondence reveals the extent to which he struggled and strove at what he believed to be a worthy "cause."[50] For example, he boasted of the risks and costs associated with the publications ("The property was entirely my own; nor could that property be considered very despicable when I cleared six hundred pounds by the speculation"), and elsewhere he cast his efforts in terms of heroic self-sacrifice ("They were distributed by me gratuitously, but have averaged nearly 2*l*. per copy at book sales. Such was my zeal in THE CAUSE").[51] Writing to Dibdin, Scott cautioned him against giving so many copies away ("I am well aware of the very great expense which must necessarily have been incurred in ornamenting the edition so highly & you really must not give way to your liberal feelings respecting particular friends").[52] Dibdin's correspondence also suggests that his memoir minimizes the hazards he risked through the acts of "speculation" on which this father of four partially supported a family.[53] For example, letters to Dibdin from the small army of Edinburgh artists he contracted to produce the "cuts" illustrating his "Northern Tour" book (*A Bibliographical, Antiquarian and Picturesque Tour in the Northern Counties of England and in Scotland* [1838]) suggest that he had indebted himself to assemble the expensive book before receiving a number of subscribers sufficient even to cover the costs. A manuscript listing the high costs estimated for the first volume of the work is revealing. "Plates, Artists" cost "[£]1250 < 2054," "Paper & Printing" cost £604, and promotion £100.[54] Correspondence about the project suggests its production was stressful as well as expensive. One letter suggests that Dibdin's exactness made the process challenging for others. An artist named Alexander Aikman wrote to him about the way an engraving depicted the "immodest fundament" (perhaps the buttocks) of a "currier's apprentice." Dibdin had expressed grave concern about the way the light hit the subject's "breeches."[55]

Occasionally desperate, the tone of his unpublished letters from this time ranges from obsequious to baroquely self-pitying to grotesque, but the style of this self-described "ornamental gentleman" was always emphatic. A particularly florid example of Dibdin's distressed mode appears in his correspondence in an exchange over a venture with William Nichol of the Shakespeare Press, whom Dibdin apparently owed money. Dibdin threatens that if he does not receive a reply from the publisher soon, he fears he "should *splash* you with more *bloody* parts of the contents of my abdomen."[56] Other correspondence with Nichol deals with financial difficulties. In 1821, Dibdin wrote,

> Of course, I am excepively [*sic*] anxious to hear from you; and conclude, from your silence, that the point will be arranged-tho' not, I am sure, without

difficulty, at a moment like this: and yet, I ought never to, and never will, *despair*. Whittaker's returned bill for £125 was handed up to me on Wednesday and I had not £12 in the house; by 5 o'clock that will was *paid*—but, of course, by borrowed money. Salaries, rents, arrears, all now, untouchable, but I will make a great effort and shake off 3/4ths of my incumbrances [*sic*] before the end of January.[57]

The circumstances detailed here, including an inability to pay seemingly any bills, suggest how narrowly and, indeed, incompletely Dibdin managed to avoid financial disaster in producing his tomes. Dibdin also negotiated with Nichol concerning the cost of publishing his ornate books. In a letter from 1828, Dibdin argues, "The question, my dear friend, is precisely *this*. If with about £200 I can make it a pretty, taking thing—the way of *ornament*—I shall sell the whole impression and gain a good round sum. If, without ornament, it may not sell *at all*: [] folks will expect something, of this kind, from such an ornamental Gentleman as Yours."[58] Letters also suggest he borrowed funds to cover publication expenses. In 1821, he requested £130 from George Nichol to help him out of a "pinch" until the end of the month, when a new book would appear. In the same letter, he complains about hard work on the *Aedes Althorpianae* (1822), saying, "[E]very day till 4 o'clock fagging hard ... thus you see I shall 'die, with *harness* on my back.'"[59] Another correspondent, Philip Bliss, the antiquarian and book collector who was the University Registrar at Oxford and had held positions at the Bodleian Library and the British Museum, warned Dibdin not to indulge in his "taste for embellishment" and to avoid spending his subscription earnings prior to publication.[60] Printers with whom Dibdin worked once wrote to him about a check he had sent that bounced.[61]

The public face of bibliomania was as extravagant and exorbitant as Dibdin's work was hard. The Roxburghe book auction of 1812, which inspired Dibdin's *Bibliomania; or Book Madness* (1809), represents the watershed moment for interest in this figure during the period. At the auction, James Innes-Ker sold the library of John Ker, third duke of Roxburghe, upon inheriting the dukedom after a costly legal battle. So notorious was the sale that articles about it appeared in the press well into the Victorian period. Collectors had eagerly anticipated the auction due to the war's inhibiting effect on the supply of rare books from the Continent and to a widely circulated auction "preface" written by George Nicol.[62] Napoleon may have sent a representative to bid on his behalf. In *The Bibliographical Decameron, or, Ten Days Pleasant Discourse upon Illuminated Manuscripts, and Subjects Connected with Early Engraving, Typography, and Bibliography* (1817), Dibdin quotes newspaper accounts of this agent's bidding £2000 for the *Decameron*, calling it "the only great *desideratum* of Napoleon's library."

Comparing the auction to the biblical flood, Dibdin says the auction lasted *"two and forty* successive days—with the exception only of Sundays" in the deceased duke's dining room. Dibdin's rendering of the auction echoes Beckford's use of the mock-heroic to describe bookish jousting:

> The arena is filled: closely wedged stand the champions: the trumpet sounds; the falchions glitter, and they are commingled in desperate conflict. Atticus [Heber] leads the van. He little expects such a "tug of war." *The Boke of the most Vyctoryous Prince Guy of Warwicke*, printed by his beloved *Copeland* . . . stands temptingly before him: and the purchaser is resolved to be as "victorious" as the Prince whose deeds are recorded in such precious black-letter strains. The contest is fierce; but Atticus is triumphant . . . yet not without "empurpling the plain" with his blood.[63]

According to Dibdin, the sale's unprecedented concentration of very rare incunabula led to price inflation. With typical flair, Dibdin describes this phenomenon as the spread of an infectious "BOOK-MADNESS," or "biblioma-niacism," among the bidders. He says that within the genre of English poetry alone, the representation of Chaucer (a *"lovely MS.* of that Bard") and works from the printers Caxton, Pynson, De Worde, and Copeland meant "that between one's finger and thumb there might be held somewhere between 5 or 600*l*. worth of books." A book other than the Boccaccio attracting a great deal of attention was *Recuyell of the Historyes of Troye* (folio, 1471), described by Dibdin as the first book printed in English.[64]

Reflecting the excitement created by the catalog, the price paid for the Valdarfer Boccaccio by its winner, the Marquis of Blandford, £2,260 (or around $190,000 in today's dollars), was the highest paid for a single book until J. Pierpont Morgan purchased a 1459 Mainz Psalter for $24,750 in 1884.[65] In writing about the sale, Dibdin sounds like someone as interested in the excitement shared by the participants as the books themselves. Observing global notice of the amount at the time, Dibdin writes, "The price given for the VALDARFER BOCCACCIO of 1471 may be truly said to have astonished the whole BOOK-WORLD. Not a living creature could have anticipated it: but this might be called the grand æra of BIBLIOMANIA."[66] The subsequent history of the Boccaccio affirmed Dibdin's sense of the auction's singularity—and his observation of the resulting inflation of values (the "courage, slaughter, devastation, and phrensy" on display).[67] When financial difficulties forced the Marquis to sell the book soon after the auction, the buyer, none other than his former competitor Lord Spencer, paid only £918.15s, or approximately $77,000).[68] By the time it ended on July 4, 1814, the auction had generated £23,397.10s6p from 9,353 items (approximately $1.6 million).[69] Its figures dwarfed other book auctions, but such feverish contests were common during the book boom. During one twelve-month period prior to the Roxburghe sale (from November 1806 to November 1807), 149,200 books were sold at auctions in London.[70]

Dibdin's celebration of the auction reflects his role as a booster and recorder at bibliomaniacal court as interested in literary materiality as in male bodies and pounds paid. Perhaps because he was not a significant collector himself, he served as the secretary of his own collecting society. This marginal status in the community helps one glimpse a source of the quasi-pornographic tone of his bookish discourse about Morocco, vellum, Tyrian dye, figurative swords, and excited bidders. In *A Bibliographical Antiquarian and Picturesque Tour in France and Germany*, for example, Dibdin narrates sensual pleasures in literary spaces among other collectors. He describes his "ecstacy [sic] of admiration" upon entering, as he says in all-capitals, a "LIBRARY OF MANUSCRIPTS," graphically details his bodily response to the sight of rarities—repeatedly recounting his unspeakable pleasure as "sighs"—and references an antiquary's "*hungry* eye."[71] Adding to the uncanniness is the fact that the enraptured consumption Dibdin records is often second-hand—a granular record of other men's shared pleasures. More abstractly, his works served in the role of a fetish—a literary substitute for the tactile pleasures of handling incunabula and other rare things ("explicit" being one of his terms for his approach to bibliography). A fellow Roxburghe Club member, Joseph Haslewood, wrote Dibdin in 1808 to praise him for his skill at reproducing this kind of experience: "There appears as might expected from you much information and amusement blended in the notes, and certainly the whole is a happy specimen of imitating early typography; the *letters gothique* and coffee stained paper is only wanting to puzzle the hunter for B.L. [black letter]."[72] A bill to Dibdin from some printers indicates he explored using imitation parchment paper in his works.[73]

While he enjoyed the fame that he did achieve, the community itself seems to have held more importance for him. Dibdin credited himself with the boom in his *Reminiscences*.[74] Less a conventional memoir than a collection, this "TYPOGRAPHICAL narrative" details the production of his works and reproduces letters written to Dibdin by prominent figures, which he calls "ornaments of grace unto my head."[75] Judging from the negative reactions of some correspondents in letters he received following the book's publication, he included at least some of the letters without prior permission. In this context Dibdin seems to want credit not only for a concrete impact on the collecting world but also for desires and feelings shared by collectors. He claims that his best-known production, the mock-heroic *Bibliomania*, "excit[ed] a general curiosity in rare and precious volumes" upon its appearance.[76] He also speaks of the book's impact on the Roxburghe sale's prices: "[T]here can be no doubt of the [*Bibliomania*'s] having been largely instrumental to the increase of the prices of this sale."[77] His best-selling production, it continues to be the work for which Dibdin is best known. New editions appeared in 1811, 1842, 1856, 1876, and 1903, and the subscription list for the 1809 edition includes King George III, 233 others, and eighteen libraries.[78] The congratulatory "effusion[s]" of subscribers such as Isaac D'Israeli, author of *Curiosities of Literature*, and Dr. John Ferriar (1761–1815) appear prominently in the text.[79]

Bibliomania may have found wide circulation among collectors, but one must take Dibdin's claims of influence with a degree of skepticism. For example, Ferriar anticipated his overall approach with *The Bibliomania* (1809), a poem that Dibdin admits inspired him.[80] Unlike what one finds in Dibdin, sharp ironies in Ferriar's poem make it satirical. Rather than a celebration of shared pleasure in objects, Ferriar's poem is a critique, and the pleasure and excitement of collectors are not the focus. Whereas in Dibdin collectors appear as warrior-capitalists with grand, if sometimes tragic, compulsions, the practices of Ferriar's collector are simply problematic:

In vain might HOMER roll the tide of song,
Or HORACE smile, or TULLY charm the throng;
If cross'd by Pallas' ire, the trenchant blade
Or too oblique, or near, the edge invade,
The Bibliomane exclaims, with haggard eye,
"No margin!" turns in haste, and scorns to buy.[81]

Here, collectors are cowards (capable of being scared by an imaginary "blade" that strays too close) and fetishists who prize desirable features of the book-object (wide margins) more than the most sublime and beautiful narratives, even by Homer, Horace, and Tully. Ferriar, incidentally, shared Dibdin's interest in medicine. A Manchester physician, Ferriar would later pen a work about the psychological causes of ghost sightings entitled "An Essay Towards a Theory of Apparition" (1813).[82]

Commentary such as Ferriar's suggests that the auction and subculture could have been just as widely known had Dibdin not written *Bibliomania*. Thomas De Quincey also wrote about the auction. The event made a strong enough impression on the seventeen-year-old, a precocious book collector at the time (of new fiction rather than incunabula), to prompt him to discuss it at length later in *The Logic of Political Economy* (1844). Like Ferriar's, De Quincey's focus is not on male pleasure but on an external phenomenon it illustrates. As is typically the case with De Quincey, the near accuracy of this account is remarkable given his forced dependence on memory:

In 1812 occurred the famous Roxburghe sale, in commemoration of which a distinguished club was subsequently established in London. . . . [I]n the series of books stood one which was perfectly unique in affirmative value. . . . The book was the VALDARFER BOCCACCIO. . . . The contest soon rose buoyantly above the element of little men. It lay between two "top-sawyers," the late Lord Spencer and Lord Blandford [George Spencer-Churchill, fifth duke of Marlborough], and finally was knocked down to the latter for two thousand two hundred and forty pounds . . . It illustrates the doctrine on which we are now engaged that the purchaser some few years later, when Duke of Marlborough, and in personal embarrassments . . . sold the book to his old competitor, Lord Spencer, for one thousand guineas. Nothing is more variable than the affirmative value of objects which ground it chiefly on rarity. It is exceedingly apt to pall upon possession. In this case there was a secondary value—the book was not only rare, but was here found in its integrity: this one copy was perfect; all others were mutilated. But still such a value, being partly a caprice, and in the extremist sense a *pretium affectionus*, or fancy price, fluctuates with the feelings or opinions of the individual.[83]

De Quincey's version of the auction and subsequent history of the *Decameron* notably differs from Dibdin's portrait of the collector. De Quincey does not describe the collector's pleasures and relations with other men but uses the collector to theorize the point of extremity at which the logic of political economy runs aground. This collector is a man of sensibility, so the contours of a more preferable type of book-consumer emerge by way of negation of the former's stigmatized tastes. "Caprice," "feelings," and "opinions" rule his determinations of value rather than reason. These compromising impulses issue in the "fancy price," or *pretium affectionus*, of the rare book. According to the *Oxford English Dictionary*, "fancy" was used to describe a dandyish man, and "fancy man" could refer to a kept man or pimp. In this light, De Quincey's rendering of the book collector as an effeminate subject of unaccountable whims not only feminizes but also sexualizes him.

This rendering belongs to a long tradition of sexualized representations of collectors. The history of representations of collectors and the history of sexuality are tightly interwoven. In *The History of Sexuality*, Foucault famously locates the first appearance of the subject of sexuality in the early modern period, when sexuality came to be defined by the "stirrings . . . of desire," rather than behavior.[84] Coincident with this development was the construction of the dissident collector. The seventeenth-century virtuoso was an Italianate and effeminate collector figure who kept "knacks." The word "knack" could refer to the attractive but merely ornamental (and hence, in Sontag's view, the camp) object, the male genitalia, or to the affected yet empty personality of the sodomitical fop.[85] The fop of the early modern stage was, to a certain extent, an antiquarian consumer—outmoded in personal style as well as superficial and artificial. As Thomas King has said in *The Gendering of Men*, the fop harkened back to a time when social status was a function of the externalities defining court politics, in which one's physical proximity to the king's body determined one's status.[86] Romantic bibliomania, an enthusiastically retrospective discourse, invokes this history and context through its focus on the aristocracy along with male aristocrats' physicality and embodied interactions. King's larger point in *The Gendering of Men* helps explain the uncanny queerness of bibliomaniacal discourse: the logic of court hierarchy, theatrically based on physicality (specifically in the form of proximity to the monarch, dress, and posture) residually persisted in gay male typology. Dibdin's Tory politics and focus on the spaces and habits of aristocrats uncanny summoned queer types that continue to have currency.

This sexual history of the collector suggests that, in Romantic conceptions of difference, gender is only one part of the equation. When De Quincey's representation of the book collector locates desire in the unaccountable "caprice" of the "individual," which is a prototypically sexological conception of desire, this should not be understood in terms of feminization alone. Theorists besides Foucault have encouraged skepticism about relying on any one lens for historicizing desire. Sedgwick remarks in *Tendencies* that within any "complex social ecology . . . the presence of different genders, different identities and identifications" are possible.[87] This multiplicity is richly evident in constructions of the bibliomaniac. This is not to say that close attention to sexuality's inconsistency and diversity enables one to see past the operation of power to a hidden, true being. From a Foucauldian perspective, such would amount to another production of meaning, another manufactured identity. As Elfenbein has said of Foucault's theory, the discourse of sexuality functions by "multiplication: a dispersion of sexualities, a strengthening of their disparate forms, a multiple implantation of 'perversities.'"[88]

Complicating matters further is the materiality of the objects of bibliomaniacal passion. In sexualizing consumerism, Dibdin makes queer innuendo inevitable. The humanization of the objects and shared pleasures of the male subjects make reading the "curious" works of Dibdin a singular experience. While seeming to demand a reading in terms of conventional identities and desires, of modern sexuality identity per se, they confront one with the arbitrariness of any such imposition. In humanizing the objects of consumerist desire and weaving them into the fabric of human affective life and relations, they compel one to look for human referents for human desires. This is a discourse that is queer on the level of form but not content—the stuff of style and posture but also protective deniability and screens. One of Dibdin's correspondents, Charles Clark, praised his facility with innuendo.[89] Tellingly,

Dibdin's discourse seems to register anxiety about its potential suggestiveness and provocations:

> It is reported of an Indian, while incautiously gliding in his canoe, towards the rapids which are within a short distance of the falls of NIAGARA, that, finding himself within the irresistible vortex of those falls, he ceased making any efforts of resistance: but, placing his paddle by the side of him, within his little bark, and lying on his back, he quietly awaited the fate which it was impossible to escape:—and was precipitated into eternity . . . down the central horse-shoe fall. The author of this work is not very unlike the Indian in question . . . in regard to being propelled by an irresistible *bibliographical* impulse. . . . I find myself inevitably, but safely and pleasantly, I trust, borne down those rapids that precipitate themselves into the might ocean which encircles the globe, and which sustained the vessels of COLUMBUS, VASCO DE GAMA, COOK and PEROUSE.[90]

Here, in *The Library Companion; or, The Young Man's Guide, and the Old Man's Comfort, in the Choice of a Library* (1824), Dibdin describes bookishness as a potentially fatal enterprise with the stakes of colonial exploration. In the background, desire, shame, and panic all color a narrative attending closely to the posture and movements of a male form. Meanwhile, the stakes are comically mismatched with the situation, creating camp effects, and the quasiclinical language creates additional, sexual suggestions as the passage casts passion as a deep-seated "impulse" leading its subject to an "irresistible vortex." That the stakes are impossibly high also compels the reading that, for Dibdin, they actually were high—that this discourse of shared book love is actually about something much more scandalous and fatal than books. Such is the inevitable suggestiveness of Dibdin's discourse about bodies and things.

Hence, passages like this one are teases. They tempt one to "over-read" them in terms of homosexual panic or innuendo, especially considering the "pleasant" acquiescence Dibdin is happy to admit. The themes are as irresistible as the falls: in the context of a Wildean pairing of male desire and fatality, a male gaze ricochets off the body of the indigenous person into a meditation on the dangers of desire. At the same time, however, a queer reading of such a typical passage, leaving aside the problem of ahistoricism, could be said to be literally minded or, worse, willfully obtuse: any suggestiveness, surely, could be "the point" of Dibdin's mock-heroic prose and, hence, should not be the point of a critical reading. Both the reservation and the reading are problematic: such an objection to grappling directly with what Dibdin might or might not (very strenuously) intend has an uncomfortable nearness not only to the suppression of dissident representations of human affective life but also to the reduction of the prose to a simplistic, binary choice, reducing the text's meaning to a stable signified and ignoring both the bookish context and the potential for exchange between this clear set of references and the sexual suggestiveness of the text. How, then, to account for the uncannily queer effects of a typical passage in Dibdin? Making the attempt means confronting a discourse simultaneously pregnant with sexual suggestion and stubbornly opaque to analysis in terms of sexuality—a challenge to interpretation that confronts one with the imposition constituted by the structure of any categorical sexuality and the limitations built into conventional notions of sexual being. The challenge in this case is similar to that posed by the Ladies' ornamental community. In that case, the ambiguity around romantic friendship and inextricability of human and nonhuman attachments made gay readings similarly irresistible, while suggesting the circulation of dissident desire beyond the human and across time and space. The experience of reading Dibdin's "Decameronic pages" about conspicuous consumption is, likewise, a rare, if frustrating, pleasure—one as stimulating as curious.[91] Nonetheless, the suggestiveness of Dibdin's enraptured accounts of men's shared pleasure can be breathtaking, not unlike the Ladies' journal entries about their conjugal bliss. In Dibdin's *The Bibliographical Decameron*, Lisardo asks Philemon, referring to a rare copy of *Roman de la Rose*, the "cream" of the Harleian Collection, "Can you indulge us with a sip of this cream?" Philemon replies, "Fortunately it is in my power to gratify you with a pretty good taste of it."[92] Not surprisingly, some feared association with Dibdin, and critics of the bibliomaniacs played up and leveraged the liberated sensuality of their homosocial world.

Multiple correspondents of Dibdin's asked that their names be omitted from subscription lists. A correspondent of Dibdin's even expressed the fear that mail from him would be identified by postal workers.[93] The activities of Dibdin's collecting society attracted a harsh attack in the periodical press, as we will see. While editor of the *Edinburgh Review*, Macvey Napier responded to a request from Dibdin for a review of a recent work by telling him of a personal attack on Dibdin that he had suppressed:

> When your "Reminiscences" appeared, two proposals from different writers, one them a most able and [], were made to me, both having it in view to write, as I ~~believed~~ suspected, a rather *cutting* article, to use a slang phrase. Now, though I [had?] not at that time had the pleasure of seeing you I had read your books, and derived both amusement and information from them, in such way as to produce a kindly feeling towards their author. In truth, I dislike articles personally severe, and never print any such, if I can possibly help it. I therefore *refused* to accept either of the proposed articles, saying, as my only excuse, that I did not intend to [review?] the book at all, by which, I believe, I disobliged one of the parties; so that it would be *impossible* for me now to insert an article, without

giving serious offense. You are obliged to me, you see, tho' not *for* an article. Time may come when I shall be more unfettered. I hope it will. I hope you will not mention any of the booklovers here, in a way to make the *profane* scoff at us. For my own part, I care nothing for merely curious or rare books; but I like [dearly?] to get hold of a *fine* copy of a standard work.[94]

While Napier was willing to protect his friend, he was also unwilling to review Dibdin and embarrassed by the way he represented their circle ("I hope you will not mention any of the booklovers here, in a way to make the *profane* scoff at us"), going so far as to distance himself from Dibdin and his world ("I care nothing for merely curious or rare books").

Another letter from Napier gently criticizes the incautious way Dibdin represents collectors and offers some advice. Unfortunately, the handwriting is not entirely legible:

Generally speaking, I have as yet seen little more than the *exterior* of your work, which is eminently imposing and beautiful; but I have glanced over some half of a chapter, and am much grieved to discover a tone of [laudation?] and *personal* [] which, in as far as concerns myself, puts it out of my [favor?] to [commend in return?]. Your good nature, and kindness of temper, have really led you much too far in this direction; and I hear that some individuals complain of being brought before the public in a way that may expose them to some laughter, in this derisive age.[95]

Napier's obliqueness ("in a way that may expose"), which his letter shares with others to Dibdin on the same topic, suggests he is unwilling, for an unclear reason, to name the issue with Dibdin's representation of collectors. Others objected more strongly to Dibdin's rendering of them. Joseph Sams, for example, complained about how he appears in *Reminiscences*. His letter, like Napier's, only hints at what is problematic and suggests that he was hurt by the tastes and manners attributed to him:

It is not four days since thy reference to me in the "Reminiscences," first met my eye—& I think it will not give thee pleasure to know, such notice has produced considerable pain, & surprise. I am, I hope, a man of serious manners. I am consequently very sorry to see my name coupled either with foolish talking, or writing. My motives in visiting of Egypt, Palestine, &c., were I hope good, & by no means called for such reference. I traveled partly for the benefit of health, & partly to collect important Biblical & Classical MSS. . . . I am not however about to enter into an account at present, of these things. But why an extensive & difficult Journey, with such views, or the person who undertook it, should be referred to, as thou has done, I am at a loss to conceive.—As to the reference to

Paris, it is not only disgusting to me to see, but there is certainly no particle of truth in it.—Were it possible to do away, or alter these painful things, I should no doubt, be very glad.[96]

The writer's evident terror at association with Dibdin's "manners," "foolish talking, or writing," when, as he says, he was merely touring Egypt for the purposes of research implies a degree of panic—and not at the thought of being associated with the idle rich. Instead, Sams expresses panic at association with the "disgusting" and "foolish" behavior of some men and their preferred kinds of amusement when abroad. The dread ("Were it possible to do away . . .") conveys that the reputational stakes were quite high. Another correspondent, Sir Cuthbert Sharp, reacted with frank "horror" at the possibility that he would be included in one of Dibdin's books: "I have received your note & remark with unmingled 'horror' that you intend to put me in the *heads* of Chapter 5."[97]

The bibliomaniac mobilized more pointed reactions beyond Dibdin's circle. For example, in 1834, *The Athenæum* published an anonymous attack on the Roxburghe Club in which innuendo seems to link one of the club's members to the practice of sodomy. The bibliophile in question was Heber, the dedicatee of Dibdin's *Bibliomania* and a collector of collections who owned as many as 150,000 volumes.[98] The article refers to a scandal stemming from Heber's rumored relationship with a younger man named Charles Henry Hartshorne (1802–1865). The affair compelled Heber to remove himself from Parliament and flee England for the Continent, where he remained in exile until 1831.[99] Sharing space in the article with the construction of Heber as a sodomite is a differently threatening image of the generalized book collector—that of a literary consumer who has forgotten his practice's importance to the solidification and maintenance of the emerging national canon. Momentarily, I will examine this article in more detail.

A RARE, UNFINISHED POEM ABOUT BOOKISH INITIATION

Despite their striking continuities with bibliomaniacal consumption, Dibdin's early works actually distinguish the practice of bibliography from that of rare book collecting. As I will argue in what follows, a privately circulated poem entitled *Bibliography: A Poem. In Six Books* (according to the title page, "not published" and printed in "fifty copies only"), only one book of which is known to have appeared, offers a glimpse at both the particular homosocial sphere of book collecting and the book-collecting fandom that inspired Dibdin's creation of the Roxburghe Club. The poem also differentiates

Dibdin's particular sensualist discourse from the practices of collectors, a distinction that occasions a subtextual form of transgressive erotica. Finally, *Bibliography* aptly illustrates Dibdin's striking style—a prolix, camp sensibility immediately recognizable by frequent use of typographical emphasis, especially small capitals.

The mock-epic narrates the stirrings in a young man (Palermo) of an appreciation for the "London Pleasures" of "LITERARY CONVERSE social," an urban, homosocial society cast in terms of the ancient symposium. Palermo's entrance into this highly sensual community anticipates narratives of homosexual self-realization—the bookish seduction of Dorian Gray, another collector, comes to mind—in the way that it requires initiation and constitutes a fall from social propriety. The scene of Palermo's fall into this world of sensual delights (in typically understated fashion, Dibdin describes it as "the bliss" of a life lived among "BOOKS, / And those that vend them") is "a sale / Of curious BOOKS, by AUCTION." As Palermo views the "curious" lots, he develops a thrilling new taste and disposition toward new pleasures:

First comes a splendid lot, in coat of Tyrian dye
(Morocco purple, by the vulgar call'd)
And burnish'd gold; which, as th' assistant shews
In order round, throws far its glittering hues
To tempt the unwary.
Quick PALERMO speaks,
And hopes to' [*sic*] obtain the prize.[100]

Like Odysseus, Palermo has entered dangerous waters. In order to qualify for the "genuine" appreciation of "LORE CAXTONIAN" (bibliography as opposed to bibliomania), Palermo must learn to temper his initial infatuation, which has alienated him and provoked feelings of guilt ("Enamour'd much of books, and of their worth," he wanders the streets aimlessly in a "pensive mood" after the sale), with a different mode of consumption. This is accomplished by a visit to another vendor, "the BIBLIOPOLIST," who provides Palermo with a "pile . . . of such needful books, / And elementary, as teach the mind, / Unfledg'd, to clothe itself with plumage fit / For flight of [bibliography]." Palermo's initial fall into the sensual pleasures of book collecting is in this way purified by a practice characterized not in terms of the mind, even though the text mentions the "mind," but rather as a different form of embodiment.[101] Palermo must change his "plumage"—find the "fit[ting]" costume—for bibliography, the mind's embodied experience of unrestrained movement through space. (And, of course, Palermo must also buy a stack of books.) This "flight" of fancy recalls the excessively embodied subject described as luxuriant, hypersensual, and "empty" in the classical discourse of effeminacy, the *effeminatus*, while conflating mind and body, a staple of the discourse of sensibility.[102] In addition to making body into mind, however, the poet invites the reader to anticipate the possibility of a movement away from the "bliss" of forbidden physical pleasures toward its ostensible opposite, the scholar's life of the mind. What the poem provides instead is a refusal of this possibility. The materiality of the literary is at once a source of shame and the horizon of possible relations with literature.

Ultimately, then, the poem presents a fatalist version of a fall—a rite of passage down a dead-end street. Here, bookishness resembles an inevitable, preordained perversion—a problem of desire and aims in the context of an individual's psychosexual development—born of a crisis. Hence, the poem offers a high-stakes drama about consumerism with the formal structure of sexuality that simultaneously acknowledges the Romantic crisis of materiality, the tension between materialist bibliography and the emerging dominance of what Foucault famously terms the "author-function."[103]

There is something uncannily queer about the story of a literary materialist trying and failing to redeem his wayward sensuality, but in this case, one should probably resist the temptation to reduce the text's referents to a latent queer signified, either communal or individual, much less to an anticipation of the late-nineteenth-century construction of homosexual identity. Lee Edelman's observation of the imbrication of textuality in the production of sexuality helps account for the queer effects of such a passage without positing a latent and coherent queer referent lurking behind the text. In *Homographesis*, Edelman says:

> [S]exuality is constituted through operations as much rhetorical as psychological—or, to put it otherwise, . . . psychological and sociological interpretations are necessarily determined by the rhetorical structures and figural logics through which "sexuality" and the discourse around it are culturally produced. . . . [H]omosexuality is constructed to bear the cultural burden of the rhetoricity inherent in "sexuality" itself; the consequence . . . is that a distinctive literariness or textuality, an allegorical relationship to the possibility—and, indeed, the mechanics—of representation, operates within the very concept of "homosexuality."[104]

What registers as queer about Dibdin's bibliomaniacal discourse in this light can be said to stem from a literariness intrinsic to sexuality, because queerness is the materiality of sexuality's literariness. Queerness is the signifier and allegory in the domain of sexuality, the aspect bearing the repressed rhetoricity of sexuality in general ("the cultural burden of rhetoricity"), and Palermo faces but cannot transcend a crisis of representation—a temptation by the signifier that reveals itself as his ultimate horizon of possibility. In this way, Palermo's lesson and failed redemption trope the nature of the relationship between queerness and normativity, while they hint at the crisis of materiality in the broader culture, which enveloped Dibdin personally. Like Dibdin himself, Palermo is taught to desire the signified and fear the signifier but cannot exit the realm of the signifier, remaining a dissident and fetishist. All of this is uncanny and oblique because the narrative of Palermo's fall casts desire in the framework that constitutes sexuality itself. His inescapable fetishism of the literary signifier, an implication Dibdin may or may not intend, explains the effective sexualization of his shame.

A striking passage encapsulates the poem's linkage of desire, consumption, and materialism. The trope of illicit sensuality associated with bibliomania extends to the scene of the character's awakening to the stirring pleasures of bibliography:

He gradually felt within the' electric spark
That sets on flame the' enthusiastic mind
To ancient lore devoted: and he own'd
That he should love such curious tomes to gain,
Which, with quaint colophon of time and place
And printer's name, spake something to the soul
Resistless, and delightsome. Now his heart
'Gan flutter at an impulse he before
Was utter stranger to.[105]

Here, the language of intellectual passion ("electric spark," "enthusiastic mind") describes not learning but possession ("gain"), which is equated with the practice of bibliography and has a mystical connection to the self ("spake something to the soul"). Even this quasireligious rendering of consumption gets constrained by the language of sensual pleasure ("resistless," "delightsome"). The poem presents bibliography, in the fullest sense, as a consumerist sensibility. The sensibility is bookish: desire for the book ("quaint colophon") is caught up in a vaguely Christological drama in which sensual pleasure and possession define a dark form of self-fulfillment, which appears here as quasievangelical transformation of the soul ("sets on flame"). As will also be relevant to discussion of Charles Lamb's proto-bohemian bookishness in the next chapter of this book, the recurrence of religious conceptions of the self is a noted feature of consumerism in the Romantic period.[106]

The dark trope of initiation ("an impulse he before / Was utter stranger to") adds dissident implications to the text's wedding of sensuality to spiritual awakening. The representation of Palermo's conversion to bibliography as an initiation invokes phobic yet common queer narratives of self-realization and coming out. Due to the fact that it appears precisely as a literary initiation, however, a more precise echo is, aptly, allusive: Dorian Gray's captivation by Henry Wotton in *The Picture of Dorian Gray* (1890). Henry gives a copy of Joris-Karl Huysmans' *À Rebours* (translated as *Against Nature*) to Dorian, who becomes obsessed with collecting and lavishly rebinding it.[107] Phallic imagery ("flame" and "electric spark") overdetermines this dissident thread of dark, uncannily queer initiation stretching across time. Dibdin once again makes an ahistorical queer reading irresistible while repelling it. Bookishness is the thread of an ontological queer real glimpsed through innuendo, but bookishness is simultaneously the thorn that makes this referent impossible. What remains is the remorselessly tempting queer thing: the book-object, a material signifier.

Queer phobia and innuendo also shaded public representation of Dibdin's ornamental community during the period. Phobic representation of bibliomaniacs by outsiders is the subject of the next section. The author of an anonymous article ostensibly reviewing a manuscript by a member of Dibdin's Roxburghe Club, Joseph Haslewood (1769–1833), applies to the figure of the bibliomaniac a matrix of deterministic idealization. This has the effect of reducing the queer indeterminacy of the bibliomaniac to an object of representation that resembles a coherent, rather than tantalizingly frayed, dissident sexual identity.

BIBLIOMANIACS IN THE PRESS

The first meeting of Dibdin's Roxburghe Club took place on June 17, 1812.[108] Members of the club, as recorded by antiquary and club member Joseph Haslewood, included Dibdin, the honorary president Lord Spencer, the Marquis of Blandford (the winner of the Valdarfer Boccaccio on the day of the auction), and a small number of other "choice bibliomaniacal spirits."[109] Yearly meetings usually occurred on the same day as the first, June 17, at various London taverns, the first being Saint Alban's.[110] Membership was available on an invitation-only basis, and the number of members capped, initially at twenty-four, then thirty-one. One of the invitees was Heber, whose immense collection gave him expertise in English literature sought by Scott and Wordsworth.[111] Heber spent an estimated one hundred thousand pounds on his collection, which served as the foundation for several popular editions of English poetry.[112] Another notable invitee was "the Unknown Author of Waverley," to whom the club asked Walter Scott to extend its invitation to fill a new vacancy in 1823.[113] In one of two letters written in reply, Scott promises a "reprint, or such-like kickshaw," apologizes for the unlikelihood of the author's appearance anytime soon, and offers himself in his stead.[114] According to a notice in *The Morning Chronicle* from 1834, Scott attended an 1825 meeting.[115] Members present at the first meeting included Sir Francis

Freeling, a book collector and postal administrator; Sir Mark Masterman Sykes, owner of a 1469 "Rome Livy"; Sir Egerton Brydges, antiquarian, topographer, poet, and novelist of spurious nobility who wrote *Topographical Miscellanies* (1792); and Edward Vernon Utterson, the editor of multiple collections of early English poetry who owned three Shakespeare folios.[116] Although initially social in purpose, business conducted at dinners included planning a monument to William Caxton, the first English printer, and outlining and divvying up the club's publications. These works, described by the club as reprints of "scarce piece(s) of ancient lore," often featured expensive ornaments, including vellum.[117]

In 1834, an article about the club appeared in *The Athenæum* and attacked the club and its membership. The long anonymous piece appeared between January 4 and 18 and was republished soon after in abridged form in *The Morning Chronicle*. The piece's overt purpose was to review a posthumous, unintended work by Haslewood, *Roxburghe Revels*, but Haslewood's text serves mainly as an occasion for the author to focus on the club. The full title of the MS, as quoted in *The Athenæum*, reads: "*Roxburghe Revels; or, an Account of the Annual Display, culinary and festivous, interspersed incidentally with Matters of Moment or Merriment. Also, Brief Notices of the Press Proceedings by a few Lions of Literature, combined as the Roxburghe Club, founded 17th June, 1812*."[118] Haslewood's text is not a satire of the club, as has been thought, but rather a manuscript record of the club's early activities that was sold at auction along with other items from Haslewood's library following the antiquarian's death. James Silk Buckingham may have authored the attack in *The Athenæum*, to which the Roxburghe Club issued a privately printed reply in 1837 edited by Haslewood's friend James Maidment.[119]

The article's insinuations yoke a nationalist perspective on British culture to a sexually phobic representation of one of the members, aligning bibliophiles linked to the club with a perverse materialism that threatens the health of the national culture. Hence, as phobic as it is in some ways, the attack suggests deeply ambivalent feelings about the activities of collectors, whose practices were fundamentally important to the construction of the same national culture that the article suggests these collectors threaten. Descriptions of the club's meetings cast the book collectors as irrational gluttons more interested in "eating and drinking" and "gourmandizing and guzzling" than in the genuine "cause of letters."[120] Their perversion of literature to the impulses of a monstrous body reflects a perverse yet alarmingly insatiable constitution: "It seems, that feasting and drinking once a year, and that to no ordinary excess, did not satisfy the appetite and thirst of some of the 'Lions of Literature.'"[121] The anonymous author links this luxurious self-indulgence to the club's more properly cultural offenses: "[T]he realm of letters is, ought to be, and always will be, a republic—an oligarchy is not only odious, but impossible to be preserved."[122] In other words, the acquisitive cultural practice celebrated by the club—collecting—represents a threat to the national literary heritage, which ought to be a public, rather than a private, resource, and the threat stems from a problem with the club's mode of aesthetic appreciation—from their taste. But they have not simply taken the gustatory metaphor for the aesthetic disposition too literally by imbibing too heavily. Their faulty stewardship of the culture reflects a deeper problem with their sensual lives—a problem with their desires.

The piece also attributes to bibliomaniacs desires quite different from literary tastes. In Georgian England, in the midst of the classical revival, the representation of effeminacy, the gendered dimension of which is a staple of the collector type invoked by De Quincey in the *Logic*, could refer to gender as well as forbidden sexual practices such as *paiderastia*.[123] Another figure, the genius, supports the notion that effeminacy and sodomy could intersect within a dissident typology. As Elfenbein has argued in *Romantic Genius*, this figure, a prototypically homosexual type, illustrates a similar conjunction of effeminacy and the practice of sodomy. As Elfenbein says, "certain developments in the eighteenth century helped to push effeminacy closer to sodomy." These include biblical commentary reading Paul to imply that the "abusers" referred to in 1 Corinthians were "similar" to another group, the effeminate. As Elfenbein also observes, a literary connection also existed between hermaphroditism and sodomy. More specifically, the author of *The Ten Plagues of England* and *Faustina; Or, the Roman Songstress* "made clear that 'luxury and effeminacy' included sodomy."[124]

In *The Athenæum*, the suspect sensuality of the *effeminatus* appears in the context of a sideways reference to the sexual scandal that enveloped Heber. As Arnold Hunt has recounted in in *Book Collector*, rumors of Heber's affair with Hartshorne, who had paid visits to the collector and politician in London and Oxford in 1821 and 1824, began to circulate in 1824. These included a reference to the affair in the Tory periodical *John Bull* that made an implicit reference to sodomy (later, Hartshorne, with the aid of Heber's fortune, successfully sued the paper for libel). Subsequently, Heber resigned from Parliament, where he had served as the member from Oxford, and fled to Europe.[125] *The Athenæum* refers to this scandal and, in the guise of reserving judgment, describes Heber in terms that suggest effeminacy, in the specifically classical sense of the *effeminatus*, whose associations included immorality, martial inadequacy, and sexual dissidence: "Mr. Heber . . . was a man of profound, as well as elegant scholarship—a gentleman by nature, as well as by education, but of a mind peculiarly and painfully sensitive, and, like many literary men, without that moral strength which would enable him to meet a calumny of the kind, and which could only be repelled by being courageously encountered."[126] This portrait of Heber as an effeminate scholar does not merely imply that Heber is womanly nor associate him with immoral proclivities. Instead, while invoking the classical associations of "virtue" (the root of which is *"vir,"* Latin for "man") with a martial form of masculinity, Heber is a preciously empty volume ("profound" and "elegant") whose lack of "moral strength" explains his inability to resist an assault on his person (to meet the "calumny" circulated by his adversaries).[127] The passage in this way implicitly distinguishes this effete "literary [man]" feminized by an overly refined sensibility (one whose effeminacy is suggested by his description as "elegant" and "peculiarly and painfully sensitive") and the ideal "gentleman," who is unencumbered by Heber's limitations; furthermore, martial diction and imagery permeate this oblique reference to sodomy. Significantly, the passage's diction implies that if the field of British letters is a battlefield, Heber is, like the classical republican *effeminatus*, incapable of fighting on it.

The article's characterization of the club's meetings as "symposia" further supports the notion that this phobic portrait of Heber has such a specifically classical antecedent as the *effeminatus*.[128] The reference appears in the context of a reference to Hartshorne as the editor of a "curious volume."[129] This could be a work Hartshorne had had privately printed in 1825, *A Geyfte ffor the Newe Yere, or a playne, plesaunte, and profytable Pathewaie to the Black Letter Paradyse. Emprinted over the grete Gatewaie off Saincte Jhonnes College*, or either of two other antiquarian books he edited in the 1820s.[130] Scott refers to one, *Ancient Metrical Tales*, in the introduction to *Ivanhoe*.[131] Through this slight about a slight book, the excessive materiality of the *effeminatus* is hinted at by the form and content of bibliomaniacal culture. The implication of this bibliomaniacal turn of phrase about a book is that Hartshorne is himself a "curious volume," just as Heber is "profound."

By invoking Heber and Hartshorne's scandal, the piece binds the figure of the bibliomaniac to the logic of sodomitical effeminacy, involving the figure in the history of sexual dissidence. In doing so, the text illustrates the role played by classical effeminacy in the history of sexuality. The figures of Heber and Hartshorne are sexual beings, not simply sexual actors, illustrating the operation of a logic of identity. As Foucault characterizes it in *The History of Sexuality*, this form of interiority was the culmination of a gradual shift in thought about erotic behavior beginning in the early modern period. A conception of eroticism casting this in terms of disconnected acts became one casting it in terms of essential identity. Sketching the process, Foucault says that "[a] twofold evolution tended to make the flesh into the root of all evil, shifted the most important transgression from the act itself to the stirrings—so difficult to perceive and formulate—of desire."[132] The bibliomaniacs' inadequacies reflect rooted deficiencies, not simply disconnected choices—hence Heber's "peculiarly sensitive" mind.

The classical touches in the article contribute to a general cloud of decadence and dissipation, but they also convey specific facets of the *effeminatus* figure. In *Hellenism and Homosexuality in Victorian Oxford*, Linda Dowling describes the figure's classical origins: "The classical *effeminatus* functioned as the negation of the classical republican warrior—comprising 'the entire sphere of social existence' made up of those who could not fight (including 'boys, girls, slaves, eunuchs, hermaphrodites, and all others perceived as unsuitable to or incapable of discharging the martial obligation to the polis')."[133] Eventually, conservative deployment of this figure in Britain in the eighteenth and nineteenth centuries (in the context of Pope's poetry, *Blackwood's* attack on the Cockney School, and Robert Buchanan's diatribe against the Fleshly School of poetry in *The Baviad*, for example) reflected this fluid, "composite," and "empty" character of the non-warrior as constructed in ancient Greek culture.[134] In keeping with this plasticity, Heber's masculinity is deficient, but he is not simply a deficient man. His delicate depths and martial inadequacies layer his dubious "elegance" with a suggestion of moral culpability for the illegal act hinted at by the language of the passage itself, which concludes with a performative metaphor for Heber's alleged crime, plumbing his depths while describing his penetration by libel ("without that moral strength which would enable him to meet a calumny of the kind, and which could only be repelled by being courageously encountered"). This language not only feminizes Heber but also suggests that this behavior has a connection to an intrinsically compromised interiority.

Dowling claims that conservative use of the type laid the foundation for modern conceptions of homosexuality in sexological discourse:

> [T]he great and important paradox is that such works as Ward's *History* and John Dunton's "The He-Strumpets" . . ., operating all the while within the classical republican category of "effeminacy" in its symbolic relation to the warrior ideal, had nonetheless been helping to produce "homosexuality" in the twentieth-century sense as an unintended effect of their own discourse.[135]

Dowling traces this genealogy through an intellectual caricature, the Oxonian aesthete, which became at the end of the nineteenth century, partly as a result of the Wilde trials, one element of modern conceptions of homosexuality. Although Dowling focuses on the Victorians, *The Athenæum*'s treatment of Heber suggests the possibility that the *effeminatus* is part of a longer genealogy in which another intellectual type, the book collector, plays a role.

Ironically, *The Athenæum* piece, published twenty-five years after *Bibliomania*, focuses bibliomaniacal desire as it hints at Heber's alleged transgression, positing a scandalous but stable, as well as human, object where Dibdin's discourse resists such determinations. Consequently, the text, which has posited bibliomania as a threat to the "republic" of letters, makes its attack on bibliomaniacal values without compromising representational idealism, converting the bookman's polymorphous perversity into the signifier of a more familiar kind of fetishism. This representational fixity and idealism affirm Klancher's thesis in "Wild Bibliography" as to the sources of Dibdin's change of fortune in the 1820s. Klancher locates the degradation of bibliomania and the fall of Dibdin in the supersession of a codex-based bibliography by one based on "author, meaning, and ownership."[136] Repression and the representational idealism intrinsic to singular authorship are reflected in the deterministic rhetoric on display in the attack on Heber. In converting bibliomania into a signifier and displacement (of a "real" object of the mania), the article resists the subculture's *real* threat, to invoke Lacan—its provocative focus on the surface of the signifier, its black-letter love.

The source of this provocation becomes clearer in light of the broader historical context of the early nineteenth-century book boom, which shared a moment with the theorization of singular authorship as well as with the construction of literature as a form of public property. Instrumental in the codification of copyright, this discourse, as Russett has argued, involved the "repression—by all parties in the [copyright] debate—of language in its dimension as mere letters or sound-clusters."[137] In *Fictions and Fakes: Forging Romantic Authenticity, 1760–1845*, Russett claims that Samuel Taylor Coleridge's *Biographia Literaria* contains the seed for our sense of the inalienable artistic product and that Coleridgean originality, or "untransslateableness," was but one strand of a larger discourse concerned with the distinction between public and private literary culture, whose conceptual framework rested on the opposition between matter and spirit and the "repression" of literary materiality.[138] Russett also sketches the legal dimension of this discourse. Within the juridical discourse on the question of literary property, the elaboration of the author-function was bound up with the theorization of the textual "spirit" (this being William Warburton's word), which in turn involved the denomination of the "merely" material dimensions of language).[139] One can trace this "metaphysical division" between the material and the ideal, universally adopted despite its paradoxical implications, as far back as William Blackstone's "canonical statement on literary identity" in his 1774 ruling on *Donaldson v. Beckett*: "The Identity of a literary Composition consists entirely in the *Sentiment* and the *Language*," Blackstone intones.[140] A foil for the new authorship in his embodiment of a mode of possessiveness that stifled rather than contributed to the dissemination of literature and that ignored the implications of his greed for the health of British letters, the figure of the bibliomaniac in his materialism and alleged monopolization of literature propped up the actual monopolies enabled by copyright and the idealization of language instrumental in their formation. In this light, the "curious" side of the bibliomaniac's culture suggests the possibility that the evolving conceptions of authorship and modern personhood were intertwined—that sexuality, in other words, has a literary history as well as a clinical one. The relations between materiality and idealism in the modern subject of sexuality—the bright, unbending line connecting the stirrings of the flesh to the contents of the soul, as Foucault describes this subject—take on new resonance in light of the vexed status of the materiality of the literary in the copyright debate as well as in the anxious hand-wringing over bibliomania.[141] The bibliomaniac's subjective incompleteness is, in the context of its representation in *The Athenæum*, yoked to semantic incompleteness, as it were: a short circuit in the transmission of meaning implicit in the bibliomaniac's alleged disregard for literary "content" corresponds to a frustration of the teleological development of the person. Blasphemous inattention to the spirits lodged in the leaves of books partakes of the erection of a soul around the body of the sexual dissident.

NOTES

1. Dibdin, *A Bibliographical Antiquarian and Picturesque Tour in France and Germany*, 1.236.
2. Dibdin, *Bibliographical Decameron; or, Ten Days Pleasant Discourse upon Illuminated Manuscripts, and Subjects Connected with Early Engraving, Typography, and Bibliography* (London: W. Bulmer and Co. Shakspeare Press, 1817), 3.62.
3. Dibdin, *Reminiscences of a Literary Life* (London: John Major, 1836), 599.
4. Dibdin, *Bibliographical Antiquarian*, 1.205 (emphasis added).
5. Jeffrey Weeks, *Coming Out: Homosexual Politics in Britain, from the Nineteenth Century to the Present* (London: Quartet Books, 1977), 36.
6. Walter, *My Secret Life* (Amsterdam: 1888–1894), vol. 8, chap. 3 (emphasis added), http://www.my-secret-life.com/sex-diary-0803.php.
7. Benedict, *Curiosity*, 2.
8. Benedict, *Curiosity*, 2.
9. Benedict, *Curiosity*, 14, 9.
10. Eve Kosofsky Sedgwick, *Tendencies* (Durham, NC: Duke University Press, 1993), 123.
11. Foucault, *History of Sexuality*, 17.
12. Lennard J. Davis, Obsession: *A History* (Chicago: University of Chicago Press), 121. Davis discusses the French origins of "bibliomania."
13. Deidre Shauna Lynch, "'Wedded to Books': Bibliomania and the Romantic Essayists," in *Romantic Libraries: A Romantic Circles Praxis Volume*, ed. Ina Ferris (Romantic Circles, February 2004), 1, http://www.rc.umd.edu/praxis/libraries/lynch/lynch.html.
14. George S. Rousseau, *Nervous Acts: Essays on Literature, Culture and Sensibility* (Hampshire, UK: Palgrave Macmillan, 2004), 61.

15. Foucault, *History of Sexuality*, 32.
16. Foucault, *History of Sexuality*, 34.
17. Davis, *Obsession*, 122.
18. Stewart, *On Longing: Narratives of the Miniature, the Gigantic, the Souvenir, the Collection* (Durham, NC: Duke University Press, 1993); Jean Baudrillard, *The System of Objects*, trans. James Benedict (London: Verso, 1996).
19. Brant, *Ship of Fools*, xviii.
20. Dibdin, *Bibliomania*, xi.
21. Connell, "Bibliomania."
22. Walter Scott to Dibdin, n.d., mssDI 533, H. E. Huntington Library, San Marino, CA.
23. Scott, *Antiquary*, 28.
24. Scott, *Antiquary*, 178 (emphasis in original).
25. Connell, "Bibliomania," 27.
26. Connell, "Bibliomania."
27. Lynch, "Wedded to Books," 4.
28. Lynch, "Wedded to Books," 1 (emphasis in original).
29. Thomas De Quincey, *The Works of Thomas De Quincey*, vol. 2.
30. Grevel Lindop, *The Opium-Eater: A Life of Thomas De Quincey* (New York: Taplinger Publishing Co., 1981).
31. Lynch, "Wedded to Books."
32. Lynch, "Wedded to Books," 8–10.
33. Margaret Russett, *De Quincey's Romanticism: Canonical Minority and the Forms of Transmission* (Cambridge: Cambridge University Press, 1997).
34. Leah Price, "Introduction: Reading Matter," *PMLA* 120, no. 1 (2006): 12, MLA International Bibliography.
35. Lorraine Piroux, "The Encyclopedist and the Peruvian Princess: The Poetics of Illegibility in French Enlightenment Book Culture," *PMLA* 121, no. 1 (2006): 120, 108, MLA International Bibliography.
36. Price, "Introduction: Reading Matter," 11.
37. Jon P. Klancher, "Wild Bibliography," in *Bookish Histories: Books, Literature, and Commercial Modernity, 1700–1900*, ed. Ina Ferris and Paul Keen (London: Palgrave, 2009), 21.
38. Klancher, "Wild Bibliography," 19 (emphasis in original).
39. N. Katherine Hayles, *Writing Machines* (Cambridge, MA: MIT Press, 2002).
40. Price, "Introduction: Reading Matter."
41. Ferris, *Book-Men, Book Clubs, and the Romantic Literary Sphere*.
42. Ina Ferris, "Introduction," in *Romantic Libraries: A Romantic Circles Praxis Volume*, ed. Ina Ferris (*Romantic Circles*, February 2004), 3–4, https://romantic-circles.org/praxis/libraries/intro.html.
43. Heather Jackson, "What Was Mr. Bennet Doing in his Library, and What Does It Matter?" in *Romantic Libraries: A Romantic Circles Praxis Volume*, ed. Ina Ferris (*Romantic Circles*, February 2004). http://www.rc.umd.edu/praxis/libraries/jackson/jackson.html.

44. John V. Richardson, Jr., "Dibdin, Thomas Frognall (1776–1847)," in *Oxford Dictionary of National Biography*, http://www.oxforddnb.com/view/article/7588.

45. George Eliot, *Middlemarch*, ed. Rosemary Ashton (New York: Penguin, 1994).

46. Klancher, "Wild Bibliography," 19, 24, 20.

47. Dibdin, *Reminiscences*, 7, 42, 48, 50, 81, 165, 152–53, 211, 231–36, 253, 296, 673.

48. James Raine to Dibdin, 15 September 1837, mssDI 492, H. E. Huntington Library, San Marino, CA.

49. John Windle Karma Pippin, *Thomas Frognall Dibdin, 1776–1847: A Bibliography* (New Castle, DE: Oak Knoll Press, 1998), xii.

50. Dibdin, *Reminiscences*, 280.

51. Dibdin, *Reminiscences*, 338.

52. Walter Scott to Dibdin, 2 February 1810, mssDI 531, H. E. Huntington Library, San Marino, CA.

53. Dibdin, *Reminiscences*, 280.

54. Dibdin, Northern Tour Financial Documents, 8 March 1838, mssDI 1-642, H. E. Huntington Library, San Marino, CA.

55. Alexander Aikman to Dibdin, 27 January 1838 (emphasis in original), mssDI 1-642, H. E. Huntington Library, San Marino, CA.

56. Dibdin to William Nichol, 16 October 1828, 11 November 1823 (emphasis in original), Letters to William Nichol, H. E. Huntington Library, San Marino, CA.

57. Dibdin to William Nichol, February 1821 (emphasis in original), Letters to William Nichol, H. E. Huntington Library, San Marino, CA.

58. Dibdin to William Nichol, 16 October 1828, Letters to William Nichol, H. E. Huntington Library, San Marino, CA.

59. Dibdin to George Nichol, 1822 (emphasis in original), Letters to William Nichol, H. E. Huntington Library, San Marino, CA.

60. Philip Bliss to Dibdin, 14 May 1837, mssDI 62 (emphasis in original), H. E. Huntington Library, San Marino, CA.

61. Leith & Smith to Dibdin, n.d., mssDI 377, H. E. Huntington Library, San Marino, CA.

62. Dibdin, *Bibliographical Decameron*, 3.50; Dibdin, *Reminiscences*, 355–56.

63. Dibdin, *Bibliographical Decameron*, 3.50, 3.66, 3.51.

64. Dibdin, *Bibliographical Decameron*, 3.57, 3.57, 3.66 (emphasis in original).

65. Basbanes, *Gentle Madness*.

66. Dibdin, *Bibliographical Decameron*, 3.65.

67. Dibdin, *Bibliographical Decameron*, 3.59.

68. Basbanes, *Gentle Madness*, 116.

69. Basbanes, *Gentle Madness*, 114.

70. Basbanes, *Gentle Madness*, 114.

71. Dibdin, *Bibliographical Antiquarian*, 2.145, 2.265, 3.189 (emphasis in original).

72. Joseph Haslewood to Dibdin, 13 July 1808, mssDI 299 (emphasis in original), H. E. Huntington Library, San Marino, CA.

73. Leith & Smith bill to Thomas F. Dibdin, n.d., mssDI 373, H. E. Huntington Library, San Marino, CA.
74. Dibdin, *Reminiscences*, 338.
75. Dibdin, *Reminiscences*, 284, vii.
76. Dibdin, *Reminiscences*, 272.
77. Dibdin, *Reminiscences*, 336.
78. Klancher, "Wild Bibliography," Klancher provides the book's publication history; Dibdin, *Reminiscences* contains a list of subscribers.
79. Dibdin, *Reminiscences*, 300–12.
80. Dibdin, *Reminiscences*.
81. Ferriar, *Bibliomania*, 38–43.
82. Basbanes, *Gentle Madness*, 25.
83. Thomas De Quincey, "The Logic of Political Economy," in *Political Economy and Politics: Being Volume IX of His Collected Writings*, ed. David Masson (New York: Augustus M. Kelley, 1970), 167–68.
84. Foucault, *History of Sexuality*, 19–20.
85. King, *Gendering of Men*, 2.98–100.
86. King, *Gendering of Men*.
87. Sedgwick, *Tendencies*, viii.
88. Elfenbein, *Romantic Genius*, 8.
89. Charles (Chas) Clark to Thomas F. Dibdin, n.d., mssDI 105, H. E. Huntington Library, San Marino, CA.
90. Dibdin, *Library Companion*, 365 (emphasis in original).
91. Dibdin, *Reminiscences*, 617.
92. Dibdin, *Bibliographical Decameron*, ccxi–ccxii.
93. F[rances] Currer to Dibdin, 6 November 1836, mssDI 146, H. E. Huntington Library, San Marino, CA.
94. Macvey Napier to Dibdin, n.d., mssDI 451, H. E. Huntington Library, San Marino, CA.
95. Macvey Napier to Dibdin, 22 May 1838, mssDI 453, H. E. Huntington Library, San Marino, CA.
96. Joseph Sams to Dibdin, 7 July 1837, mssDI 508, H. E. Huntington Library, San Marino, CA.
97. Sir Cuthbert Sharp to Dibdin, 26 March 1838, mssDI 539, H. E. Huntington Library, San Marino, CA.
98. Arthur Sherbo, "Heber, Richard (1774–1833)," in *Oxford Dictionary of National Biography*, http://www.oxforddnb.com/view/article/12854.
99. Sherbo, "Heber, Richard."
100. Dibdin, *Bibliography: A Poem. In Six Books* (London: Harding and Wright, 1812), ll. 141, 143, 145, 143–44, 158–59, 164–69.
101. Dibdin, *Bibliography: A Poem. In Six Books*, ll. 287, 279, 255, 252, 275, 276–79, 277.
102. Dowling, *Hellenism and Homosexuality in Victorian England*, 8; George Haggerty, *Men in Love: Masculinity and Sexuality in the Eighteenth Century* (New York: Columbia University Press, 1999).

103. Michel Foucault, "What Is an Author?" trans. Donald F. Bouchard and Sherry Simon, in *The Norton Anthology of Theory and Criticism*, ed. Vincent B. Leitch (New York: Norton, 2001), 1629.

104. Edelman, *Homographesis*, xiv.

105. Dibdin, *Bibliography: A Poem*, ll. 303–12.

106. Colin Campbell, *The Romantic Ethic and the Spirit of Modern Consumerism* (Oxford: Blackwell, 1987).

107. Oscar Wilde, *The Picture of Dorian Gray*, ed. Robert Mighall (London: Penguin, 2003).

108. Dibdin, *Reminiscences*.

109. Dibdin, *Reminiscences*, 370.

110. Dibdin, *Reminiscences*.

111. Sherbo, "Heber, Richard."

112. Connell, "Bibliomania."

113. "Sir Walter Scott & the Roxburghe Club," *Morning Chronicle [London]* (6 January 1834). 19th Century British Library Newspapers Gale Cengage Learning.

114. "Sir Walter Scott & the Roxburghe Club."

115. "Sir Walter Scott & the Roxburghe Club."

116. G. B. Smith, "Freeling, Sir Francis," in *The Oxford Dictionary of National Biography*, ed. David Cannadine (Oxford: Oxford University Press, 2004), http://www.oxforddnb.com/view/article/10144; "Sykes, Sir Mark Masterman, Third Baronet (1771–1823)," in *Oxford Dictionary of National Biography*, http://www.oxforddnb.com/view/article/26869; K. A. Manley, "Brydges, Sir (Samuel) Egerton, First Baronet, Styled Thirteenth Baron Chandos (1762–1837)," in *Oxford Dictionary of National Biography*, http://www.oxforddnb.com/view/article/3809; Arthur Sherbo, "Utterson, Edward Vernon (bap. 1777, d. 1856)," *Oxford Dictionary of National Biography*, http://www.oxforddnb.com/view/article/28039.

117. Buckingham?, Rev. of *Roxburghe Revels*, 2.

118. Buckingham?, Rev. of *Roxburghe Revels*, viv.

119. Alan Bell, "Haslewood, Joseph (1769–1833)," in *Oxford Dictionary of National Biography*, http://www.oxforddnb.com/view/article/12551.

120. Buckingham?, Rev. of *Roxburghe Revels*, 2.

121. Buckingham?, Rev. of *Roxburghe Revels*, 45.

122. Buckingham?, Rev. of *Roxburghe Revels*, 2.

123. Louis Crompton, *Byron and Greek Love: Homosexuality in Ninteenth-century England* (Berkeley: University of California Press, 1985), 85. Crompton helpfully discusses the classical revival.

124. Elfenbein, *Romantic Genius*, 21–22.

125. Sherbo, "Heber, Richard."

126. Dowling, *Hellenism and Homosexuality in Victorian Oxford*; Buckingham?, Rev. of *Roxburghe Revels*, 46.

127. Dowling, *Hellenism and Homosexuality in Victorian Oxford*, 8.

128. Buckingham?, Rev. of *Roxburghe Revels*, 45.

129. Buckingham?, Rev. of *Roxburghe Revels*, 45.

130. "Hartshorne, Charles Henry (1802–1865)," in *The Dictionary of National Biography*, ed. Leslie Stephen and Sidney Lee (New York: Macmillan, 1908), 25.75, Google Books.
131. "Hartshorne, Charles Henry."
132. Foucault, *History of Sexuality*, 20.
133. Dowling, *Hellenism and Homosexuality in Victorian Oxford*, 8.
134. Dowling, *Hellenism and Homosexuality in Victorian Oxford*, 8.
135. Dowling, *Hellenism and Homosexuality in Victorian Oxford*, 11.
136. Klancher, "Wild Bibliography," 35.
137. Russett, *Fictions and Fakes*, 78.
138. Russett, *Fictions and Fakes*, 72.
139. Russett, *Fictions and Fakes*, 77.
140. Russett, *Fictions and Fakes*, 77, 76, 77.
141. Foucault, *History of Sexuality*.

Chapter 3

The Punk Antiquarianism of Charles Lamb

As we have seen, the practices of the Ladies and the Roxburghe circle suggest that bookishness played a role in the imagining of dissident possibilities irreducible to conventional notions of human sexuality. For the Ladies, the collecting served a queer, heterosocial, and intergenerational revision of domesticity in Wales. In Dibdin's circle, bookish discourse uncannily thematized male love in representations of a homosocial, ornamental community of book collectors. Along with books, physical spaces figured prominently in these dissident subcultures organized around things. The Ladies' community reflected the existence of demand for experiences in the rural North attributable in part to developments in printing technology. Travel to picturesque locales similarly enabled and fostered Dibdin's ornamental culture.

The once-canonical Romantic essayist Charles Lamb, a bachelor and marginally middle-class writer who made a living by writing essays for the *London Magazine* and other periodicals, supplemented by clerking, practiced a camp form of antiquarianism both in his famed Elia essays and in his personal book collecting. Like the antiquarianism practiced by the ornamental communities we have already explored, Lamb's dissident antiquarianism hewed closely to place. For the famously urbane Lamb, London provided matter for a camp authorial persona and collecting practice.

The fullness of Lamb's antiquarian sensibility, the focus of this chapter, has a prototypically punk edge that has been obscured by a critical tradition invested in the timelessness of the Elia essays, casting Lamb as an enduring curiosity. In contrast, this chapter explores how Lamb presented a dissident style and worldview closer to his time and place. More specifically, I argue that Lamb's personal style and essays suggest a dandiacal and parodic attitude toward conventional antiquarianism, including the style of book collecting celebrated by Roxburghe Club members and their acolytes. Anticipating the politics of punk style, Lamb's dandyism gravitated toward discarded and degraded by-products of the consumer economy, including secondhand books and decaying, repurposed buildings. Appropriately enough for denizens of such spaces, the theme of disgust figured prominently in Lamb's camp aesthetic.

This effort to analyze the punk aspects of Lamb's style begins with a discussion of Lamb's urban and materialistic take on eco-poetics as represented by the essay "On Some of the Old Actors" (1823) where Elia presents a defiantly dissident style of masculinity. Next, the argument turns to the dandiacal style ("antiquarian coolness," to borrow a phrase from Elia) illustrated by a number of essays and a close reading of "My First Play" (1821). Finally, analysis of the punk dimensions of Elia's antiquarianism visible in Lamb's self-consciously dissident style of collecting uncovers a punk and bohemian style of conspicuous consumption.

A *FLÂNEUR*'S OBJECT-CENTERED ECOLOGY

Not only during his own life but also for decades after, Charles Lamb was a literary lion—in personal reputation "heroic," in artistic reputation a "genius," and in commercial terms titanic.[1] When a Penguin Classics edition of selected works appeared in 2013, however, no other edition of collected works, for the trade or scholars, was in print. Charting the rise and fall of Lamb's status in relation to the canon helps uncover the complicated networks that joined, while straining, the ties between Lamb and luminaries such as Wordsworth and Coleridge. In exploring such relationships, one can see how Lamb used the familiar essay to present an object-centered alternative to Romantic transcendentalism. Lamb's take on a theme of Romantic poetics was, furthermore, bound up with the period's gendered politics of nature and nature writing. Such were the broader politics of the field and Lamb's personal relationships within it that, in rejecting nature and its typical representation and choosing the city as a topic, Lamb could reclaim a sense of masculinity imperiled by precisely the city itself. The essays' antiquarian and urban revision of Romantic eco-poetics—a revision that should be seen as camp—is the focus of this section.

At one time in the history of nineteenth-century publishing, Lamb enjoyed a singular status. By one measure, the "hero of the *London*" was the best-compensated writer of his generation. Critics classed Lamb alongside Coleridge, Hazlitt, and even Shakespeare. John Forster said Lamb and Coleridge were "two of the most original geniuses in an age of no uncommon genius."[2] Likewise, Bryan Waller Proctor, writing as Barry Cornwall, compared Hazlitt, Coleridge, and Lamb: "They were all three extraordinary men. Hazlitt had more of the speculative and philosophical faculty . . . whilst Coleridge was more subtle and ingenious than either."[3] In the same piece, Cornwall compares Lamb favorably to Shakespeare: "it was a combination of humor with pathos . . . such as I do not remember elsewhere to have met with, except in Shakespeare."[4] Leigh Hunt said that Lamb "would have been worthy of hearing Shakespeare read one of his scenes to him, hot from the brain."[5]

More recently, critical discussion of Lamb has focused on ways he differed from his peers rather than ways he led them or echoed great poets. Some critics have read the period's celebration of Lamb as a species of sentimentalism focused on his "eccentricity," while relying on a notion of Lamb's exceptional status vis-à-vis the central themes and figures of Romanticism. As Brent Russo has said, Joseph Riehl and David Russell have made similar arguments maintaining that the commonplace sentimental rendering of Lamb (as in the important work of E. V. Lucas) served to neutralize a thread of radicalism running through the works. In taking issue with these arguments' implication of a critical conspiracy, Russo has sought to reclaim the "love" Lamb's readers feel for him and his eccentricity, identifying this sentimental attachment as a logical response to Lamb's "power" as an essayist, which consists in a "liberal project . . . to [expand] interest in and affection for individuality."[6]

Lamb's readers once viewed his gifts more conventionally, and he belonged to the canon.[7] Lamb's critical fortunes changed dramatically not long after his death, and students of Romantic critical theory have, since the nineteenth century, been largely uninterested in the hero of the London, despite his mastery of the familiar essay and his former status.[8] The same could also be said of Romantic scholarship in general.[9]

Lamb's works' ties to the themes of canonical Romanticism include the essays' marked retrospection. Not simply nostalgic, some of the Elia essays ("Elia," transposing "a lie," being the ironic pen name with which Lamb signed them) are antiquarian documents—specific enough in their representation of London to have proven useful in historical studies of the city. However detailed, the essays do not simply describe the city as Elia experiences it, nor idealize its past, nor strive for strict accuracy in representation. Instead, Elia's ambivalent attraction to urban decay and his materialistic perspective depart in significant ways from antiquarian discourse of his day and the themes of transcendentalism. Nonetheless, Lamb's urban focus ironically links his work to key subjects of Romantic poetry: memory and the environment.

Here is Elia describing Gray's Inn, a place Lamb knew well, in "On Some of the Old Actors":

> I am ill at dates, but I think it is now better than five-and-twenty years ago that walking in the gardens of Gray's Inn—they were then far finer than they are

now—the accursed Verulam Buildings had not encroached upon all the east side of them, cutting out delicate green crankles, and shouldering away one of two of the stately alcoves of the terrace—the survivor stands gaping and relationless as if it remembered its brother.[10]

The retrospection ("better than five-and-twenty years ago") and the speculative sense of loss ("as if it remembered") make Elia resemble *Tintern Abbey*'s (1798) dislocated speaker. As it is one of my goals here to demonstrate, however, Lamb's speaker offers an urban, feminine, and materialistic alternative to Wordsworthian melancholy.

Recent events in Lamb's life may explain the funereal tone. Close to the same time that Lamb published the first version of the piece, "The Old Actors" (1822), he wrote to Wordsworth on the subject of grief (March 20, 1822), remarking "a certain deadness to every thing" and how "[d]eaths overset one and put one out long after the recent grief. Two or three have died within this last two twelve months."[11] Lamb's friend and regular whist partner Captain James Burney (Fanny Burney's brother), who sailed with James Cook on multiple voyages, was among the deceased.[12]

Both the essay and Wordsworth's *Tintern Abbey* tie the themes of spiritualization and sibling intimacy to a recollection, along with intimations of mortality. *Tintern*, also a meditation on a changing physical space, transforms a natural environment into spiritual solace. There, remembrance of a vista becomes a ghostlike "wanderer through the wood" that provides redemption to an older Wordsworth alienated in the city (all of which coming from the perspective of a still older Wordsworth). "Actors" literalizes and objectifies the theme of spiritualization, the description converting a commercial space into temple niches, one filled and forlorn, one vacant. Furthermore, the essay playfully inverts the dynamics of Wordsworthian spiritualization. Rather than imagine himself spiritually cleansed by a memory, as Wordsworth's speaker does (being transformed into a "living soul" who can "see into the life of things"), Elia animates an object ("the survivor stands gaping"). Spirituality becomes a literary effect on the environment rather than a natural one on human subjects, and the world of objects orients the focus, not the inner life of emotions.

Another parallel appears in the texts' imagining of a sibling bond affected by loss. Both texts represent a brother's passing: Wordsworth's speaker looks forward in time to a moment when Dorothy will remember him as he had been in life and take from his example of nature-worship "healing thoughts," giving the "sylvan Wye" another life in human memory (and Wordsworth himself a kind of afterlife through Dorothy), but Elia imagines the remaining alcove as Dorothy with a difference—a "relationless" sibling mourning her brother. The essay departs from Wordsworth's poem in imagining the impact of this fraternal loss. Unlike Dorothy, this "survivor" has only the memory and none of the consolation Wordsworth hopes his sister will find in remembering him. Hence, the opposite of redemption—namely, an irremediable lack ("gaping")—marks this object's anthropomorphizing perspective. Ultimately, at the same time, that it seems to parody and darken Wordsworthian transcendence in this way, Elia's urban conservationism moves the theme of traumatic memory from the country to the city and from mind to matter. In this way, Elia's reverie offers an urban, embodied alternative to Wordsworth's transcendent melancholy. While revealing ties between Lamb's work and prominent themes of canonical Romanticism, the essay illustrates Lamb/Elia's critical stance toward these themes and his orientation toward the world of objects.

As in *Tintern Abbey*, in Lamb's familiar essay, the prospect of death prompts a humanization of the environment, but Lamb's upside-down "nature" writing fetishizes its objects, taking an object-centered approach to a retrospective and urban mode of ecological discourse. Notably, Elia himself is mourning, but he is mourning perceived change to the urban environment rather than the death of a person. This urban ecology reflects an enthusiasm for urban space running through the Elia essays. Although Lamb is often identified closely with London, where he lived in multiple neighborhoods, one critic has challenged the urbanity of his writing about the city. Invoking "gentle" Lamb's dissident gender style, Simon Hull has argued that Elia's urban enthusiasm renders the city a "paradoxically domesticated" space that draws on the "emancipatory spirit" of the *flâneur* and the liberalism of the countryside rambler.[13]

The particular role played by gender identity in Elia's perspective on London is inseparable from the gendered politics of nature and nature poetry among the Romantics. Lamb's focus on the city and creation of a *flâneur* in Elia involved him in the gendered politics of the urban-rural divide among Romantic writers. He embraced the urban and, in doing so, made a choice freighted with dissident implications and tied to his close relationship with Coleridge. As I will discuss in more detail in a moment, correspondence between the two suggests that Lamb's consistent identification with the city rather than the country may have stemmed from a crisis in his intimacy with Coleridge related partly to the latter's criticism of Lamb's urbanity. In subsequently choosing urban space as the consistent setting of his prose poems on antiquarian themes, Lamb/Elia seems to have embraced as liberating what Coleridge viewed as feminizing. While, in this light, suggesting the appropriative and ironic gestures of camp, Lamb's attention to urban spaces manifested a form of masculinity at once independent and defiantly dissident.

The gendered politics of the Romantic literary sphere were such that geography, gender identity, class position, and the question of a poet's legitimacy all intersected in the context of magazine reviews, Keats being the best-known case of a poet subjected to this critical matrix. Philip Cox has shown how Keats's allies, such as Leigh Hunt, and detractors, including John Gibson Lockhart and Hazlitt, alike sought to portray his claims to poetic (il) legitimacy with reference to his gender performance. In the case of Lockhart, writing in *Blackwood's*, Keats's illegitimacy was a function of analogy to "unmarried women" and "farm-servants"; for Hunt, acknowledged stylistic deficiencies signified feminine weakness.[14] Keats's Cockney rhymes left him vulnerable to these gendered and classed attacks.

Gender, in addition, could become a stake in critical judgments about where one wrote or where one wrote *about*. Lamb experienced the kind of discrimination that wounded Keats. The sentimental rendering of Lamb in "This Lime Tree Bower My Prison" (1797), where "gentle-hearted Charles" receives praise for his patient suffering of city life and alienation from nature, would have been, as Lamb's angry reaction to the poem shows, hard to find complimentary.[15] In the poem, Coleridge, as Hull observes, patronizingly diagnoses Lamb's problem as that of "passive" acquiescence to the city's oppressive confinement.[16] Coleridge's speaker says that Charles has longed

And hungered after Nature, many a year
In the great city pent, winning thy way
With sad yet patient soul.[17]

A history of intimacy between the two writers suggests that Coleridge's condescension, along with Lamb's subsequent reaction, had deeper sources than received notions of nature writing. The pitch and implications of Lamb's reaction to "Lime Tree Bower," a reaction recorded in letters to Coleridge in August 1800, suggest that passivity in relation to Coleridge's genius and a choice to write, like Coleridge, about nature carried with it a sense of compromised masculinity that, ironically, Lamb may have resisted by defiantly claiming the feminized identity of the urban writer. Furthermore, additional correspondence about the two from the period suggests that Lamb had personal reasons for reacting defensively to Coleridge's veiled swipes at his masculinity. For example, in addressing the poem with Coleridge soon after, Lamb suggests his gladness at having recovered from a very different kind of hunger:

> For God's sake (I never was more serious), don't make me ridiculous any more by terming me gentle-hearted in print, or do it in better verses. It did well enough five years ago when I came to see you, and was moral coxcomb enough at the time you wrote the lines, to feed upon such epithets; but, besides that, the meaning of gentle is equivocal at best, and almost always means poor-spirited,

the very quality of gentleness is abhorrent to such vile trumpetings. My *sentiment* is long since vanished. I hope my *virtues* have done *sucking*.[18]

Clear from this is Lamb's distaste for the feminized pleasure he once took in Coleridge's flattery. While suggesting a new sobriety, this pleasure Lamb also expresses in terms of drunken (a slang meaning of "suck" being "to drink") and infantile dependence on the milk of Coleridgean condescension.[19] In this light, the letter renders Lamb's former relations with Coleridge in sexually phobic terms: Lamb regrets "sucking" on Coleridge's "vile trumpetings." Subjection to Coleridge's famous (or, depending on the account, infamous) conversation implied embodied, feminized, and addictive debility.

Other letters between the friends suggest shame on Lamb's part stemming from the relationship with Coleridge. Around the time of Lamb's institutionalization in Hoxton following a nervous breakdown, the two exchanged a series of letters, some of which Lamb later burned.[20] Those that survive from the period suggest a deep yet, to Lamb, troubling intimacy. In *Double Life: A Biography of Charles and Mary Lamb*, Sarah Burton speculates that Lamb's "passionate ambivalence toward Coleridge's influence" prompted Lamb to destroy the letters. Among those remaining, one in particular, from which Burton quotes, speaks to the intensity of their bond at that time: "[Y]ou were repeating one of Bowles's sweetest sonnets in your sweet manner, while we two were indulging sympathy, a solitary luxury, by the fireside at Salutation. Yet I have no higher ideas of heaven. Your company was one 'cordial in this melancholy vale'—the remembrance of it is a blessing partly, and partly a curse." Lamb later tells Coleridge that he burned or hid their correspondence out of fear of its discovery by his older brother John. John would later blame Coleridge's seductive "wit"—"whose brilliant, fiery, delectable particles, when used as a will o' th' wisp to mislead, [is] dazzling and most dangerous"—for Lamb's mental instability.[21] In these lines, John imagines Coleridge as more charming snake than snake charmer, a talker of dangerously phallic potency who is not to be trusted. Lamb and John reacted defensively to suggestions of Lamb's feminized passivity in relation to Coleridge, and the reactions and actions of Lamb (and John) hint at a personal history between the two men that Lamb evidently felt he had reason to suppress. Considered alongside Lamb's correspondence with Coleridge, the manner of John's expression of anxiety serves as another illustration of a sexualized discourse about Lamb's history with Coleridge and the Lake District.

Animating a similarly repressive energy, the Lake poets' reverence for nature, like the memory of intimacy with Coleridge, may have represented a problematically feminine mode of domesticity. The "green-sick sonneteer" referenced later in the above letter—a figure from whom Lamb strenuously distinguishes himself—clearly suggests an antipathy to nature poetry.[22] One can find confirmation of this sentiment elsewhere in Lamb's correspondence, where writing about nature resembles self-emasculation. In letters from 1800 to Thomas Manning, for example, Lamb says, "I am not romance-bit about *Nature*. The earth, sea and sky (when all is said), is but a house to dwell in. . . . Hills, woods, Lakes and mountains, to the Eternal Devil. I will eat snipes with thee Thomas Manning."[23] Like his angry swipe at Coleridge, this rejection aligns nature and domesticity ("but a house to dwell in") with feminized, addictive subjection ("romance-bit").

The broader perspective and opinions in this gendered discourse on nature and nature poetry illuminate a thread uniting the Elia essays—namely, the personality of an urban sophisticate—likely has a foundation in themes central to Romantic poetry and, rather than being merely an eccentric choice, served defensive aims reflecting Lamb's closeness to the Lake poets. Not so surprising is Lamb's rejection of nature in terms similar to those with which Coleridge condescends to Lamb. More notably, in creating Elia, Lamb seems to have coopted the very identity that made him vulnerable to such slights on his masculinity. In such a gesture, one sees the irony of camp. Camp also appears in Elia's choice of topic, the city, in itself—a choice that appears more transgressive in light of the gendered politics of the Romantic literary community, where effeminacy was in multiple ways associated with the city as a literary topic or home. Lamb's creation of Elia thus recalls the gendered polarities of the urban/rural divide as seen in Keats's reception and the Ladies' transgressive and transgendered embrace of the rural and the ornamental cottage in their own use of space.

A HARD-BOILED FETISHIST

Far from being restricted by virtue of his urbanity as Coleridge represents Lamb in "Lime Tree Bower," Elia moves through space like a *flâneur*. He conducts an eccentric and dandiacal mode of this, however—one marked by ambivalence and revulsion rather than straightforward enjoyment of the world. Hull has argued that, with his style of atypical *flânerie*, Lamb offers an alternative to Thomas De Quincey's and the Lake poets' ambulatory images of liberal democracy. Lamb's eccentric version of *flânerie* departed from the example of De Quincey's opium-eater's "night-time wanderings" as described in the *Confessions of an English Opium-Eater*, on the one hand, and the Lake poets' countryside rambler, on the other. Lamb made of the city a kind of sitting room—an external domestic interior.[24] While the rough edges of Elia's *flânerie* resist identification with notions of domesticity, this hardness does reflect a queer illiberalism—specifically, the dandy's aristocratic bearing. Furthermore, Elia's moralistic discourse about the uses and abuses of cultural products implies an avant-garde and dissident style also suggestive of the dandy. For Elia, as for bibliomaniacs for whom things and spaces have afforded dissident self-expression, these products are often antiques.

The distaste Elia expresses in "On Some of the Old Actors" illustrates his general ambivalence. Ambivalence is also the dandy's signature affect, with nonchalance paradoxically comprising one rule in his rigid code. Historically, the code of a dandy like Charles Baudelaire represented a compromise between the culture of the aristocracy and that of the middle class. As Baudelaire says in "The Painter of Modern Life" (1863), the dandy, a self-disciplining "tyrant" belonging to a "cult of the self" rather than of a king or class, reifies aristocratic materialism: "For the perfect dandy these things [the toilet and material elegance] are no more than symbols of his aristocratic superiority of mind."[25]

As Colin Campbell observes in *The Romantic Ethic and the Spirit of Modern Consumerism*, in the dandy the cultivation of a "noble 'self'" gained priority over the "principle of noble birth." Beau Brummell's fastidiousness, regimented personal style, and competitiveness with other dandies, for example, exemplified a fusion of the aristocratic (evident in the neoclassical emphasis on rules, order, and logic) and the bourgeois. Furthermore, both the Restoration period's Cavalier poet and the eighteenth-century neo-Stoic re-emerged in the dissident figure, whose peers expected not only the "nonchalance" of the former but also the extreme self-control in obedience to rules of style and comportment that were a legacy of the latter.[26]

A more directly relevant historical legacy of the dandy's dissident mingling of aristocratic and bourgeois culture is available to those seeking to understand Elian style. As Campbell has also argued, aspects of the dandy persisted in the nineteenth-century bohemian, an inheritor of the dandy defined by hedonism, which was the animating "spirit" making possible the Romantic period's "consumer revolution." In a seemingly contradictory fashion, a hedonistic ethic developed out of bohemianism's Protestant roots, which an emphasis on self-denial and self-control (the Protestant ethic in Max Weber's sense of this) reflected. In this ethic, the aristocratic aspects of the dandy reappeared alongside spiritually inflected values. Citing Weber, Campbell says that the modern consumer's individualistic, expressive, and pleasure-centered ethic has a foundation in bohemianism and, consequently, in Christianity as such and as a precursor to the Romantic transformation of the Christian "drama of salvation and redemption" into—this being M. H. Abrams' view—a subjective experience and a form of pantheism or mysticism.[27] The complex history of the bohemian are aptly summarized by Pierre Bourdieu's label for bohemians: "aristocracy of culture."[28]

Although bohemianism may seem to fit poorly with what is known of Lamb's personality and his biography, uncanny parallels exist between "gentle" Charles and this dissident subculture within the middle class. In multiple ways, Lamb's frequently noted eccentricity had an ironically noble cast. He was nicknamed "Gentle Charles" by friends and not, it seems, for a gentle disposition. In fact, he had a reputation for a caustic wit that alienated some, including Keats. The Walpolian lisp celebrated as youthful and innocent by Edward Bulwer-Lytton recalled the world of the court.[29] Lamb never owned property, but Thomas Hood jokingly referred to the Islington home Lamb rented, Colebrooke Cottage, as his "cottage of Ungentility."[30] Lamb's collecting practices, a topic of this chapter's last section, invoked aristocratic practices by opposing them almost exactly, such was the extent of his parody of bibliomania through a studiously "ragged" collection.[31] This ironic collecting practice found a parallel in Lamb's aristocratic perspective on his downwardly mobile employment. While clerking for the East India Company and writing (with much notice and at a high rate) for the periodical press, Lamb adopted a posture of aristocratic disdain toward "hack work." While his bookish and ironic boast that his "true works may be found on the shelves of Leadenhall Street, filling some hundred folios" may suggest shame about his day job, it also implies that only this work was actual work.[32]

In focusing on Elia, one can see that a number of essays suggest that Lamb's cracked-glass persona belongs to this lineage that fused spiritually inflected consumerism and aristocratic style. "Superannuated" Elia's cool affect in "That We should Rise with the Lark" (1833) suggests a form of self-pricking and tonally spiritual, but ultimately secular, hedonism—an unpleasure tinged with quasispiritual renunciation. In this essay, Elia complains dramatically about past disappointments that have robbed reality of its interest. Hard-boiled Elia, for whom "disappointment early struck a dark veil between us and [the world's] dazzling illusions," would rather, like Raymond Chandler's dandiacal urbanite Philip Marlowe, "dally with visions." Elia goes on darkly, "The sun has no purposes of ours to light us to. Why should we get up?" Regardless, Elia is "never much in the world" in the first place.[33] A vague spiritualism ("never much in the world," "dally with visions") suggests that an unspecified otherworldliness lies behind the comically morose tone ("The sun has no purposes," "struck a dark veil"). This dark tone and Elia's decadently resigned posture are the focus, not a transcendence at which he superficially gestures.

Serving to distract Elia from the present, objects and antiques in particular are elemental to Elia's style. The detachment afforded by time's passage receives praise in the antiquarian-themed essay "Barrenness of the Imaginative Faculty in the Productions of Modern Art" (1833), where Elia lauds the passage of time for its ability to temper emotion. Thanks to the passing of a "thousand years" since the devastation of Pompeii, contemporary artists representing the ruins of the island "are at leisure to contemplate the weaver fixed standing at his shuttle, the baker at his oven, and to turn over with antiquarian coolness the pots and pans." "Antiquarian coolness" is a dandiacal and bohemian phrase tinged with melancholy and detachment while suggestive of promise: with it, Elia implies that temporal and spatial distance from the "eclipsing moment" prevents artistic vision from being perverted by limiting "feeling."[34]

Elia's tendency to critique his surroundings ("the survivor stands gaping and relationless") marks his "antiquarian coolness" with a meditative focus on objects. Elia experiences hedonistic revulsion—pleasurable disgust—as he richly details and critiques the objects around him. Walter Pater gravitated toward Elia's attentive gaze on the world of things, saying in *Appreciations* (1889) of Lamb that, like Keats, he "[works] ever close to the concrete, to the details, great or small, of actual things, books, persons, and with no part of them blurred to his vision."[35] An antiquarian such moment occurs in "The Old Benchers of the Inner Temple" (1823) where Elia compares and contrasts the appearance of clocks and sun-dials, lamenting the displacement of the latter by the former: "What a dead thing is a clock, with its ponderous embowelments of lead and brass, its pert or solemn dulness of communication, compared with the simple altar-like structure, and silent heart-language of the old dial!"[36] "Altar-like structure" and "silent heart-language" give this critical antiquarian discourse the form but not the substance of spirituality. In its place is a mode of nostalgia flowing from meditative object-love.

Through materialistic enthusiasm expressed with unspecific religious imagery, this observation invokes an emotional but ultimately secular mysticism. The sentiment also glancingly implies neo-Gothic priorities indicative of what Stuart Piggott has referred to as "soft" primitivism, which suffused the Gothic revival. This style of antiquarianism privileged the emotions over any scientific or analytic perspective and located in British antiquities and ancient cultures a vector for melancholic pleasure in the transience of life. The discourse similarly elevated mysticism above reason. Marked by the categories and preoccupations of the picturesque, soft primitivism betrayed "irrational beliefs of Gothick romance and a past full of Noble Savages and mystical Druidry." In addition, a new appreciation of decay figured centrally. According to Piggott, this could serve emotional as well as political aims.[37]

While showing Elia taking particular pleasure in the study of decay, "The South-Sea House" (1823) illustrates the fact that Romantic antiquarian discourse had such a political dimension. As Elia describes the "melancholy," "magnificent relic" of the South-Sea House, a once-grand trading firm, noting its general "desolation" and "worm-eaten tables" along with its "stately porticos" and "imposing staircases," a contrast emerges between the building's regal past and its lowly present, on the one hand, and the obvious affection for its dirty, neglected condition, on the other. Beauty lies in the desolation, which Elia focuses on as he lovingly describes a new, insectivorous class of tenant: "The moths, that were then battening upon the obsolete ledgers and day-books, have rested from their depredations, but other light generations have succeeded, making fine fretwork among their single and double entries."[38] In keeping with what Piggott says about the politics of antiquarianism more generally, Elia is describing a ruin as a by-product of the waning of old power structures ("obsolete ledgers and day-books").[39] Elsewhere, Elia's antiquarianism displays politics more overtly and clearly marked by bohemianism.

MY FIRST PLAY

Illustrating Elia's politics is the essay "My First Play," which merges Elia's consumerist hedonism with a suggestively bohemian theory of the aesthetic. Before exploring this implicit theory, the opening of the essay should be noted for offering another example of Elia's critical, object-centered gaze. In it, he uncovers traces of a more glorious architectural past in the city of the present: "At the north end of Cross Court there yet stands a portal, of some architectural pretensions, though reduced to humble use, serving at present for an entrance to a printing office." Here, Elia campily takes evident pleasure in the decayed and "humble" state of a formerly grand urban ruin, tracing its history across layers of habitation. Notably, Elia's hedonism here involves not only an ostensible sense of regret concerning the decay but also subjective identification *with* it: "I never pass it without shaking some forty years from off my shoulders, recurring to the evening when I passed through it to see *my first play*."[40] Lamb's reverie idealizes the past at the cost of the present but does so in such a way that the subjective experience of the decay itself, rather than any idealized space of the past, takes center stage.

This self-consciousness makes Elia's urban antiquarianism seem strikingly fresh. Not unlike a contemporary dandiacal figure—the maligned "hipster" identified with urban architectural contexts similar to those frequented by Elia—Lamb finds pleasure in and identifies with the experience of urban despoliation.[41] Hip, as well as camp, is his rejection of middle-class priorities (comfort, cleanliness, order, and futurity) in favor of grime, decay, and retrospection, but such rejection should itself be seen as fundamentally middle-class: however dissident in his personal style, this *flâneur* is nonetheless a materialistic hedonist.[42] Such tensions also appear where Elia articulates a proto-bohemian critical theory in "My First Play." This theoretical perspective renders Elia's relationship with the theater in terms of property relations, and, at the same time, the essay distinguishes Elia's "stock" from that of a proper bourgeois (much less an aristocrat). Elia's compromise makes him a landlord (a "freeholder") without land.

In "My First Play," Elia explicitly classes himself at the margins of the middle class, relating how he temporarily came into possession of a small estate in Hertfordshire. This his godfather, "F.," an implausibly cultured "oilman" who had known Sheridan, willed to him.[43] This anecdote's larger context relates another "testamentary beneficence" of the godfather: Elia's love of the theater. F. had sent him to the first play of the title, *Artaxerxes* (Thomas Arne's 1762 adaptation of Metastasio's *Artaserse*). The maturation of Elia's appreciation for the theater serves as the essay's main focus. This aesthetic development the essay presents is in terms of suggesting social, rather than individual, maturation occurring along multiple axes. One is geographical. In keeping with the Persian setting of Arne's opera, Elia's initial, youthful exposure to the theater he renders in Orientalist terms. As a youthful theater-goer, he was a "devotee" worshipping at a "temple." Young Elia also had the tastes of a sensualist: he imagined that the theater's shiny columns were made of "sugar-candy." This mistake speaks to a youthful naivety also reflected in his appreciation of the plays he attended. In his immaturity, Elia says, he did not, as one might expect, mistake signs for signifieds so much as mistakenly imagine nonrepresentational things to be signifiers—fabricating, Elia says, an "emblem" or "reference" where there was none. Looking back on his former self, the mature Elia calls his mature self a "rationalist" rather than a cultist.[44] He now understands that actors are signifiers—"men and women painted"—and the turning on of the orchestra lights is not magic but "a clumsy machinery" operated by people. In this way, the essay maps maturation, along with the mind-body dichotomy, along an East-West axis, with superstition, naivety, sensuality, and immaturity clustered in the "East" of Elia's past. The lesson maturity has taught him, however, is where the proper boundaries around idealism lie. In this way, the lesson involves property relations rather than simply the suspension of disbelief. Gerald Monsman, drawing parallels between "My First Play" and an earlier *Reflector* essay, "On the Tragedies of Shakespeare" (1811), has claimed that the essay's nostalgia idealizes the childhood experience in a more straightforward way: "[H]is main thrust centers on the loss of the child's innocent credulity and the ensuing impoverishment of the original dream."[45] While the essay does not simply favor the "rationalist" perspective, neither does it seem to settle very clearly on young Elia's representational naivety.

The essay's concluding sentences reveal that the ostensibly mature, "rationalist" Elia represents only a temporary stop on the way to a fully mature taste. In closing, Elia describes a moment in his theater-going in which cynical disillusionment yielded to a more sophisticated posture: the suspension of disbelief. Elia says,

> Perhaps it was fortunate for me that the play of the evening was but an indifferent comedy, as it gave me time to crop some unreasonable expectations, which might have interfered with the genuine emotions with which I was soon after enabled to enter upon . . . Comparison and retrospection soon yielded to the present attraction of the scene; and the theatre became to me, upon a new stock, the most delightful of recreations.[46]

Now the reason for the seemingly digressive anecdote about having received property from F. becomes clearer. Upon inheriting the bequest, Elia had taken himself for "an English freeholder" when, in fact, he had merely been playing the part: "When I journeyed down to take possession, and planted foot on my own ground, the stately habits of the donor descended upon me, and I strode (shall I confess the vanity?) with larger paces over my allotment . . . with the feeling of an English freeholder." Elia goes on, "The estate has passed into more prudent hands, and nothing but an agrarian can restore it."[47] Elia suggests that class position dictates whether or not one is entitled to the bounty of England's material patrimony—only an "agrarian" could play the part Elia was mistakenly given, that of the "freeholder"—but, considered alongside the descriptions of Elia's theater-going (a parallel invited by the diction "crop"), this notion of ownership applies to both culture and land. (Incidentally, Lamb played with this notion of cultural inheritance as property elsewhere, inscribing a copy of *The Last Essays of Elia* (1833) to his friend John Forster with the phrase, "a legacy from Elia.")[48] More specifically, a mature Elia has realized when to "crop" his expectations regarding theatrical signifiers—or, in other words, that some fields are appropriate for "recreation," and some not. In other words, the wasteful consumption practices of a youthful sensualist have matured into a more worldly, hard-boiled mode.

Furthermore, Elia's bohemian self-identification as a lord of the theater who has failed as a landlord suggests his notions of theater-going derive their sense from economics and, specifically, a bohemian take on the logic of capitalist accumulation: cultural consumption is profitable, meaning appropriately pleasurable and efficient, when the consumer can manage her desire and the distribution, as it were, of her disbelief. Developing an awareness of the gap between sign and signified is a crucible of maturity, but this gap is uncannily like the one between the products of factory production and their producers—anonymous bodies reduced (or, here, elevated) to the form of commodities ("men and women painted"). Hence, mature taste appears as a more enlightened fetishism—the profit from "a new stock" of emotion yielded by the gap between laborer and product. In this view, one form of fetishism (cultic worship) has given way to another (commodification), and different forms of pleasure and alienation share a horizon defined by objects, property, and ownership. Ultimately, Elia suggests that a mature consumer is

akin to a cultural capitalist whose maturity represents a loss of innocence—
a fall into worldly sophistication—that is actually a gain on a metaphorical
ledger. This view of consumption seems cynical and hard but, for this reason,
dandiacal and bohemian: skilled consumption merits a badge of personhood
and a spiritually inflected, yet ultimately secular, transformation centered on
the disciplining of desire for things. At the same time, the personhood and
its tastes belong to a world apart ("a cult of the self" inured to the world's
"illusions," to borrow from Baudelaire's description of the dandy), and the
question of its superiority compared to a more conventional, or at least more
conventionally privileged, way of life is a preoccupying theme.[49]

The essay's recurring agricultural metaphor derives from not only capitalist but also imperialist conceptions of property. An excess of credulity serves
to mark the uncultivated mind, and intellectual poverty (a notion the passage
literalizes) is placed on congruent axes of development and accumulation: the
play-goer who takes every signifier to refer to a signified (who, in Elia's view,
fabricates an "emblem" or "reference") is not simply naive but also immature
and wasteful. Such a consumer, who knows not when to work or when to
play, failing to distinguish fallow fields from rich ones, lacks an authentic
claim to cultural products and to the value they offer. Simply put, as the end
of the essay suggests pointedly, the rightful claimant bears a version of the
"white man's burden" that might not unfairly be called the white collector's
burden, instead: in the final sentences, a mature Elia reflects contentedly on
the cultural bounty (the "new stock") that his enlightened materialism represents—this being the capitalized pleasure of a jaded consumer whose wealth
is the product of his survival of dangerously seductive cultural products.[50]
His version of survival amounts to an acculturation to the conventions of a
discourse and habituation to the idealisms specific to it. In the case of the
theater, he understands the ways the organization of space intersects with the
conventions of representation. This parallels his learning the lessons of when,
where, and how much to invest in signifiers. For Elia, the kinds of representational idealism that eclipsed Dibdin's polymorphous materialism—such
as the idealism of the author-function, a framework for what aspects of the
book are signifiers and what signifieds they can correspond to—amount to a
form of enlightened materialism and a cult of self abstracted from matter yet
indissolubly linked to it. Melancholy colors this narrative of disillusionment
featuring an overt equation of art with capital.

In this economistic worldview, one's ability to accrue cultural capital is
a function of one's distance from the crude tastes of the kind of sensualist
who mistakes the space of the theater for a Coleridgean pleasure dome—a
"temple" akin to Kubla Khan's "miracle of rare device."[51] Yet the mature
Elia condescending to his younger, stereotypically non-Western self also
reminds one of a sensualist—a hoarder of credulity minding his stock. Such

is, seemingly, the raced and classed perspective implicit in this aesthetic theory. Hence, Elia's implicit motives and goals suggest that his discourse is sufficiently dissident to fall outside the traditional domain of the aesthetic. Considering how calculating he is and how ultimately material his calculations, Elia's ironic approach to theater-going seems the opposite of a "pure" or disinterested judgment, the criterion of aesthetic judgment as classically defined.[52] Rather, he recalls Weber's description of the capitalist in *The Protestant Ethic and the Spirit of Capitalism*, in which the "spirit of capitalism" is "the idea of a duty of the individual toward the increase of his capital which is assumed as an end in itself. Truly what is here preached is not simply a means of making one's way in the world, but a peculiar ethic."[53] For Elia, taste equates to wealth management or home economics—a process of developing self-control and experience to maximize gratification. In this light, Elia's taste resembles less an aesthetic than a bohemian and dandiacal *ethic*, one that embraces possessiveness in the name of "delight." From this view, Elia narrates his inheritance of a merely cultural form of wealth.

The resignation is of a piece with Elia's general, calculating self-denial. Elia's representation of his calibrated incredulity suggests that his capital results from careful divestment of belief in signifiers, not investment. In other words, he hoards his credulity along with his expectations. Furthermore, Elian jadedness, his consumerist unpleasure, reveals a paradoxical vacuity fundamental to the Elia persona: neither simply disappointed nor pleased, Elia does not so much constitute himself in the consumption process as evacuate himself, or relieve himself, into being. Such is his anal as well as bohemian character.

In keeping with this anality, Elia's good taste is the ironic reward of aesthetic bean-counting. The playful reduction of art to a process of accounting (suitable for a clerk) recalls the collector's fetishistic attachments. Rather than recalling the stereotypical tastes of an aristocratic collector, the piece invokes the world of bibliography described by Dibdin in the sense that, there, the expression of aesthetic enjoyment results in uncannily androcentric eroticism. Like Dibdin, Lamb is more of a materialist than a capitalist. Elia's cynical-seeming calculations make a comment on the nature of taste: recalling Baudelaire's analysis of the dandy, Elia holds and expresses fetishistic attachments while maintaining distance from merely conspicuous consumption.

Therefore, "My First Play" exemplifies an alteration, not absence, of the bibliomaniac's characteristic fetishism of cultural commodities in representing a cultic fetishism of things that leads to a more "enlightened" yet still materialistic taste. At the beginning of the essay, one image in particular succinctly sums up Lamb/Elia's conflicted attitude toward the materiality of media. Elia describes how a printer's office now occupies the former "pit entrance" to the Old Drury Theater, an antique structure the sight of which serves Elia as a monument and "portal" to the past ("I never pass it without shaking some forty years from off my shoulders"). Ironically, a new tenant at odds with the history of the place has defaced this feature of the environment not fundamentally unlike Keats's Grecian urn, which also troubles the distinction between aesthetics and ethics ("Beauty is truth, truth beauty").[54] This modern reuse of space would seem simply degrading ("reduced to humble use") and Elia simply lamenting, if not for the fact that the offensive blight is a synecdoche for contemporary cultural production: a "printing office." Hence, it mirrors Lamb/Elia's own production, a materialization of cultural memory and historic theatrical productions in essay form. For Elia in *flâneur* mode, everything in view is potentially a material signifier, as his meditative prose inspired by the built environment demonstrates—here and throughout the essays. The printer's occupation of Old Drury embodies the suggestion that Elia has ironically realized the dream of his younger self, who fantasized that everything in the theater could potentially be a material object for entertaining consumption—a virtual dessert buffet for the eyes ("sugar-candy"). The image embodies Lamb's capital, implying that his reproduction of his own memories of Old Drury and Garrick in the pages of a magazine makes him not fundamentally different from a youthful sensualist. For Lamb, often condescended to as a diverting "stylist" and craftsman (Coleridge saying of him, "His genius is talent, and his talent is genius"), signifiers were material in a vexed sense.[55] This image of a printer's jarring occupation of a meaningful cultural space likely registers Lamb's unease with his material dependence on the culture that moved him and fired his imagination in the past; here, in the present, he profits from reproducing those experiences. At the same time, the powerful extension afforded by the medium of print may have been on Lamb's mind, as well. Indeed, the central theme of the essay is the remarkable power of media to transport an audience, and Lamb/Elia's evident purpose is to take the reader back in time and space to Old Drury as it once was. Such was the power of the theater then that he wants to realize for the reader now: of the gift of "orders" to attend a performance, Elia says, "little wondrous talismans!—slight keys, and insignificant to outward sight, but opening to me more than Arabian paradises!" While sating appetites, Elia suggests, print radically extends the reach of cultural memory, making one person's experience of Old Drury and David Garrick available to another generation. Such is Elia's ambivalence about cultural materiality, however, that even the theater, while magical and powerful, is also vaguely transgressive and his youthful love of it shaded with darkness and the perils of excess.

Lamb's well-known angst about his material dependence on the periodical press adds more weight to this textual detail, as does the essay's textual history. In the earlier version of the piece that appeared in *London Magazine*, the building's new occupant is a "wine vault," affirming the autobiographical resonances of the detail for a writer who was known for and wrote about his own alcoholism.[56] In fact, the metaphor of alcoholism elsewhere represents Elia's material dependence on the press. For example, in "Oxford in the Vacation" (1820), Elia suggestively casts Lamb's magazine writing as a perversely material relationship with print culture: he "sucks his sustenance, as certain sick people are said to do, through a quill."[57] Here, Elia admits a form of dependence similar to Lamb's aforementioned, regretted taste for Coleridge's flattery. In that case as well as this one, addictive dependence is shaded with sexually dissident imagery. The textual history of "My First Play" similarly suggests that one form of substance abuse could imply the other and that writing for the magazines was its own form of substance abuse. The essays evince awareness and perhaps anxiety about Lamb's exploitation of cultural memory for material gain. A fetishist, he substituted means for ends.

The essay's meditation on the material exploitation of culture, on fetishism, and on addictive debility signifies that Elia approaches media like an ornamental consumer, meaning that his point of view emphasizes the power as well as the dissident implications of medial matter. Lamb's evident anxieties about his own uses and abuses of culture departed from while resembling the anxieties circling the activities of the so-called "bookmen." The figure of the bibliomaniac and Lamb's image of his own parasitical relation to the culture were a subset of a broader anxiety about materiality. Affirming that the bibliophile was a queer figure, Lamb's representation of alcoholism elsewhere links materiality and queerness.

Exploring this connection to sexuality helps avoid the sort of moralistic judgment about Lamb's alcohol use shared by Lamb, his contemporaries, and some critics. Lamb was not pleased by his habitual drinking and smoking, as suggested by his repeated pledges, often made to Coleridge, to quit both.[58] Nonetheless, Lewis May opens his biography of Lamb by calling his subject "disgracefully addicted to gin and tobacco."[59] During Lamb's lifetime, his drinking attracted unwelcome notice when his authorship of "Confessions of a Drunkard" (1813) became publicly known.[60] Even though, as Winifred Courtney notes in *Young Charles Lamb, 1775–1802*, he had published it in the high-toned *Philanthropist*, possibly intending an ironic effect, some critics read the essay reductively as straightforward autobiography.[61] In the essay, the corporeality of addiction (its "constitutional tendency") serves as the basis of the Drunkard's appeal to the "sturdy moralist" on the subject of alcoholism: "Alas! the hand to pilfer, and the tongue to bear false witness, have no constitutional tendency. . . . O pause, thou sturdy moralist, thou person of stout nerves and a strong head, whose liver is happily untouched, and ere thy gorge riseth at the *name* which I have written, first learn what the *thing* is."[62] The "thing" is the embodied experience of dependence, which he could have avoided through stricter attachment to another thing, the book. Before he met the boon companions whose habits and audience would lead him into addiction, books and bookish people were his companions ("My companions were chiefly books, or at most one or two living ones of my own book-loving and sober stamp"). These were healthy substitutes for the kind of sociality that led him, the type of person "least fitted" to alcohol, to the substance. Alcohol supported his object in this new circle: to play the fool. Rather than offering transcendence, "fancy" and "wit" acted as gateway substances ("a tickling relish upon your tongue," "a preternatural flow of ideas") an addiction to which turned him to drink.[63] Here, Elia casts the book as a relatively healthy fetish object and bookishness as a prophylactic for a benign kind of sociopath—a recourse for the kind who would otherwise need another, more harmful substance to socialize in the usual way. The horizon of possible relations is material, as in Dibdin's discourse, and the promise of transcendence is a false idol leading the weak to more harmful forms of dependence.

This self-conscious mode of bookish discourse—bibliomania in bad faith—typifies Lamb's bookishness. Like Lamb's urban tour in "My First Play," this discourse on books concerns not simply book-objects and possessiveness but also a sociology of the ornament in the abstract. To bibliomania what political economy is to capitalism, this abstraction is ideological in form and content, ideological by virtue of its abstraction and, therefore, a bourgeois version of bibliomania. This style of bookishness takes additional forms in Lamb's works. The most overt is perhaps Elia's voice—a signature, highly ornamental formalism that embodies bookish antiquarianism in a new way. For Dibdin, stylistic bookishness is a feature primarily of design—fonts, margins, materials, and scale—and superficial stylistic gestures on the level of language. Lamb incorporates bookishness into authorship, making the former integral to an eccentric personality. Through Lamb's version of it, bookishness moves from the description of activities, bodies, and objects in space to the interior and abstract space of an authorial persona, Elia. From this vantage, one can see a version of bibliomania and ornamental community persisting while being transformed. In this case, the objects that attract narrative focus, trigger rumination, and prompt shame organize a personality defined by self-consciously eccentric taste. In this way and others, including its abstraction from the bibliomaniacal aesthetic to a generalized ethic, Lamb's cultural consumption practices not only reflected but also transformed the overt materialism of aristocratic fetishists such as the Ladies, Richard Heber, Horace Walpole, and William Beckford. Not surprisingly, perhaps, Lamb's clearest cooptation of traditional cultural fetishism emerged in relation to the book-object.

A ROUGH TRADE IN UNGENTILITY

The materiality of the literary has come to define Lamb. One of his Victorian editors, J. E. Babson, said he deliberately did not trace allusions in order to protect the beauty of Lamb's prose—or, as Babson memorably says in the preface to *Eliana* (1864), to preserve the "blossoms of learning and observation" there.[64] In *Don't Call Me Gentle Charles!: An Essay on Lamb's Essays of Elia*, Robert Frank paints him as a deliberate aestheticist with a style that objectifies itself: "[Lamb] wanted the essays to be treated as art objects, not as the scribblings of a journalist."[65] Such views posit an absence of depth and, in the former cases, implicitly attribute this lack to labor. They resonate with some reductive, objectifying representations of Lamb's figure and personality. In addition to mocking Lamb's stutter and shuffling gait, Thomas Carlyle dismissed him as an "emblem of imbecility, bodily and spiritual."[66] Lamb emerges as a vaguely sodomitical figure, one defined by materiality and whose beautiful and feminine objects are all surface. Invoking a tradition of phobic discourse with roots in antiquity, these conceptions also draw implicitly on class difference: rather than transmit ethereal beauty, they suggest, Lamb took pains to deliver empty vessels.[67]

Frank's suggestion that the essays were out of place in the magazines speaks to an ambivalence Lamb himself evinced about publishing. A focus of the present section, this ambivalence suggests attitudes about writing that were both bookish and, literally speaking, inappropriate. Specifically, "ungentle" Lamb displayed out-of-step notions of the literary sphere. Neither polite nor professional, these were more bohemian than strictly bourgeois, and, suitably for an antiquarian, more bibliophilic than professional. Finally, these attitudes rendered Lamb vulnerable to sexually phobic characterization.

Like Elia's lamented dependence on his "quill," critics have returned often to the periodicals he wrote for and to the fact he wrote for them. Identified primarily with the essay form, Lamb is best known as a popular periodical writer—the "hero" the *London*, one of the five periodicals where the Elia essays appeared.[68] In ways subtle and obvious, critics have used this association with the periodical against him. The editor Alaric C. Watts, a contemporary, used the form to impugn his masculinity in a letter to William Blackwood: "Charles Lamb delivers himself with infinite pain and labor of a silly piece of trifling every month in this magazine [*Blackwood's*] under the signature of Elia."[69] More recent critics, while not insulting Lamb, have continued to identify him closely with the medium, with the rise in popularity of periodicals more generally, and with the professionalization of the literary field.

In *Charles Lamb and the Evolution of Elia*, George Barnett describes the context of Lamb's ascendance in the world of the periodicals. The explosive growth in popularity of a new type of periodical beginning in the late eighteenth century did lay the foundation for Lamb's eventual success. The earlier miscellanies such as *Gentleman's Magazine, Town and Country Magazine, Monthly Magazine, Critical Review, Monthly Review,* and *Blackwood's,* with their mix of politics, astronomy, and oddities, much of it reprinted from other publications, were replaced by this "new magazine." The new format was represented by the *English Review of Literature, British Critic, Edinburgh Review, British Review,* and *Eclectic Review* and allowed more space for essays and reviews. Barnett claims that a new purpose, entertainment, required more and more varied content, for which editors were willing to pay. The remarkable increase in production suggests that more was involved than simply changing tastes, however. Forty new magazines began publication in London between 1790 and 1800. By 1830, the total number exceeded 100.[70]

Lamb's own sense of his place in the literary field seems to have been more complicated than an identification of himself with the new format. Despite his success, Lamb resisted others' pigeon-holing and seems not to have seen himself as a periodical writer. We have seen ambivalence about the form in "My First Play." This reticence also emerged in his initial reluctance to work in the genre. As he said in a letter to Edward Moxon, the "serious business of life" had the power to draw him away from the "nonsense" of poetry.[71] When the weight of financial pressures lessened with the success of Elia, he returned to drama, despite the negative reception of *Mr. H.*, writing a farce, *The Pawnbroker's Daughter* (1830), and a drama in blank verse, *The Wife's Trial* (1828).[72]

Lamb's correspondence suggests that the "serious business" monopolizing his time was a badge of honor distinguishing his situation from that of more "polite" writers. In an 1822 letter to Wordsworth, he describes his work at East India House this way: "Thirty years have I served the Philistines, and my neck is not subdued to the yoke. You don't know how wearisome it is to breathe the air of four pent walls without relief day after day, all the golden hours of the day between 10 and 4 without ease or interposition."[73] A similar letter to Coleridge employs red ink for dramatic effect: "A Letter written in the blood of your poor friend would indeed be of a nature to startle you; but this is nought but harmless red ink, or, as the witty mercantile phrase hath it, Clerk's Blood. Damn 'em! my brain, guts, skin, flesh, bone, carcase, soul, Time, is all theirs."[74] The truth of the matter, testified to by Elia and obvious to both men, gives the lie to this exaggeration, but it makes the creation of Elia that much more impressive. In such lines, clerking is a yoke that shone a heroic light on Elia.

Despite such comments, Lamb seems not to have fully shared his friends' antipathy toward the kind of work he did for a living, so the Cockney label also misleads in this respect, obscuring a complete understanding of Lamb's financial situation as well as his ideas about authorship and publication.

Unlike Keats, his goal seems never to have been to subsist on his writing or to become famous for it.[75] Instead, Lamb, while working at East India House, contributed regularly but usually anonymously, in accordance with standard practice, or else under a pseudonym, to periodicals such as the *London*. Lacking the ambitions associated with the Cockneys by their critics, Lamb not only avoided the profession of the writer—preferring to depend on his East India House income and, subsequently, pension, even in the face of increasing demand and potentially lucrative pay for his writing—but also evinced in other ways a "gentlemanly" and increasingly anachronistic ambivalence about the self-publicity associated with publication.

This attitude suggests a pseudo-aristocratic ambivalence about self-exposure that, while not a reflection of what is known about Lamb's actual personality, is fully consistent with Lamb's signature—the archaic diction of the essays. The paradoxical roughness of this gentle style—the mannered and courtly features that compulsively imitate the Shaftesburian voice he denigrates in 1826's "The Genteel Style of Writing" (the "inflated finical rhapsodies" of Shaftesbury as opposed to the "plain natural chit-chat" of Temple)—suggests not only sodomitical evacuation but also art and surface.[76] In the fullest sense a sensibility, thanks to the style's antique diction, an abstract version of Dibdin's black-letter font effect, Lamb's bookish and antiquarian prose resembles that of a self-consciously "eccentric" collector. Appropriately, his efforts would have a powerful influence over the changing fortunes of the British literature of the Restoration.

This retro, "ungentle" style finds a corollary expression in choices Lamb made toward the end of his life. These have the appearance of cultural, rather than economic, nobility, appropriately enough for someone who lived in a "cottage of Ungentility." Lamb's was a comfortable but not lavish retirement: at two-thirds his former salary, Lamb's pension from India House brought in £450, a portion of which, £9, went to supporting Mary.[77] Nevertheless, Lamb complained of the economizing the pension required, telling Bernard Barton in a letter that in "cropping off wine, old books, &c. and in short all that can be called pocket money, I hope to be able to go on at the cottage."[78] He suggests in a letter to Thomas Hood that the Lambs' moves to Islington and then Enfield, progressively farther away from their beloved London, were similarly motivated.[79] Despite their financial difficulties, Lamb's output for the periodical press decreased; this was likely due in part to worsening illness. Also, Lamb was selective about the periodical commissions he undertook despite the fact that he could command a large fee. He had written his last contribution, "Stage Illusion," to the *London* in 1825, the year he retired, attributing the break in a letter to Southey to the declining quality of the magazine.[80] The year 1826 saw only the "Popular Fallacies" series from the *New Monthly Magazine*, which included the "Genteel Style" essay.[81] In 1827,

Lamb refused a commission from Barron Field to write a piece on the theater.[82] Furthermore, despite his complaints, Lamb managed to leave a significant sum to Mary upon his death, a savings derived—if, as Lucas points out, Lamb's remarks about his failure to save any of his earnings while employed are to be believed—entirely from the pension. Lamb's substantial legacy to Mary suggests that the lamented economizing was prompted not by financial strain but self-enforced discipline—a stricture all the more notable in the light of Lamb's reluctance to publish often in the periodical press despite the earning power generated by the popularity of Elia.[83] Although illness, alcoholism, and the changes brought upon him by his retirement undoubtedly contributed to the decrease in productivity at the end of his life, it also seems that a reluctance to capitalize on his earning power in the periodical press—to professionalize himself—led Lamb to turn down magazine work and focus on the less profitable and more "gentlemanly" arena of book publication.

This preference is more noteworthy given the high rate he could command. According to Bryan Waller Procter, the rate he earned for the Elia essays made him the highest paid contributor to the *London* at the time (his rate being twenty guineas per sheet, or sixteen pages), by a factor of two or three.[84] After breaking with the *London*, while writing for the periodical press on a smaller scale, Lamb focused his energies on the book projects he referred to as his "trifles." These included *Album Verses, with a Few Others* (1830), decried by some as a vanity project, and the unprofitable *The Last Essays of Elia*. At nine shillings, this was an expensive volume. Given the disappointing sales of the first collection of Elia essays (*Elia* [1823, out of print by 1834]), few expected it to sell.

The book's reception misinterpreted and sexualized Lamb's status and cross-class ambitions, constructing the book as a format unfit for unmanly types. As Joseph Riehl remarks in *That Dangerous Figure: Charles Lamb and the Critics*, William Jerdan's review of *Album Verses* in the *Literary Gazette* attributes the book's appearance to "the blinding and engrossing nature of vanity."[85] One *Monthly Magazine* reviewer's condescension was overt: "Some few years ago, there was in this metropolis a little coterie of half-bred men, who took up poetry and literature as a trade, and who . . . puffed off each other as the first writers of the day."[86] This sexually phobic critique misidentifies Lamb with the sexually suspect Cockneys and reveals this reviewer to misunderstand the economics of Lamb's choices and, hence, the nuances of Lamb's style.

This work Lamb devoted himself to rather than reliably profitable work for the magazines. The same writer who distanced himself from the ungentlemanly trade of writing also remarked ironically to a friend that fame in the East as a book author was a dream of his, and at another point expressed satisfaction about the success of a pirated Elia collection published in America

(*Elia. Second Series* [1828]), which included pieces that Lamb did not in fact write. Consistently, Lamb evinced a conflicted desire for literary fame conjoined to an (appropriately for Lamb, increasingly anachronistic) gentlemanly disdain for, on the one hand, the self-publicity associated with publication and, on the other, the commercial motives and professional identification associated with the periodical press. In writing about Lamb, Hazlitt reads Lamb's resistance to professionalization in terms of amateurism. In what may be an instance of unconscious self-loathing, he describes Lamb in a *Table Talk* piece from 1825 ("Elia—Geoffrey Crayon") as an amateur who, thanks to his venue (periodicals) and circle, has lucked into popularity.[87] Lamb's literary production, although originating in the periodicals, conformed to an ethos of gentlemanly amateurism rather than professionalism, a posture of independence from the market obtained at a not insignificant personal cost.

In his amateurism, Lamb was more "ungentle" than falsely gentle. Lamb's self-conscious rejection of literary embourgeoisment strikes a bohemian note, distinguishing him from the "professionals" with whom his work shared pages. The resistance to the forces of commercialization and prioritization of literary quality over personal profit parallels the prototypically bohemian and hedonistic aesthetic of the Romantic avant-garde. According to Campbell, the Romantic bohemian reacted simultaneously to middle-class sentimentalism (a legacy of the cult of sensibility according to which finely attuned taste took the form of an emotional expressiveness thought to indicate inner spiritual worth) and the aristocratic emphasis on the importance of conformity to rigid aesthetic norms, which was a compensation for the waning influence of neoclassicism's models. In this way, the figure, like her twentieth-century counterpart, found a middle ground—hence the avant-garde's disdain for social convention and for sentimentalism's identification of pleasurable emotional states with virtue. Pleasure, a holdover from the shift from sensibility to sentimentalism, according to which the worth of emotions consisted in the pleasure they afforded rather than the inner virtue they indicated, and creativity came to the fore, only now the pleasure being idealized was that associated with the genius' production of beautiful and true works of art, thought to be "the means by which enlightenment and moral renewal [could] be achieved."[88] In this light, Lamb's sacrificial dedication to the book format—a purer form of literary art "within bourgeois limits"—struck a bohemian note of resistance considering the moral weight and real stakes of Lamb's personal commitment to the particular commercial form that he wished for his art.[89]

While Lamb's career choices and known attitudes toward them suggestively invoke bohemian style, Lamb's collecting and essays, as I will attempt to show in what follows, similarly turn cultural consumption toward dissident ends. An influential work on the history of modern style has identified a classed and gendered mode of nonconformity in the consumption practices of certain middle-class subcultures, offering a way to understand and broadly contextualize Lamb's style. In the classic *Subculture: The Meaning of Style*, Dick Hebdige reads the countercultural styles of various subcultures (including the "teds," "punks," and "mods" of 1960s and 1970s Britain) as social salvos aimed at the symbolic order of the majority that, while subversive, were nonetheless restricted to "the profoundly superficial level of appearances." The contradiction between dominant culture and marginal culture displayed by these groups found expression through the consumption of certain commodities in deliberate, novel ways. Consequently, Hebdige sees the subversive practices of such factions as a doubly reified form of "spectacular" *bricolage*, the fashioning of a new, oppositional system of signs out of readily available consumer goods. Hebdige's analysis offers an example of bohemian consumption serving rebellious production. Among punks, the buying and repurposing of safety pins served rebellious self-expressions, including using the pins to adorn flesh, but this rebelliousness was blunted by the expressions' restriction to the sphere of signs and consumerism. Nonetheless, punks' repurposing of consumer goods represented one way that they posed challenges to the seeming naturalness of the dominant faction's aesthetic norms. Such unexpected adaptations posed challenges because, as Hebdige says, "Any elision, truncation, or convergence of prevailing linguistic and ideological categories can have profoundly disorienting effects. These deviations briefly expose the arbitrary nature of the codes which underlie and shape all forms of discourse." These codes included gender styles, which the youth subcultures initially questioned with the help of David Bowie's ambiguous personae and, subsequently, the punk styles that derived from this while also taking cues from the stylistic vocabulary of bondage and S&M.[90] Other scholars have found a more direct connection between punk style and queerness that speaks to the inextricability of queerness and bohemianism, which the dandy figure embodies.[91] Kevin Dunn, for example, has observed that punk scenes have historically made space for queer folks.[92] Tavia Nyong'o has also explored the relations between queerness and punk, identifying in the different histories of African American and white versions of punk evidence of a dynamic in which homophobia and hypersexualization haunt occluded representations of queer and black sexuality.[93] This work suggests that queerness has long been elemental to the representation and self-identification of the subculture's membership.

 Lamb's activities as a collector, which have been neglected by scholars, offer a window onto the sexual implications of his prototypically bohemian style. In their form and content, the essays themselves can be seen as extensions of these activities. Lamb's self-consciously anachronistic and, by virtue of the diction, vaguely nationalist essayistic style ("What a careless, even deportment hath your borrower!") dovetailed with his book collecting. An overtly antiquarian style was Lamb/Elia's signature. Hazlitt, writing in *Table Talk* about Lamb's archaic diction, accused Lamb of affectation: "The style of the *Essays of Elia* is liable to the charge of a certain mannerism. His sentences are cast in the mold of old authors."[94] Lamb's style could be especially vulnerable to such a charge because its archaism—incomplete and overt—coexisted with the contemporary vernacular, foregrounding the status of the archaic as a gesture. Pater expresses great affection for this "aroma of old English" in the Elia essays, along with the "noticeable echoes, in chance turn and phrase, of the great masters of style, the old masters."[95] By these echoes, this antiquarian's style was antiqued, or old-*fashioned*, rather than simply old. Hence, the essays materialize nostalgia, which is to say that their nostalgia is, famously, formal: "Hail to thy returning festival, old Bishop Valentine! Great is thy name in the rubric, thou venerable Arch-flamen of Hymen! Immortal Go-between! Who and what manner of person art thou? Art thou but a name, typifying the restless principle which impels poor humans to seek perfection in union? Or wert thou indeed a mortal prelate . . . ?"[96] Such an apostrophe, billing itself as such and as ("old," "poetic") form, insists on being read as if in quotation marks. Such words are, in a sense, antiquarian objects—old stuff that Elia has repurposed. A similar passage appears in "That We should Lie Down with the Lamb" (1826): "Marry, daylight," Elia says, "[D]aylight might furnish the images, the crude material; but for the fine shapings, the true turning and filing (as mine author hath it), they must be content to hold their inspiration of the candle."[97] Here, not only does the style objectify itself with self-consciously deployed, old-fashioned diction but the passage also thematizes literary materiality and craft ("crude material," "turning," "filing").

Noting stylistic parallels between Elia and collectors of the Roxburghe ilk, Ina Ferris has glimpsed Elia's hypermaterial style through the notion of "book fancy"—a self-conscious reflection of bookishness on the level of figuration that Lamb used to register his liminal status in the literary sphere. With bibliomaniacs, Lamb shared an "outlier" status and, hence, an alternative, more material view on the literary in contrast to the dominant idealism that defined the literary for mainstream producers. For Ferris, Lamb's style reflected not a dissident collector's posture toward the literary but an anticollector's: "Lamb contested the bibliomania's model of exclusive collection and literary possession, translating the bibliomaniac's fine library of expensive rarities into a bohemian domestic space—the site of a *reader*—where book collection marked personal attachments rather than material value."[98]

Although he read his books, Lamb adopted a style of book ownership and collecting that, while differing from a bibliomaniac's and clearly lacking the traditionally material aims of a book collection, nonetheless invested more than a reader would in his distressed tomes. As with his prose, where he preferred writers who were out of fashion, in the case of books he preferred the secondary market. In this cultivated taste for déclassé books, he recalls another noted writer for the magazines, De Quincey. Like the opium-eater's "Saturday night fever," the writer's the opium-fueled ventures into working-class London described in the *Confessions of an English Opium-Eater*, as Nigel Leask has referred to them, Lamb tended to "slum it" in London's used book stores.[99] The books he deliberately sought there were not so much bargains as seconds—the ragged detritus of the retail market. What follows discusses both Lamb's collecting itself and this activity's influence on the essays. Lamb's collecting was, like the essays, I argue, a proto-bohemian version of cross-class appropriation and consumption that anticipated the logic of punk aesthetics, in which classed and sexualized modes of dissidence have gone hand in hand.

The essays thematize his practices as a collector. Ever the "wary connoisseur," as Lamb describes the collector of prints in "Oxford in the Vacation," Lamb's refined collecting practices and general love of the book are frequent subjects of the essays and letters, where book collecting, book possession, and the material conditions and implements of cultural production are bound up with an ironic construction of a dissident authorial identity.[100] One element of this was antiquarian: Lamb was a book collector. One form of this behavior was traditional by bibliomaniacal standards. Lamb's "curious" collection, as J. Fuller Russell recalls Lamb describing his library in Russell's reminiscences of Lamb published in the *Guardian* in the 1870s, was neither a gentleman's nor a professional scholar's, and the collection's lack of utility was a source of pride for Lamb: "I have *nothing useful*."[101] While invoking, perhaps deliberately and ironically, the traditional collector's style of consumption, this statement implies an attitude toward collecting that subordinates value to the aim of self-expression—or, to use Lynch's apt description, to the acquisition of "the provisions for interiority that are furnished to the gentleman by his cabinet library."[102] At the risk of over-burdening an isolated comment, the statement sounds like one from someone for whom bookishness was less a value proposition or professional necessity than the reflection of an ironic self-concept or even a deliberate mode of consumption that served an ironic identity.

What is known about Lamb's library invokes an altered image of bibliomaniacal style in another way: the collection implies a disregard for conventional morality in favor of eccentricity and rarity. Thomas Westwood's account in *Notes and Queries* of time spent at the Lambs' home in Enfield, to which they moved in 1827, illuminates Lamb's unconventional tastes:

> I soon grew to be on intimate terms with my neighbor; who let me loose in his [Lamb's] library, and initiated me into a school of literature, which Mrs. Trimmer might not have considered the most salutary under the circumstances.

Beaumont and Fletcher, Webster, Farquhar, Defoe, Fielding—these were the pastures in which I delighted to graze, in those early years; and which, in spite of Trimmers, I believe did me less evil than good.[103]

This Mrs. Trimmer was likely Sarah Trimmer, the religious educator, children's author, and key figure in the Sunday school movement, which some criticized for its paternalistic approach to charity-based education. Trimmer also cofounded the Tory-leaning periodical *Guardian of Education*. Westwood suggests that, while being unconventionally moral ("not . . . the most salutary"), Lamb's taste was self-consciously indiscriminate.

Of his own collection, Lamb said, "I have no repugnances. . . . I can read anything which I call a book. . . . I bless my stars for a taste so catholic, so unexcluding."[104] He was proud of his exclusions, though, which he called "books which are no books"—namely, Hume ("so cold, and unnatural, and inhuman!"), Gibbon ("fine writing, so fine and composite"), and Robertson (whose style he described as "periods with three members"). Thomas Moore confirmed the absence of these three from his library.[105] Leigh Hunt recalls seeing on Lamb's shelves Chaucer, Montaigne, Sir Thomas Browne, Jeremy Taylor, Spinoza, Sidney, Southey, Jeremy Collier, Dryden, Martin Luther, Sewell, and Charles Grandison.[106] W. Carew Hazlitt lists, in addition to some of these, anthologies of Restoration drama along with Burton ("a very poor, cropped copy"), Milton, Spenser, Talfourd, William Warner (*Syrinx*, 1597), Euripides, Pope, Bacon, and Ben Johnson. W. Carew Hazlitt's descriptions of the books make reference to marginalia by both Coleridge and Lamb, noting about a copy of Thomas Holcroft's *Travels from Hamburgh, through Westphalia and the Netherlands, to Paris* (1804) that "Lamb has made these volumes, flyleaves, margins and every other imaginable space, a receptacle for a variety of observations—has, in fact, turned them into a commonplace book." He also notes some folios: Samuel Daniel (with "important notes" by Coleridge), Taylor, and Spenser.[107]

Considered at a remove, Lamb's approach to the rehabilitation of Elizabethan dramatists such as Francis Beaumont, John Fletcher, Christopher Marlowe, John Webster, and Cyril Tourneur resembles the work of a collector. First, he minimized the visibility of his roles as anthologist and editor. Pater notes the transparency of Lamb's "self-forgetful" authorial presence in this scholarly work. In *Appreciations*, Pater praises Lamb's "way of forgetting himself in his subject" while crediting him with "almost" discovering the entirety of "old English drama" for a new generation.[108]

Second, the rehabilitation of Restoration comedy that Lamb ushered in implies an approach to literature having, if not a collector's traditional motives, the appearance of speculative collecting. However genuine his fondness for Restoration comedy, Lamb's investment in the genre resembled the aristocratic collector's subordination of "content" to rarity—a prominent example of this during the period being the headline-making auction price of the Roxburghe *Decameron*—even though Lamb evidently did not seek to profit from owning copies of the dramatists' works. Like collectors' disregard for the *Decameron*'s frank representation of human sexuality in favor of the rarity and corresponding market value ultimately stemming from the same thing, Lamb's provocative tastes could be called fetishistic because they substituted the expression of eccentricity for particulars intrinsic to individual texts. In this way, Lamb's self-conscious cultivation of an eccentric reading as well as collecting style mirrored Elia's description of himself in "Mackery End, Hertfordshire" (1821): "Out-of-the-way humors and opinions—heads with some diverting twist in them—the oddities of authorship please me most."[109] Rarity reigns here, as it long had for traditional collectors, but in this case rarity operates as a criterion for the evaluation of authors and meaning, not physical copies. In other words, Lamb *reads* like a collector with an eye for authors, channeling bibliomaniacal desire through the lens of private property.

Reflecting the widespread interest in antiquarianism during the period, the renewed attention that these efforts ("Characters of Dramatic Writers, Contemporary with Shakespeare" [1808, 1818] and *Specimens of English Dramatic Poets Who Lived about the Time of Shakespeare* [1808]) brought to seventeenth-century drama nonetheless proved controversial: the New Humanists used Lamb's revival of the Elizabethans and Restoration dramatists to expel him from the canon. Irving Babbitt, like Macaulay before him, who along with C. C. Felton initiated the critical backlash against Lamb, took for a whip what he saw as the dangerous moral impurity of the Restoration playwrights.[110] In *Rousseau and Romanticism* (1919), Babbitt accuses Lamb of having insufficiently moral critical standards: "Because we are justified, as Lamb urges, in wandering imaginatively beyond 'diocese of strict conscience,' it does not follow that we may, like him, treat Restoration Comedy as a sort of fairyland; for Restoration Comedy is a world not of pure but of impure imagination."[111]

In addition to a preference for "oddness," Lamb's criticism offers examples of a self-aware and fetishistic departure from reigning standards of aesthetic judgment, including the practice of abiding by coherent standards itself. In the context of Romantic critical theory, however, Lamb's incoherent aesthetic could also accurately be called an ethic. The eccentric catholicity of Lamb's tastes, a "curious" indiscrimination, suggests the sensibility of the dilettante at the same time that it reveals the operation of an ethic of gratification, rather than an aesthetic at all. More specifically, Lamb's noted eccentricity belongs to a style and a mode of consumerism conceived in terms of personal gratification—not an aesthetic in the sense applicable to then-emergent criteria determining, for instance, Coleridge's judgments of Wordsworth's poetry in the *Biographia Literaria*. There, one finds criteria in keeping with the pure aesthetic in general and Kant's pure judgment of taste in particular. In the *Critique of the Power of Judgment* (1790), Kant describes this as an aesthetic judgment based solely on the formal properties of an object in itself, unpolluted by any impact the object has on the senses.[112] As seen in Coleridge's critique of "The Thorn," these criteria include the "heights" achieved by the poet rather than any subjective impact of the poetry.[113] In contrast, Lamb's self-conscious eccentricity ("the oddities of authorship please me most") resembles an impure ethic of gratification.

Lamb's ethic is also evident in the criticism. There Lamb announces his unabashed affection for Daniel Defoe's novels, for example ("Appreciation of De Foe's Secondary Novels" [1829]). Here, his love of Defoe illustrates one way his tastes ran in the direction of camp. As in his dramatic criticism, Lamb preferred something presently degraded, marginal, and morally "impure." In that case Lamb championed Elizabethan and Restoration drama; in this case he embraces novels by Defoe such as *Singleton, Roxana, Colonel Jack*, and *Moll Flanders*. Lamb's enthusiasm for the likes of Farquhar and Fielding, the creators of the libertine Plume and the bastard Tom Jones, respectively, finds a kin in his interest in the novel and a contentious disagreement with Coleridge about Wordsworth's "low" diction.

In the piece on Defoe, Lamb provocatively uses Coleridgean poetics to support a claim about the fidelity of Defoe's brand of realistic representation to what Wordsworth and Coleridge call "low" life. In doing so, Lamb seems to betray an awareness of the ways his tastes departed from Coleridge's:

> The narrators everywhere are chosen from low life, or have had their origin in it; therefore they tell their own tales, (Mr. Coleridge has anticipated us in this remark,) as persons in their degree are observed to do, with infinite repetition, and an overacted exactness, lest the hearer should not have minded, or have forgotten, some things that had been told before.[114]

As Lucas has said, here Lamb most likely has in mind Coleridge's chapter in the *Biographia* on Wordsworth's rustic diction in *Lyrical Ballads* (1798), where Coleridge disputes the claim made by Wordsworth in the "Preface" (1800) that in "low and rustic life" "our elementary feelings," as Wordsworth puts it, find fuller development and better expression because they find less "restraint" here than they find in cities and towns.[115]

Lamb identifies Defoe's merit with fidelity to the sphere of life declared by Coleridge to lack—due to an absence of the "cultivation" available through reading and education that elevates a people above a state where one finds "*ordinary, morbid idiocy*"—precisely the worthiness that characterizes proper subjects for art. Coleridge writes, "[I]t is not possible to imitate truly a dull and garrulous discourser, without repeating the effects of dulness and garrulity."[116] Whereas Wordsworth, in Coleridge's view, has unfortunately mixed in the "low" points of view of some narrators (Harry Gill, the Idiot Boy) with the "height" reached by his own imagination when its expression stands alone, for Lamb the "charm that has bewitched the world" that characterizes Defoe's style stems from his evident and deft handling of the perspectives of his "low" characters and their diction ("They [Defoe's narrators] bear the veritable impress of De Foe").[117] The incoherence and intermingling illustrated by Wordsworth's peasant-ventriloquism so offensive to Coleridge is for Lamb the signal mark of Defoe's artistry.

In addition to its embrace of the "low," in diction and critical judgment, and heterogeneous, Lamb's ethic also rejects the standard of distinction fundamentally important to Coleridge. Whereas, for Coleridge, Wordsworth's misplaced faith in the capacities of "the ordinary language of men" has led him into error, Lamb's embrace of Defoe's "low" language amounts to a rejection of this standard of refusal of the common, which is also a refusal of the politics of the "pure gaze."[118] Lamb's praise of Defoe is also notable for its embrace not only of the "low" diction of Defoe's narrators but also of Defoe's universal appeal, a popularity that Lamb describes in terms not of cerebral, reflective appreciation by a disinterested audience but rather of an unthinking, passive embrace (Defoe's fiction being a "charm that has bewitched the world"). Lamb's is rejecting both the standards of Coleridge's aesthetics and the mode of aesthetic appreciation they imply, a mode of consumption distinct from the unrefined kind provided by novels and that acknowledges virtues intrinsic to the art itself rather than pleasures afforded by it. This ultimate investment in an ethic of gratification suggestively presents a version of the "popular aesthetic," which "ignores or refuses the refusal of 'facile' involvement and 'vulgar' enjoyment."[119]

Lamb's own collecting practices conformed to his theory. The populist aesthetic—one doubly subversive in its citation of popularity to support a claim to artistic merit—operating there finds a corollary in his style of collecting. While aristocratic bibliomaniacs prized signifiers of rarity and exclusivity, such as uncut pages and black-letter script, the stars guiding Lamb's practices were shabbiness, affordability, and irregularity. With telling diction, Thomas Westwood, repeating an allusion to *Henry IV, Part I* in "Character of the Late Elia" (1823), describes Lamb's library as a "ragged regiment of book-tatterdemalions" that were "curious" (a term, synonymous with "desirable," favored by aristocratic collectors) and "cheap." Quoting Lamb, Westwood says, "He had, he said, a curious library of old poetry, etc., which he had bought at book stalls, cheap."[120] When a significant portion of Lamb's collection sold at auction in the United States in 1848, George L. Duyckinck took evident delight in describing the "ragged" lots in *The Literary World* (while the below quote from Duyckinck's text comes from a pamphlet about Lamb's collection issued in 1897 by the Dibdin Club). The text merits a lengthy quotation due to the details offered about Lamb's collection:

> Books beyond a certain investiture of raggedness and dilapidation, backs without corners, mutilated title-pages, and missing colophons, on ordinary occasions, command those stimulating fractions of advance, a penny on a share, for instance, which constitute liveliness on the exchange, but beget only yawns and a distaste for his profession in the jolliest of auctioneers. They are the perquisites of the basket and the street shelf; they shrink into corners of out-of-the-way streets, where they suffer a partial exposure to the weather; they are cheapened from threepence to twopence, and their last destiny is probably to be boiled in soap-vats, a fate of which their appearance is highly suggestive. They are the ill odor of auction-rooms; the fly in the ointment, the flaw in the base, the stain on the garment of the happiest of all possible professions, as illustrated by the eloquence of a Robbins or the wit of a Keese. Over a lot of the shabbiest of all known volumes the last-mentioned auctioneer was administering, but they were the books of Charles Lamb; a ragged remnant of that library which once adorned (its nakedness more attractive than the gilding of Lewis or the tooling of Hayday) the walls of the room in the Temple where Hazlitt, Wordsworth, Coleridge, and other choice spirits assembled. . . . That copy of Chaucer in black-letter was no ordinary copy. It doubtless had its history. Lamb had eyed it afar off, shedding its luminous rays of the spirit out of the reek and dinginess of a London stall, hid from all other observers, even as a chiffonier has an appreciation of an invisible silver spoon in a gutter. He had passed it and repassed it on his daily walks, his conscience growing every day more tender over its "unhoused" condition. He felt for it as he would feel for mendicity. He could bear those pangs no longer. The three and sixpence which lurked in reluctant pockets must come forth, and the black-letter victim of age and destitution be borne to the warm shelves of the Temple, its constitution hardened by the fumigation of tobacco, its dry, worm-eaten leaves moistened with ale as a libation, or honored with the ascending incense of the punchbowl and kettle. There should it have rested—but rest was not for its aged weariness, which had long since exhibited itself in yawns that would not contract, misanthropic turnings up of leaves which would not be laid, and a protruding back bone from which the calfskin had long since vanished.[121]

Lamb's dilapidated, ragged, worm-eaten, coverless, and mutilated books had an aura of their own. The pamphlet goes on to describe some lots and their prices (including a collection of "old plays" by Wycherley and others that took $5.50) and records the total proceeds of the auction as $122.[122] Low prices would probably not have offended Lamb. The cheapness of his books was a point of pride. A certain "Mrs. FitzGerald" recalled that his books even retained the price tags affixed by the stalls where he bought them.[123]

While being as "curious" as any bibliomaniac's, Lamb's bookishness distinguished itself from that of an aristocratic collector. He was a conspicuous consumer, but his practice had an element of self-conscious departure from aristocratic and typical antiquarian taste. An edge is visible in Lamb's practice as described in these accounts, which would have been in keeping with the Elian authorial persona, but this aesthetic dissonance would have been only as radical as consumerist use of products as signifiers could ever be—radical on the level of style. This aspect of Lamb's style strikes an uncannily modern note. Deliberately leaving the price tags from used book stalls on one's preciously ragged books was like wearing or a safety pin as an earring in London in the 1970s—an aggressively stylish yet solidly middle-class version of punk taste.

Lamb's punk antiquarianism also manifested itself in the essays. Elia takes an ironic perspective on bibliomaniacal collecting practices and values in essays such as "The South-Sea House" (1820), where a description of old-fashioned accounting practices and implements aligns signifiers of literary collectability with snobbishness—a style of excess that Elia simultaneously derides and idealizes:

> But thy great dead tomes, which scarce three degenerate clerks of the present day could lift from their enshrining shelves—with their old fantastic flourishes, and decorative rubric interlacings—their sums in triple columniations, set down with formal superfluity of cyphers—with pious sentences at the beginning, without which our religious ancestors never ventured to open a book of business, or bill of lading—the costly vellum covers of some of them almost persuading us that we are got into some *better library*,—very agreeable and edifying spectacles. I can look upon these defunct dragons with complacency. Thy heavy odd-shaped ivory-handled penknives (our ancestors had every thing on a larger scale than we have hearts for) are as good as any thing from Herculaneum. The pounce-boxes of our days have gone retrograde.[124]

The modern way of doing business ("the pounce-boxes of our days") pales in comparison to a deified and classicized image of antique business practices, which are here also cultural practices. These accountants of yore are Titans of no-industry. At the same time, Elia's appreciation of the signal marks of the antique accounting book belongs to a self-satisfied style of idle consumption ("*better library*"). In a similarly ironic way, the marks of antiquity themselves are prized for their distance from a present in which commercial application and general utility determine form (specifically instanced in useless and impractical decorative touches—"heavy odd-shaped ivory-handled penknives," "formal superfluity of ciphers," "fantastic flourishes"—which the present lacks the "heart" to produce) while they reflect an outmoded and ultimately silly way of doing business. At this point, a quasianthropological voice enters the description to equate the preindustrial aura of the old implements with that of a "defunct" religious totem ("enshrining shelves," "pious sentences," "religious ancestors") shrouded in mists of superstition ("dragons").

As in "My First Play," here Elia seeks to recuperate a materialistic and "retrograde" ornamentation within limits. In both cases, Elia represents antiquarian investment implicitly in terms of reading. In that essay, Elia reminisces about the loss of youthful naivety regarding signifiers that have taken the form of assuming a referent. A mature as well as civilized state of consumption, by contrast, reflects the ability to invest properly in the utility of signifiers. Here, referentiality is similarly at stake. Specifically, the antique appears as a mode of signification whose referents, such as penknives, are simultaneously redundant (the implicit critical perspective on antique business practices being informed by the values of populism and utility) and representative of a lost ideal ("The pounce-boxes of our day have gone retrograde").

In yoking commerce to a bookish sensibility rendered in terms of excessive materiality, not only does the passage refer to Lamb's own prose style, but it also does so in terms of the antiquity and commercial viability of expression. Perhaps Lamb's aesthetic does not make sound business "sense," Elia implies, but this Quixotic hero of "retrograde" literature will, in any case, soldier on. Elia is making a winking case for bibliomania. This passage's playful image of a cultural heritage as weighty "tomes" appears in De Quincey's prose in a similar context. Both writers—writers for the magazines, collectors, and *flâneurs*—represented their literary heritage in materialistic terms. In this instance, Lamb suggestively renders himself as an obsolete but virtuous hold-out for useless matter, facing, as the reference to Herculaneum implies, the prospect of ecological disaster. "Gaping" like the empty archway in "On Some of the Old Actors," where a modern printer's occupation of an urban space signals the gap between beauty and utility, Elia watches in ironic horror as an industrial age develops beyond a tolerance for the "merely" ornamental. What distinguishes this style from aristocratic consumerism is that desire is accompanied by a knowing distance. Lamb/Elia's love of old things is to a degree a pose.

Along with this irony, one can see different criteria. For aristocratic collectors such as Heber (and "pups" such as Dibdin), an ultimately straightforward construction of the authentic object (in this case connoting the qualities of the historical—possessing a history and belonging to a tradition—and the preindustrial) determined worth, hence the special prestige of the manuscript copy, the first edition, and the vellum copy. For Lamb, by contrast, a book's status as a readily available commodity—replete with still-affixed price tags—had more worth than a book's distance from the mass market. This is not to say that Lamb's shelves were indistinguishable from those of a used book retailer of the early nineteenth century: his "ragged regiment of book-tatterdemalions" was neither simply new nor simply cheap.

Lamb's collection reflects the formation of an aura around the collectible book, but this aura is not the same one that has long determined value in aristocratic collecting circles. The criteria for collectability operating among more traditional bibliomaniacs speaks to what Walter Benjamin, in "The Work of Art in the Age of Mechanical Reproduction," calls the "aura" of the artwork. The books most sought after by aristocratic collectors share a signal characteristic: a unique existence in time and space. Benjamin says that such singularity "is the prerequisite to the concept of authenticity," a "presence" that is "outside technical . . . reproducibility."[125] Hence, within the world of aristocratic collecting, the collectability of manuscript copies (each being unique), first editions (rarer and often produced in smaller quantities than subsequent editions), and copies like the Roxburghe *Decameron* that for any reason had been rendered unique or rare. Sir Robert Cotton (1571–1631) organized his library solely around this criterion. As Basbanes says, Cotton "cared deeply for the welfare of documentary materials simply because they were irreplaceable, not for any political of theological positions they may have supported."[126]

Like the libraries of aristocratic collectors, however, Lamb's library conformed to an abstract system that shaped and regulated the contents of his collection in a way that differentiated it from an inventory of new, readily available "cheap books," to use the publisher Charles Knight's term from 1854.[127] Lamb's bibliophilia was instead an alternative mode of bibliomania—a practice on the margins of privilege that was nonetheless elite and distinguished itself from rather than approximated aristocratic practices and aesthetic standards. Lamb's differed markedly from the library of the aristocratic collector whose prize was the "irreplaceable" codex. Lamb's, by contrast, was full of books marked overtly by their circulation as readily available commodities—by tags indicating their exchange-values in a market.

Lamb's books also bore the marks of the individual histories of circulation—a "ragged" condition testifying to heavy use by multiple readers and movement within the market for second-hand books in London. The rapture of the anonymous author of the Dibdin Club's pamphlet at the long, mysterious histories of Lamb's ragged books speaks to the attractiveness of this down-market aura. These were books whose marks of distinction paradoxically constituted a refutation of distinction itself—a closing of the distance from circulation determinant in the aristocratic calculus of value. Lamb's books were marked overtly not by their mass appeal but by their distance from the elite distance from the social determinant of value in Dibdin's and Heber's worlds. This was consistent with Lamb's literary criticism, which, rather than embracing the common, rejected the rejection of the "mass of readers" by Coleridge. As in "Appreciation of De Foe's Secondary Novels," where a populist aesthetic identifies merit with popularity and the category of the "charming," in his collecting Lamb employed an aesthetic defined by its opposition to the standard of distinction fundamental to reigning standards.

Those price tags warrant further discussion. Lamb's books' signs of wear—an abstract value of use that was not a signifier of use-value but its opposite—were joined in Lamb's calculus of value by signifiers of commodification. Marking the status of Lamb's books as products intended for the rationalized market for commodities, the price tag marked Lamb's collectible book overtly as an object circulating within the social. In this way, the book collectible to Lamb might be said to be the polar opposite of the authentic art object—this object being, according to Benjamin, one whose authenticity derives historically from its original status as an object for use in magical and religious ritual.[128]

The criteria for determining value operative in aristocratic collecting circles, in the Romantic period and currently, show the circulation of such "cult value." This value has stemmed from art's occult lineage—the mystified "ritualistic basis" of art and foundation of the antique art object's aura of authenticity, a unique existence in space and time the high value of which speaks to the art object's origins in religious practice. This lineage explains the high value to bibliomaniacs not only of the unique edition but also of the perfect one. As Benjamin's theory suggests, the value of the auratic book, like the cult object from which it descends, is tied to its literal distance from the human and its metaphorical distance from human collectives such as mass movements and systems of exchange. Benjamin cites prehistoric cave paintings, whose intended audiences were "spirits" rather than humans, and modern religious practices involving representations of the Madonna: "Today the cult value would seem to demand that the work of art remain hidden."[129] This helps explain the high price fetched by the book unmarked by human hands—the "pristine" uncut copy free of "rubbing" and "bumped corners"—all being signs of human handling and use. Consequently, Lamb's "ragged regiment of book tatterdemalions" strikes a populist pose in duplicating-with-a-difference a practice descending from "cults" of exclusivity. Within Benjamin's historical narrative, the exclusivity surrounding this sacred function would eventually be undermined by the wide circulation of art made possible by its reproduction.[130] But Lamb's transformation of the collective into a sign in the context of his collecting style—its form being a badge taken from the marketplace—parodies this aura, resacralizing the book in a new way. A different sacredness, this was a fetish of the collective.

Lamb's deviations from established standards of value in his taste for the heterogeneous and "low" in literature and the commercial and "ragged" in books illustrate an opposition to dominant aesthetic values and norms. This opposition took the form not of explicit expressions of dissatisfaction or critique but of the subversive use of signs: the contradiction with the "aristocracy of culture," with its tastes for "high" diction (Coleridgean critical theory) and "pristine" uncut copies (aristocratic collecting practice), as elaborated through his collecting and criticism, was a style—simultaneously a mode of consumption and a semiotic system consisting of the commodities he consumed and the new ways these objects signified in the context of his antiquarian practices.[131] This *bricolage* was, like the punks', a practice of conspicuous consumption the internally coherent, intentional deviations of which from established modes and standards exposed aristocratic and bourgeois practice *as* cultural practice.

On the level of Lamb/Elia's prose diction, this punk and camp version of antiquarianism drew attention to the materiality of signifiers, creating dissident effects on the level of personal style and authorship. The heightened ornamentation of Elia's antiqued diction ("Yea, but [methinks I hear somebody object] if sobriety be that fine thing you would have us to understand") lends the voice a camp edge: the Elia voice is aggressively mannered, so there is something of the "residually pederastic" Restoration fop in Elia.[132] A kind of cabinet for old signifiers, Elia's material subjectivity gives a new form to the figure of the queer bookman. The ornamentation also lends to the voice a found, second-hand quality. Lynch has observed a general resistance to the author-function among Romantic writers for the magazines.[133] Lamb/Elia's antiquarian and, indeed, anthological voice (a collection on the level of diction) paradoxically makes a posture of unoriginality the source of "originality." The ostensible singularity of this authorial persona is ironic, illustrating a new way that the figure of the collector stood in contrast to the author-function. The Victorian reception of the Romantics offers another useful context for exploring the figure of the queerly bookish antiquarian. The period that ushered out Lamb enshrined Percy Shelley and Keats in the canon, and the literary societies instrumental to this process occasioned an ornamental community devoted to the Romantic corpus in the fullest sense.

NOTES

1. J. Lewis May, *Charles Lamb: A Study* (London: G. Bles, 1934), x.

2. Barry Cornwall, *Charles Lamb: A Memoir* (London: Edward Moxon & Co., 1866), 289, Google Books.

3. Cornwall, *Charles Lamb*, 298.

4. Cornwall, *Charles Lamb*, 303.

5. Leigh Hunt, *The Autobiography of Leigh Hunt: With Reminiscences of Friends and Contemporaries*, ed. Roger Ingpen (Westminster: Archibald Constable, 1903), 2.52, Google Books.

6. Brent Russo, "Charles Lamb's Beloved Liberalism: Eccentricity in the Familiar Essays," *Studies in Romanticism* 52, no. 3 (Fall 2013): 439, MLA International Bibliography.

7. Joseph E. Riehl, *That Dangerous Figure: Charles Lamb and the Critics* (Rochester, NY: Boydell and Brewer, 1998).

8. Tim Milnes, "Charles Lamb: Professor of Indifference," *Philosophy and Literature* 28, no. 2 (2004): 324. ProQuest Religion.

9. Milnes, "Charles Lamb," 324.

10. Lucas, ed., *Works*, 2.136; the essay first appeared in *London Magazine* in February, 1822.

11. J. C. Thomson, *A Bibliography of the Writings of Charles and Mary Lamb: A Literary History* (Bronxville, NY: N. T. Smith, 1979), 73; Lucas, ed., *Works*, 7.562.

12. George L. Barnett, *Charles Lamb* (New York: Twayne, 1976).

13. Simon P. Hull, *Charles Lamb, Elia and the London Magazine: Metropolitan Muse* (London: Pickering & Chatto, 2010), 55.

14. Philip Cox, "Keats and the Performance of Gender," *Keats-Shelley Journal* 44 (1995): 41–42, http://www.jstor.org/stable/30212992.

15. Cox, "Keats and the Performance of Gender," 55, 57.

16. Cox, "Keats and the Performance of Gender," 57.

17. Hull, *Charles Lamb, Elia and the London Magazine*, 57.

18. Lucas, ed., *Works*, 6.172 (emphasis original).

19. Francis Grose, *A Dictionary of the Vulgar Tongue: A Dictionary of Buckish Slang, University Wit, and Pickpocket Eloquence* (Project Gutenberg [1811] 2011), http://www.gutenberg.org/cache/epub/5402/pg5402.html.

20. Sarah Burton, *Double Life: A Biography of Charles and Mary Lamb* (London: Viking, 2003), 82.

21. Burton, *Double Life*, 83–84.

22. Burton, *Double Life*, 173.

23. Hull, *Charles Lamb, Elia and the London Magazine*, 61.

24. Hull, *Charles Lamb, Elia and the London Magazine*.

25. Charles Baudelaire, "The Painter of Modern Life," in *The Painter of Modern Life and Other Essays*, trans. Jonathan Mayne (London: Phaidon), 27–28.

26. Colin Campbell, *The Romantic Ethic and the Spirit of Modern Consumerism* (Oxford: Blackwell, 1987), 168–70.

27. Campbell, *Romantic Ethic*, 11, 182.

28. Bourdieu, *Distinction* (Cambridge, MA: Harvard, 1984), 11.

29. Pete Newbon, *The Boy-Man, Masculinity and Immaturity in the Long Nineteenth Century* (London: Palgrave, 2018); King, *The Gendering of Men*.

30. Thomas Hood, *The Works of Thomas Hood: Comic and Serious, in Prose and Verse, with all the Illustrations*, 12 vols. (London: Ward, Lock & Co., 1882–1884), 2.369n, Google Books. The context of the quote refers to the home's modest scale.

31. Lucas, ed., *Works*, 2.191. This is Thomas Westwood's description of the collection.
32. Monsman, *Charles Lamb as the London Magazine's Elia*, 44.
33. Lucas, ed., *Works*, 2.270.
34. Lucas, ed., *Works*, 2.231, 2.230
35. Walter Pater, *The Works of Walter Pater in Eight Volumes* (London: Macmillan, 1901), 5.109, Google Books.
36. Lucas, ed., *Works*, 2.83.
37. Stuart Piggott, *Ruins in a Landscape: Essays in Antiquarianism* (Edinburgh: Edinburgh University Press, 1976), 118–20.
38. Lucas, ed., *Works*, 2.1–2.
39. Piggott, *Ruins in a Landscape*.
40. Lucas, ed., *Works*, 2.97.
41. Wes Hill, *Art after the Hipster: Identity Politics, Ethics and Aesthetics* (Cham: Palgrave Macmillan, 2017).
42. Susan Sontag, "Notes on Camp," in *Against Interpretation and Other Essays*, ed. Susan Sontag (New York: Dell Publishing Co., 1969).
43. Lucas, ed., *Works*, 2.97.
44. Lucas, ed., *Works*, 2.99–100.
45. Gerald Monsman, *Confessions of a Prosaic Dreamer: Charles Lamb's Art of Autobiography* (Durham, NC: Duke University Press, 1984), 122.
46. Charles Lamb, *The Works of Charles Lamb* (New York: W. J. Widdleton, 1870), 3.141–42.
47. Lamb, *Works*, 3.138.
48. Lucas, ed., *Works*, 2.
49. Baudelaire, "Painter," 27.
50. Rudyard Kipling, "White Man's Burden," in *Kipling: Poems*, ed. Peter Washington (New York: Knopf, 2013): 96.
51. Samuel Taylor Coleridge, "Kubla Khan," in *The Norton Anthology of English Literature*, ed. M. H. Abrams et al. (New York: Norton, 1974), 2.309.
52. Bourdieu, *Distinction*, 487.
53. Max Weber, *The Protestant Ethic and the Spirit of Capitalism* (Los Angeles: Roxbury, 1996), 51.
54. John Keats, "Ode on a Grecian Urn," in *English Romantic Writers*, ed. David Perkins (Fort Worth: Harcourt Brace College Publishers, 1995), 1252–53, 1253.
55. J. E. Morpurgo, "Introduction," in *Selected Writings by Charles Lamb* (New York: Routledge, 2003), xi.
56. Lucas, ed., *Works*, 2.372.
57. Lamb, *Works*, 3.20.
58. Will Howe, *Charles Lamb and His Friends* (Indianapolis: Bobbs-Merill Co., 1944), 167.
59. May, *Charles Lamb: A Study*, ix.
60. May, 24; Winifred Courtney, *Young Charles Lamb 1775–1802* (London: Macmillan, 1984), 276, Google Books.
61. Courtney, *Young Charles Lamb 1775–1802*, 276.
62. Lucas, ed., *Works*, 1.133 (emphasis in original).

63. Morpurgo, ed., "Confessions of a Drunkard," in *Selected Writings by Charles Lamb*, 81.

64. Qtd in William Macdonald, "Preface," in *The Works of Charles Lamb*, ed. Macdonald (London: Dutton, 1903), 1.xvii.

65. Robert J. Frank, *Don't Call Me Gentle Charles!: An Essay on Lamb's Essays of Elia* (Corvallis: Oregon State University Press, 1976), 13.

66. Thomas Carlyle, *Reminiscences*, ed. James Anthony Froude (New York: Charles Scribner's Sons, 1881), 400, Google Books.

67. Dowling, *Hellenism and Homosexuality in Victorian Oxford*.

68. Edith Christina Johnson, *Lamb Always Elia* (London: Methuen, 1935), 141, Google Books.

69. Margaret Oliphant, *Annals of a Publishing House: William Blackwood and His Sons, Their Magazine and Friends* (New York: Charles Scriber's, 1897), 1.501.

70. Barnett *Charles Lamb and the Evolution of Elia*.

71. Lucas, ed., *Works*, 7.892.

72. Barnett, *Charles Lamb and the Evolution of Elia*.

73. Thomas Noon Talfourd, ed., *The Works of Charles Lamb: A New Edition* (London: Edward Moxon, 1848), 20, Google Books.

74. Lucas, ed., *Works*, 6.536

75. Thomas Hood, *The Works of Thomas Hood: Comic and Serious, in Prose and Verse, with all the Illustrations*, 12 vols. (London: Ward, Lock & Co., 1882–1884), 2.369n, Google Books.

76. Hood, *Works*, 2.199.

77. Lucas, ed., *Works*.

78. Lucas, *The Life of Charles Lamb*, 2 vols. (London: Methuen, 1905), 2.167.

79. Lucas, *Life*.

80. Lucas, *Life*.

81. Claude A. Prance, *Companion to Charles Lamb: A Guide to the People and Places 1760–1847* (London: Mansell Publishing Ltd., 1983), 370.

82. Lucas, *Life*.

83. Lucas, *Life*.

84. Lucas, *Life*.

85. Riehl, *That Dangerous Figure*, 20.

86. Riehl, *That Dangerous Figure*, 20.

87. Riehl, *That Dangerous Figure*.

88. Campbell, *Romantic Ethic*, 204–05.

89. Leon Trotsky, *The Spanish Revolution, 1931–39* (New York, 1973), 312.

90. Dick Hebdige, *Subculture: The Meaning of Style* (London, 1979), 17, 102–04, 91.

91. Campbell, *Romantic Ethic*.

92. Kevin Dunn, *Global Punk: Resistance and Rebellion in Everyday Life* (New York, 2015).

93. Tavia Nyong'o, "Punk'd Theory," *Social Text* 23.84–85 (2005). Academic Search Complete.

94. William Hazlitt, *The Spirit of the Age: or, Contemporary Portraits*, 2nd ed. (London: Henry Colburn, 1825), 403, Google Books.
95. Pater, *Works of Walter Pater*, 5.113.
96. Lucas, ed., *Works*, 2.55.
97. Lucas, ed., *Works*, 2.272.
98. Ferris, *Book-Men, Book Clubs, and the Romantic Literary Sphere*, 7, 5, 38 (emphasis in original).
99. Nigel Leask, *British Romantic Writers and the East: Anxieties of Empire* (Cambridge: Cambridge University Press, 2004), 205.
100. Lucas, ed., *Works*.
101. Lucas, *Life*, 2.271 (emphasis in original).
102. Lynch, *Loving Literature*, 131.
103. Qtd in Lucas, *Life*, 2.188–89.
104. Barnett, *Charles Lamb*, 95.
105. Barnett, *Charles Lamb*, 96.
106. Howe, *Charles Lamb and His Friends*, 114.
107. William Carew Hazlitt, *The Lambs: Their Lives, Their Friends, and Their Correspondents* (London: Elkin Mathews, 1897), 62–65.
108. Pater, *Works of Walter Pater*, 5.111.
109. Lucas, ed., *Works*, 2.295.
110. Riehl, *That Dangerous Figure*.
111. Irving Babbitt, *Rousseau and Romanticism* (Boston: Houghton Mifflin, 1919), 209, Google Books.
112. Immanuel Kant, *Critique of the Power of Judgment*, ed. Paul Guyer, trans. Paul Guyer and Eric Matthews (Cambridge: Cambridge University Press, 2000), 110.
113. Coleridge, *Biographia Literaria*, 2.52.
114. Lucas, ed., *Works*, 1.382–83.
115. Coleridge, *Biographia Literaria*, 2.43; Lucas, ed., *Works*, 1.539.
116. Coleridge, *Biographia Literaria*, 2.45, 2.48, 2.49 (emphasis in original).
117. Lucas, ed., *Works*, 1.382.
118. Bourdieu, *Distinction*, 3.
119. Bourdieu, *Distinction*, 4.
120. Lucas, ed., *Works*, 2.191, 2.271.
121. *A Descriptive Catalogue of the Library of Charles Lamb* (New York: The Dibdin Club, 1897), 12–13, Google Books.
122. *A Descriptive Catalogue of the Library of Charles Lamb*, 16.
123. Lucas, *Letters of Charles Lamb*, 3.39.
124. Lucas, ed., *Works*, 2.2–3 (emphasis in original).
125. Walter Benjamin, "The Work of Art in the Age of Mechanical Reproduction," in *Illuminations: Essays and Reflections*, ed. Hannah Arendt, trans. Harry Zohn (New York: Schocken Books, 1968), 220–21.
126. Basbanes, *Gentle Madness*, 89.
127. Charles Knight, *The Old Printer and the Modern Press* (London: John Murray, 1854), 246, Google Books.

128. Benjamin, "The Work of Art in the Age of Mechanical Reproduction."
129. Benjamin, "The Work of Art," 224–25.
130. Benjamin, "The Work of Art."
131. Bourdieu, *Distinction*, 11.
132. Morpurgo, ed., "Confessions of a Drunkard," in *Selected Writings by Charles Lamb*, 85; King, *The Gendering of Men*, 1.111.
133. Lynch, *Loving Literature*.

Chapter 4

Henry Buxton Forman and Thomas J. Wise, a Curious Pair of Bookmen

With the literary crimes of the book forgers Thomas J. Wise (1859–1937) and Henry ("Harry") Buxton Forman (1842–1917), dissident Romantic bookishness took a new form. Using a type of forgery invented by Forman, a radical publisher who edited standard editions of Keats and Percy Shelley, this pair of noted collectors and eminent bibliographers profited from their status in the literary world over the course of years of fraudulent production. They were innovators, contributing to the history of literary crime the creative forgery, or fake first edition—an unauthorized reissue with a false imprint giving it primacy in a text's publication history. Advances in forensic science, which made detecting the pair's forgeries possible, dramatically exposed Wise in his last years, a fate that Forman's earlier death spared him.

The roots of the bookmen's forgeries in Victorian antiquarian circles reveal a point of contact between the private press movement, the Victorian cult of the canonical, male Romantic poets, and a style of bookish dissidence traceable back to the Ladies of Llangollen and Dibdin's circle. Connections to Romantic bibliophiles illuminate an ornamental community extending across the century. An irony of the forgers' case is that the canonization of Romantics, including Keats and Shelley, owed a debt to the bookish fraudulence of a pair of collectors. In the spirit of Charles Lamb, the collectors exploited and exposed the discursive foundations of the author-function.

Like that of the other collectors discussed in this study, the pair's queerness is multifaceted and, to a certain degree, abstract. Lamb abstracted bibliomania to the realm of self-consciously dissident taste: bookish consumerism served Elia's eccentric worldview and style. In the case of Wise and Forman, bibliomania took the form of an editorial philosophy, a cult of authors, and a fraudulent mode of authorship—dissident bookishness in the form of production. As in other ornamental communities, in these men's world, dissidence was irreducible to conventional frameworks for understanding human sexuality. Their male love was bound up with and inextricable from book love.

More concretely, the tastes of this ornamental community enable one to chart a revolution in the collecting world since the days of the Ladies and Dibdin. On the one hand, the story of the dramatic rise and fall of the forgers illuminates broad continuities among bookish dissidents over the course of the century, in the sense that bookishness remained the ground of uncannily queer desire and the occasion of dissident community into the Victorian period. On the other, the story of the forgers, who were instrumental in the canonization of Romantic poets, speaks to the evolution of the symptomology of Romantic bibliomania. The forgers helped usher in and exploited a new taste in bibliophile collecting, one different from the affection of the Ladies, Lamb, and Dibdin for "black-letter lore" and Gothic culture. The ideological center of gravity of the antiquarianism practiced by the Ladies, parodied by Lamb, and celebrated by Dibdin, who "loved a lord almost as much as he loved an Aldine on blue paper," was located in the aristocracy, even if these figures did not all belong to this class or represent its values conventionally or uncritically.[1] As Lynch has noted, the publicity of aristocratic bibliomania provided by Dibdin had the unintended effect of "mainstreaming" the habit of book collecting, for example.[2] Compared to Dibdin's, the activities and taste of the forgers are more recognizable from a modern perspective, when first editions by recent or even living authors can be just as valuable as incunabula, auction culture is not a preoccupying theme of bibliography, and the public character of the literary world is not debated. Literary societies to which the forgers belonged sought to expand public appreciation for literature. Also, the men's collecting and celebration of rarities were but one element of a more abstract style of literary consumerism that nonetheless remain bookish—the celebration of authors. This fetishism of authors also had a dark side, as we will see. The forgers' taste for modern literature illustrates one way the story of their productions and criminal rise and fall outlines a modern form of queer ornamental community in the literary world.

In supporting this larger claim, this chapter first situates the forgers in the world of Victorian literary societies and sketches their biographies. The focus then shifts to Forman's bookish editorial philosophy and its antiquarian-inflected materialism, which put it at odds with the author-function. I claim that Forman's alternative view of cultural production shared with Percy Shelley a dialectical view of the creative process and stood in contrast to the idealist framework of singular authorship as theorized by jurists as well as by Wordsworth and Coleridge. Forman's views were consistent, furthermore, with his and Wise's collecting practices, which, as I next discuss, resembled the acquisitive yet compensatory, expressive, and subculturally binding activities of the Ladies and Dibdin's circle. Along with such queer implications of antiquarianism, the case of the forgers presents dissident implications unique to forgery, which are the focus of chapter's penultimate section. Finally, the chapter ends by recounting the strange tale of the forgers' exposure by a pair of intrepid booksellers in the 1930s.

A BOOKISH PARTNERSHIP

When the British Museum bought the library of Thomas J. Wise for £66,000 in 1937, the sale brought unflattering attention to the deceased collector. Announcing the acquisition, the *Daily Express* ran a less than subtle headline: "BRITISH MUSEUM TO GIVE BOOK FAKER MEMORIAL."[3] The breathlessness suggests that, even years after his exposure as a literary criminal, Wise's offenses could still shock. In 1934, a pair of enterprising booksellers, John Carter and Graham Pollard, published *An Enquiry into the Nature of Certain Nineteenth Century Pamphlets*, and with the innocuously titled book quickly toppled the eminent collector and scholar famed for bibliographies of modern authors and his *Ashley Library* (1922) collection of books and manuscripts. The fall of Wise shook the ground of the international collecting world: Wise had hoodwinked major U.S. collectors, including John Henry Wrenn, the Chicago businessman whose library established the renowned collections of the University of Texas at Austin.[4] Wise had advised Wrenn on many of his rare book purchases, and many of the UT library's rare items were revealed to be likely or certain fakes.

From then on, Wise's name would be synonymous with literary forgery, and Wise seen by many as the mastermind of the largest literary fraud ever perpetrated. There was still more to the story, however. Among its strange aspects is the fact that its scale became even grander as the years passed. As John Collins relates in *The Two Forgers: A Biography of Harry Buxton Forman and Thomas James Wise*, Wise gained an accomplice in the 1970s, when revelations about Forman revised his role in the pair's activities. Once considered at most an accessory, Forman was then credited with authorship of the plot. He, not Wise, had invented the pair's criminal innovation, the creative forgery, akin to a copy lacking an original.[5] Collins, one of the people responsible for exposing Forman, has helpfully compared this invention to the Piltdown Man forgery, whose human cranium and orangutan's jaw successfully filled the hypothetical gap between humans and apes for forty-one years until its exposure as a hoax in 1953. Like the Piltdown Man, Forman's creative forgery materialized "empty" bibliographical space through the production of a fake first edition of an already published text.[6] The forgers knew how easily one could detect fake books, but creating a new edition of a work precluded comparison to a real book, which often exposed traditional imitators.[7] To succeed, a creative forgery requires the falsification of publication history in the bibliographical record. Conveniently, both Forman and Wise were well-respected bibliographers. Among the passions the bibliographers shared was a love of Romantic culture and book collecting.

Long before they undertook their book fraud, the men's shared fondness for Romantic poets led them both to Frederick J. Furnivall and his literary societies, including the short-lived Shelley Society. Furnivall is generally remembered as an "eccentric" who published many reissues for which he wrote meandering prefaces.[8] Furnivall's editions of Chaucer and early English texts are well-known.[9] The Early English Text Society, probably the most influential literary society he headed, issued a facsimile edition of *Beowulf* edited by Julius Zupitza that was published in 1882.[10] An apostle and editor of early English literature, Furnivall championed the author-function and canonization more generally through energetic work establishing literary societies that celebrated authors and supported the emerging genre of author bibliography, a development that contributed to the canonization of Romantic writers and helped shape modern collecting habits.[11] Along with the New Shakespeare Society, to which George Bernard Shaw belonged, groups that Furnivall founded included the Wordsworth, Browning, and Shelley Societies.[12] The last he founded in 1886 with a widely reviewed performance of Percy Shelley's notorious verse drama *The Cenci, A Tragedy, in Five Acts* (1819).[13] Forman edited and wrote, with his brother Alfred, an introduction to a published version of the script.[14] The society's frequently told origin story concerned Furnivall's personal acquaintance with the Shelleys. As John Munro has recounted, Furnivall met Percy Shelley as a child in Egham, where Furnivall's father, a physician, treated both Mary and Percy Shelley and enjoyed spinning tales about the latter's vegetarianism and heterodox ideas about suicide.[15] William M. Rossetti was the group's chairperson.[16]

The society quickly attracted members, counting as many as 2,000 on its rolls according to club records, and plans formed for satellite groups in a number of cities around the world.[17] It disbanded in 1892, however, due to a lack of funds following a costly production of *Hellas* (1822).[18] Forman's father-in-law W. Sellé composed the score for the production.[19] Speakers at meetings of the society included Rossetti, B. L. Mosely, and Forman, whose talk at the group's inaugural meeting, "The Vicissitudes of *Queen Mab*," was attended by Shaw, who asked a question. A curious footnote to the story of the forgers is that Furnivall was among the first people to ask awkward questions about their illicit works.[20]

Wise and Forman's connection to Furnivall involved them in the broader canonization of Romantic poets that took place during the Victorian period. Furnivall's work has been called instrumental in the changing critical fortunes and increasing popularity of Shelley and Keats in particular. In *Dr. F.*

J. Furnivall: Victorian Scholar Adventurer, William Benzie describes how Furnivall's groups, like the Roxburghe Club in terms of the degree of influence they wielded on scholarship, differed in spirit from that club in being public-minded and outward-facing. Over the short life of the Shelley Society, for example, members planned or started off-shoots in Reading, New York, Auckland, and Birmingham. Through Furnivall's efforts to establish and expand the society, he championed greater public appreciation for Percy Shelley, and he lived long enough to witness and laud the fruits of this labor. "Now the tide of opinion is turning," he said approvingly, "towards reverence for Shelley's genius."[21]

Furnivall was not merely propagandizing, and the same could be said of other Romantics he championed. In *What the Victorians Made of Romanticism: Material Artifacts, Cultural Practices, and Reception History*, Tom Mole shows how Victorian editors such as Francis Turner Palgrave and Charles Mackay, while offering a distorted view due to moralistic editing and a "mismatch" between the anthology and volume formats, gave new life to Romantic writers by anthologizing their work for a broad audience habituated to the new leisure time. This reception of Romanticism "fostered ways of encountering and responding to" poets including Byron, Hemans, Keats, and Shelley. While offering a version of these poets that would have been unfamiliar to their first readers and that neglected many of the eventually canonical works, Victorian reissues gave the poets "wide cultural reach."[22]

Mole's observation that "the reception of literature is not itself always literary or literary-critical" applies aptly to the efforts of Wise and Forman, who employed unconventionally literary means to appreciate and transmit the works of the Romantics. Their licit and illicit "works" should be numbered among the objects and media that, along with the more typical modes of transmission registered by reception histories, formed the "web of reception," to borrow an apt phrase from Mole, that gave new life to writers in the Victorian period.[23] Wise and Forman did their first such work together— small-scale facsimile reproductions of Shelley's poetry—under the auspices of the Shelley Society in 1886.[24] Common among literary societies of the day, this type of private publishing is traceable back to Dibdin's Roxburghe Club. Many of the reprints that the two produced for literary societies were fairly unimpeachable, featuring clear indications of their real provenance. For example, they collaborated on a club-sponsored reissue of *Adonais* (1821), and Wise saw eleven more such legitimate reproductions through the press for the club. Forman's independent reprinting had considerable reach. His reissues of Percy Shelley influenced the international labor movement. Forman's cheap edition of *Queen Mab* (1813), the "Chartist's Bible," was known to Karl Marx, who observed its ubiquity among members of the movement.[25] Marx's daughter Eleanor Marx-Aveling quoted him as saying,

"Mr. Buxton Forman's collection of small, cheap copies [of *Queen Mab*], blackened with the finger marks of many heavy-handed tradesmen, are the proofs that Shelley became a power."[26]

Forman and Wise themselves came from the world of work. When they met, Forman was working for the post office, and Wise was climbing the ranks of the commodities firm of Herman Rubeck & Co. (also known as Rubeck's), traders in essential oils, where he had started out as an office assistant.[27] In the early 1890s, he was managing the company and acting as the cashier.[28] Letters to Wrenn and Sir Edmund Gosse about his work for Rubeck's paint a picture of someone with significant responsibilities. In 1906, he traveled to Spain to manage a distilling operation there, for example, and in 1914, he quelled a strike at the London company he led on the side with Otto Portman Rubeck, son of Herman.[29] During his tenure, the business derived significant profits from gaining a monopoly on vanillin, and he was able to retire in 1920, the owner of a large fortune.[30] His estate, excluding the value of his library, would total £138,000 upon his death.[31]

Aside from his initial work as a clerk at Rubeck's, relatively little is known about Wise's youth.[32] His grandfather, the first Thomas James Wise, was a silversmith. His father, Thomas James Wise II, called himself at various points a jeweler, tobacconist, and pencil case maker and married three times. Thomas James Wise III was born in Gravesend, England, in 1859 but grew up in the Holloway district of London. Wise's accounts of his education varied, and the version in which he attended the City of London School is unreliable. He probably attended the board school near his family home in Holloway.[33]

A precocious bibliophile and collector, Wise acquired his first rare books at seventeen. Like Charles Lamb, he started out by foraging through bins and dingy, tight stalls in areas such as Farringdon Road, Fleet Street, and the Strand. Unlike Lamb, he eventually graduated to the book dealers in the West end.[34] Although one should not rely on his recollections alone, he later said that first editions acquired in his late teens of Moore's *Epicurean* (1827) and *The Cenci* laid the foundation for the collection that would make his name.[35] This was the Ashley Library, the collection that, like Richard Heber's, was installed in the British Museum following his death, which was an honor all the more noteworthy for the fact that many of his crimes had by that time become known.[36] Wise's widow arranged the sale.[37]

Ashley Library, Wise's catalog of his Morocco-bound and gilt-edged collection, a project begun in 1905, made Wise's name in the rare book world.[38] Soon after the book's volumes began to appear, Wise received an Honorary Fellowship at Worcester College, Oxford, a profile in the 1925 *Who's Who*, and a seat in the Roxburghe Club—the last after the members made him swear (falsely, of course) that he had never profited from his collection: "[N]o man has ever regarded his books in a less mercenary manner than I have throughout my active life," he said.[39]

The admittance of Wise, praised by Richard Curle as the owner of "the foremost Private Library in England," into the Roxburghe Club provides a fitting capstone to a Dibdinesque career.[40] Wise was a bibliophile starting at an early age, his juvenilia portending bookish tendencies. He contributed to an elaborate periodical called *Pen and Pencil*, the manuscript magazine of the youth group of Camden Road Baptist Church. It features "printed rules and printed titles and half calf binding." Wise's contribution was a long poem, *Isandula*, that echoed Shelley: "That the weak are strong when oppressed by wrong / That the slave is for ever free." Wise also had printed a collection of poems entitled *Verses*. It appeared in multiple issues beginning in 1882. Notably, there were copies on lavender paper, vellum, and large paper.[41] The text also differed across the variants. Another youthful publication was more prophetic: an edition of a Romantic poem, Keats's "Ode to a Nightingale." Like *Verses*, this was privately printed by A. Fullford of King's Cross. Wise also experimented with facsimile reproduction as a young person by having J. W. Jarvis print a photolithograph of Dickens' *Sunday, under Three Heads* in 1884. He included his own preface and advertised a forthcoming bibliography of Keats, which appears not to have been completed.[42]

Relations formed through such objects left behind suggestive traces. A surviving copy from the 1886 edition of *Verses* (one of multiple editions) features a mysterious inscription to an unknown male recipient: "To my dearest friend from his 'Jonathan.'" The object may have been Walter B. Slater, to whom Wise had earlier inscribed a copy of *Verses* with "his friend's love."[43] In *Forging Ahead: The True Story of the Upward Progress of Thomas James Wise, Prince of Book Collectors, Bibliographer Extraordinary and Otherwise*, Wilfred Partington, a contemporary of Wise, seems unaware of any closeness between Slater and Wise, and he does not mention the inscription. He does devote much space to a description of an intimate friendship with a different man, Clement King Shorter, editor of the *Illustrated London News* and a neighbor to Wise on Ashley Road. A collector in his own right, Shorter gained fame for discovering Brontë juvenilia in the papers of the Rev. Arthur Bell Nicolls, briefly Charlotte Brontë's husband in the 1850s. A less august contribution to letters was his likely suggestion of *Ashley Library* as a title for Wise's catalog. Partington's broad (and, it must be said, phobic) hints as to the nature of their friendship suggest an intimacy of which the biographer claims first-hand knowledge. These "bosom pals" and "clinging pair of bookmen" recall for Partington a poem of Wise's in *Verses*, "Twin Souls," in which the poet imagines love in Platonic terms: "Two forms together clinging." They were "boon companion[s]" whose "merry company" allowed them to "relieve themselves from the tiresome poses that other contacts required: they could hail each other beneath their veneers." Partington recalls seeing "Tommy" and "Clem," their nicknames for one another, on weekly rendezvous. The two laughed and confided "like two lovers" in their visits to bookshops on the Strand. The exchange of literary rarities was a treasured ritual of these meet-ups. When it was Shorter's turn to pay the lunch bill he instead offered Wise a letter sent to him by George Meredith or Thomas Hardy, so Wise took to picking up the tab. The tension between Shorter and another Wise friend, Gosse, came to be the subject of gossip.[44] E. V. Lucas wrote some verses on the subject in *Punch* entitled "Woful [sic] Ballad of Failure."[45]

A more salacious anecdote on this theme relayed by Partington centers on Wise's allegedly exposing himself to male coworkers after a night of carousing. While discussing Wise's libertine side, Partington tells of a night spent with sailors from a steamship called the *Verona* in 1888. Wise's risky and, evidently, exhibitionist habits lead Partington to use a singular euphemism. He says that the day after such a night, Wise "insisted on showing the fevered instrument of mischance to his office colleagues, much to their embarrassment—males though they were." Partington plays the anecdote for laughs and does not provide a source.[46]

Perhaps feeling out of place among colleagues at Rubeck's, the bookish Wise did find friends in homosocial literary societies, where the love of literature was practically inseparable from love of the book-object. Wise became a member of the Browning Society in 1881 and joined its committee in 1884, giving him the privilege of meeting and interviewing Browning. Printing Wise oversaw for the society may have been his entrée to facsimile reproduction of modern poetry. In 1886, Wise edited for the society a facsimile reproduction of Browning's *Pauline* (1833) executed by Richard Clay & Sons, beginning Wise's connection to that company. At around this time, he met Furnivall and began collecting Shelley, so he was a logical choice to serve on the committee of the new Shelley Society. The association would prove unfortunate for the group. Wise embarked on an aggressive printing agenda that over seven years produced thirty-three books. Risky in itself, the plan was not helped when he billed a publication of his own to the society, had extra copies of other works printed from types paid for by the group, and sold these on the side to enrich himself. Wise's compulsive reissuing undid the society: the publications ultimately bankrupted the group and left it indebted to Clay. The debacle also left members in debt to Wise, because he had bankrolled some of the printing work. One embittered member complained in his diary portentously, "Wise is still proceeding on his wild career of reprinting or pirating Browning Shelley Swinburne &c." The episode would nonetheless leave Wise's reputation somehow undamaged.[47] Partington claims he examined the diary in person but was sworn to secrecy about the identity of the man, a well-known figure who belonged to both the Browning and Shelley Societies.[48]

Independently, Wise began an active business in reprints, duplications of expensive and rare books. A gifted speculator, Wise could capitalize on the new taste for bibliophile editions of works by modern writers. He reprinted short works in small editions of around thirty on paper and a handful on vellum, featuring clear indications of their actual provenance. These were cataloged by Wise in a way that shielded his enterprise from the appearance of a profit motive. A catalog Wise released at the time revealingly had the air of a defense: "The following list is printed as a Record, not by way of Advertisement." Authors Wise reprinted in these early years, the 1880s and 1890s, included William Morris, Edward Fitzgerald, and Andrew Lang.[49]

Wise met Forman in 1886, but Forman already knew of him.[50] Wise, who had read Forman's *Our Living Poets* (1871) as a young person, had written to Forman a fan letter in 1882 inquiring about the older man's progress on an anticipated bibliography of Shelley.[51] Forman's path to Shelley and collecting in general had been, like Wise's, indirect. Born the fifth child of a military doctor, he grew up in Devon. He started a career with the post office as a third-class clerk.[52] He would work there in various capacities from 1860 to 1907, including in the important post of surveyor of the British Post Offices in the Mediterranean.[53] There and generally, socializing presented challenges. Barker and Collins attribute this in part to his "intimidating" appearance. Acquaintances thought him "shy and secretive," and he counted the Canadian physician Richard Maurice Bucke, after whom Forman named his son, among his few friends. He did marry, and in the same letter to Bucke quoted above, he mentions the woman who would be his wife, Laura Sellé, the daughter of a German conductor and expat. They would have three children. Forman's work for the post office was not well paid, as he complained in letters to Bucke, and the most he could expect was £500. The job did put him in the company of other bookish men and relatives of well-known writers. These included the son and grandson of Leigh Hunt, the son of George Henry Lewes, Anthony Trollope, and Edmund Yates, editor of *Tinsley's Magazine* and *Temple Bar*. Forman for a time served as the Secretary of the Post Office Literary Society.[54]

Coworkers gave him access to London's literary scene, where he met George Eliot. Acquaintance with Eliot and Dante Gabriel Rossetti never flowered into close friendships, however, despite overtures to these figures as well as R. L. Stevenson, Tennyson, and Robert Browning. His relations with these and other literary figures never moved beyond a merely "formal" tone, as in the case of his correspondence with Swinburne and William Morris. He had ambitions of his own and drafted a long poem about Devon. He also published criticism, but his eccentric tastes had little influence. Pieces by Forman appeared in *Macmillan's Magazine*, the *Contemporary Review*, *Fortnightly Review*, *Tinsley's Magazine*, and *The London Quarterly Review*, but he found more success helping others see their work through to publication. Barker and Collins characterize this role as a feminized mode of surrogacy, or compensation for his own dreams of authorship. Generalizing from Forman's impersonal and unequal dealings with William Morris, they write, "He may or may not have realized his own lack of success as an interpreter of poetry, but, as the friend and confidant of poets, he turned from the intangible to the tangible."[55]

If editorship were for Forman a kind of second-chance lyricism, as this characterization suggests, the materiality of the literary would have been exceptional or compensatory rather than continuous with Forman's broader affective life. But we have seen that, in his "secretive," "awkward," and distantly "formal" relations with others, form was the content, as Edelman says of queerness in general.[56] While a person such as Lamb could make artifice into a socially and culturally powerful personality—the irony that was charming in Elia's mouth and humorous but sometimes confusing in Lamb's own—Forman's style seems not to have been playful or ironic. There being no acceptable social script available to him for a truer expression of self, his mode of self-expression could only ever seem scripted and artificial. This manner Forman shared with Wise, whose bookishness may have been similarly protective. An obituary published in the London *Times* describes Wise as "guarded" and "aloof from the themes of general conversation, but always . . . acute and tenacious as to all that concerned his beloved books."[57]

As in Wise's case, one finds traces of impossible and occluded desires in Forman's biography, throughout which books were a constant. Forman was an early and enthusiastic admirer of Whitman. He contributed to Bucke's *Walt Whitman* (1883) and collected the poet with dedication, acquiring not only the complete works but also a first edition *Leaves of Grass* (1855) and the notebook from Whitman's time as a military nurse during the Civil War. Bucke helped Forman build his Whitman collection, and the pair's correspondence reveals that Bucke fielded requests for Whitman items.[58] Forman wrote a brief biography of the poet for Lloyd Sanders' *Celebrities of the Century* (1887). Barker and Collins speculate that Bucke's request of Forman's help in obtaining a copy of Joseph Octave Delepierre's *Un point curieux* (1871), the first public discussion of sexual dissidence among the ancient Greeks, may have been made on behalf of Whitman. Evidently, Forman found the request shocking.[59]

Nonetheless, Forman's correspondence suggests that this interest resonated deeply. In 1866, he wrote to Bucke about his difficulty relating to women, with whom "so much care is wanted . . . that our friendship there is to a certain extent damped by anxiety to keep at exactly the right pitch of warmth." Bucke, however, has no reason to

> fear my becoming a renegade. . . . The fact is that life is not what it was in the glorious time we had with you, old fellow. Troubles and responsibilities increase on us all, I suppose; but at all events they have made not inconsiderable strides with us of late; and as I love the acquisition of knowledge of whatever sort more than anything else, I choose books for my anaesthesia.[60]

"I choose books": in a telling sentence, Forman identifies books as his compensation. For Forman, the love of books and Romantic literature in particular seems to have been a conscious form of recuperation for the loss of a wished-for but impossible mode of affective life.

Forman represented this impossibility publicly as well as privately. *The Books of William Morris* (1897) contains a dedicatory poem that casts Forman's feelings about Morris in dangerous terms. The first part of the poem describes Forman's memories of his son Maurice's reading Morris in Forman's library as a child, who "loved to walk about / the book-room mingling lore with chaff." Two stanzas memorialize a missed intimacy with Morris. In the first, the poet declares, "I grew to hold the man more dear / And ever loved the poet better." The second reads,

(Ah! Morris, it was well to know you—
Whatever comes of it, it was well—
Though dry the sprigs of bay I throw you,
Right fain were I to be your Boswell!)[61]

Without going into specifics, Barker and Collins say that with these lines Forman "came nearest to telling the truth about himself . . . with a candor that very nearly got him into serious trouble."[62]

Forman's fetishism of choice led him eventually to a position of eminence in editing British Romantics. The approach he took to the task was innovative and influential, while reflecting a philosophically materialist and bibliophilic perspective evocative of Romantic bibliography. Despite increasing responsibilities at the post office, he managed to produce a monumental edition of Shelley's poetry and prose beginning in 1876. A four-volume edition of the *Collected Poems* was followed by a four-volume set of *Prose Works* (1880). The eight-volume set went through multiple editions and became the standard edition of the poet for fifty years.[63] Illustrating the change in fortunes for Shelley that the collection helped usher in, the project's first reviewers expressed skepticism about Shelley's merit for Forman's pains.[64] The edition was also ground-breaking from an editorial viewpoint but, in a way that has been overlooked, traditional from a bibliophile and antiquarian one. Forman's innovative editorial methods can be seen as intrinsically Dibdinesque, because their innovations built on the materialist revolution that Dibdin's attention to the physical dimensions of the copy brought to bibliography.

Examination of the Shelley set reveals intersections between Forman's approach to editing and the bookish side of the pioneering Romanticist. Forman's innovative editorial philosophy can be called bookish because the approach relies on copies as they actually existed in time and space in order to create a text. While framed outwardly in terms of the poet's intentions, Forman's method of determining these was evidence-based and rigorously materialist. A later editor of Shelley wrote that Forman applied a "scientific exactness of method" in giving precedence to the "original" text and eschewing overt interpreting and correcting.[65] In the preface to the 1876 edition of the *Collected Poems*, Forman summarizes his goal as being "to put within the reach of students and the public generally as near an approximation as may be to the text that the poet intended to issue." Without polemicizing, Forman makes clear that the things the poet created with the aid of the press, not contemporary readers' tastes or their expectations fostered by contemporary publishers, have dictated the text he has put forth. In Shelley's case, this goal is difficult to achieve, Forman says, because manuscripts and revised proofs are unavailable in many cases. Strikingly, the solution Forman offers is an approach that is not necessarily true to the manuscript copy, which has not been Forman's basis for determining intentions; rather, the approach should be true to the corporate process of production as it should have taken place. Forman's preface merits quoting at length for a sense of this materialist and press-centric philosophy:

> Generally speaking . . . where there is no manuscript extant, the text as printed in Shelley's life-time must be accepted as the nearest obtainable approach to an authority; and even when there is a manuscript extant, it is by no means a final authority as a matter of course. The relative value of a poem as printed in Shelley's life-time and as written out by him must depend not only upon the revision of the press by the author or his substitute, but upon the technical quality of the printer's work, and the amount of care bestowed upon the manuscript. If the printed version is obviously a careless piece of typography, it loses much of its authority even if seen through the press by Shelley himself. This is preëminently the case with *Laon and Cythna*; and the extant manuscript fragments tend to shew that the printer had not one of Shelley's best manuscripts to work from. *Alastor*, on the contrary, seems to me a very creditable piece of printer's work, on the whole; and, if a manuscript of that volume were discovered, I should not expect it to authorize us in more than two important verbal alterations.[66]

Forman makes plain here that he does not need a manuscript in order to determine authorial intention and that even the former should be made subordinate to a "printer's work." What he needs ultimately is a good printer. On this score, "care bestowed upon the manuscript" is a key phrase because it recognizes any text as, to a degree, a joint production. The manuscript is not the final word but a preliminary step in a corporate process, a directive subject to further interactive work with a printer.

This emphasis in Forman's philosophy on the publication process and the physicality of culture extends to the book's arrangement of Shelley's works. The collection organizes the poetry by publication date, not by topics, titles, or themes, an innovative choice at the time. As Collins has noted, the set was also unique for the prominence of facsimile reproduction in the design, which featured minutely accurate duplications of original editions' title pages.[67] In Forman's hands, the quest for a correct, perfect text of Shelley was inextricable from bookishness, which, here, takes the form of theory: it is an editorial philosophy positing the objects and physical processes involved in the production of culture as the only practical purchase on an author. In short, Forman's overall approach reveals that he translated the bibliophile's notion of the perfect copy into a theory and mode of interpretation. The end-product was something philosophically at odds with the conceptual foundations of singular authorship, even as it collected an author's works and helped canonize him.

A useful point of contrast is Gerald Woodbury's 1892 edition of Shelley, in which Woodbury's preface offers a defense of more traditional editorial practices. In fact, Woodbury may be responding to Forman's edition when he justifies having used a heavy hand, without attention to manuscripts or proofs, in doing the editing:

> The punctuation has been revised. Shelley did not . . . give such attention to punctuation as to make it possible or desirable to follow his own hand; and, in such poems as were most carefully written in this respect, he practised a usage of his time that is perplexing or misleading to the ordinary reader accustomed to the habits of the press to-day.[68]

That Woodbury may be responding to Forman is perhaps clearer from the following passage, where he critiques the practice of including facsimile reproduction:

> The personal judgment of the editor counts for so much in any edition that a variorum text is the only just and perfect rendering of his poetry that is possible. Nevertheless, the reproduction of the originals, whether Shelley's own editions or his manuscripts or transcripts from them, need not be exact to the point of facsimile; and, with this view, it is here limited to what is material.[69]

With likely unintended irony, Woodbury calls materiality immaterial, echoing conventional Victorian moralism on the subject of literary materiality and suggesting just how radical Forman's approach was. As Price observes in *How to Do Things with Books in Victorian Britain*, "the book's physicality" was stigmatized during the period. Focusing on literature's treatment of book-objects, Price reveals that Victorian novels reify literature by making even the "awareness" of literary matter an index of characters' immorality.[70] This context illustrates how innovative and, from a mainstream Victorian perspective, even perverse Forman's privileging of materiality in his editing must have seemed to some.

Forman also presented his bookish, press-oriented theory in a talk for the Shelley Society. According to *The Notebook of the Shelley Society*, his lecture at the first meeting argued that, although *Queen Mab* provided a strong and rich foundation for the poet's later works, it deserved to be classed among his juvenilia. In making his case, Forman depicted Shelley not as the sole agency behind the poem but as a relatively helpless subject of the text and its printing history. Forman notes that Shelley denied responsibility for it by disowning it and professed ignorance of its meaning, calling it "worthless" and saying he "really hardly knew what this poem was about." In describing the textual history, Forman gives more agency to the poem than to Shelley, who is rendered as not so much the writer as the fosterer of the thing: "It was a work whose vitality he was powerless to check; a work which when he abandoned it proved that it had by no means abandoned him." In sum, Shelley did not own or control the poem that was foundational for the works that would amount to his major contributions. Human parties did wield power over *Queen Mab*, Forman suggested: the pirate William Clark, who made it more widely available, and the authorities who tried to quash it. The latter ensured its long life ("The ruling caste had not learnt that the only certain way of giving a book a career is to prosecute its author, publisher, or some one connected with it"). Forman included an edition of his own in this list of agencies ("Some years later, pocket editions were issued, intended for the use of the Radical mechanic") but did not take credit for it.[71] Although the overt topic of this talk was the proper status of *Queen Mab* in Shelley's oeuvre, the speech served as an opportunity for Forman to present a bookish, corporate view of authorship that minimized the singular author concept. In this manifestation, the theory is more far-reaching than elsewhere because, here, a text's production itself, independent of the printing and editing processes, is also a material process that can take place apart from and in spite of the text's ostensible author.

Another Romantic whose reception Forman influenced was Keats. This work took the form of multiple editions of *Letters of John Keats to Fanny Brawne* and *The Poetical Works and Other Writings of John Keats*. In editing the poet, Forman demonstrated the integral relationship in his process between editing and aggressive behavior on the market for literary rarities. He also articulated a philosophy that can be read as a bibliophile's idealism—Plato for the collector set. The importance of collecting in the work on Keats is clear from the story of Forman's acquisition of notorious unpublished correspondence. As Collins relates in *The Two Forgers*, Forman's editorship of Keats depended partially on the successful acquisition of the relevant and consequently infamous portion of Keats's correspondence relating to his scandalous relationship with Brawne, the black spot on the poet's Victorian reputation. This major acquisition Forman wrested from Fanny Brawne's descendants, enabling him to create what he referred to as a "perfect" text of the poet. A record of Keats's clandestine relationship with Brawne (1800–1865) existed in letters he wrote to her that Herbert and Margaret Lindon (children from her marriage to the businessman Louis Lindon) inherited upon Brawne's death. Brawne had earlier destroyed her own letters to Keats. With the ostensible purpose of suppressing them, Sir Charles Wentworth Dilke, grandson of Keats's friend Charles Wentworth Dilke, bought the letters along with other Keats memorabilia following Louis Lindon's death in 1872. When quotations from the correspondence began circulating, Herbert Lindon recovered it, and Forman obtained it thereafter. Forman may have encouraged Lindon to get the letters back from Dilke in order to buy them himself. Later, in 1890, Dilke claimed to Forman that he owned letters from Keats to Brawne that he had refused to return to Lindon; Forman tried but failed to obtain these for the second edition of the *Letters*.[72] At the time, Forman received criticism from many quarters for publishing the correspondence. Matthew Arnold and Swinburne were among the prominent figures who disagreed with the notion that the correspondence was required for a complete view of the poet.[73] Arnold described the publication as "inexcusable" and then quoted from one of the letters at length before dismissing it as "the love-letter of a surgeon's apprentice" and characterizing Keats's manner as "ignoble" and "underbred."[74] Forman defended himself from the attacks by writing in an 1895 edition of Keats's collected letters, "I still think Keats's letters without those to Fanny Brawne very much like *Hamlet* without the Prince of Denmark. When I made up my mind, after weighing the whole matter carefully, to publish those letters in 1878, I was fully alive to the risk of vituperation and not particularly solicitous on that branch of the subject."[75]

With *Letters of John Keats to Fanny Brawne* (1878, 1890), Forman demonstrated the dependence of his innovative approach to Romanticism on a collector's shrewd negotiation of the market for literary rarities and, hence, the blurred boundaries between collector and scholar as well as text and book.[76] The episode additionally reveals an irony of literary history: a bibliographer who theorized textual purity and helped canonize Romantic poets did so by relying on the skills of a savvy book collector and speculator (as in the case of the Shelley set, Forman's own money was at stake) with a willingness to defy Victorian sexual mores.[77] Forman's editorial framing makes plain the relationship between scholarship and bibliophile brinksmanship.

His brief introduction to the book justifies the publication of the letters by presenting them as a tool for enhancing critical understanding of the poet: "[W]e who love him unknown except by faith in what is written, must alike rejoice in the good hap that has preserved, for our better knowledge of his heart, these vivid and varied transcripts of his inner life during his latter years."[78] This justification further implies that bibliophile collecting of unpublished or suppressed documents by a poet, even on taboo subjects, is a moral good because it adds material to the only available source of love on the part of the audience ("what is written"), whose image of the poet is an act of "faith" in the archive. Correspondence has a privileged place in this spiritual dynamic between poet and audience because it paradoxically offers an unmediated relationship with the poet's inner life ("vivid and varied transcripts"). Forman justifies publication of the letters with the claim that the collecting of media is a process that, if perfected, can overcome the limitations intrinsic to media. In a letter to Fanny Llanos, Keats's sister, Forman casts this idea in terms of "perfect speech." The nature of perfect speech is such that an editor faces a choice between consigning the poet to "oblivion" and granting his "whole story to posterity." A partial portrait is no different than none.[79] Hence, as an editor, he was obligated "to gather together everything I could find from the hand of the poet, and to establish the text as nearly as possible in accordance with what the poet wrote or meant to write."[80] This is a bookish kind of idealism—a bibliomaniacal revision of phonologism in which pure speech is not opposed to media, as in Plato's *Phaedrus* (370 BCE), but the product of total ownership of a poet's archive.[81] Materiality is not distinct from the poet's "inner life" but the means of access to it.

However contrary a bibliomaniacal editorial philosophy may seem to the themes of canonical Romantic poetry, Forman's elevation of materiality can be seen as consistent with Shelley's thinking on medial materiality. Although the *Defence of Poetry* (1821, published in 1840) can be read as consigning materiality to the dustbin of the creative process (as in the line "Poetry . . . may be defined to be 'the expression of the imagination'"), this text and other philosophical works by Shelley, as Terence Allan Hoagwood argues in *Skepticism and Ideology: Shelley's Political Prose and Its Philosophical Context from Bacon to Marx*, can also be read as representing poetry as the product of an exchange between the self and the material circumstances and contexts of production. Reflecting the influence of ancient Greek thinkers, Shelley suggests that mind and matter exist in dialectical, rather than oppositional, relation.[82] Affirming Hoagwood's general thesis is the discussion of reason and the imagination in the *Defence*, where an Æolian harp serves as an analogical point of contrast. Unlike a human being, this instrument acts simply as a medium and, hence, produces only "melody." A human being, in contrast, is a medial substrate that does more than receive sense impressions. These impressions produce "harmony," meaning that, in receiving sense impressions, a human being in turn augments reality by producing culture, which is an effect of external reality as received and reproduced through the working of reason and the imagination ("apprehension"). (In Shelley's poem "Mutability" [1816], this process similarly appears as the sound of "forgotten lyres, whose dissonant strings / Give various response to each varying blast."[83]) Reality, now transformed by humans through culture, continues to act upon the human medium, which responds in kind, complicating the dynamic of sense impression and representation ("image") until these become indistinguishable. In a ringing sentence, Shelley suggests that medium and message exist not in opposition but in dynamic interplay: "language, gesture, and the imitative arts, become at once the representation and the medium, the pencil and the picture, the chisel and the statue, the chord and the harmony." Being among the impressions that apprehension transforms into culture, cultural materiality is not "mere" matter. In fact, the distinction between matter and spirit cannot theoretically hold.[84]

Forman's Shelleyan skepticism about absolute distinctions between literary materiality and ideality—and, hence, this theory's integration of materiality not simply as an adjunct to textual production but as a lauded means of access to poetic genius—is also notable for its inconsistency with the ideology of singular authorship. In *Fictions and Fakes: Forging Romantic Authenticity, 1760–1845*, Margaret Russett describes how this ideology, partly a product of the Romantic period, depended on a notion of immaterial authorial voice. Coleridge's *Biographia Literaria* contains the seed for the modern sense of this immaterial and inalienable artistic product, but Coleridgean originality, or "untranslateableness," was one strand of a larger discourse concerned with a distinction between public and private literary culture that relied on an opposition between matter and spirit. The juridical discourse on the question of literary property was similarly bound up with the theorization of the textual "spirit" (William Warburton's word), and this involved the denomination of the "merely" material dimensions of language. What Russett terms a "metaphysical division" between the material and the ideal, universally adopted despite its paradoxical implications, is perceivable as far back as William Blackstone's 1774 ruling on *Donaldson v. Beckett*. A thorny issue for jurists was positing a singular authorial subject, a supersensible agency apart from the work, while preserving the sense of language as capable of constituting a *work*. This presented a problem: if the author's idea is what should be regarded as unique, then in what consists the value of the material copy, which is at the same time the only tangible manifestation of the idea? Implicitly, a work, like land, was thought to be owned by virtue of authorial labor, reflecting Locke's theory of private property. Language, unlike land, could not simply be parceled out, however, so distinguishing the public from the private in this case presented a significant conundrum. How could an author's use of the common language—an author's plot of language—be enclosed? If what identifies a literary work as property is, to use a term from Blackstone's ruling, the "sentiment," then what renders the merely material, printed copy unique? Either the copy is an "impostor," or the author-function loses coherence.[85]

As Russett says, the strategies used by jurists to navigate this terrain varied. William Enfield distinguished between the common stock of words and unique thoughts, for example. For Enfield, literary property was a product of the animation matter by a spiritual agency. In a similarly Gothic vein, Wordsworth, in "Essays upon Epitaphs," theorized originality as ideas made incarnate in language.[86] The impact of these novel conceptions of authorship can be seen in the "new reading strategies" that appeared simultaneously.[87] As Martha Woodmansee argues in *The Author, Art, and the Market*, the "radically new" notional uniquity of the monograph—the Romantic author-function—spawned not just one strand of modern textual criticism but the guiding principle of all literary theory since the eighteenth century. This founding concept is the notion that the text conveys not a general truth with which a reader can identify and which is held to be representative but rather a glimpse at the interior life of "an Other." Pope's "Essay on Criticism" (1711) illustrates the former, neoclassical view by positing literary truths as mirror images of readers' minds. In contrast, Johann Gottfried Herder's theory of reading as a spiritual glimpse at an author's soul represented the theoretical innovation. The Byronic authorial persona could also be cited, because the instant celebrity of this notorious author—mad and bad, according to Lady Caroline Lamb—who in his self-representations also trafficked in the exotic, testifies to the pervasiveness of a mode of reading that posited an author who was, as Herder imagined, strange and utterly singular.[88]

More of a ghost than a divine spark, the spectral author hovering behind these theories of writing and reading illustrates the extent of the problem posed by the materiality of the literary for efforts to postulate an owner of signifiers. From a psychoanalytic perspective, as Russett observes, authorial incorporeality "*symptomizes* the repression" of the materiality of language, including the spoken word.[89] The phonocentric notion of singular authorship—founded on the concept of voice—codified in British copyright law and theorized by Coleridge resembles, then, a kind of neurosis. When Lord Charles Camden stressed the need for sure footing for rulings concerning literary property in "the old black Letter of our Law, . . . on some solid written

Authority, preserved in their books" he unwittingly wished to unleash the author's existential double.[90] This perverse literary Id, obverse of the "pure" and disembodied author, is the paradoxically empty, because too full, subject of the materiality of the literary. Another figure for this queer "subject" ("object" would be more apt) seems to have been a literary criminal. In the context of the copyright debate, the pirate played this role.

In the eighteenth century, what Woodmansee has termed "the debate over the book" (the ontological status of this *object* being central to the copyright debate) explicitly yoked the ideality of the literary to authorship and materiality to piracy. Opponents of the emergent conception of authorship, which in addition to spiritualizing literature imagined it as the outcome of an individual rather than corporate process and hence as the author's property, asserted that books were constituted by material elements rather than ideal ones. One anonymous such theorist of piracy (a "zealous mercantilist") is very plain: "The book is not an ideal object. . . . It is a fabrication made of paper upon which thought symbols are printed. It does not contain thoughts; these must first arise in the mind of the comprehending reader. It is a commodity produced for hard cash."[91] As such, an author has no claim to it once the manuscript leaves her hands.

Forman theorized authorial voice not exactly in the spirit of such apostates and criminals, but, as we have seen, his theory of editing, along with the view of authorship it suggests, made allowances for the unique material property of the collector, along with the unique ideal property of the author. In his theory and practice, authorial voice does not exist on a plane apart from the material. Instead, voice, while ideal, exists for posterity only in material form. Implicitly, collectors and editors have a crucial role to play in preserving materialized productions of genius. Poetic genius may be singular, but one's only access to it comes from material and corporate processes.

In light of his views on editing and authorship, Forman's enthusiasm, rather than shame, over the financial aspects of collecting and editing expressed in his correspondence are intellectually consistent with his views on the proper stewardship of classic texts and authors. In a letter to Bucke, Forman follows a list of his farsighted purchases of original editions of Shelley with the odd-sounding statement, "You will see I am in earnest about editing!"[92] The previous sentence of the letter brags of the bargain-basement price he had paid for a copy of "Rosalind" (Shelley's *Rosalind and Helen*?): "When I die, mine will likely fetch £5.5s!" For Forman (and perhaps also Bucke), it could go without saying that property speculation was integral to the editorial process. Collins' reading of this correspondence implies that such statements point to a criminality latent in Forman, a pathological personality that, like murder, would out, but one can also see such statements as illustrating the frankness and skepticism with which Forman viewed the roles of editor and author.

Similarly, the bibliomaniacal touches on Forman's legitimate productions drew attention to the materiality of the medium and enabled him to earn more profit from the works—perhaps to a degree more commensurate with the importance of editors' and collectors' roles in the production process as he represented these. These flourishes included special "short issues" (individual runs of facsimile reproductions included in his editions) that, like the creative forgeries to come, were speculative productions based on the principle of artificial scarcity. In the case of the edition of Shelley's complete works, Collins reasonably speculates that Forman proposed the printing of a vellum copy and "twenty-five special copies on Whatman paper in a white rather than blue binding," because, as Forman wrote to Bucke, "they will of course be eagerly taken up: 'short issues' always are."[93] Forman also had the text of *Epipsychidion* (1821) from his edition of Keats, including a facsimile of the original's front matter, printed separately in a batch of twelve in a variety of formats, including one on vellum.[94] In this process, one can see continuities between collecting, editing, and, as we will see in a moment, forgery. Collins implies that this kind of activity was parasitic or exploitative (Forman "milked [the edition of Shelley] for all it was worth"), which is true to the extent that the materiality of the literary must be seen as instrumental—more or less purely a substrate.[95] If, as Shelley says in the *Defence*, the imagination and the materiality of the medium are mutually constitutive and ultimately indistinguishable, however, then applying creative energy to the material dimensions of a work as Forman did can be seen as enlivening rather than corrupting. Forman's approach potentially enhances an audience's understanding of the totality of the creative process behind any work. The approach is also Shelleyan. In drawing attention to himself as a printer, editor, and collector, Forman also illustrates Shelley's suggestively social view of cultural production in the *Defence*, where culture appears not as a unique property of an individual but as an image of external reality that bears the imprint of societal influence, which is reflected by the poet. From this perspective, Forman's bibliophile aesthetic in the design of his editions of the Romantics and his "bibliophilic flourishes" come to seem less supplementary than collaborative.[96] Forman's attention to the materiality of the literary foregrounded the material, social, and external dimensions of the literary occluded by the author-function. Ironically, Forman himself, through his editing and bibliography, like Wise, profited from and supported the "author-reader dyad" in his collaborative editing and reprinting of other authors.[97]

In being guided by a social, printer- and press-centered, and materialist editorial philosophy and practice at odds with the author-function, Forman appears not only as an innovatively bookish editor of his own time but also as a fundamentally traditional bookman of the old school whose legal and extralegal works recall Romantic bibliography and the work of Dibdin in particular. Ina Ferris has insightfully argued in *Book-Men, Book Clubs, and the Romantic Literary Sphere* that the prominence of collaboration in Romantic bibliography—between printers and scholars, for example—contributed to the genre's negative reputation. Specifically, a source of Dibdin's and the broader bibliographical culture's provocation lay in its heretical mingling of univocal narrative with materialist, collaboratively produced printing history. Dibdin's works highlight their intertextuality and shared authorship. *Typographical Antiquities: Or, The History of Printing in England, Scotland, and Ireland* is an example cited by Ferris, who aptly calls it a "seamed" text and notes that Joseph Ames, William Herbert, and Dibdin all appear on the work's title page. Dibdin's collaboration with others and mixing of the cultures of the shop and the study brought the degraded work of printers and engravers uncomfortably close to the authorial plane—the literary proper. We have already seen how provocative, as well as uncannily queer, Dibdin's focus on shared male love of literary materiality was. More abstractly, Ferris says that Dibdin's focus on "the experience of print (letterpress, illustration, page) central to the experience of the book" was also problematic because it made the medium visible, troubling the ideological supports of the author-function.

Specifically, Dibdin's works are "odd hybrids" that merge the discourses of printing history and literature, challenging the notional invisibility of the medium linking authors to readers. Through attention to typography and ornaments and by employing in his productions printing history's anthological and joint model of production, Dibdin transgressed by bringing the material, workaday realm of the printer's workshop into contact with the ethereal plane of the properly literary arts. The irritation attendant upon this classed violation of the "protocols" of the Romantic cultural sphere received a tellingly harsh response from reviewers. Ferris quotes from a *Quarterly Review* piece about Dibdin that chastises him for "lower[ing] himself into a sort of walking puff for booksellers and book-collectors, engravers and auctioneers" and by failing to "exercise his own talents" exclusively in producing his tomes.[98]

The form taken by Forman's extracurricular celebration of Romantic authors reflected his Dibdinesque and material investments in the medium. He not only produced works in the spirit of Romantic bibliography but also made fetishism of authors a personal mission, extending his interest in the materiality of poetry to the physical lives of the poets whose texts he rendered hypermaterial. As Altick has noted, Forman and Wise were among the first to collect first editions by modern writers, but his collecting was remarkable in other ways, embracing relics associated with Romantic authors.[99] One such relic in particular points to the degree to which the repressed body of the literary should be seen as integral to these forgers' influential Romanticism.

When Forman's library was sold off in piecemeal fashion around 1920, some remarkable but conventionally desirable rare books and manuscripts, including *Queen Mab* in Shelley's hand and Keats's presentation copy of Hunt's *Foliage* (1818), came to light. A somewhat less conventional collectible was a part of Shelley's body, described this way: "portion of the remains of Shelley, after his cremation: in a cardboard box."[100] Indeed, collecting such relics and using them to adorn books was a curious habit of Forman's. Similar objects in his collection included a lock of Keats's hair and locks of Mary and Percy Shelley's hair, which he used to decorate Mary's account of Percy's death, and a gold watch once owned by Sir Timothy Shelley.[101]

In *The Hummingbird Cabinet*, Pascoe relates the story of Forman's competition with the U.S. collector Edward Silsbee for such Shelley relics from the collection of Claire Clairmont in Italy, which was in the possession of Claire's niece Paola at the time. An enthusiastic collector of Romantic relics, Silsbee owned one of the most-desired Romantic relics, the guitar Shelley gave to Jane Williams. Silsbee also notoriously inserted himself into the Clairmont family in the hope of acquiring a cache of Shelley rarities, including papers, an inkstand, notebooks, and even bodily remains. These machinations of Silsbee's inspired Henry James's *The Aspern Papers*.[102]

Pascoe describes the competition and ensuing bitterness that enveloped the eventual transfer of Clairmont's relics to Forman, who won out over Silsbee because the former could pay for the lot in cash. The items joined a collection notable for its association objects. Along with the Clairmont items, Forman owned "a toupee's worth of romantic hair" grown by the Shelleys, Allegra Byron, and Fanny Brawne.[103] As described by Wise in *A Shelley Library* (1924), a particularly unusual item was a book attributed to Mary Shelley, *The Last Days of Percy Bysshe Shelley, including an account of his Shipwreck and Cremation*, bound with a doublure (an ornamental lining) displaying pieces of Percy Shelley's skull. The volume is said to contain a letter from E. J. Trelawny to Jane Clairmont in which Trelawny writes of a gift of Shelley's ashes—the ones included in the doublure—and mentions that he has given Shelley's heart to Mary.[104]

Photographic reproductions of the book's cover in *A Shelley Library* reveal encased locks of hair and an urn-shaped doublure enclosing what appear to be arrayed bone fragments. Beneath is a label: "Fragments of the ashes of P. B. Shelley." Wise's description of the book reads in part:

> The volume is bound by Sangorski and Sutcliffe in ruby-red levant morocco, with dark green levant morocco doublures and silk fly-leaves. . . . Inserted in the end doublure, under glass in an urn-shaped frame, are the Ashes of Shelley (including a fragment of the skull) given by Trelawny to Claire. . . . The tiny

heap of Shelley's ashes, including fragments of his skull, inserted in the end cover of the volume, is an object of deep and pathetic attraction, and stands unique as a memorial of one of the greatest of the English poets. . . . It is sufficient to state that the ashes were given by Trelawny to Jane Clairmont at the time he was pressing his claims to her affection; that they were included in the sale of Claire's effects made by Paola Clairmont to Buxton Forman; and that from Forman they passed to me.[105]

As the description makes clear, Wise also eagerly collected Romantic relics. Wise almost certainly bound this ornate volume, as the style reflects his expensive taste and, as some of his contemporaries thought, ostentatious and irresponsible habits when it came to rebinding rare books. Pascoe opposes Wise and Forman's academic collecting of relics to the amateurish and generous enthusiasm of collectors such as Silsbee, who preferred to give away rather than hoard the association objects they collected. Pascoe suggests that such an attitude reflected a genuine appreciation of Shelley, whose poetry "advocates a lofty remove from earthly things." In contrast, the antiquarianism of Wise and Forman was "greedy," obsessive, and clinical in the way that it sought to capture and retain as much Shelleyana as possible.[106]

Although, as Pascoe says, the seemingly insatiable possessiveness of Wise and Forman has an air of "compulsion" and seems ungenerous compared to the actions of a benefactor like Silsbee, we have seen that conspicuous consumption can serve aims other than exclusive ownership or mastery.[107] Percy Shelley's own writing explores the expressive potential of materiality, and ornamental communities have indeed found the expressive aspects of consumerism useful in discovering and fostering common cause and identity. Poignant in the story of such communities bound by a love of literature is the evident fact that more conventional literary expressions of selfhood have been unavailable or impossible for dissident persons within these groups. Communities such as the one rooted in the Ladies' ornamental cottage in Llangollen have taken productive recourse to ironic appropriation of existing expressions of selfhood, in the process exposing and revising the rhetoricity and materiality of gender and self. In the case of Wise and Forman, one can identify a similarly productive intersection of dissidence and expressive consumption. As their joint forgeries reveal, a bookish and materialist mode of authorship exploited the author-function's reification of signifiers. Continuous with the collective fandom that initially brought the pair of collectors together, this unsanctioned echo of authorship embraced and reclaimed the materiality of the substrate *qua* substrate from the disembodied "voice" of the author-function.

FORGERY IN THEORY

Exploring the illicit work of Forman and Wise calls to mind the degraded and dissident status of materiality in the Romantic literary world, where many perceived the expression of material investment in literature as a badge of disqualification from authorship. The career of Keats is a case in point. Hostile critics writing for conservative publications such as *Blackwood's* and the *Quarterly Review* found ammunition in signs of his background, including "Cockney rhymes" and signals of a nonelite education.[108] Keats famously exposed himself in the sonnet "On first looking into Chapman's Homer" (1817), where the poet describes a grand tour strikingly and unapologetically different from the elite version. It has been a virtual and bookish one taken through an English translation of Homer: "Oft of one wide expanse had I been told / That deep-brow'd Homer rul'd as his demesne; / Yet did I never breathe its pure serene / Till I heard Chapman speak out loud and bold." Taking to the cultural ramparts in the last lines, the poet compares himself to the explorer and colonizer Hernán Cortés, who appears surrounded by a crew of other men eyeing each other "with a wild surmise" as they view the Pacific for the first time.[109] With this image, after confessing his doubly mediated access to classical culture, the poet boldly stakes a claim, seemingly on behalf of his class, to a literary career. As Susan J. Wolfson has observed, conservative critics responded to Keats by impugning his masculinity and questioning the legitimacy of Keats and the rest of the "Cockney school" of poets.[110] At issue in the attacks was the fact of his material interest in poetry—the ambition and need that reflected his class position. The attacks could be said to reflect the ideological structure of the literary field, materiality being the repressed foundation of singular authorship.

We have seen how Forman took a heterodox view on materiality as it related to authorship, offering Shelleyan skepticism about the author-function even as he contributed to the cult of Romantic poets and played a role in enshrining authors in the canon. In this section, I will explore ways that Forman and Wise's criminal activity in its own right can be seen as a heterodox, as well as dissident, echo of authorship. A superficial thread linking marginalized authors such as Keats to provoking materialists such as Forman and Wise was the thorny issue of material self-interest.

In the world of antiquarianism, mixing collecting and selling was verboten among collectors. Wise was a particular offender. However angrily he disputed Partington's suggestion that he was ever in the business of selling books ("This is a statement in keeping with his angry protestation to me: 'I am NOT a bookseller'"), it is difficult, as Partington says, to see another purpose for *Ashley Library*, the famous description of Wise's own collection that resembles an auction catalog.[111] Tellingly, Wise's framing of it offers defenses against any commercial intention. In the introduction to the 1922 edition, Richard Curle casts Wise as someone who puts value on a plane wholly above cost but, revealingly, cannot resist trumpeting Wise's profits from collecting and gifts as a speculator (Wise is "often ahead of his time and . . . able to buy the rarest of books at prices which now appear fantastically low"). Wise's collecting is said to be similarly disinterested, even altruistic. As "the most generous of collectors," Wise is doing a service to history, science, and the public by collecting and presenting his collecting in the form of bibliography: "[P]eople are learning more and more that scientific bibliography is not a mere fad of collectors of first editions, but that it affords unique glimpses of the inner story of the authors concerned."[112] In contrast, Wise's general style of collecting suggests disinterest in this inner story.

Defensive protests notwithstanding, both he and Forman sought to make literature into a profitable enterprise. It might be argued that Wise was more successful—because he was less scrupulous and more ambitious—than his collaborator. Even his legitimate literary activities bore the mark of the profiteer's agenda. This commodities broker who, lacking a share in Rubeck's, actually earned his considerable fortune from a potentially risky sideline—the capital-intensive business of manufacturing essential oils, in which he was a partner of Otto Portman Rubeck, the son of the owner of Rubeck's—likewise had an uncanny knack for successfully speculating on the market for rare books.[113] Luckily for Wise, he began collecting at exactly the time when rarities were still available at affordable prices while an increase in demand for them was readily foreseeable. First editions of Shelley's works, for instance, could be bought for as little as a shilling. Wise guessed correctly that such books in original condition or with association interest, as in the case of presentation copies, would soon be much harder to find and more valuable.[114]

Even in their above-board dealings, both Wise and Forman repeatedly broke this rule, but their tendencies were at least consistent. Forman's legitimate productions were similarly profane—heretically mongrel from the perspective of either the bookman or the scholar. Forman freely mixed the collector's "materialistic" priorities and values, such as profit and speculation, with the editor's supposedly pure investments. We have already seen how the books he designed, not unlike Keats's poetry, showcased the material investments and realities integral to their production. Dilke, with whom Forman had become entangled over some of Keats's correspondence, sneered that Forman was a "bookmaker" rather than a real intellectual.[115]

With this attack, Dilke summons the author-function's existential double, the creator of a book without text. In doing so, his comment hints at a broader set of ideas in which the forger and author both played roles. This double invokes both the *effeminatus* and the conservative stereotype of the Cockney author and appears in the annals of literary crime as the forger. The forger is kin to these other literary dissidents because a tradition has defined the figure in terms of material transgressions. Rather than a false claim of authorship, a falsification of the self, the forger's crime is a falsification of property and, specifically, documents. Consequently, as Anthony Grafton says in *Forgers and Critics*, a forger's crime more properly constitutes obscenity than theft: "[A] forger is in fact often caught because of the 'unnatural' relations between himself or herself and [a] document."[116] Like Thackeray's diagnosis of Squire Pitt's fetishism in *Vanity Fair*, the "unnaturalness" of the specific type of forgery committed by Wise and Forman, the creative forgery, a copy lacking an original, is encapsulated by the literal meaning of "obscene": "off-stage," or "out of place." Once identified, a creative forgery is obscene in an author's bibliography, and the creative forger, the author of a book but not a text, is similarly exposed.

If "unnatural," the forgery's obscenity is at least organic, because it suggests Jacques Lacan's notion of the "*sinthome*"—a pathology that is nonetheless the source of "consistency" and "support" in the world.[117] Forgery and, in particular, the creative forgery, traffic in the materiality of the literary, as Grafton has observed, while the author-function requires the repression of this.[118] In this light, the still relatively new status of the organization of the field around the author may explain the high pitch of the animosity directed at literary materialists of all stripes in the nineteenth century.[119] The reification of materiality in the context of the codification of authorial property—the *fetishism* identifiable in the construction of meaning as the singular, inalienable product of one mind—perhaps required the displacement of fetishism onto the figure of the alleged materialist, whose obscene relations with books contradicted yet enabled the modern concept of authorship. The history of literature reveals this relationship between forgery and authorship to be concrete as well as abstract.

Scholars who have studied literary forgery have pointed to the close historical relationship between forgery and authorship. As Russett has argued, early fiction shared many features with forgeries, including the found manuscript topos, impostor narrative, and false attribution (*The Castle of Otranto* illustrating all three). The genealogies of forgery and fiction are so intimately connected, in fact, that forgery arguably made the novel possible. Forgery, Russett says, "provided the conceptual measure against which the epistemological experiment of the novel could be understood." The relevance of forgery extends to the evolution of the author-function. The Romantic account of authorship, which emphasizes discovery and reception rather than labor, bears the hallmarks of forgery, which also posits the author as an accidental "inheritor." The forger Thomas Chatterton's manuscript "discoveries" are echoed not only by Walter Scott's story about happening upon the manuscript of *Waverley* in "an old writing desk" while looking for "some fishing-tackle" but also by Wordsworth's theory of poetry in *Lyrical Ballads* and "the Shelleyan account of labor as the recovery of buried inspiration."[120]

Being the right kind of alienated subject, the right kind of vacuum, the figure of the author uncannily resembles the forger, who could serve the notion of an alternative, obscene version of transmission identifiable as wholly unoriginal. Another materialist, the collector, played a similar role. As textuality was reified in the context of copyright law, the materiality of the literary could be displaced onto the disturbed mental landscape of the deviant—the subject of a "curious" affective life.

Like the collector and Cockney poet, the forger has been cast as the subject of pathological desires, and psychoanalysis offers a window onto this aspect of the forger's symptomology. In *Emotional Growth*, Phyllis Greenacre concludes that the impostor's symptom is the fetishism of materiality: he mistakes the penis for the phallus. The biographies of several famous impostors, including two forgers, support this generalization about the incomplete psychosexual development of impostors. Similarly to the posthumous Chatterton, Titus Oates (1649–1705), the probable mastermind of the "Popish Plot," lost his clergyman father (a "psychopathic scoundrel") to the separation of his parents at age six. The Formosan poser and friend of Johnson Psalmanazar, whose real name remains unknown, experienced the separation of his parents when he was six. Lastly, the presumed father of the coconspirator of Oates, William Fuller, died when the boy was six months old.[121]

Greenacre concludes that a subjective "incompleteness" can result, and imitative performance becomes the means by which the impostor copes with this deficiency in later life, imitating the father so as to kill him "symbolically." It is in this way that the chronic impostor continually restages the family romance. The resulting personality acquires a theatrical cast, charming in the adult, as "an interest in gesture and imitation" characterize the impostor's underdeveloped mode of engagement with reality.[122] Misidentification of the phallus also manifests itself in the role of material gain in a forger's works. Chatterton's inadvertent exposure to Horace Walpole of a financial motivation behind his invention of the fifteenth-century monk Thomas Rowley ultimately undid him: having received a positive reply from the antiquarian after sending Walpole a Rowley manuscript, Chatterton rashly followed up with a sad story and a plea for aid. Now skeptical, Walpole shared the manuscript with more knowledgeable friends, who spotted the forgery for what it was. To Greenacre, the false self-identification combined with a materialistic agenda marks Chatterton's fraud as typical of imposture. Rather than a normal identification with the father in the form of an ego-ideal, the impostor's desire for "material advantage" means the forger wishes "to rob the overthrown father of his penis, which, it is imagined, furnishes a better equipment than the inferior infantile one which the impostor feels himself to have." Unable to see himself as the creator of Rowley's works, Chatterton devised the monkish authority in order both to defeat the paternal power Rowley represented and to exploit his (imaginary) stature.[123]

Chatterton's incomplete development resulted in a bookish fantasy life. He showed his first interest in culture and forecasted his eventual career when he took an interest in trunks of "old parchments and ancient writings" thrown out by the Church of St. Mary Redcliffe in Bristol and in an "old musical folio" that his father had left behind. His mother said Thomas "fell in love with the illuminated capitals."[124] Hence, Chatterton's perversity seems polymorphous: his object was not simply the phallus—in Lacanian terms the "letter," or the "Master Signifier, the signifier of the symbolic authority founded only in itself"—much less his actual father; it was also the concretized letter, the materiality of the Master Signifier.[125] The case of Chatterton shows how, from a psychoanalytic perspective, forgery is bound up with literary fetishism, and the fetishism of the materiality of the literary is elemental to the forger's pathology.

Chatterton's love of the thing (rather than the Thing) puts him in the wrong in relation to subjective wholeness—an abjection that immediately calls to mind the axiomatic emptiness of other Romantic literary materialists and that offers a way toward some conclusions about the dissidence of this general typology. The *effeminatus*, bibliomaniac, and Cockney poet were dissident types defined by a sensuality that, in objectifying these subjects, actually verged upon the limits of the concept of the sensual itself, because sensuality assumes a feeling subject. As described by Lacan, the normal subject of the symbolic order is already empty. This "existential *cogito*," or subject "*qua* 0*,*" is in a constant state of becoming ("the subject can never fully 'become himself'") because he is a "void" that "ex-sists" as a negation ("as the void of a distance from the Thing").[126] Contrasted to this subject, the literary materialist, like a "doubting Thomas" who must put "[his] finger into the *print* of the nails," is paradoxically empty by virtue of lacking emptiness.[127]

Hence, the transcendental subject is haunted by a differently empty subject, which reflects the paradox located by Lacan at the foundations of subjectivity. Drawing on Marx's concept of the proletarian, Lacan identifies castration as a symptom of alienation (in Marx's terminology, objectification).[128] The "pure" subject is a castrated subject, a subject reduced to insubstantiality (being "devoid of all objective conditions of the productive process") by exchange. In Slavoj Žižek's words, "the paradox [of subjectivity] is that what is alienated (the dimension of subjectivity) is literally constituted by way of alienation." This is the source of castration anxiety, which reflects not a horrific other but the alienation of the self. As exemplary of castration, the woman is at once the pure subject of patriarchy and the return of the repressed: "she epitomizes what the Cartesian male subject . . . is compelled to 'repress,' namely the *Versagung* [frustration] which forms the hidden reverse of his freedom."[129] She returns the material conditions of subjectivity: market capitalism.

Rather than the return of the male subject's repressed objectification, or "pure" vacuity symptomatic of capitalist modernity, the imposturous forger, in his axiomatic emptiness, voices an echo, or "real" version in the Lacanian sense, of authorship—an absolute denial of the phantasmatic author-function, premised on the repression of materiality and the dream of singularity. In this way, the forger represents the apotheosis of the vexing materialists discussed in this study. This figure presents a modern form of the materialist's obscenity, or unnatural relationship to literature, because his dissident literary sensibility violates not only a norm but also the law. He, like the ornamental collector and bibliomaniac, is too interested in filthy lucre and too "curious" about "folded leaves," but he is also subject to a scientific and forensic regime. The story of Forman and Wise's fall reveals how this regime made the fetishist into a criminal.

FORGING AUTHORSHIP

Forman and Wise's illicit productions, which the two sold to credulous, often U.S. collectors, frequently for very large sums, exploited the "missing" links in the publication histories of, usually, contemporary poets such as Swinburne, Tennyson, Dante Gabriel Rossetti, and the Brownings. Unlike Chatterton, the pair posed as actual authors and falsified only books, not texts. These perfectly bookish works were continuous with Forman's innovative editing, because they arguably extended Forman's notion of pure speech to its logical conclusion: with the kind of forgery they pioneered, editing assumed something like the status of authorship, absent the production of text. Their first such project, undertaken in 1887, dealt with a Romantic, Percy Shelley. It reprinted in book form some works by Shelley that had just appeared in print for the first time in an 1886 biography of the poet by the Irish scholar Edward Dowden. For their spurious edition the pair invented an editor, "Charles Alfred Seymour," and made him a member of the equally imaginary Philadelphia Historical Society. The place of publication was not actually Philadelphia, as described, but the location of the printer Wise and Forman used for legitimate reprinting for the Shelley Society: London. Oblivious to their aims, the pair's usual printers, Clay and Sons, did the printing.[130] The paper, Whatman, is an English brand, but this is conveniently explained in "Seymour's" preface.[131]

This particular "first edition" has an unusual history, even for the forgers, because Wise later acknowledged and tried to explain it, using bibliography to construct his own responsibility rather than someone else's. As Partington says, the book tellingly lacks an entry in the 1905–1908 edition of Wise's *Ashley Library*, but the 1922–1936 edition includes a description in which Wise says that he, "Dowden, Rossetti, Forman, and *other friends*" wished to have the Shelley poems "in a convenient form," so they produced a reprint. Effectively laundering the forgery, Wise puts an innocent gloss on the false imprint and the fictitious Seymour by claiming that he and his friends had sought to shield themselves from the ire of Lady Shelley, who had "expressed dissent" with their plans even though "she held no interest whatever in the copyright of the verses." The story is typically weak on its face, as would become clear in the cases of other works years later when many similar forgeries came to light. Lacking any claim, why would Lady Shelley's permission have been sought at all? The forgery is typical for another reason: it was immediately suspect. Another continuity was Wise's chutzpah. Remarkably, he sent Dowden himself a copy of the forgery. In a letter thanking Wise, "a gentleman of the road," for the gift, the scholar not only exposes the fiction of any cooperation on his part but also hints broadly at what he suspects to be Wise's real game. Dowden asks Wise to send a barbed message to "Seymour," whom the scholar has clearly seen through: "He [Seymour] has done his work with the greatest care and correctness as far as I can see, and I hope you will greet him from me in the words of Shelley in his Homeric hymn which tells of the light-fingered doings of the first of pirates. . . . I will keep the veil of darkness over his misdeeds, but I fear I cannot help him to the 'other songs.'" As Partington observes, "No gentleman of the road, wise or unwise, could have mistaken the sarcasm here."[132]

Wise and Forman would become notorious for this kind of creative forgery, issuing fake first editions of dozens of works by mainly Victorian writers over the course of their illicit career.[133] In the process, they carved a parodic form of authorship out of bibliography, in their own way perfecting bookishness as a creative style. Through their rise and fall, they also performed a queer history of the author-function by revealing the workings of the discourse of authorship: a new form of forensic bibliography ultimately exposed them, turning the pair of eminent bibliographers and collectors into fraudulent producers. Their best-known work is probably the "Reading 1847" collection of sonnets by Elizabeth Barrett Browning, first published legitimately in the 1850 edition of Browning's *Poems*.[134] Due to the fame of the poems, the choice suggests the irrationality and provocation implicit in the pair's Keatsian claim to pseudo-authorship. This particular fraud, undertaken before the invention of methods to date paper, was so daring because it sought to capitalize on a work with a provenance narrative whose fame had already reached legendary proportions.[135] Fruit of "the most celebrated literary love story of Victorian England," the story of the book went that Elizabeth had composed its poems during Robert and Elizabeth's courtship in the home of her father, a star-crossed romance culminating in elopement and flight to Italy.[136] After they had arrived in Pisa, she shared the poems with Robert, who insisted on publication.[137] The means by which Wise and Forman inserted this pamphlet into history and ensured its value on the market for literary rarities, which would rise as high as $1,250, illustrates their methods.[138]

With the probably unwitting support of the writer and former Librarian to the House of Lords Sir Edmund Gosse, Wise publicized a new version of the work's printing history in order to account for the new first edition.[139] Gosse told the story in his introduction to Dent's 1894 edition of Elizabeth Browning's *Sonnets* and then three more times in *Critical Kit-Kats*.[140] Furnivall was an unwitting accomplice in spreading the tale. In it, upon first reading the poems over breakfast in Pisa in 1847, Robert passionately refuses to deprive the public of "the finest sonnets written in any language since Shakespeare's."[141] Soon Elizabeth's friend Mary Russell Mitford was enlisted to have some copies printed privately, but for an unknown (and inexplicable) reason sent the manuscript to Reading to have the printing done there, rather than in Italy where they were.[142] Then, rather than send all the copies to the Brownings to distribute themselves, as one might expect, she sent some copies to Dr. William Cox Bennett, Wise's stated source for his copy. The title page of the slender volume reads: "Sonnets/by/E.B.B./Reading/Not for Publication/1847,/an octavo of 47 pages."[143] The 1922 edition of *Ashley Library* contains detailed descriptions of multiple copies of the forgery and photographs of a copy rebound in Wise's flamboyant style.

Ashley Library was a source of Wise's fame in the collecting world as well as an authoritative source for information about rare books and manuscripts. Consequently, it could serve Wise, acting as his own fence, as a means of authorizing the forgeries. Wise's description of one copy of "Reading 1847" in the 1922 edition of *Ashley Library* illustrates how Wise used bibliography to insert spurious issues into publication histories and thereby profit from the forgeries. Most accounts of the forgeries neglect the specific ways Wise and Forman used bibliographic discourse, focusing instead on the fact of a forgery's appearance in a bibliography or letter. The *Ashley Library* description of "Reading 1849" includes a transcription of an "A. L. S." (autographed letter signed) allegedly inserted into the copy that contained "much chatty news about the Brownings." Below the transcription is a reproduction of a Mitford signature and handwritten date in 1854. Wise does not reproduce the rest of this manuscript. The revealing letter is said to be from Mitford, who died in 1855, to Dr. Bennett, who died in 1895, but they were not known to be very close, posing a problem for the narrative used to explain the forgery.[144]

Mitford is quoted, "Also I have a long letter from Mrs. Browning. They are kept in Florence for want of money, want so absolute that they cannot get to the Baths of Lucca. She says if it had been otherwise she would have come, if only to see me. The letter is really affectionate."[145] The letter serves the justifying notion that intimate ties bound the Brownings, Bennett, and Mitford, because it relays news of a letter of a highly personal nature from Elizabeth Browning to Mitford about the Brownings' financial hardship and mentions Bagni di Lucca, a place central to the romantic history of the "Reading 1847" sonnets.

This Browning forgery was the starting point for a pair of booksellers, John Carter and Graham Pollard, in their investigation of a number of suspicious pamphlets in the 1930s.[146] Carter and Pollard described later how their suspicions were raised initially while studying John Ruskin's bibliography. They noticed that two Ruskin pamphlets, *The National Gallery* (1852) and *The Queen's Gardens* (1864), had been identified as fakes around 1903 by the editors of the standard edition of Ruskin. Those editors, who had also come to suspect other Ruskin items, noticed that the texts of the works were based on subsequent, revised editions. Their discoveries had made no impact outside a small circle of Ruskin scholars, perhaps because Ruskin's collectability was waning.[147] Upon reading about the suspicious Ruskin pamphlets, Carter and Pollard were reminded of an uncommon series of events attracting notice in the rare book world: pristine first editions had been improbably appearing for sale in batches and winning large sums. Rumors swirled around the pamphlets in part because, improbably, none had been known of prior to 1880, and, despite being preprints, they lacked inscriptions.[148]

Carter and Pollard's investigation of the Elizabeth Barrett Browning sonnets yielded a puzzle in the sonnets' history. They learned that, in correspondence, Robert Browning said the romantic breakfast-table scene in which Elizabeth shared the poems with him took place in Bagni di Lucca in 1849, not in Pisa in 1847. Seeking confirmation, Carter and Pollard turned to an eminent authority on Browning bibliography, T. J. Wise, author of *Bibliography of the Writings in Prose and Verse of Elizabeth Barrett Browning* and *A Browning Library*. There, Wise tells Gosse's story from the 1894 introduction and explains that Wise paid Dr. Bennett all of £25 for his copy. Then, Bennett allegedly sold about a dozen more to other collectors. Wise's narrative made sense on the surface but raised questions. For example, who was Gosse's source for the printing history? He does not name the friend who supposedly told him about the pamphlet's being printed in Reading rather than Italy, where the couple was at the time. Carter and Pollard could neither find explanations for other odd parts of the story, such as Mitford's keeping copies logically intended for Elizabeth Browning and the gift to Dr. Bennett. Also, the Brownings never discussed the edition in their correspondence, no copy existed in Robert Browning's library, and the pamphlet's trail disappeared prior to 1885. Wise's story did not account for all the copies in existence by the early 1930s, and prior to the 1890s, the consensus among Browning scholars was that the sonnets' publication history began in 1850.[149] Turning to the extant copies of the suspicious pamphlets, the booksellers noted some striking anomalies. First, no presentation copies were known to exist, despite the fact that presentation copies are statistically more common in the case of privately issued books and that both Brownings left behind presentation copies of all their other works. Second, no copy contained period inscriptions or ownership marks of any kind, which, while suspicious in any case, was especially noteworthy in the case of a highly personal and rare gift such as each pamphlet would have been.[150]

Carter and Pollard had more reason than they needed to undertake a forensic analysis of the pamphlet. In the process, they created methods used to this day that, as Altick says, "now form an insuperable obstacle in the path of bookmen with intent to defraud." The pair's chief innovation was paper-dating. Previously, dating had only ever been applied to ink.[151] In writing the *Enquiry*, they conducted a history of commercial paper-making and concluded that paper containing esparto grass could not have been produced prior to 1861, nor paper containing chemical wood pulp prior to 1874 (Pollard later revising the latter date to 1883 based on new information, resulting in the identification of fifteen new forgeries).[152] Their methods for analyzing the paper were unavailable during the period when Forman and Wise produced the bulk of the forgeries.[153] Consulting chemists for microscopic analysis, they learned that the paper in "Reading 1847," along with twelve other suspected pamphlets, contained primarily chemical wood pulp, damning them all.[154]

Next, Carter and Pollard consulted the St. Bride Foundation Library in London in an effort to date the type. They learned that kernless fonts had not been in use by any printers prior to 1880. The innovation had come at the instigation of Richard Clay, founder of the company that would become R. Clay and Sons, on account of the fragility of kerned fonts. Armed with this information, the booksellers turned to the suspicious pamphlets and could identify sixteen as fraudulent, as all were kernless yet featured dates prior to 1880. A typographer named Stanley Morison, whom the pair had consulted, pointed out a quirk of the font used in "Reading 1847": the misaligned question mark. The unusual mark meant that the font was a hybrid combining fonts from two foundries in one particular way, narrowing the possible printers down to exactly one. Identifying the printer responsible for some or all of the pamphlets would help them track down the forger or forgers, but identifying the true printer based solely on a font seemed impossible. Luckily, the pair happened to be examining a reprint from the

1890s of a Matthew Arnold poem, *Alaric at Rome* (1840). They found the identical font, down to the atypical question mark. It had been edited by Thomas J. Wise and printed by Richard Clay and Sons in 1893.[155] Clay and Sons confirmed to Carter and Pollard that they were using the font in the 1880s, but, unfortunately, the company had lost all records of activity at the firm prior to 1911, so they could offer no information about the party behind "Reading 1847."[156] Clay was not under suspicion, and, given the amount of facsimile reproduction they had been doing, no one at the firm would have had any reason to view requests to print fictitious imprints with skepticism.[157]

Although they could not yet identify the forger, Carter and Pollard used this method to identify some 500 items as forgeries. Some were exposed not by chemical wood pulp but esparto. In the process, the men created a profile of their forger. This person would have had impressive knowledge of literary history and bibliography and known enough about the biographies and works of authors to insert relatively seamlessly a new work into a modern writer's bibliography and to choose a writer who, if living, would be unable or unwilling to expose the fraud. Even those then alive, such as Ruskin, debilitated by mental illness, could not refute the story concocted to legitimize the forgery. Being new first editions, the forged books could not be exposed by comparison to existing editions.[158]

Gradually, the amateur detectives built a case linking Wise to the suspicious first editions. Some of the evidence came from examining Clay's private printing for literary societies. Not only was facsimile reproduction a specialty of the firm, but it served the Furnivall's societies in their small-run reissues of rare texts. Among these, the Browning and Shelley Societies' reprints closely resembled the forged productions, and Wise had been responsible for some of the societies' works printed by Clay. Carter and Pollard also knew that Wise had acquired extensive experience doing this kind of legitimate work, seeing over 250 such reproductions through the press in his career. If the firm were innocent, which seemed all but certain, the guilty party must have been well-known to the company and seemingly trustworthy. Like Wise's history with Clay, Wise's efforts in the area of bibliography connected him to the forgeries. The authors of bibliographies that included the forgeries acknowledged Wise's assistance in writing their books; Wise himself along with William Robertson Nicoll published a book, *Literary Anecdotes of the Nineteenth Century*, that discussed the pamphlets; and Wise's many otherwise reliable contributions to the field of bibliography, including *Ashley Library*, integrated them into the relevant authors' bibliographies. Finally, Wise had donated copies of the suspect pamphlets to the collections of Cambridge University and the British Museum. In the process, as Altick says, they became "official."[159]

The circumstantial evidence linking Wise to the forgeries was by this time compelling, but Carter and Pollard had not yet discovered how the spurious editions first reached the rare book market. A curious aspect of the case was the fact that they appeared for sale in batches lacking ownership histories, as if some party were deliberately supplying the market. Clues from sales records eventually pointed to Herbert Gorfin, who assisted Wise in the bookselling and essential oils businesses as a young person. Initially a suspect, Gorfin ended up cooperating with the booksellers. Records he shared with Carter and Pollard revealed that he had unknowingly purchased hundreds of fakes from Wise over a three-year period. He had started out with Wise as an office assistant and salesperson who earned a commission from selling pamphlets.[160]

The eventual exposure of Wise was no less dramatic than the investigation. Armed with this evidence of Wise's closeness to the fraud, Carter and Pollard approached the seventy-four-year-old collector and shared their suspicions. They told him they intended to publish but, in fairness to the accused, wanted to include his version of events. Expressing shock, Wise pledged to consult his papers. Waiting for months but hearing nothing from him, Carter and Pollard went ahead, publishing their findings approximately eight months later with none other than Richard Clay & Sons. The case they presented took a subtle tack. Lacking direct evidence of Wise's personal involvement, the booksellers chose to declare the case inconclusive while painting Wise as a forty-year dupe of the unknown forger.[161] As Carter would say later in the *Atlantic*, "Mr. Graham Pollard and I did not . . . accuse Wise of being a witting accessory; nor did we suggest in print that he might actually have been himself the forger, in spite of our private conviction that he was."[162] They could not at that time demonstrate that, while being responsible for marketing, establishing, and promoting the forgeries, he also created them.[163]

The book, *An Enquiry into the Nature of Certain Nineteenth Century Pamphlets*, is a classic that makes "superb use of unrelenting, icily polite irony," making obvious that Wise was the culprit while understating the case against him.[164] As Carter later wrote, the book exposes upwards of fifty ostensible first editions of writers including, in addition to the Brownings, Rudyard Kipling, R. L. Stevenson, William Morris, George Eliot, and Algernon Charles Swinburne. Mostly "pre-firsts" in pamphlet form, the books had been seen as legitimate for a generation. In the wake of the book's revelations, the editors of the *British Museum Catalogue* revised the pamphlets' status in that record, a rare event.[165]

Before Carter and Pollard's book appeared, Wise tried to enlist Gorfin's help in creating an alibi, proposing a deal in which, in exchange for £400, Gorfin would return all his unsold pamphlets to Wise and back up a new explanation for the forgeries: the late Henry B. Forman was the real forger.

The forgeries had come to Wise from an unnamed agent who had tried to sell them to the firm of Robson's in London as publisher's remainders, but, Robson's not wanting them, the agent was referred to Wise, who bought the lot for £5.[166] Unbeknownst to Wise, Gorfin consulted Carter and Pollard, who advised him to accede to the request for the books but not the plan to blame Forman. Then, the book still not out, Wise mounted a self-defense in the *Times Literary Supplement*, presenting the story about Forman that Gorfin had already contradicted but citing Gorfin in support. Indignant, Gorfin published his own letter in *TLS* denying that Wise ever mentioned Forman's involvement prior to buying back the leftover pamphlets in 1933.[167] Wise was cornered, but his effort to blame Forman found support from a strange quarter, Forman's son Maurice Buxton Forman. The Keats scholar and George Meredith bibliographer wrote two public letters in support of Wise's overall argument implicating his father.[168]

As Carter would say later, Wise's tendered a weak defense; he clearly did not understand the forensic methods applied by Carter and Pollard to the forgeries. While signed by Wise, the letter was actually the work of Frederick Page of Oxford University Press, a Wise ally who approached Carter and Pollard after the letter had appeared, demanding to be shown records of their meetings with Gorfin. The booksellers shared their evidence with Page and cautioned that continued attacks on Gorfin or baseless accusations against Forman would result in the publication of yet more damaging evidence against Wise, including his efforts to pressure Gorfin. Page immediately changed course, breaking with Wise in a letter that unfortunately misrepresented Carter and Pollard's position.[169]

The prospect of Carter and Pollard's book raised many objections and defenses from powerful entities in the book world. Carter related later that the book's publisher was pressured if not threatened ("warned . . . in the friendliest and but weightiest way") to suppress it. Understandable questions were raised about Wise's possible motives. At the time, he enjoyed not only eminence but great wealth. Why would he have committed such reckless crimes? Carter observes that Wise had always dealt in rare books as a sideline and that in the 1890s Wise's financial situation was quite different. His income then amounted to only £500, and this had to support both himself and his wife.[170]

Among the revelations to follow from the book's publication was the discovery of new forgeries. Roland Baughman at the Huntington Library found a new fake first edition, of Tennyson's *Becket*, along with evidence that Wise attempted a traditional forgery—the faking of an existing book. Imprudently, the way he went about this was by copying and retailing his own *Alaric at Rome* reprint as the real thing in 1893.[171]

In the years after the exposure of Wise, potential coauthors were identified. The first was Forman. Evidence of his relationship to the forgeries came out after an article erroneously referred to in Carter and Pollard's *Enquiry* as the work of Nicoll and Wise, "The Building of the *Idylls*," was identified as actually being the work of Forman. Then, the noted collector Carl H. Pforzheimer found the proofs and manuscript for "The Building of the *Idylls*" in his collection. What he found shed light on Forman's role in the forgeries, but Pforzheimer suppressed their contents for the next ten years. Despite holding them back from the public for reasons only he knew, Pforzheimer invited Carter to inspect them but forbade him from publishing their contents. Carter could only say later that one document "convicts Wise in his own handwriting of the responsibility for one of the forgeries and includes Forman in the responsibility."[172]

Only in 1945 was Fannie E. Ratchford successful at persuading Pforzheimer to publish what the documents contained: a conversation between Wise and Forman that implicated both in an Alfred Lord Tennyson forgery. The eventual book, entitled *Between the Lines: Letters and Memoranda Interchanged by H. Buxton Forman and Thomas J. Wise*, included an introduction and notes by Ratchford and appeared from the University of Texas Press in 1945. It presents reproductions and transcriptions of interlinear conversations between Wise and Forman on proofs of a project being undertaken by them in collaboration with William Robertson Nicoll, *Literary Anecdotes of the Nineteenth Century*. This project's volumes—two only out of a projected ten—describe many forgeries, suggesting that one of its purposes was to authorize them.[173] In a foreword to *Between the Lines*, Pforzheimer only vaguely refers to the forgeries as a "sordid episode" and does not explain his delay in publishing the documents. He does suggest that he changed his mind due to "rumours about [the letters] which may have led to some erroneous inferences."[174] The introduction by Ratchford provides the history of Wise, Forman, and Nicoll's collaboration and appears intended to frame the "sordid episode" in a way favorable to Wise and harmful to Forman. She reads Forman's discussion of details of pamphlets—typography, printing history, textual variants—very closely, finding not a bibliographer's professional analysis but a veiled subtext of "bold" satire and malignant teasing of a collaborator.[175] Ratchford says that Forman's version of the story of the printing of "Reading, 1847" is similarly satirical and that his discussion of the forgery's typography was malignant in observing its difference from that of Elizabeth Browning's usual printer, Bradbury and Evans. When Forman says that a Tennyson forgery, *The Last Tournament*, is identical to other, legitimate works as far as "the lay eye" can see, this implies for Ratchford that Forman was tweaking Wise.[176]

Requiring no such analytical pressure is the trove's fairly damning exchange about how Wise intended to describe the size of print run of one of his legitimate facsimile productions. Forman takes issue with Wise's decision to understate the size of the run. Wise's response is striking. He writes dismissively, "Quite so. And we print 'Last Tournament' in 1896, and want 'some one to think' it was printed in 1871! The moral position is exactly the same! But there is no 'dishonesty'"[177] With that, Wise seals his and Forman's fates. The find was particularly notable because not only did it finally offer concrete evidence of Wise's guilt, but it also exposed Forman as an accessory if not an accomplice.[178] Ratchford uses this evidence of Forman's participation in *The Last Tournament* to paint him as an equal partner in every one of the forgeries. At the end of the introduction, she writes that a bibliographer and scholar such as Forman must have known the other forgeries, many examples being in his own library, by the same "peculiar hybrid font" of the Tennyson pamphlet.[179]

In revealing Forman's role in one forgery with near certainty, the discovery bolstered the case that Ratchford had already made against Forman, along with Gosse, in *Letters of Thomas J. Wise to John Henry Wrenn. A Further Inquiry into the Guilt of Certain Nineteenth-century Forgers* (1944). Carter publicized the discovery in his 1945 article while observing that "the degree and nature of [Forman's] complicity remain speculative."[180] He also points out that Ratchford "is naturally at pains to vindicate the main bulk of the Wrenn Library" at the University of Texas, where Ratchford worked: in his services to Wrenn, Wise "supplied perhaps three quarters of the volumes."[181] One way she could do that, Carter implies, is by expanding the circle of the guilty to a conspiracy, or, in Ratchford's terms, a "workshop."[182] Indeed, Carter remained highly dubious of Ratchford's argument implicating Forman and Gosse on the same footing as Wise. A damning remark in a proof aside, Forman was expected to have been able to make the distinction among typefaces that took decades, the skills of Morison, "the most expert living analyst of type," and the pure luck of Carter and Pollard's stumbling upon the same hybrid typeface in a legitimate reprint for the same distinction to come to light. This should have been believed along with the notion that possession of the forgeries was incriminating. If this were the case, Carter writes, then the British Museum, the Huntington Library, and the University of Texas Libraries all would be guilty.[183]

Scholars also debated Gosse's culpability. Ratchford's case against him hung on one handwritten word on a proof sheet of a forgery (Elizabeth Browning's "The Runaway Slave at Pilgrim's Point") and the fact that Gosse's history of *Sonnets from the Portuguese* served Wise's aims in legitimizing the "Reading 1847" forgery. Few saw the handwriting evidence as compelling. As Altick notes, the Texas Department of Public Safety declined Ratchford's request to undertake an analysis of the case when she brought it to that office, citing the small sample size.[184] William O. Raymond makes the point that the "s" in the word matches Gosse's initial "s," not his terminal one.[185] Pollard reviewed a copy of the specimen and found it more like Wise' handwriting than Gosse's.[186] The evidence against Gosse as an assistant in Wise's propagation of a false history for the *Sonnets* centered on the fact that Gosse aided Wise in spreading the lie about the earlier printing of the sonnets crucial to the success of the "Reading 1847" forgery. The story appeared in print on four separate occasions, and Gosse does not name his source. This can be attributed to Gosse's being the too trusting friend of Wise and does not automatically implicate him. The story Gosse also told about the writing, rather than the printing, of the sonnets raises a separate issue, which is the fact that, like Wise, Gosse misrepresents the circumstances of the composition (Pisa in 1847 rather than Bagni di Lucca in 1849) while attributing the information directly to Robert Browning. As Raymond says, there are reasons to think this was simply an error that actually predated the printing of "Reading 1847." For all his strengths as a writer, Gosse made errors of fact. Also, the Robert Browning biographer William Sharp, likely relying on Gosse's authority, made the same error in 1890, when Gosse could not have known about the forgery. It is perhaps more likely that Wise exploited the error than that Gosse coconspired, especially in light of Gosse's known criticisms of Wise's editorial carelessness and habitual reprinting of rarities that lacked complete and transparent publication information. Finally, letters between the two about four forgeries strongly suggest Gosse's complete ignorance of their status as such.[187] Carter reproduces two letters about a Ruskin, George Eliot, and Swinburne forgery in which Wise can be seen to employ the same tactics used on Wrenn and Gosse to be wholly duped. As Carter says, "If Gosse was a partner . . . why does he write in 1909 like a delighted amateur to a benevolent professional?"[188] While there is general agreement that Gosse did not conspire with Wise in or know about the forgeries, there is reason to think he lied in print to increase the value of rare Robert Louis Stevenson materials in Wise's collection.[189]

Another associate who has been accused subsequently is William G. Kingsland, who promoted Wise's productions in England and the United States. Kingsland also belonged to the Browning Society. As Lyle Kendall, Jr., has found, Kingsland used publications such as *Poet Lore* to advertise legitimate and illegitimate works by the pair. In fact, evidence suggests that his promotional copy about the "Reading 1847" sonnets in the pages of *Poet Lore* was the first published mention of that forgery.[190] The most noteworthy addition to the conspiracy was, of course, Forman. The Pforzheimer discovery did not establish Forman as a partner in the forgeries, but it removed any doubts about his knowledge of them. As Donald Gallup has written in "The Carter-Pollard 'Enquiry' Fifty Years After," a fuller understanding of Forman's role was not possible until the sale of his son Maurice Forman's library in the 1970s. His father's papers in the collection revealed that, if

Wise was the chief executor of the fraud, Forman had built the fortune. In fact, Forman could be called the "chief brains at the start of the whole enterprise."[191] These papers were made available to Carter and Pollard in 1972, when most of them were bought by Bernard Quaritch. Pollard and Quaritch collaborated on a catalog, and Carter and Pollard planned to issue a working paper and revision of the *Enquiry* in light of the new material. All the plans were halted by the death of Carter in 1975 and Pollard in 1976. Nicolas Barker and John Collins continued the work with Pollard's and the pair's executors' blessing. Barker and Collins soon discovered that the existing draft chapters could not be simply augmented by the new evidence, and they needed a fundamentally new approach. This would take the form of Barker and Collins's *A Sequel to an Enquiry into the Nature of Certain Nineteenth Century Pamphlets by John Carter and Graham Pollard* (1983).[192]

The new evidence suggested that Ratchford's overarching argument about Forman's being on equal footing with Wise, if not all her claims, was sound: Forman was the criminal genius who hatched the scheme. The conspiracy was also, as Ratchford had claimed, akin to, if not a "workshop," then a cottage industry. The fraud encompassed Forman's brother, Alfred, who worked in paper manufacturing.[193] As Gallup says, the first creative forgery the forgers produced, a new first edition of Richard Horne's *Galatea Secunda*, demonstrates Forman's role and the perverse or even inscrutable motives behind the frauds. Strangely, Forman seems to have deliberately chosen to use paper with a watermark dated 1873 for an edition featuring the publication date of 1867. Another production, a forgery of William Morris' *Socialists at Play* was just as puzzling. Its stated publication date was 1885, its paper dated 1896. Did Forman want to be found out?[194] The probing questions Forman asks in *Literary Anecdotes* about the pair's own forgeries, as noted by Ratchford, suggests the possibility.[195] The same could also be asked about Wise, whose behavior was in some ways even more reckless. He stole leaves from the British Museum and left them in the collection that he intended to bequeath to the same institution.[196]

This behavior raises questions about the pair's motives, which many have puzzled over. A crime requires a motive, but, in the case of literary crime, motive would seem to be as difficult to assign as a text's intention, because both require certitude about ownership of signifiers. Determining the motives of Wise and Forman would be as difficult as determining with certainty their "authorship" of the forgeries. The conventional way of discussing their relationship to the forgeries, which has been adopted here, reflects the most recent and agreed-upon convention, but the attribution represents a change and addition. Foucault observes in "What Is an Author?" that an author "is a function of discourse," and the evolving attributions of the works for which Wise and Forman have been held responsible testifies to the discursive quality of this attribution akin to authorship.[197] From one perspective, the new methods employed by Graham and Pollard, then by Barker and Collins, uncovered the fact of the pair's responsibility, and, hence, in a real sense, their authorship. But from another, despite their evident guilt, they could never be cited as guilty parties. Elizabeth Browning authored the "Reading 1847" sonnets, and nothing the forgers produced changed the nature of this relationship, just as William Clark's pirating of *Queen Mab* in no way challenged Shelley's designation as the author of that text. In a strict version of author-centric attribution, the only thing about a book that could "matter" would be the text. Neither Browning nor Shelley (nor any buyer of a pamphlet sold by Wise) could logically make a claim of harm. On the other hand, to propose Elizabeth Browning be held even partly responsible for "Reading 1847" might seem preposterous, but such would also be consistent with the author-function.

Granting the conventional distinction between text and book that has shaped discussion of the forgers, authorship nonetheless enters into the discussion of their works because they were, if not conventional authors, ironic ones whose books drew attention to the artifice of one of literature's sacred yet still relatively new dogmas. As collectors, editors, and bibliographers, they found a way to make a "virtue of necessity," as Bourdieu says of bohemians in *Distinction*.[198] They turned their second-class status relative to the author-function, their over-closeness to the materiality of the literary, into a profitable parody of authorship. These likely queer men simultaneously turned their palliative, compensatory bookishness ("I choose books") into a vehicle for powerful, if hidden and illicit, agency over those whom society had rewarded with wealth and standing. Forman had anticipated his invention of the creative forgery not just in his private reprinting but also in his editing, which offered a challenge to the author-function by drawing attention to the corporate, as opposed to singular, process behind printed works and emphasizing the materiality of the medium. The pair's ornamental culture—their work conducted under the sign of the fetish in the tradition of the queer collectors who came before them—recall camp aesthetics by appropriating and playfully degrading a legitimate form of art.

In the narrower context of Romanticism, intriguing about this case of literary fraud is the enmeshment of these fraudulent authors in the cult of the Romantic author produced during the Victorian period. While Collins has viewed the pair's forgery through the lens of addiction, one could also view it through the lens of Romantic canon-formation, which centered on fetishism, one form of which being the author-function itself. Forman, the "brains" behind the operation, was a devout fetishist of the canonical poets. Indeed, the adoration of Keats and Shelley, for instance, to which Forman in particular contributed through his legitimate collecting, editing, and reprinting, undoubtedly made the pair's crimes more profitable. More abstractly, the genus in relation to which the cult was a species, singular authorship, made possible the crimes and the identification of Wise and Forman as the criminals—the identification of them as the sole "owners" of the forged signifiers. What from one perspective was simply a criminal enterprise was from another perspective a capitalization on the author-function by people whose role in the literary field was to reify precisely this form of fetishism. What they exploited was the reification of signifiers into immaterial property in the juridical discourse of copyright, the foundational separation of author from medium and text from copy.

The forgery as they produced it was continuous with collecting. Collectors in general are parasites on the author-function who reclaim value for the copy from the text. They exist in an aftermarket for signifiers, a Fleet Street to the author-function's Piccadilly. Forman and Wise conceived of a way to author the copy but not the text, breaking the author's monopoly on signifiers and, in the process, replacing one form of fetishism, authorship, with another, forgery. In personal terms, their authorship of forgeries extended the Victorians' love of the Romantic corpus. In *Crimes of Writing*, Susan Stewart theorizes forgery as a crime of writing stemming from a problematic relationship to a document.[199] One could, following Stewart, call the forgers' relationship to documents emblematic of Victorian adoration of the Romantic poets—an exaggerated form of obsessive or possessive attachment that refused to be satisfied with only the Lacanian Real. They wanted the real, as well. Hence, their productions could be seen as an extension, not a perversion, of the Victorian celebration of the Romantics. They found a way to capitalize on the broader culture's possession of Romanticism.

NOTES

1. John Carter and Graham Pollard, *An Enquiry into the Nature of Certain Nineteenth Century Pamphlets*, ed. Nicolas Barker and John Collins, 2nd ed. (London: Scolar Press, 1983), 99.

2. Lynch, *Loving Literature*, 113.

3. Wilfred Partington, *Forging Ahead: The True Story of the Upward Progress of Thomas James Wise: Prince of Book Collectors, Bibliographer Extraordinary and Otherwise* (New York: G. P. Putnam's Sons, 1939), 272.

4. Richard D. Altick, *The Scholar Adventurers* (New York: Macmillan, 1950).

5. Collins, *Two Forgers*.

6. Collins, *Two Forgers*, 43.

7. John Carter, "Thomas J. Wise and His Forgeries," *Atlantic Monthly* (February 1945).

8. Hans Aarsleff, Rev. of *Dr. F. J. Furnivall: A Victorian Scholar Adventurer* by William Benzie, *Victorian Studies* 29, no. 1 (Sept. 1985): 176.

9. Aarsleff, Rev. of *Dr. F. J. Furnivall*, 176.

10. J. R. Hall, "F. J. Furnivall's Letter to the Royal Library, Copenhagen, Asking that the Thorkelin Transcripts . . .," *Notes & Queries* 45, no. 3 (1998), MLA International Bibliography.

11. Carter and Pollard, *Enquiry*.

12. Archibald Henderson, *George Bernard Shaw: Man of the Century* (New York: Appleton-Century-Crofts, 1956); John Munro, "Biography," in *Frederick J. Furnivall, A Volume of Personal Record*, ed. Munro et al. (Oxford: Oxford University Press, 1911).

13. Munro, "Biography."

14. *The Notebook of the Shelley Society*, ed. the Honorary Secretaries (London: Reeves and Turner, 1888).

15. Munro, "Biography."

16. Henderson, *George Bernard Shaw*.

17. *The Notebook of the Shelley Society*.

18. Munro, "Biography."

19. Barker and Collins, *A Sequel to an Enquiry into the Nature of Certain Nineteenth Century Pamphlets*, ed. John Carter and Graham Pollard (London: Scolar Press, 1983).

20. Lyle H. Kendall, "The Not-So-Gentle Art of Puffing: William G. Kingsland and Thomas J. Wise," *The Papers of the Bibliographical Society of America* 62, no. 1 (1968), http://www.jstor.org.uri.idm.oclc.org/stable/24301873.

21. William Benzie, *Dr. F. J. Furnivall: Victorian Scholar Adventurer* (Norman, OK: Pilgrim Books, Inc.), 251–52.

22. Tom Mole, *What the Victorians Made of Romanticism: Material Artifacts, Cultural Practices, and Reception History* (Princeton, NJ: Princeton University Press, 2017), 187, 195.

23. Mole, *What the Victorians Made*, 2, 3.

24. Collins, *Two Forgers*, 75.

25. Henderson, *George Bernard Shaw*.

26. Henderson, *George Bernard Shaw*, 148.

27. Barker and Collins, *Sequel to an Enquiry*.

28. Partington, *Forging Ahead*.

29. Barker and Collins, *Sequel to an Enquiry*.

30. Barker and Collins, *Sequel to an Enquiry*.

31. Partington, *Forging Ahead*, 271.

32. Collins, *Two Forgers*, 102, 66.

33. Barker and Collins, *Sequel to an Enquiry*.

34. Partington, *Forging Ahead*.

35. Barker and Collins, *Sequel to an Enquiry*.

36. Partington, *Forging Ahead*; Collins, *Two Forgers*.

37. Donald Gallup, "The Carter and Pollard 'Enquiry' Fifty Years After," *Papers of the Bibliographical Society of America* 78, no. 4 (1984).

38. Collins, *Two Forgers*.

39. Collins, *Two Forgers*; Partington, *Forging Ahead*, 232.

40. Richard Curle, "Introduction," in *The Ashley Library: A Catalogue of Printed Books, Manuscripts and Autograph Letters Collected by Thomas James Wise* (London: Printed for Private Circulation Only, 1922), 1.vii.
41. Collins, *Two Forgers*, 67.
42. Barker and Collins, *Sequel to an Enquiry*.
43. Collins, *Two Forgers*, 73.
44. Partington, *Forging Ahead*, 102–3.
45. E. V. Lucas, "Woful Ballad of Failure," *Punch, or the London Charivari* 161 (July 13, 1921), http://www.archive.org/details/punchvol160a161lemouoft.
46. Partington, *Forging Ahead*, 72.
47. Barker and Collins, *Sequel to an Enquiry*, 48.
48. Partington, *Forging Ahead*.
49. Barker and Collins, *Sequel to an Enquiry*.
50. Barker and Collins, *Sequel to an Enquiry*.
51. Collins, *Two Forgers*.
52. Barker and Collins, *Sequel to an Enquiry*.
53. Collins, *Two Forgers*.
54. Barker and Collins, *Sequel to an Enquiry*, 27, 26.
55. Barker and Collins, *Sequel to an Enquiry*, 28, 30.
56. Barker and Collins, 27; Edelman, *Homographesis*.
57. "Mr. T. J. Wise," *The Times (London, England)*, (May 14, 1937): 17, Times Digital Archive.
58. Collins, *Two Forgers*, 213, 33.
59. Barker and Collins, *Sequel to an Enquiry*.
60. Collins, *Two Forgers*, 39–40.
61. Harry Buxton Forman, *The Books of William Morris* (London: Frank Hollings, 1897), Google Books.
62. Barker and Collins, *Sequel to an Enquiry*, 39.
63. Collins, *Two Forgers*.
64. Barker and Collins, *Sequel to an Enquiry*.
65. Thomas Hutchinson, "Preface," in *The Poetical Works of Percy Bysshe Shelley* (London: Henry Frowde, 1905), vi, Google Books.
66. Harry Buxton Forman, "Preface," in *The Poetical Works of Percy Bysshe Shelley*, ed. Harry Buxton Forman (London: Reeves and Turner, 1876), 1.xi, 1.xii, Google Books.
67. Collins, *Two Forgers*.
68. Gerald Woodbury, "Preface," in *The Complete Poetical Works of Percy Bysshe Shelley*, ed. Gerald Woodbury (Boston: Houghton, Mifflin and Company, 1892), 1.viii, Google Books.
69. Woodbury, "Preface," 1.vii.
70. Leah Price, *How to Do Things with Books in Victorian Britain* (Princeton, NJ: Princeton University Press, 2012), 77.
71. Anon., *Notebook of the Shelley Society*, 26, 28.
72. Collins, *Two Forgers*.
73. Barker and Collins, *Sequel to an Enquiry*, 33.

74. Matthew Arnold, *Essays in Criticism*, ed. Susan Sheridan (Boston: Allyn and Bacon, 1896), 33.
75. Harry Buxton Forman, ed., *Letters of John Keats* (London: Reeves and Turner, 1895), xiv, Google Books.
76. Collins, *Two Forgers*.
77. Barker and Collins, *Sequel to an Enquiry*.
78. Harry Buxton Forman, ed., *Letters of John Keats to Fanny Brawne: Written in the Years DCCCXIX and MDCCCXX and now Given from the Original Manuscripts* (New York: Scribner, Armstrong, 1878), x, Google Books.
79. Collins, *Two Forgers*, 53.
80. John Keats, *The Poetical Works of John Keats*, ed. Harry Buxton Forman (London: Reeves and Turner, 1884), xvii, Google Books.
81. Jacques Derrida, *Of Grammatology*, trans. Gayatri Chakravorty Spivak (Baltimore, MD: Johns Hopkins University Press, 1976).
82. Terence Allan Hoagwood, *Skepticism and Ideology: Shelley's Political Prose and Its Philosophical Context from Bacon to Marx* (Iowa City: University of Iowa Press, 1988).
83. Percy Shelley, "Mutability," in *The Poetical Works of Percy Bysshe Shelley*, ed. Harry Buxton Forman (London: Reeves and Turner, 1876), 1.52.
84. Percy Shelley, "A Defence of Poetry," in *The Works of Percy Bysshe Shelley in Verse and Prose*, ed. Harry Buxton Forman (London: Reeves and Turner, 1880), 7.100–102, Google Books.
85. Russett, *Fictions and Fakes*, 72, 76, 77.
86. Russett, *Fictions and Fakes*.
87. Woodmansee, *Author, Art, and the Market*, 55.
88. Woodmansee, *Author, Art, and the Market*, 55.
89. Russett, *Fictions and Fakes*, 78 (emphasis in original).
90. George Ticknor Curtis, *A Treatise on the Law of Copyright in Books, Dramatic and Musical Compositions, Letters and Other Manuscripts, Engravings and Sculpture, as Enacted and Administered in England and America; with Some Notices of the History of Literary Property* (London: A. Maxwell and Son, 1847), 65, Google Books; Russett, *Fictions and Fakes*.
91. Woodmansee, *Author, Art, and the Market*, 47, 49.
92. Collins, *Two Forgers*, 45.
93. Collins, *Two Forgers*, 47.
94. Collins, *Two Forgers*.
95. Collins, *Two Forgers*, 47.
96. Collins, *Two Forgers*, 47.
97. Ina Ferris, *Book-Men, Book Clubs, and the Romantic Literary Sphere*.
98. Ferris, *Book-Men*.
99. Altick, *Scholar Adventurers*.
100. Altick, *Scholar Adventurers*, 213.
101. Barker and Collins, *Sequel to an Enquiry*; Collins, *Two Forgers*.
102. Pascoe, *Hummingbird Cabinet*.
103. Pascoe, *Hummingbird Cabinet*, 171.

104. Thomas J. Wise, *A Shelley Library: A Catalogue of Printed Books, Manuscripts and Autograph Letters* (New York: Haskell House Publishers, 1971), 9–10.
105. Wise, *Shelley Library*, 11.
106. Pascoe, *Hummingbird Cabinet*, 11, 172.
107. Pascoe, *Hummingbird Cabinet*, 172.
108. [John Gibson Lockhart], "On the Cockney School of Poetry. IV," *Blackwood's Edinburgh Magazine* 3, no. 17 (August 1818): 522.
109. Keats, *Poetical Works of John Keats*, 54.
110. Susan J. Wolfson, "John Keats," in *The Cambridge Companion to English Poets*, ed. Claude Rawson (Cambridge: Cambridge University Press, 2011).
111. Partington, *Forging Ahead*, 121–22.
112. Curle, "Introduction," viii, ix.
113. Collins, *Two Forgers*.
114. Partington, *Forging Ahead*.
115. Collins, *Two Forgers*, 52.
116. Grafton, *Forgers and Critics*, 24.
117. Slavoj Žižek, *The Sublime Object of Ideology* (London: Verso, 1989), 75 (emphasis original).
118. Grafton, *Forgers and Critics*.
119. Price, *How to Do Things with Books*.
120. Russett, *Fictions and Fakes*, 14, 29, 28, 29.
121. Greenacre, *Emotional Growth*, 100, 538, 102, 94, 101, 95, 102.
122. Greenacre, *Emotional Growth*, 102, 101, 507, 103.
123. Greenacre, *Emotional Growth*, 512, 105.
124. B. P. Carton, "The Palace of Art," *Irish Monthly* 17, no. 315 (Sept. 1899): 456, 454.
125. Slavoj Žižek, *Enjoy Your Symptom!: Jacques Lacan in Hollywood and Out* (London: Routledge Classics, 2008), 119.
126. Žižek, *Enjoy Your Symptom!*, 207.
127. *The 1769 King James Bible*, John 20: 25 (emphasis added), https://en.wikisource.org/wiki/Bible_(King_James)/John#Chapter_20.
128. Žižek, *Enjoy Your Symptom!*, 196.
129. Žižek, *Enjoy Your Symptom!*, 196–97.
130. Partington, *Forging Ahead*, 56.
131. Collins, *Two Forgers*, 81.
132. Partington, *Forging Ahead*, 56–57.
133. Altick, *Scholar Adventurers*.
134. Collins, *Two Forgers*.
135. Altick, *Scholar Adventurers*.
136. Collins, *Two Forgers*, 105.
137. Carter and Pollard, *Enquiry*.
138. Altick, *Scholar Adventurers*.
139. Fred B. Warner, "'The Hanging Judge' Once More Before the Bar," *The Papers of the Bibliographical Society of America* 70, no. 1 (1976), http://www.jstor.org.uri.idm.oclc.org/stable/24302258; Collins, *Two Forgers*.

140. W. O. Raymond, "The Forgeries of Thomas J. Wise and Their Aftermath," *The Journal of English and Germanic Philology* 44, no. 3 (1945), http://www.jstor.org.uri.idm.oclc.org/stable/27705213.
141. Collins, *Two Forgers*, 105–7.
142. Altick, *Scholar Adventurers*, 41–42.
143. Collins, *Two Forgers*, 107.
144. Altick, *Scholar Adventurers*.
145. Thomas J. Wise, *The Ashley Library: A Catalogue of Printed Books, Manuscripts and Autograph Letters Collected by Thomas James Wise* (London: Printed for Private Circulation Only, 1922), 1.97.
146. Altick, *Scholar Adventurers*.
147. Carter and Pollard, *Enquiry*.
148. Altick, *Scholar Adventurers*.
149. Altick, *Scholar Adventurers*.
150. Carter and Pollard, *Enquiry*.
151. Altick, *Scholar Adventurers*, 43.
152. Carter and Pollard, *Enquiry*; Barker and Collins, *Sequel to an Enquiry*.
153. Carter, "Thomas J. Wise and His Forgeries."
154. Carter and Pollard, *Enquiry*.
155. Carter and Pollard, *Enquiry*.
156. Altick, *Scholar Adventurers*.
157. Carter and Pollard, *Enquiry*.
158. Altick, *Scholar Adventurers*.
159. Altick, *Scholar Adventurers*, 52.
160. Altick, *Scholar Adventurers*.
161. Altick, *Scholar Adventurers*.
162. Carter, "Thomas J. Wise and His Forgeries," 93.
163. Carter, "Thomas J. Wise."
164. Altick, *Scholar Adventurers*, 54.
165. Carter, "Thomas J. Wise."
166. Carter, "Thomas J. Wise."
167. Altick, *Scholar Adventurers*.
168. Carter, "Thomas J. Wise."
169. Carter, "Thomas J. Wise."
170. Carter, "Thomas J. Wise," 94.
171. Carter, "Thomas J. Wise."
172. Carter, "Thomas J. Wise," 97.
173. Fannie Ratchford, "Introductory Essay," in *Between the Lines: Letters and Memoranda Interchanged by H. Buxton Forman and Thomas J. Wise* (Austin: University of Texas Press, 1945).
174. Carl Pforzheimer, "Foreword," in *Between the Lines*, xi.
175. Ratchford, "Introductory Essay," 7.
176. Ratchford, "Introductory Essay," 9.
177. Harry Buxton Forman and Thomas J. Wise, *Between the Lines*, 31.
178. Altick, *Scholar Adventurers*, 61.

179. Ratchford, "Introductory Essay," 11.
180. Raymond, "Forgeries of Thomas J. Wise"; Carter, "Thomas J. Wise," 97.
181. Carter, "Thomas J. Wise," 97.
182. Carter, "Thomas J. Wise," 100.
183. Carter, "Thomas J. Wise," 98.
184. Altick, *Scholar Adventurers*.
185. Raymond, "The Forgeries of Thomas J. Wise."
186. Carter, "Thomas J. Wise."
187. Raymond, "The Forgeries of Thomas J. Wise."
188. Carter, "Thomas J. Wise," 100.
189. Warner, "'Hanging Judge' Once More Before the Bar."
190. Kendall, Jr., "The Not-so-Gentle Art of Puffing."
191. Gallup, "Carter and Pollard 'Enquiry' Fifty Years After," 455.
192. Barker and Collins, *Sequel*.
193. Gallup, "Carter and Pollard 'Enquiry' Fifty Years After."
194. Gallup, "Carter and Pollard 'Enquiry' Fifty Years After."
195. Ratchford, "Introductory Essay."
196. Gallup, "Carter and Pollard 'Enquiry' Fifty Years After."
197. Foucault, "What Is an Author?," 1628, 1629.
198. Bourdieu, *Distinction*, 220.
199. Susan Stewart, *Crimes of Writing: Problems in the Containment of Representation* (New York: Oxford University Press, 1991).

Bibliography

Aarsleff, Hans. Rev. of *Dr. F. J. Furnivall: A Victorian Scholar Adventurer* by William Benzie. *Victorian Studies* 29, no. 1 (Sept. 1985): 175–78.

Abrams, M. H., E. Talbot Donaldson, Hallett Smith, Robert M. Abrams, Samuel Holt Monk, Lawrence Lipking, George H. Ford, and David Daiches, eds. *The Norton Anthology of English Literature*. 3rd ed. 2 vols. New York: Norton, 1974.

Allan, David. *A Nation of Readers: The Lending Library in Georgian England*. London: The British Library, 2008.

Altick, Richard D. *The English Common Reader: A Social History of the Mass Reading Public, 1800–1900*. Chicago: University of Chicago Press, 1957.

Altick, Richard D. *The Scholar Adventurers*. New York: Macmillan, 1950.

Appadurai, Arjun. "The Thing Itself." *Public Culture* 18, no. 1 (2006): 15–21.

Arnold, Matthew. *Essays in Criticism*. Edited by Susan Sheridan. Boston: Allyn and Bacon, 1896.

Babbitt, Irving. *Rousseau and Romanticism*. Boston: Houghton Mifflin, 1919. Google Books.

Barker, Nicolas and John Collins. *A Sequel to an Enquiry into the Nature of Certain Nineteenth Century Pamphlets by John Carter and Graham Pollard*. London: Scolar Press, 1983.

Barnett, George L., *Charles Lamb*. New York: Twayne, 1976.

Barnett, George L., *Charles Lamb and the Evolution of Elia*. Bloomington: Indiana University Press, 1964.

Basbanes, Nicholas A., *A Gentle Madness: Bibliophiles, Bibliomanes, and the Eternal Passion for Books*. New York: Henry Holt, 1995.

Basbanes, Nicholas A., *Patience and Fortitude: A Roving Chronicle of Book People, Book Places, and Book Culture*. New York: HarperCollins, 2001.

Baudrillard, Jean. *The System of Objects*. Translated by James Benedict. London: Verso, 1996.

Beckford, William. *Rare Doings at Roxburghe Hall. A Ballad*. London: J. F. Dove, 1821.

Benedict, Barbara M. *Curiosity: A Cultural History of Early Modern Inquiry*. Chicago: University of Chicago Press, 2001.

Benjamin, Walter. "The Work of Art in the Age of Mechanical Reproduction." In *Illuminations: Essays and Reflections*, edited by Hannah Arendt, translated by Harry Zohn, 217–52. New York: Schocken Books, 1968.

Benzie, William. *Dr. F. J. Furnivall: Victorian Scholar Adventurer*. Norman, OK: Pilgrim Books, Inc., 1983.

Bourdieu, Pierre. *Distinction: A Social Critique of the Judgement of Taste*. Translated by Richard Nice. Cambridge, MA: Harvard University Press, 1984.

Brant, Sebastian. *Ship of Fools*. Edited by T. H. Jamieson. Translated by Alexander Barclay. Edinburgh: William Paterson, 1874. http://www.gutenberg.org/.

Brideoake, Fiona. "'Extraordinary Female Affection': The Ladies of Llangollen and the Endurance of Queer Community." *RAVON*, 36–37 (November 2004, February 2005). http://www.erudit.org/revue/ron/2005/v/n36-37/011141ar.html?vue=resume.

Brideoake, Fiona. *The Ladies of Llangollen: Desire, Indeterminacy, and the Legacies of Criticism*. Lewisburg, PA: Bucknell University Press, 2017.

Brown, Bill. "Objects, Others, and Us (The Refabrication of Things)." *Critical Inquiry* 36, no. 2 (Winter 2010): 183–217. http://www.jstor.org/stable/10.1086/648523.

Brydges, Sir Samuel Egerton. *The Autobiography, Times, Opinions, and Contemporaries of Sir Egerton Brydges*. Vol 2. London: Cochrane and McCrone, 1834. Google Books.

[Buckingham, James Silk?]. Rev. of *Roxburghe Revels*. *The Athenæum* 323–25 (January 1834): 1–6, 28–31, 45–47, 60–64.

Burke, Edmund. *Reflections on the Revolution in France*. Edited by J. C. D. Clark. Stanford: Stanford University Press, 2001.

Burton, Sarah. *Double Life: A Biography of Charles and Mary Lamb*. London: Viking, 2003.

Butler, Eleanor, Sarah Ponsonby, and Caroline Tighe Hamilton. *The Hamwood Papers of the Ladies of Llangollen and Caroline Hamilton*. London: Macmillan, 1930.

Butler, Judith. *Gender Trouble*. New York: Routledge, 1990.

Butler, Marilyn. *Maria Edgeworth: A Literary Biography*. Oxford: Clarendon Press, 1972.

Buzard, James. "The Grand Tour and After (1660–1840)." In *The Cambridge Companion to Travel Writing*, edited by Peter Hume and Tim Young, 37–52. Cambridge: Cambridge University Press, 2002.

Byron, George Gordon Lord. *Byron's Letters and Journals*. Edited by Leslie A. Marchand. 12 vols. Cambridge, MA: Belknap Press of Harvard University Press, 1977.

C., J. P. "Introduction." In "The Trimming of Thomas Nash, Gentleman." In *Miscellaneous Tracts*, i–vi. 1807?. Google Books.

Campbell, Colin. *The Romantic Ethic and the Spirit of Modern Consumerism*. Oxford: Blackwell, 1987.

Cannadine, David, ed. *The Oxford Dictionary of National Biography*. Oxford: Oxford University Press, 2004. https://www.oxforddnb.com.

Carter, John. "Thomas J. Wise and His Forgeries." *Atlantic Monthly*, February 1945.

Carter, John, and Graham Pollard. *An Enquiry into the Nature of Certain Nineteenth Century Pamphlets*. Edited by Nicolas Barker and John Collins. 3rd ed. London: Scolar Press, 1983.

Carton, B. P. "The Palace of Art." *Irish Monthly* 17, no. 315 (Sept. 1899): 454–64.

Castle, Terry. *The Literature of Lesbianism: A Historical Anthology from Ariosto to Stonewall*. New York: Columbia University Press, 2003.

Clarke, William. *Repertorium Bibliographicum; or, Some Account of the Most Celebrated British Libraries*. London: W. Clarke, 1819.

Coleridge, Samuel Taylor. *Biographia Literaria, or Biographical Sketches of My Literary Life and Opinions*. Edited by James Engall and W. Jackson Bate. In *The Collected Works of Samuel Taylor Coleridge*. Edited by Kathleen Coburn and Bart Winer. Vol. 7. London: Routledge & Kegan Paul, 1983.

Coleridge, Samuel Taylor. *The Statesman's Manual; or the Bible the Best Guide to Political Skill and Foresight: A Lay Sermon, Addressed to the Higher Classes of Society*. Edited by R. J. White. In *The Collected Works of Samuel Taylor Coleridge*. Edited by Kathleen Coburn and Bart Winer, 6.3–117. London: Routledge & Kegan Paul, 1983.

Collins, John. *The Two Forgers: A Biography of Harry Buxton Forman and Thomas J. Wise*. New Castle, DE: Oak Knoll, 1992.

Connell, Philip. "Bibliomania: Book Collecting, Cultural Politics, and the Rise of Literary Heritage in Romantic Britain." *Representations* 71 (2000): 24–47.

Cook, Blanche Wiesen. "'Women Alone Stir My Imagination': Lesbianism and the Cultural Tradition." *Signs* 4, no. 4 (1979): 718–39. https://www.jstor.org/stable/3173368.

Cornwall, Barry. *Charles Lamb: A Memoir*. London: Edward Moxon & Co., 1866. Google Books.

Courtney, Winifred. *Young Charles Lamb 1775–1802*. London: Macmillan, 1984. Google Books.

Cox, Philip. "Keats and the Performance of Gender." *Keats-Shelley Journal* 44 (1995): 40–65. http://www.jstor.org/stable/30212992.

Crompton, Louis. *Byron and Greek Love: Homosexuality in Nineteenth-century England*. Berkeley: University of California Press, 1985.

Crowell, Ellen. "Ghosting the Llangollen Ladies: Female Intimacies, Ascendancy Exiles, and the Anglo-Irish Novel." *Éire-Ireland* 39, no. 3 (2004): 202–27.

Curle, Richard. "Introduction." In *The Ashley Library: A Catalogue of Printed Books, Manuscripts and Autograph Letters Collected by Thomas James Wise*, edited by Thomas J. Wise, vii–xiii. London: Printed for Private Circulation Only, 1922.

Curtis, George Ticknor. *A Treatise on the Law of Copyright in Books, Dramatic and Musical Compositions, Letters and Other Manuscripts, Engravings and Sculpture, as Enacted and Administered in England and America; with Some Notices of the History of Literary Property*. London: A. Maxwell and Son, 1847. Google Books.

Cvetkovich, Ann. *An Archive of Feelings: Trauma, Sexuality, and Lesbian Public Cultures*. Durham, NC: Duke University Press.

De Quincey, Thomas. "The Logic of Political Economy." In *Political Economy and Politics: Being Volume IX of His Collected Writings*, edited by David Masson, 118–294. New York: Augustus M. Kelley, 1970.

De Quincey, Thomas. *De Quincey's Works*. London: James Hogg, 1856. Google Books.

De Quincey, Thomas. *The Works of Thomas De Quincey*. 21 vols. London: Pickering & Chatto, 2000.

Dane, Joseph. *The Myth of Print Culture*. Toronto, ON: University of Toronto Press, 2003.

Darnton, Robert. *The Business of Enlightenment*. Cambridge, MA: Belknap Press of Harvard University Press, 1979.

Darnton, Robert. *The Case for Books: Past, Present, and Future*. New York: PublicAffairs, 2010.

Davis, Lennard J. *Obsession: A History*. Chicago: University of Chicago Press, 2008.

D'Emilio, John. "Capitalism and Gay Identity." In *Powers of Desire: The Politics of Sexuality*, edited by Christine Stansell, Ann Snitow, and Sharan Thompson, 100–113. New York: Monthly Review Press, 1983.

Derrida, Jacques. *Of Grammatology*. Translated by Gayatri Chakravorty Spivak. Baltimore, MD: Johns Hopkins University Press, 1976.

Dibdin, Thomas Frognall. *A Bibliographical Antiquarian and Picturesque Tour in France and Germany*. London: Shakespeare Press, 1821.

Dibdin, Thomas Frognall. *Bibliography: A Poem. In Six Books*. London: Harding and Wright, 1812.

Dibdin, Thomas Frognall. *Bibliomania, or, Book-madness: A Bibliographical Romance, in Six Parts, Illustrated with Cuts*. London: Mssrs. Longman, Hurst, Rees, Orme, and Brown, 1811.

Dibdin, Thomas Frognall. *Bibliomania, or, Book-madness: A Bibliographical Romance, in Six Parts, Illustrated with Cuts*. 2nd ed. London, 1842.

Dibdin, Thomas Frognall. *Letters, 1807–1810*. San Marino, CA: H. E. Huntington Library.

Dibdin, Thomas Frognall. *Letters, 1813–1844*. San Marino, CA: H. E. Huntington Library.

Dibdin, Thomas Frognall. *Library Companion, or the Young Man's Guide, and the Old Man's Comfort in the Choice of a Library*. London: Harding, Triphook and Lepard, 1824.

Dibdin, Thomas Frognall. *Northern Tour Financial Documents*. San Marino, CA: H. E. Huntington Library.

Dibdin, Thomas Frognall. *Reminiscences of a Literary Life*. London: John Major, 1836.

Dibdin, Thomas Frognall. *The Bibliographical Decameron, or, Ten Days Pleasant Discourse upon Illuminated Manuscripts, and Subjects Connected with Early Engraving, Typography, and Bibliography*. London: W. Bulmer and Co. Shakespeare Press, 1817.

Dobson, Austin. *Horace Walpole: A Memoir*. New York: Dodd, Mead and Co., 1893. Google Books.

Dowling, Linda, *Hellenism and Homosexuality in Victorian Oxford*. Ithaca, NY: Cornell University Press, 1994.

Dunn, Kevin. *Global Punk: Resistance and Rebellion in Everyday Life*. New York: Bloomsbury, 2015.

Edelman, Lee. *Homographesis: Essays in Gay Literary and Cultural Theory*. New York: Routledge, 1994.

Edelman, Lee. *No Future: Queer Theory and the Death Drive*. Durham, NC: Duke University Press, 2004.

Eisenstein, Elizabeth L. *Divine Art, Infernal Machine: The Reception of Printing in the West from First Impressions to the Sense of an Ending*. Philadelphia: University of Pennsylvania Press, 2011.

Eisenstein, Elizabeth L. *The Printing Press as an Agent of Change: Communications and Cultural Transformations in Early-modern Europe*. Cambridge: Cambridge University Press, 1979.

Elfenbein, Andrew. *Romantic Genius: The Prehistory of a Homosexual Role*. New York: Columbia University Press, 1999.

Eliot, George. *Middlemarch*. Edited by Rosemary Ashton. New York: Penguin, 1994.

"Extraordinary Instance of Female Friendship." *Parental Monitor*, 1796, 98–101. Adam Matthew Digital Database.

Febvre, Lucien and Henri-Jean Martin. *The Coming of the Book*. Translated by David Gerard London: Verso, 1976.

Felski, Rita. "Object Relations." *Contemporary Women's Writing* 1, no. 1–2 (2007): 185–91. https://academic-oup-com.uri.idm.oclc.org/cww.

Ferriar, John. M. D. *The Bibliomania, an Epistle, to Richard Heber, Esq*. London: T. Cadell and W. Davies, 1809. Google Books.

Ferris, Ina. "Book-love and the Remaking of Literary Culture in the Romantic Periodical." In *Bookish Histories: Books, Literature, and Commercial Modernity, 1700–1900*, edited by Ina Ferris and Paul Keen, 111–25. Basingstoke, UK: Palgrave Macmillan, 2009.

Ferris, Ina. "Introduction." In *Romantic Libraries: A Romantic Circles Praxis Volume*, edited by Ina Ferris. Romantic Circles, February 2004. http://www.rc.u md.edu/praxis/libraries/intro/html.

Ferris, Ina. *Book-Men, Book Clubs, and the Romantic Literary Sphere*. Basingstoke, UK: Palgrave Macmillan, 2015.

Forman, Harry Buxton, ed. *Letters of John Keats to Fanny Brawne: Written in the Years MDCCCXIX and MDCCCXX and Now Given from the Original Manuscripts*. New York: Scribner, Armstrong, 1878. Google Books.

Forman, Harry Buxton, ed. *Letters of John Keats*. London: Reeves and Turner, 1895. Google Books.

Forman, Henry Buxton. *The Books of William Morris*. London: Frank Hollings, 1897. Google Books.

Forman, Henry Buxton and Thomas J. Wise. *Between the Lines: Letters and Memoranda Interchanged by H. Buxton Forman and Thomas J. Wise*. Edited by Fannie Ratchford. Austin: University of Texas Press, 1945.

Foucault, Michel. "What Is an Author?" Translated by Donald F. Bouchard and Sherry Simon. In *The Norton Anthology of Theory and Criticism*, edited by Vincent B. Leitch, 1622–1636. New York: Norton, 2001.

Foucault, Michel. *The History of Sexuality: Volume I: An Introduction*. Translated by Robert Hurley. New York: Vintage, 1990.

Frank, Robert J. *Don't Call Me Gentle Charles!: An Essay on Lamb's Essays of Elia*. Corvallis: Oregon State University Press, 1976.

Freeman, Elizabeth. *Time Binds: Queer Temporalities, Queer Histories*. Durham, NC: Duke University Press, 2010.

Freud, Sigmund. "Character and Anal Erotism." Translated by James Strachey. In *The Freud Reader*. Edited by Peter Gay, 293–97. New York: Norton, 1989.

Freud, Sigmund. "From the History of an Infantile Neurosis ('Wolf Man')." Translated by James Strachey. In *The Freud Reader*, edited by Peter Gay, 400–426. New York: Norton, 1989.

Fulford, Tim. "Virtual Topography: Poets, Painters, Publishers and the Reproduction of the Landscape in the Early Nineteenth Century." *RAVON* 57–58 (February–May 2010). https://id.erudit.org/iderudit/1006512ar.

Funke, Jana, et al. "Illustrating Phallic Worship: Uses of Material Objects and the Production of Sexual Knowledge in Eighteenth-century Antiquarianism and Early Twentieth-Century Sexual Science." *Word & Image* 33, no. 3 (2017): 324–37. https://www.tandfonline.com/doi/full/10.1080/02666286.2017.1294952.

Gallup, Donald. "The Carter-Pollard 'Enquiry' Fifty Years After." *The Papers of the Bibliographical Society of America* 78 no. 4 (1984), 447–60.

Gambold, William. *A Compendious Welsh Grammar, or a Short and Easy Introduction to the Welsh Language*. Bala, UK: R. Saunderson, 1833.

Goggin, Maureen Daly. "Introduction: Threading Women." In *Women and the Material Culture of Needlework and Textiles, 1750–1950*, edited by Maureen Daly Goggin and Beth Fowkes Tobin, 1–12. Abingdon, UK: Routledge, 2016.

Goode, Mike. *Sentimental Masculinity and the Rise of History, 1790–1890*. Cambridge: Cambridge University Press, 2009.

Gordon, Mary. *Chase of the Wild Goose*. New York: Arno Press, 1975.

Grafton, Anthony. *Forgers and Critics: Creativity and Duplicity in Western Scholarship*. Princeton: Princeton University Press, 1990.

Gramsci, Antonio. *Selections from the Prison Notebooks*. Edited and translated by Quintin Hoare and Geoffrey Nowell Smith. New York: International Publishers, 1971.

Greenacre, Phyllis. *Emotional Growth: Psychoanalytic Studies of the Gifted and a Great Variety of Other Individuals*. New York: International Universities Press, Inc., 1971.

Grose, Francis. *A Dictionary of the Vulgar Tongue: A Dictionary of Buckish Slang, University Wit, and Pickpocket Eloquence*. N.p.: Project Gutenberg, (1811) 2011. http://www.gutenberg.org/.

Haggerty, George. *Men in Love: Masculinity and Sexuality in the Eighteenth Century.* New York: Columbia University Press, 1999.
Haggerty, George. *Queer Gothic.* Champaign: University of Illinois Press, 2006.
Halberstam, Jack. *Female Masculinity.* Durham, NC: Duke University Press, 1998.
Halberstam, Jack. *In a Queer Time and Place: Transgender Bodies, Subcultural Lives.* New York: New York University Press, 2005.
Hall, David D. *Culture of Print: Essays in the History of the Book.* Amherst: University of Massachusetts Press, 1996.
Hall, J. R. "F. J. Furnivall's Letter to the Royal Library, Copenhagen, Asking That the Thorkelin Transcripts." *Notes & Queries* 45, no. 3 (1998): 267–63. MLA International Bibliography.
Halperin, David. *How to do the History of Homosexuality.* Chicago: University of Chicago Press, 2002.
Halperin, David. *Saint Foucault: Towards a Gay Hagiography.* New York: Oxford University Press, 1995.
Hayles, N. Katherine. *Writing Machines.* Cambridge, MA: MIT Press, 2002.
Hazlitt, William Carew. *The Lambs: Their Lives, Their Friends, and Their Correspondents.* London: Elkin Mathews, 1897.
Hazlitt, William. *The Spirit of the Age: Or, Contemporary Portraits.* 2nd ed. London: Henry Colburn, 1825. Google Books.
Hebdige, Dick. *Subculture: The Meaning of Style.* New York: Methuen & Co., 1979.
Henderson, Archibald. *George Bernard Shaw: Man of the Century.* New York: Appleton-Century-Crofts, 1956.
Hesiod, *Theogony and Works and Days.* Translated by M. L. West. Oxford: Oxford University Press, 1988.
Hicklin, John. *The Ladies of Llangollen, as Sketched by Many Hands: With Notices of Other Objects of Interest in that Sweetest of Vales.* Chester, UK: Thomas Catherall, 1847. Google Books.
Hill, Wes. *Art after the Hipster: Identity Politics, Ethics and Aesthetics.* Cham: Palgrave Macmillan, 2017.
Hoagwood, Terence Allan. *Skepticism and Ideology: Shelley's Political Prose and Its Philosophical Context from Bacon to Marx.* Iowa City: University of Iowa Press, 1988.
Hood, Thomas. *The Works of Thomas Hood: Comic and Serious, in Prose and Verse, with all the Illustrations.* Edited by his son and daughter. 11 vols. London: Ward, Lock & Co., 1882–1884. Google Books.
Howe, Will. *Charles Lamb and His Friends.* Indianapolis, IN: Bobbs-Merill Co., 1944.
Hull, Simon P. *Charles Lamb, Elia and The London Magazine: Metropolitan Muse.* London: Pickering & Chatto, 2010.
Hunt, Leigh. *The Autobiography of Leigh Hunt: With Reminiscences of Friends and Contemporaries.* Edited by Roger Ingpen. Vol. 2. Westminster: Archibald Constable, 1903. Google Books.
Hutchings, Kevin. *Romantic Ecologies and Colonial Cultures in the British Atlantic World. 1770–1850.* Montreal: McGill-Queen's University Press, 2009.

Hutchinson, Thomas. "Preface." In *The Poetical Works of Percy Bysshe Shelley*. Edited by Thomas Hutchinson. London: Henry Frowde, 1905. Google Books.

Jackson, Heather. "What Was Mr. Bennet Doing in his Library, and What Does It Matter?" In *Romantic Libraries: A Romantic Circles Praxis Volume*, edited by Ina Ferris. Romantic Circles, February 2004. http://www.rc.umd.edu/praxis/libraries/jackson/jackson.html.

Jackson, Heather. *Marginalia: Readers Writing in Books*. New Haven: Yale University Press, 2001.

Jackson, Heather. *Romantic Readers: The Evidence of Marginalia*. New Haven: Yale University Press, 2005.

Johnson, Edith Christina. *Lamb Always Elia*. London: Methuen, 1935. Google Books.

Kalter, Barrett. *Modern Antiques: The Material Past in England, 1660–1780*. Lewisburg, PA: Bucknell University Press, 2011.

Kant, Immanuel. *Critique of the Power of Judgment*. Edited by Paul Guyer. Translated by Paul Guyer and Eric Matthews. Cambridge: Cambridge University Press, 2000.

Keats, John. *The Poetical Works of John Keats*. Edited by Harry Buxton Forman. London: Reeves and Turner, 1884. Google Books.

Kendall, Lyle H. "The Not-So-Gentle Art of Puffing: William G. Kingsland and Thomas J. Wise." *The Papers of the Bibliographical Society of America* 62, no. 1 (1968): 25–37. http://www.jstor.org.uri.idm.oclc.org/stable/24301873.

King, Thomas A. *The Gendering of Men, 1600–1750*. 2 vols. Madison: University of Wisconsin Press, 2004.

Kipling, Rudyard. *Kipling: Poems*. Edited by Peter Washington. New York: Knopf, 2013.

Klancher, Jon P. "Wild Bibliography." In *Bookish Histories: Books, Literature, and Commercial Modernity, 1700–1900*, edited by Ina Ferris and Paul Keen, 19–40. London: Palgrave, 2009.

Klancher, Jon P. *The Making of English Reading Audiences, 1790–1832*. Madison: University of Wisconsin Press, 1987.

Knight, Charles. *The Old Printer and the Modern Press*. London: John Murray, 1854. Google Books.

Knight, Richard Payne. *A Discourse on the Worship of Priapus, and Its Connection with the Mystic Theology of the Ancients to which is added an Essay on the Worship of the Generative Powers during the Middle Ages*. London: Privately Printed, 1865. Google Books.

Lamb, Charles. *The Works of Charles Lamb*. Vol. 3. New York: W. J. Widdleton, 1870. Google Books.

Lanser, Susan S. "'Put to the Blush': Romantic Irregularities and Sapphic Tropes." In *Historicizing Romantic Sexuality: A Romantic Circles Praxis Volume*, edited by Richard C. Sha. Romantic Circles, 2006. https://romantic-circles.org/praxis/sexuality/lanser/lanser.html.

Lanser, Susan S. "Bluestocking Sapphism and the Economies of Desire." *Huntington Library Quarterly* 65, no. 1/2 (2002): 257–75. https://www.jstor.org/stable/3817740.

Lanser, Susan S. *The Sexuality of History: Modernity and the Sapphic, 1565–1830*. Chicago: University of Chicago Press, 2014.
Leask, Nigel. *British Romantic Writers and the East: Anxieties of Empire*. Cambridge: Cambridge University Press, 2004.
Lehman, Peter. *Running Scared: Masculinity and the Representation of the Male Body*. Detroit: Wayne State University Press, 2007.
Levine, Peter A. and Ann Frederick. *Waking the Tiger: Healing Trauma*. Berkeley: North Atlantic Books, 1997.
Lichfield, Richard [Gabriel Harvey]. "The Trimming of Thomas Nash." In *The Old Book Collector's Miscellany: or a Collection of Readerly Reprints of Literary Rarities, Illustrative of the History, Literature, Manners, and Biography of the English Nation*, edited by Charles Hindley, i–64. 3 vols. London: Reeves & Turner, (1597) 1871–1873. Google Books.
Lieberman, Hallie. "Intimate Transactions: Sex Toys and the Sexual Discourse of Second-Wave Feminism." *Sexuality & Culture* 21, no. 1 (2017): 96–120. Academic Search Complete.
Lindop, Grevel. *The Opium-Eater: A Life of Thomas De Quincey*. New York: Taplinger Publishing Co., 1981.
Lister, Anne. *I Know My Own Heart: The Diaries of Anne Lister, 1791–1840*. New York: New York University Press, 1992.
Lockhart, John Gibson. "On the Cockney School of Poetry. IV." *Blackwood's Edinburgh Magazine* 3, no. 17 (August 1818): 519–24.
Lucas, E. V. "Woful Ballad of Failure." *Punch, or the London Charivari* 161 (July 13, 1921). http://www.archive.org/details/punchvol160a161lemouoft.
Lucas, E. V. *A Swan and Her Friends*. London: Methuen & Co., 1907.
Lucas, E. V. *The Life of Charles Lamb*. 2 vols. London: Methuen, 1905.
Lucas, E. V., ed. *Letters of Charles Lamb: to which are Added Those of His Sister, Mary Lamb*. London: J. M. Dent, 1935.
Lucas, E. V., ed. *The Letters of Charles and Mary Lamb*. 3 vols. New York: AMS, 1968.
Lucas, E. V., ed. *The Works of Charles and Mary Lamb*. 7 vols. London: Methuen, 1903.
Lynch, Deidre Shauna. "'Wedded to Books': Bibliomania and the Romantic Essayists." In *Romantic Libraries: A Romantic Circles Praxis Volume*, edited by Ina Ferris. Romantic Circles, February 2004. http://www.rc.umd.edu/praxis/libraries/lynch/lynch.html.
Lynch, Deidre Shauna. "Canons' Clockwork: Novels for Everyday Use." In *Bookish Histories: Books, Literature, and Commercial Modernity, 1700–1900*, edited by Ina Ferris and Paul Keen, 87–110. Basingstoke, UK: Palgrave Macmillan, 2009.
Lynch, Deidre Shauna. *Loving Literature: A Cultural History*. Chicago: University of Chicago Press, 2015.
Macdonald, William, ed. *The Works of Charles Lamb*. 12 vols. London: Dutton, 1903. Google Books.
Malton, James. *An Essay on British Cottage Architecture: Being an Attempt to Perpetuate on Principle, that Peculiar Mode of Building, which was Originally the Effect of Chance*. London: Hockham and Carpenter, Booksellers, 1798.

Marrone, Gaetana, Paolo Puppa, and Luce Sonigli. *Encyclopedia of Italian Literary Studies*. New York: Routledge, 2007.

Marx, Karl. *Capital: A Critique of Political Economy*. Edited by Frederick Engels. Translated by Samuel Moore and Edward Aveling. 2 vols. New York: International Publishers, 1967.

Matheson, C. S. "'Ancient and Present': Charles Heath of Monmouth and the Historical and Descriptive Accounts . . . of Tintern Abbey 1793–1828." In *Travel Writing and Tourism in Britain and Ireland*, edited by Benjamin Colbert, 50–67. Houndmills, UK: Palgrave Macmillan, 2012.

Mavor, Elizabeth. *The Ladies of Llangollen: A Study in Romantic Friendship*. London: Michael Joseph, 1971.

May, J. Lewis. *Charles Lamb: A Study*. London: G. Bles, 1934.

McLuhan, Marshall. *Understanding Media: The Extensions of Man*. New York: McGraw-Hill Book Company, 1964.

Milnes, Tim. "Charles Lamb: Professor of Indifference." *Philosophy and Literature* 28, no. 2 (2004): 324–41. ProQuest Religion.

Milton, John. *Paradise Lost*. Edited by Gordon Teskey. New York: Norton, 2005.

Mizukoshi, Ayumi. "The Cockney Politics of Gender—The Cases of Hunt and Keats." *Romanticism on the Net*, 14 (May 1999). http://users.ox.ac.uk/~scat0385/cockneygender.html.

Mole, Tom. *What the Victorians Made of Romanticism: Material Artifacts, Cultural Practices, and Reception History*. Princeton: Princeton University Press, 2017.

Monsman, Gerald. *Charles Lamb as the* London Magazine*'s Elia*. Lewiston, NY: Edwin Mellon Press, 2003.

Monsman, Gerald. *Confessions of a Prosaic Dreamer: Charles Lamb's Art of Autobiography*. Durham, NC: Duke University Press, 1984.

Moore, Lisa. *Dangerous Intimacies: Toward a Sapphic History of the British Novel*. Durham, NC: Duke University Press, 1997.

Morpurgo, J. E., ed. *Selected Writings by Charles Lamb*. New York: Routledge, 2003.

"Mr. T. J. Wise." *The Times (London, England)*. May 14, 1937. The Times Digital Archive.

Munro, John. "Biography." In *Frederick J. Furnivall, A Volume of Personal Record*, edited by John Munro et al. Oxford: Oxford University Press, 1911.

Murray, David. "The Challenge of Home for Sexual Orientation and Gendered Identity Refugees in Toronto." *Journal of Canadian Studies* 48 (2014): 132–52. Academic Search Complete.

Nagle, Christopher. *Sexuality and the Culture of Sensibility in the British Romantic Era*. New York: Palgrave Macmillan, 2007.

Nash, Catherine Jean. "Trans Experiences in Lesbian and Queer Space." *Canadian Geographer* 55 no. 2 (2011): 192–207. Academic Search Complete.

Newbon, Pete. *The Boy-Man, Masculinity and Immaturity in the Long Nineteenth Century*. London: Palgrave Macmillan, 2018.

The Notebook of the Shelley Society. Edited by the Honorary Secretaries. London: Reeves & Turner, 1888.

Nyong'o, Tavia. "Punk'd Theory." *Social Text*, 23, no. 84–85 (2005): 19–34. Academic Search Complete.

Oliphant, Margaret. *Annals of a Publishing House: William Blackwood and His Sons, Their Magazine and Friends*. New York: Charles Scriber's, 1897. Google Books.

Partington, Wilfred. *Forging Ahead: The True Story of the Upward Progress of Thomas James Wise: Prince of Book Collectors, Bibliographer Extraordinary and Otherwise*. New York: G. P. Putnam's Sons, 1939.

Pascoe, Judith. *The Hummingbird Cabinet: A Rare and Curious History of Romantic Collectors* Ithaca, NY: Cornell University Press, 2006.

Penny, Nicholas. "Richard Payne Knight: A Brief Life." In *The Arrogant Connoisseur: Richard Payne Knight 1770–1824*, edited by Michael Clarke and Nicholas Penny, 1–18. Manchester: Manchester University Press, 1982.

Pforzheimer, Carl. "Foreword." In *Between the Lines: Letters and Memoranda Interchanged by H. Buxton Forman and Thomas J. Wise*. Edited by Fannie E. Ratchford. Austin: University of Texas Press, 1945.

Piggott, Stuart. *Ruins in a Landscape: Essays in Antiquarianism*. Edinburgh: Edinburgh University Press, 1976.

Piozzi, Hester Lynch. *The Piozzi Letters: Correspondence of Hester Lynch Piozzi, 1784–1821 (Formerly Mrs. Thrale)*. Edited by Lillian D Bloom. Vol. 3 (1799–18). Newark: University of Delaware Press, 1991.

Piroux, Lorraine. "The Encyclopedist and the Peruvian Princess: The Poetics of Illegibility in French Enlightenment Book Culture." *PMLA* 121, no. 1 (2006): 107–23. MLA International Bibliography.

Pocock, William F. *Architectural Designs for Rustic Cottages, Picturesque Dwellings, Villas, &c*. London: J. Turner, 1807.

Prance, Claude A. *Companion to Charles Lamb: A Guide to the People and Places 1760–1847*. London: Mansell Publishing Ltd., 1983.

Price, Leah. "Introduction: Reading Matter." *PMLA* 120, no. 1 (2006): 9–16. MLA International Bibliography.

Price, Leah. *How to Do Things with Books in Victorian Britain*. Princeton: Princeton University Press, 2012.

Punter, David. "The Picturesque and the Sublime: Two Worldviews." In *The Politics of the Picturesque: Literature, Landscape and Aesthetics since 1770*, edited by Stephen Copley and Peter Garside, 220–39. Cambridge: Cambridge, University Press, 1994.

Quincey, Thomas. *A Short Tour in the Midland Counties of England; Performed in the Summer of 1772. Together with an Account of a Similar Excursion, undertaken September 1774*. London: M. Lewis, 1775.

Ratchford, Fannie E. "Introductory Essay." In *Between the Lines: Letters and Memoranda Interchanged by H. Buxton Forman and Thomas J. Wise*. Edited by Fannie E. Ratchford. Austin: University of Texas Press, 1945.

Raymond, W. O. "The Forgeries of Thomas J. Wise and Their Aftermath." *The Journal of English and Germanic Philology* 44, no. 3 (1945): 229–38. http://www.jstor.org.uri.idm.oclc.org/stable/27705213.

Rev. of *Repertorium Bibliographicum*. *Gentleman's Magazine* (May and June 1819): 434–35, 631–32. ProQuest British Periodicals.

Reynolds, Nicole. *Building Romanticism: Literature and Architecture in Nineteenth-Century Britain*. Ann Arbor: University of Michigan Press, 2010.

Riehl, Joseph E. *That Dangerous Figure: Charles Lamb and the Critics*. Rochester, NY: Boydell and Brewer, 1998.

Roberts, Gwyneth Tyson. "'Under the Hatches': English Parliamentary Commissioners' Views of the People and Language of Mid-nineteenth-century Wales." In *The Expansion of England: Race, Ethnicity and Cultural History*, edited by Bill Schwartz, 171–97. London: Routledge, 1996.

Ross, Andrew. *No Respect: Intellectuals and Popular Culture*. Abingdon, UK: Routledge, 2014.

Rousseau, George S. *Nervous Acts: Essays on Literature, Culture and Sensibility*. Hampshire, UK: Palgrave Macmillan, 2004.

Rowley, Gordon E. "Enchantresses of Wales Still Lure Visitors." *Chicago Tribune* (22 May 1977): C15. ProQuest.

Rubin, Gayle. "Thinking Sex: Notes for a Radical Theory of the Politics of Sexuality." In *The Lesbian and Gay Studies Reader*, edited by H. Abelove, M. A. Barale, and D. M. Halperin, 3–44. New York: Routledge, 1993.

Russett, Margaret. *De Quincey's Romanticism: Canonical Minority and the Forms of Transmission*. Cambridge: Cambridge University Press, 1997.

Russett, Margaret. *Fictions and Fakes: Forging Romantic Authenticity, 1760–1845*. Cambridge: Cambridge University Press, 2006.

Russo, Brent. "Charles Lamb's Beloved Liberalism: Eccentricity in the Familiar Essays." *Studies in Romanticism* 52, no. 3 (Fall 2013): 437–57. MLA International Bibliography.

Savage, Mike. "Status, Lifestyle, and Taste." In *The Oxford Handbook of the History of Consumption*, edited by Frank Trentmann, 551–67. Oxford: Oxford University Press, 2013.

Sawyer, Ethel R. *Books Are People: A Bookman's Credo*. Portland, OR: Berncliff Press, 1951.

Scott, Sir Walter. *The Antiquary*. London: Ward, Lock & Co., 1883.

Sedgwick, Eve Kosofsky. *Between Men: English Literature and Male Homosocial Desire*. New York: Columbia University Press, 1985.

Sedgwick, Eve Kosofsky. *Tendencies: Essays*. Durham, NC: Duke University Press, 1993.

Seward, Anna. *Letters of Anna Seward, Written Between the Years 1784 and 1807*. Vol. 4. Edinburgh: Archibald Constable and Co., 1811. Google Books.

Sha, Richard C. *Perverse Romanticism: Aesthetics and Sexuality in Britain, 1750–1832*. Baltimore: Johns Hopkins University Press, 2009.

Shelley, Percy. *The Poetical Works of Percy Bysshe Shelley*. Edited by Harry Buxton Forman. London: Reeves and Turner, 1876. Google Books.

Shelley, Percy. *The Works of Percy Bysshe Shelley in Verse and Prose*. Edited by Harry Buxton Forman. London: Reeves and Turner, 1880. Google Books.

Silver, Sean R. "Visiting Strawberry Hill: Horace Walpole's Gothic Historiography." *Eighteenth Century Fiction* 21, no. 4 (2009): 535–64. Academic Search Complete.

Sinclair, Catherine. *Hill and Valley: or, Wales and the Welsh*. 4th ed. Edinburgh: W. Whyte and Co., 1848. Google Books.

Singer, Rita. "Through Wales in the Footsteps of William Gilpin: Illustrated Travel Accounts by Early French Tourists, 1768–1810." *European Romantic Review* 30, no. 2 (2019): 127–47. Academic Search Complete.

"Sir Walter Scott & the Roxburghe Club." *Morning Chronicle [London]* (6 January 1834). 19th Century British Library Newspapers, Gale Cengage Learning.

Sontag, Susan. "Notes on Camp." In *Against Interpretation and Other Essays*, by Susan Sontag. New York: Dell Publishing Co., 1969.

Southey, Robert. *Joan of Arc*. London: Henry Vizetelly, 1853. Google Books.

St. Clair, William. *The Reading Nation in the Romantic Period*. Cambridge: Cambridge University Press, 2004.

Stephen, Leslie and Sidney Lee, eds. *The Dictionary of National Biography*. New York: Macmillan, 1908. Google Books.

Stewart, Susan. *Crimes of Writing: Problems in the Containment of Representation*. New York: Oxford University Press, 1991.

Stewart, Susan. *On Longing: Narratives of the Miniature, the Gigantic, the Souvenir, the Collection*. Durham, NC: Duke University Press, 1993.

Stone, Amy L. "Flexible Queers, Serious Bodies: Transgender Inclusion in Queer Spaces." *Journal of Homosexuality* 60, no. 12 (2013): 1648–65. Academic Search Complete.

Talfourd, Thomas Noon, ed. *The Works of Charles Lamb: A New Edition*. London: Edward Moxon, 1848. Google Books.

Thackeray, William Makepeace. *Vanity Fair*. Edited by John Sutherland. Oxford: Oxford University Press, 1998.

Thomson, J. C. *A Bibliography of the Writings of Charles and Mary Lamb: A Literary History* Bronxville, NY: N. T. Smith, 1979.

Thrale, Hester Lynch. *Thraliana: The Diary of Mrs. Hester Lynch Thrale (Later Mrs. Piozzi), 1776–1809*. Vol. 2 (1784–18). Oxford: Clarendon Press, 1951.

Townshend, Dale. *Gothic Antiquity: History, Romance, and the Architectural Imagination, 1760–1840*. Oxford: Oxford University Press, 2019.

Trentmann, Frank. "Knowing Consumers—Histories, Identities, Practices." In *The Making of the Consumer: Knowledge, Power, and Identity in the Modern World*, edited by Frank Trentmann, 1–30. Oxford: Berg Publishers, 2005.

Trentmann, Frank. *Empire of Things: How We Became a World of Consumers, from the Fifteenth Century to the Twenty-first*. New York: HarperCollins Publishers, 2016.

Trentmann, Frank. *Free Trade Nation: Commerce, Consumption, and Civil Society in Modern Britain*. Oxford: Oxford University Press, 2009.

Vicinus, Martha. "'They Wonder to Which Sex I Belong': The Historical Roots of the Modern Lesbian Identity." *Feminist Studies* 18, no. 3 (1992): 467–97. https://www.jstor.org/stable/3178078.

Vicinus, Martha. "Distance and Desire: English Boarding-School Friendships." *Signs* 9, no. 4 (1984): 600–22. https://www.jstor.org/stable/3173613.

Volti, Rudi. *Society and Technological Change*. 4th ed. New York: Worth Publishers, 2001.

Walpole, Horace. *Horace Walpole and His World: Select Passages from his Letters*. London: Seeley, Jackson, and Halliday, 1884. Google Books.

Walpole, Horace. *The Castle of Otranto*. Edited by W. S. Lewis and E. J. Clery. Oxford: Oxford University Press, 1998.

Walpole, Horace. *The Letters of Horace Walpole, Fourth Earl of Orford*. Vol. 5. Edinburgh: John Grant, 1906. Google Books.

Walter. *My Secret Life*. Vol. 8. Ch. 3. Amsterdam: 1888–1894. http://www.my-secret-life.com/sex-diary-0803.php.

Warner, Fred B. "'The Hanging Judge' Once More Before the Bar." *The Papers of the Bibliographical Society of America* 70, no. 1 (1976): 89–96. http://www.jstor.org.uri.idm.oclc.org/stable/24302258.

Weeks, Jeffrey. *Coming Out: Homosexual Politics in Britain, from the Nineteenth Century to the Present*. London: Quartet Books, 1977.

Whale, John. "Romantics, Explorers and Picturesque Travellers." In *The Politics of the Picturesque: Literature, Landscape and Aesthetics since 1770*, edited by Stephen Copley and Peter Garside, 175–95. Cambridge: Cambridge, University Press, 1994.

Wilde, Oscar. *The Picture of Dorian Gray*. Edited by Robert Mighall. London: Penguin, 2003.

Windle, John and Karma Pippin. *Thomas Frognall Dibdin, 1776–1847: A Bibliography*. New Castle, DE: Oak Knoll Press, 1998.

Wise, Thomas J. *A Shelley Library: A Catalogue of Printed Books, Manuscripts and Autograph Letters*. New York: Haskell House Publishers, 1971.

Wise, Thomas J. *The Ashley Library: A Catalogue of Printed Books, Manuscripts and Autograph Letters Collected by Thomas James Wise*. 11 vols. London: Printed for Private Circulation Only, 1922.

Wolfson, Susan J. "John Keats." In *The Cambridge Companion to English Poets*, edited by Claude Rawson, 360–75. Cambridge: Cambridge University Press, 2011.

Woodbury, Gerald. "Preface." In *The Complete Poetical Works of Percy Bysshe Shelley, by Percy Shelley*, edited by Gerald Woodbury. Boston: Houghton, Mifflin and Company, 1892. Google Books.

Woodmansee, Martha. *The Author, Art, and the Market: Rereading the History of Aesthetics*. New York: Columbia University Press, 1994.

Wordsworth, William. "Essay, Supplementary to the Preface." In *The Prose Works of William Wordsworth*, edited by W. J. B. Owen and Jane W. Smyser. Vol. 3. Oxford: Clarendon Press, 1974.

Wordsworth, William. "Wordsworth's Prefaces of 1800 and 1802." In *Lyrical Ballads, by William Wordsworth and Samuel Taylor Coleridge*, edited by R. L. Brett and A. R. Jones, 241–72. London: Routledge, 1991.

Wordsworth, William. *The Poetical Works of William Wordsworth*. Edited by William Knight. Vol. 7. London: Macmillan, 1896. Google Books.

Žižek, Slavoj. *Enjoy Your Symptom!: Jacques Lacan in Hollywood and Out*. London: Routledge Classics, 2008.

Žižek, Slavoj. *Looking Awry: An Introduction to Jacques Lacan through Popular Culture*. Cambridge, MA: MIT Press, 1992.

Žižek, Slavoj. *The Sublime Object of Ideology*. London: Verso, 1989.

Index

Page references for figures are italicized.

Account of a Journey in Wales (Ponsonby), 36, 67–68
Adonais (P. Shelley), 163
Aedes Althorpianae (Dibdin), 91
æolian harp, 175
affect, 20; and dissidence, 3–4, 22
Against Nature (À rebours) (Huysmans), 104
Album Verses, with a Few Others (Lamb), 139
Allan, David, 6, 8
Altick, Richard D., 18, 179, 191, 193
An Analytical Inquiry into the Principles of Taste (Knight), 69
Andrew, Charlotte, 60
antiquarianism: queer phobia and, 21–22
The Antiquary (Scott), 8, 85
Appadurai, Arjun, 10, 13
"Appreciation of De Foe's Secondary Novels" (Lamb), 146–47, 152
Appreciations (Pater), 127, 144
Arnold, Matthew, 173
Ashley Library (Wise), 161, 164, 182, 189
The Aspern Papers (James), 180

Athenæum magazine, 24, 100; attack on the Roxburghe Club in, 100, 104–10
Austen, Jane: *Pride and Prejudice* (1813), 88
authorship, 16; forgery and, 198–200; legal history of, 109; monopoly of, 200; Victorian cult of, 199–200. *See also* singular authorship

Babbitt, Irving: *Rousseau and Romanticism* (1919), 145
Babson, J. E., 136
Barclay, Alexander, 84
Barker, Nicolas and John Collins, 198–99
Barnett, George, 136
"Barrenness of the Imaginative Faculty in the Productions of Modern Art" (Lamb), 126
Barthes, Roland, 42
Basbanes, Nicholas, 8, 13, 151
Baudelaire, Charles, 131, 132; "The Painter of Modern Life" (1863), 125
Baudrillard, Jean, 84
Beckford, William, 15, 43, 47, 71, 92; "Rare Doings at Roxburghe Hall, A

Ballad" (1821), 11; *Vathek* (1782), 11, 15
Benedict, Barbara M., 19–20, 82
Benjamin, Walter, 151–52
Benzie, William, 163
A Bibliographical, Antiquarian, and Picturesque Tour in France and Germany (Dibdin), 71, 81, 82, 90
A Bibliographical, Antiquarian, and Picturesque Tour in the Northern Counties of England and in Scotland (Dibdin), 71
The Bibliographical Decameron (Dibdin), 9, 81, 82, 91, 97
Bibliography (Dibdin), 24, 100–104
The Bibliomania, an Epistle to Richard Heber, Esq. (Ferriar), 8, 94
Bibliomania, or, Book-Madness (Dibdin), 9, 13, 84, 93–94, 100
bibliomaniac, figure of: criminalization of, 187; medical discourse informing, 83–84, 187; phobic response to, 100, 104, 107; political-economic discourse informing, 85–86, 109; professional writers' response to, 86; psychological version of, 13; queerness of, 96, 104, 134, 186. *See also* book collecting; book collectors; book collectors, image of; bookishness
Biographia Literaria (Coleridge), 7, 109, 146, 175
Blackstone, William, 109, 175–76
Blackwood, William, 136
Blackwood's Magazine, 86, 108
Blandford, Marquis of. *See* Marlborough, 5th Duke of
Boccaccio, Giovanni, 13, 23, 81; *The Decameron* (1471), 13–14, 91, 92. *See also The Decameron* (1471)
bohemianism, 23, 25, 125, 130
Bonaparte, Napoleon, 91
book collecting: auction culture and, 8, 92, 101; "book boom" and, 8, 83, 92–93, 109; Roxburghe book auction and, 91–95
book collectors: bibliophiles, opposition to, 4, 95, 109; genius, parallels with, 106. *See also* bibliomaniac
book collectors, image of: anti-democratic, 105; anti-social, 8, 19; aristocratic, 6, 91; dissident, 23, 35, 84–85; effeminate, 14, 105–6; fetishistic, 9, 94. *See also* bibliomaniac
Book Collector's Miscellany, 12
book history, 17–19; role in Romantic bibliography of, 87
bookishness: addiction and, 135; canonizing of Romantics, role in, 174; domesticity and, 35; history of sexuality, place in, 10, 16, 24, 83; phobia and, 2, 13, 102, 104; pornography, resemblance to, 11–12, 92, 93, 96–97; queer discourse, form of, 96–100, 101–4, 117; Romantic theme, as, 3; scientific discourse and, 24, 83–84, 110; sexual repression and, 13, 16, 19, 168–69, 181; subcultural form of, 14–16, 19, 22, 23, 88, 109. *See also* bibliomaniac, figure of; book collecting; book collectors
bookishness in literary field: affective relation and, 10, 20, 86; author-function and, 17, 109; literature and, 4–6; materialism, relation to, 88
bookish style: addiction and, 134–35; "book fancy" as mode of, 5; camp, form of, 153; collecting, parallels with, 141–42; consumerism and, 16, 150; sensibility, form of, 9–10, 138
Bourdieu, Pierre, 57, 199
Bowen, Elizabeth, 34
Bowie, David, 141
Brant, Sebastian: *Ship of Fools* (1494), 13, 84
Brawne, Fanny, 173

Brideoake, Fiona on LL:
historiographical problems posed by, 33, 34, 53, 56, 63; home of, 40, 42–43, 49–50; things, importance to, 31, 35, 52; travel and tourism of, 46
British Museum, 69, 161, 196, 198
Brown, Bill, 36, 54
Browning, Elizabeth Barrett, 26, 188–89, 196; "Reading, 1847" forgery, 188–89, 191–92, 199; *Songs from the Portuguese* (1850), 26
Browning, Robert, 166, 167; *Pauline* (1833), 166
Browning Society, 14, 166; TJW's destruction of, 166
Brummel, Beau, 125
Brydges, Samuel Egerton, 8, 10
Buchanan, Robert, 108
Bucke, Richard Maurice, 167, 168, 169, 177
Buckingham, James Silk, 14, 24, 105. See also Roxburghe Revels (1834)
Burke, Edmund, 6, 40
Butler, Eleanor, 3, 23; *Diary* (1788), 35, 38, 50–51, 59, 64; early life of, 39; masculine appearance of, 40, 50, 52. See also Ladies of Llangollen
Butler, Judith, 53
Buzard, James, 69
Byron, George Gordon Lord, 7, 38, 71, 176

Camden, Charles, 176
camp, 5, 16, 40, 44–46, 95, 97, 101; Charles Lamb's style of, 124, 128
Campbell, Colin, 25, 125
Capital (Marx), 41, 57
Carlyle, Thomas, 136
Carter, John and Graham Pollard, 190–99
Cartesianism, 86, 187
Caryll, Mary, 59–60, 62
Castle, Terry, 33
The Castle of Otranto (Walpole), 15

The Cenci (P. Shelley), 162
Chandler, Raymond, 126
Changes Produced in the Nervous System by Civilization (Verity), 84
Chappelow, Leonard, 37–38, 47, 48, 63
"Character of the Late Elia" (Lamb), 147
Charlotte Augusta of Wales, Princess, 23
Chartier, Roger, 18
Chase of the Wild Goose (Gordon), 32, 35, 61
Chatterton, Thomas, 184–86
Chaucer, Geoffrey, 92
Cheney, Lynne, 33; *Sisters* (1981), 33
Clairmont, Claire, 180
Clark, J. C. D., 6
Clark, William, 199
Cockney School of poets, 108, 137–39, 182
Coleridge, Samuel Taylor, 19; *Biographia Literaria* (1817), 7, 109, 146, 175; Kant, echoes of, 146; Lamb, relations with, 118–19, 134, 137; literary property, theory of, 109, 175; materialism, views on, 59, 131; new readers, views on, 6–7; TFD, familiarity with, 89; "This Lime Tree Bower My Prison" (1797), 122
collecting: anti-democratic image of, 85, 105; author-function and, 200; editing, role in, 177; medium, function as, 44–46, 181; modern first editions, focus on, 179; selling, prohibition against, 182
collectors: history of sexuality, place in, 95–96; Society of Dilettanti and, 69; *virtuoso* figure of, 21, 24, 55, 85, 95. See also bibliomaniac, figure of; book collecting; book collectors; effeminacy; Roxburghe Club
Collette: *The Pure and the Impure* (*Ces plaisirs*) (1932), 33
Collins, John, 161, 171, 173, 177, 178

Collins, Wilkie, 18
"Confessions of a Drunkard" (Lamb), 134
Confessions of an English Opium-eater (De Quincey), 86, 143
Connell, Philip, 85
consumerism, 3, 6, 31, 34, 41, 55–56, 130
Cornwallis, Elizabeth, 47
Cortés, Hernán, 182
cottage ornée. See ornamental cottage
Courtney, Winifred, 134
Cox, Philip, 122
Critique of the Power of Judgment (Kant), 146
Crowell, Ellen, 32, 33, 65
Curiosities of Literature (D'Israeli), 94
curiosity, 21, 82
Curle, Richard, 182
Cvetkovich, Ann, 35

dandy figure, 125, 131
Dane, Joseph, 17
Darnton, Robert, 17–19
Davis, Lennard J., 24, 84
The Decameron (Boccaccio), 13–14, 91, 92; Valdarfer edition of, 92, 95, 145, 151
Defence of Poetry (P. Shelley), 174–75, 178
Defoe, Daniel, 146
D'Emilio, John, 56
Delepierre, Joseph Octave: *Un point curieux* (1871), 168
De Quincey, Thomas (TDQ): bookish style of, 16, 20, 86; collectors and collecting, views on, 14, 94, 96, 106; *Confessions of an English Opium-eater* (1821), 86, 143; *flânerie* of, 124, 143; LL, meeting of, 38; *The Logic of Political Economy* (1844), 94; *Sketches of Life and Manners* (1834), 7; tour books, memories of, 7–8

Dibdin, Thomas F. (TFD), 65; authorship, materialist mode of, 131, 179; biography and career of, 89–90; "book boom," views on, 6, 10; book design, risks taken in, 91; camp style of, 5; *The Director*, editorship of, 89; financial difficulties and correspondence about, 90–91, 93; history of bibliography, place in, 13, 109; illustrators, correspondence with, 90; Napier, Macvey, correspondence with, 98–99; Northern tourism of, 71; queer discourse of, 100–104, 108; *Reminiscences of a Literary Life* (1836), 93; Roxburghe Club, founding of, 14, 23, 24, 25; Royal Institution, history with, 89; Sams, Joseph, correspondence with, 99–100; Sharp, Cuthbert, correspondence with, 100; Valdarfer *Decameron*, views on, 81; Walter Scott, correspondence with, 90
Dibdin, Thomas F. (TFD), works of: *Aedes Althorpianae* (1822), 91; *A Bibliographical Antiquarian and Picturesque Tour in France and Germany* (1821), 71, 81, 82, 90; *A Bibliographical, Antiquarian and Picturesque Tour in the Northern Counties of England and in Scotland* (1838), 71; *The Bibliographical Decameron* (1817), 9, 81, 82, 91, 97; *Bibliography* (1812), 24, 100–104; *Bibliomania, or, Book-Madness* (1811), 9, 13, 84, 93–94, 100; *Introduction to the Knowledge of Rare and Valuable Editions of the Greek and Latin Classics* (1827), 89; *The Library Companion* (1824), 71, 97; *Typographical Antiquities* (1816), 179; "Vaccinia," 84
Dilke, Charles W., 183
D'Israeli, Isaac, 94; *Curiosities of Literature* (1835), 94

domesticity, 15, 34, 35, 49; queer community and, 59, 83; repression and, 55; trans identity and, 50–51
Dowling, Linda, 24, 108
drag, 49–50
Dunn, Kevin, 141
Duyckinck, George L., 147–48

Early English Text Society, 162
Edelman, Lee, 6, 16, 102, 168
Edgeworth, Maria, 6, 7, 34
Edinburgh Review, 98
effeminacy, 2; bookish trait, role as, 101–2, 106; *effeminatus* figure, trait of, 14, 24, 101–2, 106–8, 184, 185; "fancy price" concept and, 95; sodomite figure, links to, 106, 136
Eisenstein, Elizabeth, 17
Elfenbein, Andrew, 43, 96, 106
Elia. *See* Lamb, Charles
Elia (Lamb), 139
Elia essays. *See under* Lamb, Charles
Eliana (Lamb), 136
Eliot, George, 167
Enfield, William, 176
Epipsychidion (P. Shelley), 178
"Essay, Supplementary to the Preface" (Wordsworth), 7
"Essay on Criticism" (Pope), 176
"Essays upon Epitaphs" (Wordsworth), 176
"An Essay towards a Theory of Apparition" (Ferriar), 94
The Excursion (Wordsworth), 70

Febvre, Lucien, 7
Felski, Rita, 55
Ferriar, John: *The Bibliomania, an Epistle to Richard Heber, Esq.* (1809), 8, 94; "An Essay towards a Theory of Apparition" (1813), 94
Ferris, Ina, 4, 19–20, 22, 87–88, 142, 179
fetishism: Romantic bibliography, role in, 92, 93; theories and image of, 2, 41. *See also* Marx, Karl

Fitzgerald, William, 167
flâneur, 23, 128, 133
Fleshly School of poetry, 108
Foliage (Hunt), 180
fop, 95–96
forgery, 17; attribution, problems with, 198–99; authorship, as queer mode of, 181, 182, 188; creative forgery form of, 3, 26, 161–62, 184, 199; forensic methods for detecting, 191; HBF and TJW, their style of, 181, 187–99; singular author, relation to, 177, 199; theories of, 184–87
Forman, Henry B. (HBF), 3, 13, 23, 25; authorship, theory of, 172; bibliographical methods of, 170, 179; *The Books of William Morris* (1897), 169; Bucke, Maurice, friendship with, 167–68; *The Collected Poems of Percy Bysshe Shelley* (1876), 169; collecting practices of, 168, 173, 177; creative forgery, invention of, 161, 198; early life and works of, 167–68; editorial philosophy of, 169–72; exposure of, 194–98; *Letters of John Keats to Fanny Brawne* (1878), 172–73; library of, 180; *Our Living Poets* (1871), 167; "perfect speech," theory of, 174, 177; *The Poetical and Other Writings of John Keats* (1884), 172; Post Office, career with, 167; *The Prose Works of Percy Bysshe Shelley* (1880), 169; relic collecting of, 180; Shelley, Percy, editing of, 163
Forman, Maurice (son of HBF), 194, 197
Forster, John, 118, 130
Foucault, Michel, 42, 53, 83, 84, 95–96, 102, 107, 110, 198
Frank, Robert, 136
Frank Chickens, 33
Freeman, Elizabeth, 22
Freud, Sigmund, 11
Fulford, Tim, 65, 69

Furet, François, 19
Furnivall, Frederick J., 14, 25, 161; canonizing Romantic poets, role in, 162–63

Gallup, Donald, 197
Garrick, David, 133
Geertz, Clifford, 19
"The Genteel Style of Writing" (Lamb), 138
George III (king), 94
George IV (king), 2
Gilpin, William: *Observations on the River Wye, and several parts of South Wales* (1782), 66
Glamorgan Pottery, 31, *32*, 67
Goggin, Maureen Daly, 19
Goode, Mike, 22
Gordon, Mary, 33, 51, 62; *Chase of the Wild Goose* (1936), 33, 35, 61
Gorfin, Herbert, 193–94
Gosse, Edmund, 164, 189, 196–97
Gothic culture, 41; collecting in, 15; LL, their version of, 34, 36, 37, 39, 67; new readers and, 6; primitivism of, 127; queerness of, 42–43, 46, 55, 83
Grafton, Anthony, 184
Gramsci, Antonio, 18
Grand Tour, 32, 34, 69. See also tourism
Greenacre, Phyllis, 185
Grumbach, Doris: *The Ladies* (1984), 33

Halberstam, Jack, 49, 62
Hall, David C., 17–19
Halperin, David, 35, 53
The Hamwood Papers (Travers), 38
Hartshorne, Charles Henry, 100, 106; antiquarian works by, 107
Harvey, Gabriel: "The Trimming of Thomas Nashe, Gentleman" (1597), 12
Haslewood, Joseph, 14, 92, 93, 104, 105
Hayles, N. Katherine, 87

Hazlitt, William, 20, 86, 118, 122, 140, 141
Hazlitt, William Carew, 144
Hebdige, Dick, 15, 25, 141
Heber, Richard, 8, 14, 85; *Athenæum*'s attack on, 100, 106–8; sex scandal of, 106, 108
Hellas (P. Shelley), 162
Hemans, Felicia, 6, 7
Herder, Johann Gottfried, 176
Hesiod, 20
Hoagwood, Terence Allan, 174
Homer, 94, 182
Home Tour, 66, 69, 70. See also tourism
Hood, Thomas, 138
Horace, 94
Horne, Richard, 198
Hull, Simon, 121
Hunt, Arnold, 106
Hunt, Leigh, 16, 119, 122; *Foliage* (1818), 180
Hunt, Lynn, 19
Huntington Library, 196
Hutchings, Kevin, 69
Huysmans, Joris-Karl: *Against Nature* (À rebours) (1884), 104

Innes-Ker, James, 91
Introduction to the Knowledge of Rare and Valuable Editions of the Greek and Latin Classics (Dibdin), 89

Jackson, Heather J., 19–20, 88
James, Henry, 57; *The Aspern Papers*, (1888), 180; *The Spoils of Poynton* (1897), 57
Jerden, William, 139
Jesus of Nazareth, 10
John, Saint (the apostle), 10
Johnson, Samuel, 20–21

Kalter, Barrett, 15, 43–44
Kant, Immanuel, 16, 21; *Critique of the Power of Judgment* (1790), 146

Keane, Molly, 34
Keats, John, 3, 26, 133; HBF's editing of, 172–73; Lamb, comparison to, 124, 127, 138; "On first looking into Chapman's Homer" (1817), 182; reception of, 122, 182
Keen, Paul, 19
Kendall, Jr., Lyle, 197
Ker, John, 91
King, Thomas A., 95–96
King James Bible (1769), 10
Kingsland, William G., 197
kitsch, 15, 16
Klancher, Jon P., 18–19, 22, 87, 89, 109
Knight, Charles, 151
Knight, Richard Payne, 69; *An Analytical Inquiry into the Principles of Taste* (1805), 69; *The Worship of Priapus* (1786), 69

de Laborde, Jean-Benjamin, 7
Lacan, Jacques, 109, 184, 186, 187, 200
The Ladies (Grumbach), 33
Ladies of Llangollen (LL), 15, 23, 25, 83, 117, 181; "A Catalog of Our Books" (1792), 52; elopement of, 34, 36, 39; "female husband" typology, subjection to, 34; icons, role as, 31–33, 36, 38, 50; library of, 63–64; queer sapphism of, 34, 52–54; "romantic friendship" thesis about, 23, 32–33, 36, 37, 38, 53; trans identity of, 46, 49. *See also* Butler, Eleanor; Ponsonby, Sarah
Lake District, 69
Lamb, Charles, 16, 20, 23, 25, 86, 117, 168; bohemianism of, 125–27, 140; canonical status of, 118; Coleridge, strained relations with, 121–24, 134; dependency as interest of, 134–35; effeminacy (alleged) of, 136; Elizabethan dramatists, rehabilitation of, 144–45; *flânerie* of, 121, 124–33; library, "ragged" state of, 143–44, 147–49, 150–53; medial materiality, views on, 132–34; New Humanists on, 145; periodicals, association with, 136–37; periodicals, views on, 137–40; reception, sentimentality in, 119; transcendentalism of, 118–24; urban focus of, 119–24
Lamb, Charles, works of: *Album Verses, with a Few Others* (1830), 139; "Appreciation of De Foe's Secondary Novels" (1829), 146–47, 152; "Barrenness of the Imaginative Faculty in the Productions of Modern Art" (1833), 126; "Character of the Late Elia" (1823), 147; "Characters of Dramatic Writers, Contemporary with Shakespeare" (1808), 145; "Confessions of a Drunkard" (1813), 134; *Elia* (1823), 139; *Eliana* (1864), 136; "The Genteel Style of Writing" (1826), 138; *Last Essays of Elia* (1833), 130; "Mackery End, Hertfordshire" (1821), 145; *Mr. H.* (1806), 137; "My First Play" (1821), 118, 128; "The Old Benchers of the Inner Temple" (1823), 127; "On Some of the Old Actors" (1823), 118, 119–20, 125, 150; "On the Tragedies of Shakespeare" (1811), 129; "Oxford in the Vacation" (1820), 25, 134, 143; *The Pawnbroker's Daughter* (1830), 137; "Popular Fallacies" (1826), 138; "The South-Sea House" (1820), 149; *Specimens of English Dramatic Poets Who Lived about the Time of Shakespeare* (1808), 145; "Stage Illusion" (1825), 138; "That We should Lie Down with the Lamb" (1826), 142; "That We should Rise with the Lark" (1833), 126; *The Wife's Trial* (1828), 137
Lamb, Mary, 138, 139
Lanser, Susan L., 34, 53–54
The Last Days of Percy Bysshe Shelley (M. Shelley), 180

Last Essays of Elia (Lamb), 130
The Last Tournament (Tennyson), 195–96
Leaves of Grass (Whitman), 168
libraries, 2, 46; circulating libraries, 7
The Library Companion (Dibdin), 71, 97
Lister, Anne, 52
Liu, Alan, 5
Llangollen Vale (Seward), 37
Locke, John, 176
Lockhart, John Gibson, 38, 122
The Logic of Political Economy (De Quincey), 94
Lolly, Amelia, 60
London Magazine, 25, 86, 117, 133, 136, 139
Lucas, Edward Verrall, 119; TJW, view of, 166
Lynch, Deidre Shauna, 9, 10, 16, 19–20, 22, 25, 83, 86
Lyrical Ballads (Wordsworth), 146, 185

Macaulay, Thomas, 44
"Mackery End, Hertfordshire" (Lamb), 145
Macvey, Napier, 98
Malton, James, 48–49
Manning, Thomas, 124
Marlborough, 5th Duke of (George Spencer-Churchill, Marquis of Blandford), 92, 95
Martin, Henri-Jean, 7
Marx, Karl, 41–42, 45, 57, 61, 186; *Capital* (1867), 41, 57; HBF, familiarity with, 163–64
materiality: authorship and, 5, 20, 87, 102, 110; canonical status and, 16; curiosity and, 82; desire, as object of, 56–57, 92; gender and, 55; human extension and, 42, 49, 58–60, 68; "material turn" and, 19; philosophy, status in, 48, 86–87; phobia and, 7, 8, 95, 102, 107; Romantic poetics, status in, 59, 175, 182; semiotics

and, 41, 95; theories of, 41–42; trauma and, 68
Mavor, Elizabeth, 32, 33, 38, 39, 46, 47, 52, 53, 60
May, Lewis, 134
McLuhan, Marshall, 41–42, 43, 44, 68; *Understanding Media: The Extensions of Man* (1964), 42
Milton, John: *Paradise Lost* (1667), 59, 64
Mitford, Mary Russell, 189–90
Mole, Tom, 163
Monsman, Gerald, 129
Montesquieu, 7
Moore, Lisa L., 34, 40
Morgannwg, Iolo, 66
Morison, Stanley, 191, 196
Morris, William, 167, 198
Moxon, Edward, 137
Mr. H. (Lamb), 137
Munro, John, 162
Murray, David, 38–39
"Mutability" (P. Shelley), 175
"My First Play" (Lamb), 118, 128
My Secret Life (Walter), 82

Nagle, Christopher, 3, 9, 19, 22
Nash, C. J., 62
Neoplatonism, 11
Nichol, George, 91
Nichol, William, 90
Nicholl, William Robertson, 195
Nyong'o, Tavia, 141

Observations on the River Wye, and several parts of South Wales (Gilpin), 66
"The Old Benchers of the Inner Temple" (Lamb), 127
"On first looking into Chapman's Homer" (Keats), 182
"On Some of the Old Actors" (Lamb), 118, 119–20, 125, 150
ornamentation, 15; book design, role in, 89, 90, 101, 180–81; capitalism

and, 56; imagination and, 46–47; queerness and, 17, 54–55, 95, 100; style and, 135
ornamental community: defined, 3–4, 181; TFD's circle, role in, 83, 87–88, 93; Lamb, role in works of, 135; LL, role in circle of, 32, 34, 35, 40–41, 60–61; Victorian forgers, role among, 153, 159–60
ornamental cottage, 36, 37, 40–41, 42, 45–48; gendered and sexualized history of, 48–49; LL, their subversion of, 50–51, 181
Our Living Poets (Forman), 167
"Oxford in the Vacation" (Lamb), 25, 134, 143

"The Painter of Modern Life" (Baudelaire), 125
Paradise Lost (Milton), 59, 64
Partington, Wilfred, 165, 188
Pascoe, Judith, 8, 180, 181
Pater, Walter: *Appreciations* (1889), 127, 144
Pauline (R. Browning), 166
The Pawnbroker's Daughter (Lamb), 137
pederasty (residual), 96, 153. See also fop
Pennant, Thomas, 7
Pforzheimer, Carl H., 195
The Phaedrus (Plato), 173
Philanthropist, 134
Phillips, Thomas, 8, 9, 10
The Picture of Dorian Gray (Wilde), 101, 103–4
picturesque, 66, 71, 117
Piggott, Stuart, 127
Piozzi, Hester Lynch, 37–38, 47, 63
Piroux, Lorraine, 87
Plas newydd, 32, 38; collection, resemblance to, 46; design of, 46–47; evolution of, 61–62; ornamentation of, 15, 40, 45; queerness of, 15, 36, 39, 45–48; situation of, 46

Plato, 174; *The Phaedrus* (370 BCE), 173
Pocock, William, 48
Pollard, Graham and John Carter, 190–99
Ponsonby, Sarah, 3, 23; *Account of a Journey in Wales* (1778), 36, 67–68; early life of, 39. See also Ladies of Llangollen
Pope, Alexander, 108; "Essay on Criticism" (1711), 176
"Popular Fallacies" (Lamb), 138
Price, Leah, 19–20, 22, 86–87, 172
Pride and Prejudice (Austen), 88
print: literature, role in conceptions of, 20; technological advances in, 7
Proctor, Bryan Waller, 118–19
punk style, 117, 141, 153
The Pure and the Impure (*Ces plaisirs*) (Collette), 33
Pynson, Richard, 85, 92

Quaritch, Bernard, 198
Queen Mab (P. Shelley), 25, 163–64, 172, 199
queerness: capitalism and, 56; class privilege and, 39; curiosity and, 82; Dibdin's bibliography, role in, 100–104; essentialism, contrasts to, 53, 108; geographical displacement and, 36, 38–39, 68; historiography and, 53; homosociality, parallels to, 8, 88, 101; literary materiality and, 6; nervous disorders and, 84; "residual pederasty" concept and, 95–96; tourism and, 69–71
Quincey, Thomas (father of TDQ), 7; *A Short Tour in the Midland Counties of England* (1775), 7

"Rare Doings at Roxburghe Hall, A Ballad" (Beckford), 11
Ratchford, Fannie E., 195–98
Raymond, William O., 196–97

reading: democratization of, 6, 7, 8, 17–18; "material turn" and, 17
Reminiscences of a Literary Life (Dibdin), 93
Ricardo, David, 41
Richardson, John V., 14
Riehl, Joseph, 119, 139
Roberts, Gwyneth Tyson, 66, 69
Robertson, G. H., 61, 62
Robins, George, 46
Ross, Andrew, 44
Rossetti, Dante Gabriel, 167
Rossetti, William M., 162
Rousseau, George S., 83
Rousseau, Jean-Jacques, 57, 66
Rousseau and Romanticism (Babbitt), 145
Rowlandson, Thomas, 22
Roxburghe Club, 4; auction commemorated by, 14, 92; first meeting of, 104; members of, 104–5; representation of, role of phobia in, 100, 104; TFD's founding of, 23–24, 82; Victorian legacy of, 25. *See also* bibliomanic, figure of; book collecting; book collectors
Roxburghe Revels (Buckingham), 14, 104, 105–10
Rubin, Gayle, 2–3
Ruskin, John, 190
Russell, David, 119
Russell, J. Fuller, 143
Russett, Margaret, 16, 17, 25, 109, 175, 184
Russo, Brent, 119

Sams, Joseph, 99–100
Savage, Mike, 57
Sawyer, Ethel R., 10
Scott, Walter, 4, 38, 107, 185; *The Antiquary* (1816), 8, 85
Sedgwick, Eve Kosofsky, 96
Sendak, Maurice, 13
sensibility, discourse of, 3, 5, 9, 10, 22, 101–3

Seward, Anna: Cornwallis, Elizabeth, relationship with, 47; LL, exchange of books with, 64–65; LL, idealization of, 37, 67; LL, inspiration by, 49, 58, 59; *Llangollen Vale* (1796), 37; Plas newydd, description of, 47
Sha, Richard C., 16, 21, 34
Shakespeare, William, 119
Shakespeare Press, 90
Sharp, William, 197
Shelley, Mary, 162, 180; *The Last Days of Percy Bysshe Shelley* (1898), 180
Shelley, Percy Bysshe, 181; *Adonais* (1821), 163; *The Cenci* (1819), 162; *Defence of Poetry* (1821), 174–75, 178; *Epipsychidion* (1821), 178; *Hellas* (1822), 162; "Mutability" (1816), 175; TJW and HBF's work on, 25–26, 177–78; Victorian love of, 14. *See also Defence of Poetry* (1821); *Queen Mab* (1813)
Shelley Society, 14, 162, 166; HBF's lecture to, 172; membership and history of, 163. *See also* Furnivall, Fredrick J.; Wise, Thomas J.
Ship of Fools (Brant), 13, 84
Shorter, Clement King, 165–66
Silsbee, Edward, 180, 181
Silver, Sean, 15
Sinclair, Catherine, 66
singular authorship, 87; bibliography, opposition to, 179; disembodiment and, 5, 16, 17, 109, 178; forgery, link to, 181, 199–200; heterosexuality, analogy to, 16; repression and, 184. *See also* authorship
Sisters (Cheney), 33
Sketches of Life and Manners (De Quincey), 7
Sloane, Hans, 21
Smith, Adam, 41
Society of Dilettanti, 69
Songs from the Portuguese (Browning), 26

Sontag, Susan, 43–44, 95
Southey, Robert, 38, 64, 89
"The South-Sea House" (Lamb), 149
Spacks, Patricia Meyer, 22
Specimens of English Dramatic Poets Who Lived about the Time of Shakespeare (Lamb), 145
Spencer, 2nd Earl (George John Spencer), 10, 24, 85, 95
The Spoils of Poynton (James), 57
"Stage Illusion" (Lamb), 138
Stanhope, Philip (Lord Chesterfield), 83
St. Clair, William, 6, 17, 19–20
Stevenson, Robert L., 167
Stewart, Susan, 84, 200
Stone, Amy L., 62
Strawberry Hill, 15, 23, 40, 43–45, 71. *See also* Walpole, Horace
Swinburne, Algernon C., 167
Symonds, John Addington, 84

technology, 117; camp and, 5; determinism and, 17; sensibility and, 9
Tennyson, Alfred Lord, 167, 195; *The Last Tournament* (1872), 195–96
Thackeray, William M.: *Vanity Fair* (1847), 1–3, 184
"That We should Lie Down with the Lamb" (Lamb), 142
"That We should Rise with the Lark" (Lamb), 126
"Tintern Abbey" (Wordsworth), 119
"To the Lady E. B. and the Hon. Miss P" (Wordsworth), 36–37
tour books, 7, 65
tourism, 23, 32, 34, 46, 65, 68–69
Townshend, Dale, 43
Travers, John: *The Hamwood Papers* (1930), 38
Trentmann, Frank, 57
Trimmer, Sarah, 144
"The Trimming of Thomas Nashe, Gentleman" (Harvey), 12

Trollope, Anthony, 167
Tully, 94
Typographical Antiquities (Dibdin), 179

Understanding Media: The Extensions of Man (McLuhan), 42
University of Texas, 161, 196
Un point curieux (Delepierre), 168

"Vaccinia" (Dibdin), 84
Vanity Fair (Thackeray), 1–3, 184
Vathek (Beckford), 11, 15
Verity, Robert, 84; *Changes Produced in the Nervous System by Civilization* (1839), 84

Wales, 39, 40, 46, 65–66; commodified image of, 23, 32, 66–67; LL, their move to, 15, 31; Romantic tourism, role in, 65–66, 69, 71
Walpole, Horace, 35, 40, 42–45, 185; *The Castle of Otranto* (1764), 15
Walter: *My Secret Life* (1888–1894), 82
Warburton, William, 175
Ward, Edward, 82
Watt, Alaric C., 136
Weber, Max, 57, 125
Westwood, Thomas, 143, 147
Whale, John, 69
Whitman, Walt, 168; *Leaves of Grass* (1855), 168
The Wife's Trial (Lamb), 137
Wilde, Oscar, 97, 108; *The Picture of Dorian Gray* (1890), 101, 103–4; trials of, 108
Williams, Richard Lloyd, 61
Wise, Thomas J., 3, 23, 25; *Ashley Library* (1922), 161, 164, 182, 189; commodities career of, 164, 183; collecting practices of, 181, 183; early life and works of, 164–65; exposure of, 193; Furnivall's societies, work for, 166–67; library, sale of, 161; relic collecting of, 181;

Roxburghe Club, admittance to, 164–65; *A Shelley Library* (1924), 180; *Verses* (1886), 165–66
Wolfson, Susan J., 182
Woodbury, Gerald, 171–72
Woodmansee, Martha, 17, 176, 177
Woolf, Leonard, 33
Woolf, Virginia, 33
Wordsworth, Dorothy, 120–21
Wordsworth, William, 36–37, 38, 48, 49, 58, 69, 86, 137; "Essay, Supplementary to the Preface" (1815), 7; "Essays upon Epitaphs" (1810), 176; *The Excursion* (1814), 70; Lamb, contrasted to, 120–21; "low diction" of, 146–47; *Lyrical Ballads* (1798), 146, 185; "Tintern Abbey" (1798), 119; "To the Lady E. B. and the Hon. Miss P" (1824), 36–37; *The Worship of Priapus* (Knight), 69
Wrenn, John Henry, 161, 164
Wrenn Library, 196

Yates, Edward, 167
Yorke, John, 61, 62

Žižek, Slavoj, 12, 186

About the Author

Michael Robinson teaches in the Writing and Rhetoric Department of the University of Rhode Island. He is the author of scholarly articles on Charles Lamb, Thomas F. Dibdin, and Shirley Jackson. He has taught in the fields of English, humanities, and writing at the University of Southern California, Boğaziçi University (formerly Robert College) in Istanbul, UMass Dartmouth, California Lutheran University, and elsewhere. He is the past recipient of a Mellon Fellowship for study at the Huntington Library in San Marino, California.

www.ingramcontent.com/pod-product-compliance
Lightning Source LLC
Chambersburg PA
CBHW050903300426
44111CB00010B/1353